The Measurement of Delinquency

PATTERSON SMITH SERIES IN
CRIMINOLOGY, LAW ENFORCEMENT & SOCIAL PROBLEMS
PUBLICATION NO. 209

The Measurement of Delinquency

Thorsten Sellin
Marvin E. Wolfgang

Reprinted with a new introduction by Stanley Turner

Patterson Smith   Montclair, New Jersey   1978

HV
6253
.S4
1978

First published 1964 by John Wiley & Sons, Inc.
Copyright © 1964 by John Wiley & Sons, Inc.

Reprinted 1978, with permission, by
Patterson Smith Publishing Corporation
Montclair, New Jersey 07042

New material copyright © 1978 by
Patterson Smith Publishing Corporation

Library of Congress Cataloging in Publication Data

Sellin, Johan Thorsten, 1896-
   The measurement of delinquency.

   (Patterson Smith series in criminology, law enforcement, and social problems. Publication no. 209)
   Reprint of the 1964 ed. with a new introduction.
   Includes bibliographical references.
   1. Classification of crimes.   I. Wolfgang, Marvin E.,
1924- joint author.   II. Title.

[HV6253.S4   1977]   364.36'01'2   77-4336
ISBN 0-87585-209-2

Introduction to the Reprint Edition

For almost fifteen years the Sellin-Wolfgang scale of seriousness has stood as the most sophisticated measure of an extraordinarily elusive social variable: the relative seriousness of criminal events. Demographers may have better—i.e., more precise—measures (death rates, birth rates, etc.) because they deal with relatively simple and more immediately apparent phenomena. On the other hand, sociologists are often in pursuit of data relating to more evanescent concepts (e.g., anomie) which can be but crudely approximated or measured. Throughout the vast history of criminal law—from Ur-nammu to the latest criminal codes—a fundamental notion has persisted that all prohibited criminal acts are not equal in seriousness and, accordingly, the punishment which society applies to each should vary correspondingly. The distinctive contribution of Sellin and Wolfgang has been to demonstrate with rather remarkable precision and with astonishing reproducibility the extent to which one crime is more "serious" than another.

Perhaps the most striking aspect of this work has been the claim that the scale was more or less invariant across different populations. Thus the ratings of Philadelphia police officers as to comparative seriousness of criminal acts are said to be only slightly different (a linear transformation) from the judgments of the same events rendered by such disparate groups as delinquents in Puerto Rico or office workers in Montreal.

It is this notion of the universality of the scale values that affronts our preconceptions. When the study was undertaken, the authors had to face the possibility of some "unpleasant" findings. If two discrete groups (such as upper-class and lower-class respondents) should differ significantly in their perceptions of seriousness of crime, which set of values would be the "right" ones? Such diversity of opinion is an unfortunate commonplace of comparative sociology and anthropology. The Bindibu have sets of values significantly at variance with those of the Dobuans, who in turn are not all like the Cree. It is the shibboleth of the sociologist that "our" values can be regarded as universal only if we have immersed ourselves in parochialism and naive ethnocentrism. But it is precisely at this unlikely point where the study has seemingly most brilliantly succeeded. The original research represented by this volume found that although various dissimilar populations did indeed assign somewhat different numerical values to the same offense, the ratio of seriousness of one offense compared to other offenses was constant (or approximately so). This hitherto unsuspected unanimity of the judgments of diverse groups was found to be quantitative in nature, not just qualitative.

The methods used in this volume might well serve as a model in cross-cultural assessment of the invariance behind seeming diversity in group perceptions. A plethora of research, particularly that dealing with comparative cultures, aims at finding group differences and ceases when the differences are found. As if it were not the aim of science to find underlying patterns rather than differences! In linguistics, for example, it is the fundamental task of that science to show not how languages differ one from the other, but rather to demonstrate the invariance rules which seem to lurk behind the seemingly endless heterogeneity of languages.

Another thread running through Sellin and Wolfgang's work (and the Manual that was subsequently prepared as a practical aid in the use of the Scale) was the comparison of their approach with the *Uniform Crime Reports* published by the Federal Bureau of Investigation. The authors claim (rather unconvincingly, it must be admitted) that they do not wish their scheme of measurement to supplant the *Uniform Crime Reports* system, only to supplement it. It is argued that the two methods differ— that the Uniform Crime Statistics Index in the *Uniform Crime Reports* is predicated upon an implicit scale of seriousness (all seven "index crimes" are equal to each other in that each counts equally in the construction of the overall rate of crimes known to police), that the index crimes omit many serious offenses and include many trivial offenses (e.g. auto theft), and that the index focuses on the most glaring or distinctive elements of a crime and omits subsidiary features.

These serious criticisms of the *Uniform Crime Reports* had been leveled before, but what made Sellin and Wolfgang's work unique was that it actually proposed a feasible alternative to it. The Sellin-Wolfgang scale could be calculated from data elements found on typical police complaint forms. Thus, the scale was never intended to be one more empty methodological demonstration but was proposed as an operational device to be used and judged in the arena of criminal justice.

In summary, Sellin and Wolfgang have put forth the strong claim that they have created a scale of the relative (numerical) seriousness of crimes which is virtually invariant across diverse populations within a culture and even between cultures. They also claim that their scale could (should) be used by agencies dealing with crime at no or very little additional cost.

Before examining these claims and the criticism to which they were subjected, we may briefly review Sellin and Wolfgang's aims and methods.

In the late 1950s the authors undertook in Philadelphia the basic research, which essentially combined two fundamental ideas: 1) the use of silhouette descriptions of offenses, which tersely describe the "bare bones" of selected criminal offenses against respondents, and 2) a measurement technique devised by S. Smith Stevens, an eminent authority in psychophysics. Psychophysics had long been preoccupied with the problem of how the "outside" gets "inside," that is, how the objective, exterior event correlates with the subjective interior event; it aimed at ascertaining the fundamental law which connects what things "are" with what they "seem to be." Stevens had proposed and popularized the concept that there is an astonishingly simple relationship between the objective and subjective—between how heavy an object truly is and how heavy it seems to be. The law suggests that for a broad class of stimuli if the "objective" were increased by a certain percentage, the "subjective" would regularly increase by the same percentage. (Mathematically speaking, the relationship between the two is a power function.) This simple relationship was found again and again in a large number of investigations of sensory perceptions. The present work was made possible only by assuming that the same method would work in an area in which there was no objective standard of seriousness.

Sellin and Wolfgang drew 141 offense silhouettes from the full range of crimes handled by the *Uniform Crime Reports* (both index and non-index crimes). They included single versions of some legal offenses like disorderly conduct and multiple versions of other offenses like robbery. Numerous silhouettes were constructed for those crimes which seemed to be both serious and heterogeneous, (i.e., where there was much diversity of behavior concealed behind a single legal label). The 141 offenses ranged throughout the whole continuum of seriousness—from truancy and corner-lounging to rape and murder. (This is not to say that the selection of offenses seems in retrospect entirely appropriate in all respects: there was included only a single silhouette for arson, for example.)

The listing of the offense silhouettes appears in Appendix D of this volume. It will be seen that the descriptions are extremely sparse, giving only those details needed to differentiate one event from another. Characterizing the offender was scrupulously avoided, not because the offender was deemed unimportant, but because 1) to do so would have unbelievably complicated an already extremely complex research design; 2) the primary focus of the study was on offenses (the acts not the actors); 3) in real-life police operations knowledge of the offender's identity is often vague or completely lacking, in which case the seriousness of the offense must be evaluated without it.

One group of subjects was asked to rate the full range of offenses on an equal-interval scale of 11 steps ranging from "least serious" to "most serious." From these responses the internal scale was generated. Another group of respondents was asked to rate each offense by writing down a number which indicated how many times more serious each silhouetted offense was compared to a single fixed-standard (modulus) offense. The standard offense (a form of auto theft) was always assigned a score or value of ten; therefore, a response of 50 for a given offense would mean that the subject judged that offense to be five times more serious than the standard, while a scale of 5 meant the crime was regarded as half as serious as the standard auto theft. From these responses the ratio scale was generated.

The reader should carefully distinguish between two quite different senses in which one can discuss the Sellin and Wolfgang scale. First there is the set of numbers derived from the offense silhouettes themselves. Though the number of silhouettes changes from 141 to 21 and undergoes other changes, the basic approach is the same: the authors present the silhouettes and the subjects themselves provide the scale scores. But since not all possible versions of all possible offenses were (or could be) utilized the authors concocted an alternative device which they also refer to as the Sellin-Wolfgang Scale; this version is quite different from the straightforward version described above. In the alternative scheme, described in Appendix F of this volume, the authors present a series of elements (degree of bodily harm inflicted on victims, value of property stolen or damaged, etc.) along with weights for each of these elements which when summed are supposed to produce a number that is proportional to the number that would have been derived from the basic procedure if the event had been one of the standard silhouettes. It is suggested that these weights are appropriate for scoring *any* conceivable criminal offense that could ever occur. As a further extension, offenses within an area over a period of time can be thus scored, aggregated, and related to population to derive an index of delinquency appropriate to that area.

This very ambitious extension of the scaling technique would, if valid, make the Sellin-Wolfgang scale much more flexible. It is important, however, to notice that its derivation has never been adequately explained by the authors nor its correctness demonstrated. Indeed it is highly unlikely that the elements and weights they suggest are optimal even for their own data. The most impressive part of Sellin and Wolfgang's work is the scoring derived from the basic silhouettes themselves and *not* the particular additive version that they impose on it. Further research, using multivariate analysis, is needed to determine the appropriate data elements and their weights.

The techniques employed and the conclusions drawn by Sellin and Wolfgang did not long go unchallenged. Let us consider the most important of them, giving most of our consideration to those studies which criticize the work rather than to those studies which are relatively routine extensions.

Blumstein[1] examines the relationship between the FBI's *Uniform Crime Reports* and the Sellin-Wolfgang scale for the period

[1] Alfred Blumstein, "Seriousness Weights in an Index of Crime," *American Sociological Review* **39** (December 1974): 854-864.

1960 through 1972. He takes the FBI data directly from the figures published by the agency for the relevant period. The *UCR* rate for a given population would simply be the sum of the frequencies of all relevant offenses like criminal homicide, forcible rape, etc. A rate based on Sellin and Wolfgang would weight each relevant offense by a weight proportional to its seriousness. Thus the *UCR* rate would be based on a sum and the Sellin-Wolfgang rate would be based on a weighted sum. Blumstein assumes that the Sellin-Wolfgang rate can be approximated by taking the frequencies from the *UCR* and the average weights from a study by Heller and McEwan[2] of 9728 reported crimes committed in St. Louis in 1971. Blumstein finds the Sellin-Wolfgang scale is almost exactly linearly correlated with the FBI data and so concludes that the Sellin-Wolfgang scale contributes little additional information. As the author realized, this is in part due to the use of weights which he himself held constant. Thus the only thing left to vary was the proportional distribution of offenses and since this mix is known not to vary much the results he found were no surprise. But with characteristic ingenuity Blumstein analyzed what would be the case if the weights were to vary by a fairly large order of magnitude. The same conclusion is still reached.

Some objections can be raised to Blumstein's contention. First, he does not calculate the Sellin-Wolfgang scale as its authors do. It is simply not true that the Sellin-Wolfgang scale can be represented as a series of weight-times-frequency of seven index offenses. Many offenses which Sellin and Wolfgang would count are not FBI index offenses and some offenses they count, the FBI does not. The point could be raised in rebuttal that different Sellin-Wolfgang offenses and *UCR* offenses are strongly intercorrelated, but it remains that Blumstein's argument rests on assumptions which do not have to be made (given better data) and which may be crucial to his conclusion. Second, and more important, Blumstein's contention is only rarely relevant. The operational setting to which he implicitly refers seems to be one in which a decision-maker would survey the whole nation and decide whether crime was increasing or decreasing. Blumstein's advice to such a decision-maker is "Use the *UCR*; it is simpler

---

[2]Nelson B. Heller and J. Thomas McEwan, "Applications of Crime Seriousness Information in a Police Department," *Journal of Criminal Justice* **1**, no. 3 (Fall 1973): 241–253; also in *Journal of Research in Crime and Delinquency* **12**, no. 1 (January 1975): 44–50.

and cheaper." But how much decision-making takes place on such a plane? Most decisions in the criminal justice system are about individuals—whether to arrest them, what offense to charge them with, whether to prosecute them, what sentence to pass on them. In such a case how would Blumstein's advice fare? Pretty poorly. The district attorney, say, must decide which of two defendants to proceed against, and the character of the offense each is suspected of is probably the most important single variable affecting his decision. (In a district attorney's office, the number of offenses to be dealt with at any one time is constant; what is free to vary is the assessment of their seriousness.) Application of the Sellin-Wolfgang scale would suggest proceeding against the more serious. Similarly, sentencing is influenced by the relative severity of the offense and the relative extensiveness of the previous criminal history of the defendant. Blumstein has shown, in short, that the *UCR* and Sellin-Wolfgang scale point to the same decision in certain contexts, but these contexts do not include the day-to-day operations wherein uniform crime reporting is useless.

Rossi et al.[3] used 140 offense silhouettes, some or all of which were judged as to seriousness by 200 adult respondents in a household sample in Baltimore in 1972. The offenses were very briefly described and were judged on a scale of 9 gradations. Principally the authors studied how race, sex, social class, and education affected the judgment of seriousness. They conclude that most (68%) of the variance in seriousness is accounted for by "binary" legal characteristics of the offense: Was the offense against property or against the person? Was it a victimless crime? Was drug-selling involved? etc. They found overall agreement between the races and the sexes regarding the seriousness of offenses. Slight differences noted were: blacks found offenses in general somewhat more serious than whites, and females found them more serious than males. Using the demographic variables (age, race, and sex) in a regression analysis, they found that *these variables* accounted for only about 5 percent of the variance. Thus Rossi and his associates have buttressed the work of Sellin and Wolfgang and have demonstrated that that consensus on the seriousness of criminal offenses is real, wide-

---

[3]Peter H. Rossi, Emily Waite, Christine E. Bose, and Richard E. Berk, "The Seriousness of Crimes: Normative Structure and Individual Differences," *American Sociological Review* 39 (April 1974): 224-237.

spread among diverse subgroups, and stable over individual respondents.

Marlene Hsu[4] replicated the Sellin-Wolfgang scale in the city of Taipei, Taiwan. She translated 20 offenses into Chinese and transformed the money-values mentioned in the offenses into equivalent purchasing power in Taiwan currency (yuans); she also substituted motorcycle theft for the (in Taiwan) uncommon crime of auto theft. Offenses were presented in a randomized sequence for blocks of ten raters consisting of college students, judges, and policemen, as in the original study. As an innovation male and female college students were admitted into the replication. The final data were based on 203 male college students, 53 female students, 59 police, and 32 judges. The geometric means of offense scores for the four groups were found to be highly correlated (correlation coefficients ranging from 0.84 to 0.95). The slopes of the regression lines between students and police, students and judges, and police and judges were very close to 1.0, indicating that the three groups responded with very similar mean scores for each of the offenses (with the exception of homicide). One of the few differences among groups was that female students judged forcible rape as much more serious than did male students.

Another piece of evidence that the relative rating of crimes is similar across groups is offered by the work of Sechrest.[5] In 1965 at a California correctional institution, Sechrest gave 142 men 30 offense labels (forcible rape, grand theft, auto theft, etc.) and had them indicate seriousness on a 0 to 10 scale. A comparison of the medians showed extensive agreement among inmates, staff members, correctional officers, and parole agents for most offenses, though inmates disagreed most with correctional officers and parole agents. The offenses were grouped into six offense categories (sex, drugs, offenses against the person with and without profit, offenses against property, and false pretenses), and 142 inmates were asked to judge their own offenses. In general the actual offender saw his offense as having the same severity as other inmates did. But for two categories (drugs and false pretenses) the actual offender saw his own offenses as far less serious than did other inmates.

[4]Marlene Hsu, "Cultural and Sexual Differences in the Judgment of Criminal Offenses: A Replication of the Measurement of Delinquency," *Journal of Criminal Law and Criminology* **64,** no. 3 (1973): 348.

[5]Dale Sechrest, "Comparisons of Inmates' and Staff's Judgments of the Severity of Offenses," *JRC&D* **6,** no. 1 (January 1969): 41-55.

Michael Hindelang[6] has proposed a similar view to that of Blumstein, pointing out that using Sellin-Wolfgang weights will produce results similar to the *UCR* since about five out of six offenses are property offenses and the weights for property offenses are generally similar.

Walker[7] has voiced suspicion that the sample on which Sellin and Wolfgang based their findings was biased (as it no doubt was). G. N. G. Rose has the same reservation.[8] In response, it must be admitted that the authors never took a random sample of the universe; it is hard even to specify the "universe." Is it the United States population in 1970? The world? It is unlikely that any such populations will ever be sampled and subjected to laboratory control. This means that if one is set against measuring the seriousness of crime one can always reject the results out of hand since they do not meet a high standard of methodological purity. But the rest of humanity would, I think, be convinced of the acceptability of measuring the seriousness of crime if a large number of studies, most admittedly nonrandom, were to be performed for diverse groups in diverse settings. This is just what has occurred with the Sellin-Wolfgang scale. Its strength is that is has stood up under replication, and much of the original criticism is blunted by these findings.

But to say that the Sellin-Wolfgang research has stood up over time is not to say that the follow-up studies have found identity. Far from it. What they have found in the main is that the Sellin-Wolfgang magnitude scale when applied to two diverse populations typically finds the relationship between the two populations to be positive, linear on log-log paper, and with an impressively high correlation coefficient. This does not imply that "seriousness" is stable within or between societies. History is replete with examples of change in public attitude toward specific offenses. For example, Savitz, Turner, and Roberts (in a study not yet published) have completed a replication of the basic 21 offenses plus a large number of drug offenses. The results show that although juvenile delinquents, college stu-

[6]Michael Hindelang, "The Uniform Crime Reports Revisited," *JCJ* 2 (1974): 1-17.

[7]Nigel Walker, "Psychophysics and the Recording Angel," *British Journal of Criminology* 11, no. 2 (April 1971): 191-194.

[8]G. N. G. Rose, "Concerning the Measurement of Delinquency," *BJC* 6 (1966): 414-421; G. N. G. Rose, "The Merits of an Index of Crime of the Kind Devised by Sellin and Wolfgang," in *The Index of Crime: Some Further Studies* (Strasbourg: Council of Europe, 1970).

dents, self-confessed heroin addicts, and police officers in the sample overwhelmingly agree with each other and with the original study, this agreement is limited to the basic offenses and does not include drug offenses. Attitudes toward the latter, espe-·cially among college students, have apparently shifted with time. It was presumably for such a reason that S. Smith Stevens suggested that the primary need for such studies as Sellin and Wolfgang's was "replication, replication, replication."

Another issue raised by the critics of the scale is "additivity." Among others Pease, Ireson, and Thorpe,[9] and Rose[10] have raised objections. Perhaps the case is best stated by Pease, Ireson, and Thorpe, whose remarks we may paraphrase and amplify to exhibit two assumptions that are implicit in the Sellin-Wolfgang scale.

Assumption 1: The total scale score for an event can be derived by adding the scale scores for the constituent elements of the offense. Thus if an event entails physical injury and property damage, the total scale is the addition of the score that observers would have given had they been asked to rate the parts separately. Or to put the matter differently, if the Sellin-Wolfgang scale is the dependent variable then a close-fitting linear regression model would contain no interaction terms.

Pease, Ireson, and Thorpe present data to show that additivity does not hold. They presented 147 subjects with booklets which described events in which one offender commits an act twice and another offender commits it only once. Subjects were asked how many more times as serious were the actions of the recidivists. Most subjects thought it was less than twice as serious. But this evidence though persuasive, is not conclusive. One might object that it rather unfairly highlights the offender and in effect asks, "Do you think that Offender A is twice as 'bad' as Offender B if A commits an offense twice while B does it only once?" That is to say, the experimental arrangements may have measured the *blameworthiness* of acts rather than their seriousness. There comes a point when an increase in a sentence is not accompanied by an increase in suffering. In the convict's phrase, "The first hundred years are hardest."

Assumption 2: Sellin and Wolfgang have discovered the proper

[9]Kenneth Pease, Judith Ireson, and Jennifer Thorpe, "Additivity Assumptions in the Measurements of Delinquency," *BJC* **14,** no. 3 (July 1974): 256-263.
[10]Rose, "Concerning the Measurement of Delinquency."

weights for the elements. It could be true that seriousness is additive yet the authors did not discover the proper weights. The derivation of the weights is not properly explicated by the authors and stands as one of the more dubious aspects of their work. What is needed here is sophisticated analysis of the data already collected, yet none has appeared. Such analysis would answer whether an additive or non-additive model would better fit the data, what the "best" weights of the variables are, and how closely a best-fitting model will account for all the variation. It is my opinion that the best scale would not be additive and that the weights would differ from those proposed. Yet this does not alter the main work of Sellin and Wolfgang, which is formulating a scale based on offense silhouettes themselves and not the particular version of the scale they finally present. The task at hand seems to be to find a better set of elements and weights with which to build a model on those very offense silhouettes.

Nugent and Chansley[11] used 23 students as subjects. Fifteen offense descriptions from Appendix E-1 of *The Measurement of Delinquency* were formed into 15 x 14/2 = 105 pairs, and subjects were asked to rate the similarity of each comparison on a 10-point scale. Their analysis based on a multi-dimensional non-metric scaling procedure suggests that people take two considerations into account when making discriminations between offenses: first, the extent of physical injury and property theft (these are the building blocks of "seriousness" in Sellin and Wolfgang's scale) and second, the extent to which the victim is responsible for the results of the crime. They suggest that being hurt at all (regardless of degree of injury) is not considered to be equivalent to property offenses which have the same or even greater seriousness scores on the Sellin-Wolfgang scale. That physical injury and property theft or damage, though admitted to be major components of social disutility, should perhaps not be added together is a point made by other critics as well. Blumstein[12] suggests that it is preferable to have two components, "violent crimes" and "property crimes." Walker[13] makes a similar point about the desirability of separate indices. Thus we might have one, two, or any number of indices. Which approach

[11]James Nugent and Norman Chansky, "A Multiple Analysis of Social Perceptions of Criminal Behavior" (manuscript).

[12]Blumstein, "Seriousness Weights."

[13]Walker, "Psychophysics."

is right? Perhaps the answer lies in the decision which must be made when using the scale. If we focus (as few critics have) on the "micro" uses of the scale, then clearly the problem of lumping events together really only reaches significance when the previous record of the individual is being considered. His instant offense is most often a single offense, his previous record is not. Thus the question might be phrased, "How do people make up their minds about an offender when faced with reaching a decision on selecting one of a few alternatives for him?" Do they add together the principal components or not? On a macro level the caveats of the critics are well taken, and the scale should embody a set of components. But a close reading of Sellin and Wolfgang shows that they suggest this repeatedly and in fact list three major components (A events, or crimes with physical injury; B events, or crimes with property theft; and C events, or crimes with property damage).

Some cautions have been raised concerning the difficulties of replication, particularly cross-cultural replication. The warning could be made that currency values used in replications should be adjusted for differences in purchasing power. To make single-offense comparisons more meaningful, offenses might be calculated in some standardized form. The raw scores of magnitude estimates might for instance be logarithmically transformed and then further transformed into Z scores. If appropriate, this would allow comparisons of single crimes unaffected by differences in average level or range of response.

However such transformations may not be desirable. If for instance we set the value of larceny of one dollar equal to one unit of seriousness we have arbitrarily removed one source of variance between two countries and may cover up interesting differences. Clearly the employment of such techniques by Normandeau[14] deserves reappraisal and some of his methods for making international comparisons need improvement.

Lesieur and Lehman[15] conducted a replication using 563 students at several universities in New England. They used offense silhouettes borrowed from the original study with three main changes: 1) they inserted "intentionally" into a version of crimi-

[14]Andre Normandeau, "Crime Indices for Eight Countries," *Revue International de Police Criminelle* **234** (1970): 15-18.
[15]Henry Lesieur and Peter Lehman, "Remeasuring—A Replication and Overdue Essay" (manuscript).

nal homicide, a negligible change; 2) they had more than one offense per page, a questionable innovation; and 3) they selected a new modulus or comparison offense. They eliminated the responses of 53 subjects who had obviously misunderstood the questions. When plotted on log-log paper, the results showed an impressive consistency and agreement between the original studies and their replication. Nonetheless Lesieur and Lehman claim that the consistency and agreement is illusory and is merely the consequence of averaging the data. They found no consistency when looking at individual data. But the real reason they found less consistency on an individual basis is because each single person's response is a function of *both* the seriousness of the offense and the order of presentation during the test procedure. One of the reasons for "averaging" the data taken on randomly presented stimuli is to remove the sequence effect and reveal the subject's response to the seriousness of the offense only. Similarly Lesieur and Lehman try to show a lack of consistency in individual judges' scores by plotting the scale scores for sets of individuals but do so for only two offenses: homicide and theft of $5,000. But looking at just two offenses is not the best means of examining consistency between raters. Their procedure is like looking at only a part of a scatter diagram: within some small section of the diagram the relation may seem random but reveals a clear correlation when the whole range of data is viewed. Rossi et al.[16] have subjected the data to a better test of consistency by sampling the entire range of response.

The remaining replications by other investigators[17] essentially support at least the minimum claim: when the appropriate mea-

[16]Rossi et al., "Seriousness of Crimes."

[17]See for instance: Dogan Akman, Andre Normandeau, and Stanley Turner, "Replication of a Delinquency and Crime Index in French Canada," *Canadian Journal of Corrections* 8, no. 1 (January 1966): 1-19: Dogan Akman and Andre Normandeau, "Towards the Measurement of Criminality in Canada: A Replication Study," *Acta Criminologica* 1 (January 1968): 135-260; and Angel Velez-Diaz and Edwin I. Megargee, "An Investigation of Differences in Value Judgments between Youthful Offenders and Non-Offenders in Puerto Rico," *Journal of Criminal Law, Criminology, and Police Science* 61, no. 4 (1970): 549-553. For closely related articles see: Jon McConnell and J. David Martin, "Judicial Attitudes and Public Morals," *American Bar Association* 55 (December 1969): 1129-1133; R. Carroll, S. Pine, and B. Kleinhaus, "Judged Seriousness of Watergate-Related Crimes," *Journal of Psychology* 86 (1974): 235-239; and L. Rosen and A. Carl, "The Decision to Refer to Juvenile Court for a Judicial Hearing," in Marc Riedel and Terence P. Thornberry, *Crime and Delinquency: Dimensions of Deviance* (New York: Praeger, 1974).

sures of central tendency are plotted against the original study or between groups within the study, the logarithms of the scores will be positively and linearly related. These replications extend the geographical range of the samples to Canada, the Belgian Congo, and Puerto Rico and, in addition, they extend the range of types of subjects: lower-class Spanish-speaking boys, Canadian office workers, etc. Beyond that little that is novel is introduced.

The operational uses to which the scale has been put add something which the above replications do not. They test the usefulness of the scale. PROMIS (Prosecutor's Management Information System) in Washington, D.C., utilized a measure of the urgency of a case for prosecution. Under previous procedures, this measure was based on the subjective assessment of a series of closed cases by an experienced prosecutor. Joan Jacoby and Stanley Turner[18] found that this subjective appraisal could be estimated very well by three variables with their appropriate weights. The relationship (excluding some variables of trivial importance) took the following form:

$$U = pw^1 SW + pw^2 BE,$$

where

  U = judged urgency of the case for prosecution,

  p = subjective probability of winning the case,

  SW = seriousness of the offense on the Sellin-Wolfgang Scale,

  BE = base expectancy, a measure of the likelihood of the offender's recidivism, based on the excellent work of Gottfredson, et al.,[19]

w^1, w^2 = weights appropriate to seriousness and base expectancy, respectively.

The weight w^1 was found to be approximately .22 and w^2 approximately .09, indicating that in judging urgency for prosecution,

[18] Joan E. Jacoby, *A System for Manual Evaluation of Case Processing in the Prosecutor's Office* (First Annual Report, National Center for Prosecution Management, Washington, D.C., 1972).

[19] Don M. Gottfredson and Robert F. Beverly, "Development and Operational Use of Prediction Methods in Correctional Work," *Proceedings of the American Statistical Association, Social Statistics Section* (1962), pp. 54-61.

seriousness was considered much more important than base expectancy. In such applications the Sellin-Wolfgang scale was of demonstrated effectiveness in simulating the decisions of a prosecutor through the use of formulas which "make sense" in their interpretation.

In a symposium, sponsored by the *Journal of Criminal Law and Criminology*,[20] Charles F. Wellford and Michael Wiatroski ("On the Measurement of Delinquency," pp. 175-188) review the development of the Sellin-Wolfgang scale, consider the implications of the many replications of the scale, review data on the question of scale additivity, and comment upon the usefulness of a seriousness scale. They conclude that Sellin and Wolfgang have established a useful research model that measures offense seriousness. In their view, the original seriousness scale is an important advance in that it has provided the foundation for the development of a science of behavior.

Robert M. Figlio ("The Seriousnes of Offenses: An Evaluation by Offenders and Nonoffenders," pp. 189-200) presents a study of the subjective severities of various criminal offenses as judged by three groups: "hard-core" convicts, youth offenders, and college students. Figlio notes that the three groups evidence strong agreement about which offenses are serious in both magnitude and sequence. He finds the relationship between the groups is logarithmic. He also examines the manner in which student views have changed in the ten years following the development of the original Sellin-Wolfgang scale. In this examination he discovers time trends and determines that the more recent studies view offenses less seriously.

Marc Riedel ("Perceived Circumstances, Inferences of Intent and Judgments of Offense Seriousness," pp. 201-208) studies the effect of perceptions of circumstances on judgments of the seriousness of offenses. Riedel concludes that while respondents had little difficulty inferring intent from the perceived circumstances, there is little support for the theory that different circumstances lead to a differential willingness to attribute intent. He also finds little evidence that inferences of intent alter judgments of seriousness and concludes that perceivers assess the seriousness of

[20]Symposium on the Measurement of Delinquency, *Journal of Criminal Law and Criminology* **66**, no. 2 (1975): 173-221.

criminal events in ways that make unimportant any inferences about whether the offender intended the act.

Kenneth Pease, Judith Ireson and Jennifer Thorpe ("Modified Crime Indices for Eight Countries," pp. 209-214) examine Andre Normandeau's attempts to provide an international comparison of judgments of offense seriousness by use of the Sellin-Wolfgang scale. They conclude that Normandeau's methods of comparison are misleading in two important ways. First, he incorrectly assumes that all national groups agree on the seriousness of larceny of one dollar. Second, a direct comparison of scores of national groups is meaningless because ranges over which seriousness judgments are spread differ between national groups.

George S. Bridges and Nancy S. Lisagor ("Scaling Seriousness: An Evaluation of Magnitude and Category Scaling Techniques," pp. 215-221) demonstrate the similarity between magnitude and category scaling techniques in measuring the seriousness of offenses. The authors observe that the relationship between the scaling techniques is logarithmic and, consequently, similar results are generated when either scaling technique is applied. The authors note that similar distributions and estimates of seriousness magnitude are produced regardless of which technique is utilized.

Summary

In the decade and a half since the pioneering work of Sellin and Wolfgang many attempts have been made to verify or criticize the scale. What may be concluded from these efforts? I believe that it may fairly be stated that the authors' final version (the elements and their additive weights) is not the best representation of their data. Further it may be conceded that the techniques for making international comparisons have not been fully thought out. But the original study has held up under repeated replications on diverse populations. It is also likely that national (macro-level) comparisons over time or between jurisdictions will add very little to present schemes. In addition demographic and socio-economic variables appear to affect the scale values only in a very slight way.

All this is to say the minimum claim advanced by Sellin and Wolfgang has not been successfully challenged. The scale (or some version of it) appears distinctively useful for making decisions about individuals in the criminal justice system. Of how many endeavors is this true? How many have survived replication and criticism? It may be said of Sellin and Wolfgang's work what was said of it when first reviewed: It is probably the most sophisticated attempt in sociology to measure an elusive yet important variable.

STANLEY TURNER

January 1977

Preface

At least since the early part of the nineteenth century, when criminal statistics first began to be collected in some European countries on a uniform basis, the problem of measuring the frequency and seriousness of offenses has occupied scholars. Different solutions have been offered but all have been found wanting for various reasons. One obstacle has been the difficulty of devising a classification and a differential weighting of the seriousness of offenses that would be in some way independent of the specific technical labels given to crimes by the law. The research, which is the subject of this book, has been done with a view to find a means of overcoming this obstacle and develop a firmer basis for constructing an index to delinquency.

We are most grateful to the Ford Foundation, which in 1960 initiated our inquiry and has generously defrayed its cost. We owe a special debt in that connection to Mr. David Hunter and Professor Jackson Toby. During the study we also enjoyed the benefit of the professional advice of several consultants. Mr. Ronald H. Beattie, formerly head of the Bureau of Criminal Statistics, State of California, and now chief of the statistical service of the Administrative Office of the United States Courts, Washington, D. C., was involved in the early planning of the design and in some of our discussions of theoretical issues in index construction. Professor Eugene Galanter, now chairman of the Department of Psychology, University of Washington, Seattle, aided us in constructing the category and the magnitude estimation scales, in applying the lessons from psychophysics to our data, and in analyzing some of the results. Portions of his assistance were provided by the Office of Naval Research

NONR contract 551(37) between the University of Pennsylvania and the Office of Naval Research. Mr. Leslie T. Wilkins of the Home Office Research Unit, London, was in the United States during 1962–1963, and we profited from his insight and advice in connection with statistical problems. Some of his suggestions prompted us to add statistical manipulations that enhanced the value of our data, and his positive view of the project was much appreciated. We are also grateful to Professor Nathan Fine, Department of Mathematics, University of Pennsylvania, and Assistant Professor Harvey Smith, Department of Mathematics, Drexel Institute of Technology, for useful advice.

We were assisted throughout the project by a small staff of workers, consisting of a full-time research associate and several half-time assistants who were graduate students working for the degree of Master of Arts in criminology. During the first two years Dr. Norman H. Johnston was our research associate; his sound judgment greatly facilitated our contacts with police authorities and aided us in the construction of our research design. During the third year, Mr. Stanley Turner, research assistant from the beginning of the project, took Dr. Johnston's place. His statistical skill and his inventive mind have been invaluable and are reflected in almost all parts of the study.

For varying periods of time our research assistants have been: Mr. Ian Lennox, now on the staff of the Philadelphia Crime Commission, Mr. Tokuhiro Tatezawa, member of the research staff of the Supreme Court in Japan, Mr. S. K. Mukherjee, Mr. Wayne Mucci, Mr. Bernard Cohen, Miss Judith Hart, and Miss Marianne Karnafel.

Most statistical tabulations were performed by our staff, but we are gratefully acknowledging the capable and ready assistance given by Mrs. Carolyn Ganschow and Mr. Ronald H. Cohen of the Wharton School of Finance and Commerce who provided us with many machine tabulations from our punch cards. Arrays and manipulations of data were performed on UNIVAC tape, partly through the help of Mr. Thomas Angell, senior programmer, and Mr. James Guertin, manager of the Computing Center of the University of Pennsylvania, and especially by Mr. Lawrence McGinn, director of the Computing Center of the Franklin Institute, Philadelphia.

Our research could not have been done without the very generous and always cordial cooperation of members of the Philadelphia Police Department, which gave us not only access to the files of the Juvenile Aid Division but consulted with us, answered innumerable questions, and have now introduced the system we have proposed for constructing an index of delinquency. We are happy to acknowledge this cooperative relationship which was at the outset established with the then Commissioner of Police, Mr. Albert N. Brown, and subsequently with Commissioner Howard R. Leary.

Throughout the research we were fortunate in having the willing assistance of capable police administrators in strategic positions, such as Inspector Joseph Max, head of the Juvenile Aid Division, Inspector Wilfred Faust, in charge of Central Records, and Captain Edward Doran, Central Records. When we were assembling data, the following persons were especially helpful: Captain Frank A. Scafidi of the Morals Squad; Sergeant Herbert Hoffman and Mr. John Woodland of the Juvenile Aid Division; Mr. Charles Anderson, Central Records; and Mr. Vincent Rossi, Youth Conservation Services. Dr. E. Preston Sharp, director, and Mr. Howard Pindell, Intake Supervisor of the Youth Study Center kindly provided us with valuable information missing from our own files.

During the first two years, Miss Francine Spiegel, and later Miss Jean Wilmot, performed the often difficult and always necessary tasks of an office secretary with dispatch and devotion, and after the completion of the manuscript Mrs. Lenora Wolfgang and Mrs. Annette Jacobson aided us by checking it for typing and other formal errors.

THORSTEN SELLIN
MARVIN E. WOLFGANG

June 1964

Contents

1

Introduction: the problem

A grave concern for what appears to be a continuous increase in juvenile delinquency is felt in nearly all countries. The anxiety is being expressed in the daily press and reflected in popular magazines and other media of mass communication. Scholars discuss the problem in learned and scientific journals, remedies are debated in legislative committee rooms and assemblies, and local communities design programs and initiate projects to combat it.

It is little consolation to know that we are dealing with no recent or new phenomenon. People have always been worried about the misbehavior of adolescents. Whether or not we are more sensitive today than people were formerly and more eager to promote the moral health of our children and youth are matters that could perhaps be debated, but there is no doubt that we are keenly aware of the extent of juvenile delinquency and are trying to prevent or reduce it by a variety of means. No matter what forms these efforts take, we hope that they will have a salutary result, but we have not yet discovered any reliable way of gauging their effectiveness. Therefore, in order to expend most purposefully and usefully the time, thought, energy, and public and private funds required for the organization and operation of programs that are expected to prevent or reduce delinquency, there is obvious need of some instrument or device that, alone or in conjunction with other devices, can be used to test the effectiveness of these programs. Such an instrument must, as accurately as possible, measure or provide an index to the degree and the nature of changes in delinquency over a period of time in a population exposed to the preventive activity.

Broadly speaking, preventive activity in this connection can be divided into two types: general and individual. General activity aims to affect a juvenile population or a segment thereof without focusing on any specific individual in that population, in the hope that all, most, or many of those affected will benefit morally from their experience. Individual activity consists of social, psychological, or psychiatric "casework" with specific individuals who are in danger of or have already engaged in delinquency, in the hope that such treatment will be therapeutic. In either instance, it would be desirable to determine the effectiveness of the activity. If either activity, alone or in conjunction with the other, were successful, the effect on delinquency in the population should be measurable by the instrument mentioned.[1]

There are many difficult problems involved in the construction of measurements of offenses against the law including offenses committed by juveniles. All such offenses do not become publicly recorded, which means that the recorded offenses are only a sample of those actually committed. Whether we consider all offenses or specific kinds of offenses, there is always a hidden dimension that must be taken into account. This unknown quota, when added to the recorded proportion, results in a total which constitutes the volume of *real* criminality.

Since we can only count the offenses that are recorded—the publicly known criminality—yet wish to obtain a measure of the real criminality, the question of the statistically representative nature of the recorded samples must be considered. When a universe of data studied by the statistician is fully known, he can, by observing certain rules, take a sample of it that will give him an accurate miniature picture of that universe. If he ignores these principles he may end up with a biased sample that so distorts the miniature that it is impossible to tell what the universe it is supposed to mirror looks like and what its real properties are. To what degree, then, and under what circumstances can we assume that the recorded samples of the real—and partly unknown—criminality are unbiased and, therefore, representative, so that we may assume that if it were possible to secure a complete census, year after year, of the real criminality the only thing that would happen would be that we would have a record of more offenses and therefore higher rates, while trends and other characteristics of the offenses would remain the same? Unless it is possible to assume that the hidden and the recorded offenses maintain

---

[1] The specific effect of individual therapy may be ascertained by comparative research based on individual case studies, but this is a problem which lies outside the scope of the research which is the subject of this monograph.

invariable proportions, measurement in the sense used in this discussion is a vain hope.[2]

We are also faced with a problem when we consider the recorded offenses alone, for they present us with a different hidden quota. An offense may be reported to the public authorities and may even be investigated by these authorities and its actual occurrence validated. However, the person or persons who committed the offense may be unknown or may never be found. The dimension of the quota of recorded offenses committed by unknown or never apprehended persons varies with the type of offense and a variety of other factors. And, so long as the offender remains unknown, it is of course impossible to describe his attributes.

When we begin to think in terms of the measurement of offenses committed by juveniles or adults, males or females, whites or colored, rich or poor, still another problem arises. Now we are compelled to operate with data pertaining to only those offenses among the total of hidden and recorded ones that can be attributed to specific persons who are taken into custody and subjected to questioning or investigation, during which their age, sex, race, occupation, etc., can be ascertained. The measurement of the delinquency of juveniles, therefore, can be based only on that recorded sample of real offenses actually attributable to them. The representative nature of this sample of offenses must, of course, be determined.

The problems so far mentioned are connected with the *basis* of the measurement of criminality or delinquency. Usually it is thought that this basis should be the offenses recorded by one or more of the public authorities directly concerned with criminal law enforcement and the administration of justice. However, in many countries it is felt that the basis must be widened to include certain forms of conduct which are analogous to criminal offenses (e.g., vagrancy, prostitution, and drunkenness) but are unknown or unrecorded by the authorities mentioned because they are not considered as crimes in their legislations; these offenses would be recorded by other responsible public agencies. In recent years voices have also been heard demanding that the basis should be broad enough to include

[2] In the first criminologically important statistical research report published, Adolphe Quetelet wrote, "I do not hesitate to say that all we possess of statistics of crimes and misdemeanors would have no utility if we did not tacitly assume that *there is a nearly invariable relationship between offenses known and adjudicated and the total unknown sum of offenses committed.*" *Recherches sur le penchant au crime aux différens ages* (87 pp. Brussels, 1831), pp. 18–19.

even offenses known to certain private agencies but not brought to the attention of public authorities. The feasibility as well as the utility of such an enlargement of the basis for measurement should be examined and determined.

Even if it were decided that the offenses recorded by public agencies or authorities should be the sole basis for measurement, there are still questions to be answered. Records of offenses committed are found in the registers of the police, the prosecutor's office, and the clerks of courts, to mention only the most important depositories. Should basic data for measurement purposes be drawn from *all* of these sources or only from *one* of them? If one source alone were to be used, which one should be chosen? The selection of a single source could either be made in the belief that any one of the sources is equally serviceable, or because the particular source is believed to possess basic data that are most pertinent and valid for the purpose in view and therefore superior to other sources. In any case, the choice must be founded on a thorough analysis of the elements involved.

Having selected the source of basic data, we must determine what data to extract from registers. At least two aspects of offenses must be considered, the quantitative and the qualitative aspects. Offenses may vary numerically in the sense that more or fewer would occur from one period to another, but they may also vary qualitatively in that they would become more or less serious. The frequency of delinquent acts is an indispensable datum; but unless some weight based on a scale of relative seriousness of such acts is assigned to them, an important ingredient of measurement will be lost. And, as we shall see later, when all these and other matters will be discussed in more detail, the problem of the proper classification of the law violations studied intrudes itself, whichever aspect is dealt with.

Finally, when we are specifically concerned with how to measure juvenile delinquency, i.e., the illegal conduct of persons who fall within a certain age range of, for instance, 7 to 18 years, should we apply the measurement:

(a) to the total delinquency attributable to this age group during a specified period of time, usually a year, so that a similar measure applied in subsequent comparable periods to a similar age group would indicate possible changes? In this connection it must be recalled that each year the group changes by the entry of a new cohort at the bottom and the disappearance of one at the top of the age group and that therefore, in successive years, we are applying the measure to age brackets that may contain populations different in composition as to race, economic status, specific ages, etc.

(b) retrospectively to the total delinquency of the cohort which has passed through the juvenile age period and is leaving it? Some claim that since many juveniles do not come into conflict with the law every year, an accurate measure of delinquency can only be secured by taking into account all recorded violations committed by them during the entire span of their life as "juveniles."

(c) to each cohort entering the age span, measuring its delinquency during the first year and in each subsequent year until it enters adulthood so far as the law is concerned?

A desire to find some solution to the problem briefly sketched in the preceding pages prompted the study described in this report. Various reasons caused us to restrict the research to one metropolitan community, Philadelphia, which in 1960 had a population of 2,002,509. First, juvenile delinquency is chiefly an urban problem; it is in the largest cities that it exhibits the greatest variety of forms and induces the strongest demands by citizens for preventive measures. Second, we were convinced that by studying a single community we could become, in the fullest measure possible, aware of and able to understand all aspects of the administrative structures and functions that relate to the maintenance and use of recorded data in the public agencies that deal with juvenile delinquency, thus equipping ourselves better to employ and interpret these data. Third, we knew from close contacts with these agencies that their records contained the information we believed would be adequate for our needs. And, fourth, we were assured by those in charge of the agencies that their records would be at our disposal and that we could count on complete cooperation. Therefore, with the encouragement of the Ford Foundation which provided generous financial support for the project over a period of three years, the study was begun in the fall of 1960.

It was decided to base the research on data pertaining to the year 1960, which was selected primarily because the population census of that year would furnish information needed for the computation of certain rates. We realized that the decision would preclude any attempt to test the efficiency of any measurement device at which we might arrive—since such an experiment would require data derived from delinquency records covering a series of years, as well as a study of one or more specific preventive action programs initiated in the community during those years—but we believed that the nature of the problem justified the decision.

As the study progressed, we assembled not only information that we regarded as essential for the purpose of constructing measurements of delinquency, but also a mass of data of more peripheral interest to measurement but potentially valuable for investigating some aspects of delinquency that received more or less and sometimes no attention in earlier studies. Therefore, it seemed proper to us, in planning our report, to devote the present volume to the specific question of measurement and to leave for a second volume the analysis of certain spatial and temporal features of delinquency and the more detailed study of the sex, specific age, residence, race, recidivism, etc., of the delinquents.

In subsequent chapters we shall first cast a glance at the history of measurement—the various sources of data, the choice of data, the qualitative appraisal of offenses, and, more specifically, how these matters have been considered by those concerned with juvenile delinquency. A discussion of what delinquency means in legal terms follows. Thereafter, it seems necessary to describe the organization of the Juvenile Aid Division of the Police Department of Philadelphia, its policies and record system, since our data were drawn from its records and the interpretation of these data requires a knowledge of how they came to be recorded.

Our research design is based on a number of theoretical assumptions, which we discuss somewhat at length, followed by a chapter describing how we went about drawing the 10 per cent sample of juvenile offenses, compared it with a similar sample based on the total of juvenile offenses known to the police, and established operational definitions of the categories of data to be transcribed from the offense reports. A chapter on our operational classification of delinquent conduct follows, and on the basis of this classification a series of chapters are devoted to an analysis of who discovered the offenses, the sequence and locus of discovery, and offenses involving bodily injury or property loss or damage, in particular.

Our belief that measurement of delinquency must take into account both the frequency and the degree of seriousness of delinquent acts led us to develop a design for the scaling of offenses, which is fully described as is its application to our data. Finally we shall discuss the construction of an index of delinquency, the reliability and validity of the scaling results, and the theory of measurement as related to delinquency.

2
The Historical Background: sources of data

We indicated in our introductory chapter some of the issues that require study in order to determine the feasibility of measuring criminality or delinquency and of devising means of measuring them. Most of these issues have been known and discussed for a century or more. It may be of some interest and value to learn how they have been viewed in the past and what suggestions have been made for coping with them. Although we are specifically concerned with juvenile delinquency, the fundamental principles governing its measurement have emerged in the study of criminality in general with the aid of criminal statistics. We shall begin, therefore, with an examination of the problems of measuring *criminality* in general and then see how the principles so disengaged may be applicable to the measurement of juvenile delinquency.

The belief that certain information contained in the records of various official agencies concerned with law violations and their perpetrators could be extracted, tabulated, and made to serve as an index or measure of a people's criminality is not of recent origin. If we accept the common view that statistics originated in the 17th century, the founders of this discipline were already in search of such measures. Sir William Petty (1623–1687), for instance, called for information "by the number of people . . . [of] the number of corporal sufferings and persons imprisoned for crimes, to know the measure of vice and sin in the nation."[1]

[1] *The Petty Papers, Some unpublished writings of Sir William Petty,* edited from the Bowood papers by the Marquis of Lansdowne (2 vols. Boston: Houghton

7

More than a century later, in 1778, Jeremy Bentham (1748–1832) urged that courts be required to make reports of convictions for crime, because

the ordering of these returns is a measure of excellent use in furnishing *data* for the legislator to work upon. They will form altogether a kind of *political barometer*, by which the effect of every legislative operation relative to the subject may be indicated and made palpable. It is not till lately that legislators have thought of providing themselves with these necessary documents. They may be compared with the bills of mortality published annually in London; indicating the moral health of the country (but a little more accurately, it is hoped) as these latter do the physical.[2]

During the nineteenth century, the study of the "moral health" of nations and the search for means of gauging it by the use of statistics occupied the minds of many scholars and led to the development of a branch of vital and social statistics that actually came to be known as "moral statistics." So far as the statistics of criminal offenses and offenders were concerned, however, researchers had limited source data until France began the first systematic collection of judicial criminal statistics during the first quarter of the nineteenth century. The first annual report of these statistics, covering the year 1825, was published in 1827, beginning a series that has since then been rarely interrupted. In the introduction to this report, the director of the bureau in the Ministry of Justice that prepared it, Jacques Guerry de Champneuf (1788–1852), noted that over a period of years these statistics would

assist in determining the circumstances which cooperate in increasing or diminishing the number of crimes. Such an investigation [he wrote] is worthy of the most powerful support of Your Majesty's Government. Everything points to the fact that Your Majesty's constant concern for the development of agriculture, commerce and industry and the consequent spreading of well-being and enlightenment will weaken the common causes of crime and that these tables . . . will reflect this happy influence. But if in some part of the Kingdom, these comforting theories were to be destroyed by experience, Your Majesty would at least be sure that the first symptoms of the evil would be shown with precision.

Mifflin Co., 1927), Vol. 1, p. 197. See also E. Strauss, *Sir William Petty, Portrait of a Genius* (260 pp. Glencoe, Ill.: The Free Press, 1954), p. 196.

[2] Quoted in Leon Radzinowicz, *A History of English Criminal Law and Its Administration from 1750. Vol. I. The Movement for Reform 1750–1833* (xxiv, 853 pp. New York: Macmillan, 1948), p. 395.

The French initiative was soon imitated by other countries.[3] The French statistics also became the source of the first important analytical and correlational studies of criminality, published by André Michel Guerry (1802–1866) and Adolphe Quetelet (1796–1874), the latter of whom came to occupy a dominant role in the development of statistics as an analytical tool. Other scholars, especially in France, England, Germany, and Italy, began to exploit the data contained in the growing number of official reports on criminal statistics in their countries. Before half a century had passed, most of the issues involved in the problem of measuring criminality had been touched upon, as may be seen from the following statement by Alexander von Oettingen (1827–1905):

But what shall we in fact consider to be the symptom of the movement of criminality? The mass of the unobserved substance is not only great but the differences of viewpoints and measures of appraisal are confusing, too. Some simply want to seize upon the actual convictions, as these alone permit an ascertainment of the real mass of offenses since among those *accused* one would discover that many of those subjected to investigation are innocent. Others see in the number of officially "known offenses" the most important documentation of social morality or, rather, social immorality, since the relatively small number of detected offenders or of those actually sentenced might be, in a sense, only a proof of inferior policing or of the obtuse sensitivity of a population to illegal acts. Some prefer to look at the relative number of offenses, i.e., their intensity in relation to the population "capable of committing crime"; still others regard the relationship between acquittals and convictions as a specially characteristic expression of public morals. For some the identification of serious crime is all important for the qualitative measurement of the pathological conditions of the body politic; for others, on the other hand, the participation of the different population segments according to age, sex, and occupation are of decisive importance, so that even when there is a general decline in the number of serious offenses, for instance, an increased participation of juveniles or females or of the "educated" is seen as a particularly bad symptom. Finally, some venture to concoct criminality maps and tables for various countries and peoples based on the intensive frequency of the main types of offenses, in order to

---

[3] The first to do so was Sweden, which in 1832 published its first annual report on judicial criminal statistics, covering the year 1830. The reason for establishing this service, according to the then Minister of Justice, Mattias Rosenblad, was that the King "often desired to know if crimes had increased or decreased," a question which had been unanswerable because of the absence of the necessary facts. Otto Grönlund, "Den svenska rättsstatistikens hundraårsminne," *Statsvet. Tidsskrift* 36:133–145 (May 1933), p. 138.

rank nations according to their morality and erect, on the crude material of raw empirical international criminal statistics, an indisputable monument to their own or their people's higher level of culture. Others consciously search for an average equivalent of the value of different crimes, delicts and violations by computing this value in terms of the amount of punishment and, by using certain offense units, arrive at the most precise possible quantitative representation of the multiform crimes.[4]

Aside from some of von Oettingen's references to certain technical questions, such as the graphic presentation of statistical data and the difficulties of international comparisons, he pointed to some very fundamental problems of measuring criminality: the troublesome question of the hidden or unrecorded criminality, the choice of the series of data on which to base measurement (convictions, prosecutions, crimes officially known), the kinds of crimes selected (all offenses, serious offenses), and the matter of the qualitative weighting of different offenses in order to arrive at "the proper symptom of the movement of criminality." He even referred to the interest of some researchers in the relative criminality of population segments, including different age groups. All these are, indeed, some of the most important issues that require consideration, and among them the one that first needs study is the choice of the *source* of the data needed for measurement.

The most important sources of information about criminal offenses are, of course, the governmental agencies that are entrusted with the enforcement of the criminal law and the administration of criminal justice. In the process of carrying out the duties devolving upon them, these agencies make a record of cases submitted to them and the actions and decisions taken in regard to these cases. Police agencies receive complaints from private citizens about offenses observed by them or committed against them; the police record offenses they have themselves observed or detected and the result of their investigations of complaints. If they make an arrest, this fact is recorded, as well as the reason for the arrest, i.e., the offense or offenses which the person arrested committed or is believed to have committed. Subsequently, the agencies charged with the prosecution of offenders record information about the offenses of the accused and clerks of courts record data about the offenses involved in cases that lead to some disposition by the courts, especially in cases resulting in the

[4] Alexander von Oettingen, *Die Moralstatistik in ihrer Bedeutung für eine Christliche Socialethik* (2nd rev. ed., xvi, 784 + 82 pp. Erlangen, 1874), pp. 442–443.

conviction of an offender. In all the agencies mentioned, every offense dealt with will be given a descriptive label in conformity with the law, although that label may be changed as the case progresses from one agency to the next.

Faced with the problem of the need for establishing the extent and, more particularly, the trend of criminality in any given area, we are compelled to evaluate the sources just mentioned and determine which is likely to possess the most useful information for measurement purposes: the offenses reported to the police, the offenses established by the police as having actually been committed, the offenses committed by those prosecuted before a court, or the offenses committed by those convicted. Having made a choice, we might secure permission to consult the original records of the agency, extract the information needed, and arrange and analyze it in a manner suitable to our purpose, but we would expect to find that the agency itself had already performed these operations, had published the results, and had thereby facilitated the task. In other words, we would hope that criminal statistics[5] issued by the agency would be found to contain the necessary information, permitting the analysis to encompass different types of communities and even entire states or countries. It would seem reasonable to assume that one important function of criminal statistics would be to supply basic data for the measurement of criminality.

Considering the many decades that have passed since the need for criminal statistics was firmly recognized and the many practitioners and scholars who have produced or exploited them, we might think that by now there would be complete agreement on what basic data should be used to measure criminality. This is not the case, however. Without going into details, we might say that there are, broadly speaking, two schools of thought. One of them would rely entirely on statistics of offenses derived from court records and forming a part of what is usually referred to as judicial criminal statistics;

[5] "Criminal statistics . . . might be defined as (1) uniform data on offenses or offenders that can be expressed in numerical terms, (2) derived from records of primary official agencies, (3) classified, tabulated and analyzed to demonstrate inter-group relationships, and (4) published periodically according to a uniform plan. . . . Within criminal statistics definite classes can be recognized. For various purposes it may be useful to classify such statistics according to administrative area (municipal, county, state, etc.), procedural stage (arrest, indictment, prosecution, conviction, etc.), or dominant unit of tabulation (offense, offender)." Thorsten Sellin, "Status and prospects of criminal statistics in the United States," *Festskrift tillägnad . . . Karl Schlyter . . .* (413 pp. Stockholm: Svensk Juristtidning, 1949), 291–307, pp. 294–295.

the other would place the greatest confidence in such statistics derived from the police registers or police statistics.[6] Within each of these two approaches there are some noticeable divergences. Some of those who prefer judicial statistics would limit themselves to data on convictions, while others would include all adjudications involving offenses. Among the supporters of police statistics some are willing to use all complaints of offenses whether these complaints originate from without or from within the police services and whether they are all investigated or not; others would insist on using only statistics on offenses that the police claim have actually occurred, because they were either committed in the presence of a police officer, were otherwise discovered by him, or were determined as a result of the police investigation of complaints made by private persons.

Although many of the leading criminal statisticians of the past century were thoroughly aware of the limitations of judicial criminal statistics as a source for data usable for the measurement of criminality, they nevertheless either defended or accepted them for want of anything better. It must be recalled that criminal statistics originated as a means of portraying the work of strictly judicial agencies and in countries where the investigation of crime was entrusted to such agencies rather than to the police. Therefore it was accepted as axiomatic that the extent and trends of criminality could safely be inferred from their data. Furthermore, it seemed obvious that in view of the often intricate definitions of offenses in the criminal code, only legally trained persons would be able to give an offense the descriptive label which properly belonged to it. In most countries, indeed, the resulting statistics dealt only with offenses resulting in convictions, and when at an early date it became the custom to focus the attention on the offenders convicted of crimes, practical considerations dictated the necessity of counting them only for the most serious of their crimes, thus omitting in the tabulations the additional but less serious offenses which they may also have committed. In the countries that adopted this system, inferences about criminality had to be based on statistics of offenders rather than on data about the totality of their offenses and had to ignore information about offenses that actually had been the object of judicial investigation and ascertainment but for various reasons had never reached the stage where someone was actually convicted of having committed them.

---

[6] No reference is made to prison statistics, because it is generally agreed that they are useless for the measurement of criminality.

In some countries a broader view was taken of the scope of judicial statistics. French statistics gave data about the complaints that had reached judicial authorities, the results of the investigation of these complaints, and the results of the prosecution, including convictions. Similar data were collected in Italy. Some years ago, the chief of the bureau of criminal statistics in the Italian Ministry of Justice wrote:

The statistics of criminality . . . have the task . . . of studying the objective and subjective aspects of criminality. Their basis is the irrevocable decisions of judicial authorities, because such decisions alone permit us to determine the legal existence and the characteristics of offenses and the ones responsible for them. . . . Among definitive and irrevocable decisions are included those handed down by the investigatory magistrates and resulting in no prosecution for reasons other than the lack of proof that the offense occurred and because it is not to be dealt with in the usual way. Included among such decisions are those that result in the filing of the case because the offender is unknown.[7]

It seems clear that studies of criminality based on adjudications as inclusive as those just mentioned would be more comprehensive and useful than those based only on convictions, and that such adjudications would therefore furnish the better basis for the measurement of criminality by the use of judicial statistics.

Some countries took a position between the two extremes just mentioned and based their judicial statistics on prosecutions. Broader than statistics on convictions, these statistics nevertheless ignored the offenses that may have been judicially established as having actually occurred but which did not result in the prosecution of their perpetrators.

Those who believed that there was no way of identifying and counting criminal offenses until a judicial agency had officially recognized them had, of course, little or no confidence in the information possessed by the police authorities. "I can put no value on the data on the number of offenses that have been the subject of complaints," said W. Starke, "so long as the objective nature [of the offense] has not been determined by the court and the offender ascertained, for criminal statistics (like all statistics for that matter) lose their value unless they rest on firm and accurate primary facts." We must wait for the judge "to establish both the nature of the offense and the guilt of the accused," since many crimes reported to the police are found to be

[7] Alfredo Spallanzani, *Statistiche giudiziarie* (viii, 95 pp. Milano: Giuffrè, 1933), p. 32. The last two sentences are not found in the text. They are a typewritten addendum inserted in a complimentary copy sent by the author.

groundless and prosecutions based on a fair assumption of guilt often lead to acquittals.[8]

This attitude toward the possible value of statistics of offenses known to the police dominated among scholars during the last century. Before the First World War it was indeed uncommon to find national statistics of this character, except in Great Britain, where they had begun to be published in 1857, and in some other commonwealths of the British Empire. As late as 1917, Georg von Mayr (1841–1925), after commending the British for their policy, complained that police statistics of the kind here discussed could be found elsewhere only for a small number of large cities in a few countries.[9] The importance of such data for the measurement of criminality was stressed quite early, however, and they were actually used for index purposes by competent scholars in studies that go back to the middle of the last century.

In 1853, Frederic Hill (1803–1896), inspector of prisons in Scotland, wrote:

In order to render the statistics of crime of real value, a register is wanted of the actual offenses committed, without reference to subsequent detection and conviction. Such a record, which will be found recommended in some of my Reports, besides being of essential service in determining the amount of crime at different periods and in different parts of the country would be very useful in testing the efficiency of the police.[10]

This view was not fully shared by Hill's fellow countrymen for many decades to come but it was expressed by some of the foremost criminal statisticians on the Continent. In 1867, Mayr published a study of Bavarian criminality based on crimes known to the police,[11] believing that research on moral statistics must, so far as possible, take the mass of established offenses as the point of departure, a view

---

[8] W. Starke, "Des éléments essentiels qui doivent figurer dans la statistique criminelle et des moyens de les rendre comparables," *Bull. de l'Institut Intern. de Statistique* 4, No. 1: 69–102 (1889), p. 72. (Text in German.)

[9] Georg von Mayr, *Statistik und Gesellschaftslehre* Vol. 3. *Moralstatistik mit Einschluss der Kriminalstatistik* (viii, 1042 pp. Tübingen: Mohr, 1917), pp. 454–526, *passim.*

[10] Frederic Hill, *Crime: Its Amount, Causes and Remedies* (xvi, 443 pp. London, 1853), p. 21.

[11] Georg Mayr, *Statistik der gerichtlichen Polizei im Königreiche Bayern und in einigen anderen Ländern* (200 + 187 + 10 pp. Munich, 1867), (*Beiträge zur Statistik des Königreichs Bayern*, Heft XVI). Mayr was given a title of nobility in 1879 and thus became von Mayr.

from which he, the foremost criminal statistician of them all, never departed. In his great work on criminal statistics, published in 1917, he insisted that "both with respect to serious offenses and certain lesser ones, police reports—as exhaustive as possible—on their occurrence, regardless of the success or failure of prosecution, constitute important moral statistical data about the formation of criminality."[12]

Similar ideas were expressed by von Oettingen, another pioneer in this field. In his *Moralstatistik* he advocated the collection of police statistics on offenses, and elsewhere he stated that an important task of methodical criminal statistics was "systematically to enumerate the violations of the criminal law that have actually occurred and been reported."[13]

In 1897, William Douglas Morrison, in a paper read before the Royal Statistical Society, said:

Police statistics from our point of view may be . . . defined as a body of returns relating to the number of offenses annually reported to the police, and to the number of apprehensions . . . as a result of these reports. Statistics of this character are the most comprehensive account to be obtained of the annual dimensions of crime. . . . It hardly requires to be stated that the number of apprehensions and the number of offenses reported to the police are a more complete index of the annual volume of crime than either the statistics of trials, convictions or imprisonments. The statistics of offenses reported to the police are the most complete of all . . . a very high percentage of the cases of serious crime never get beyond the stage of being reported to the police.[14]

At that time, however, the official view, expressed in the annual reports on criminal statistics of England and Wales, still was that such statistics had little value; ten years later they were somewhat more highly regarded but not yet accepted as a substitute for statistics of prosecutions or convictions.

It would, of course, be possible to give a much more elaborate and more fully documented discussion of the earlier views concerning the relative potentialities of judicial versus police statistics for measurement purposes. Generally speaking, before the First World War judicial statistics were almost universally held to be the only ones

---

[12] *Moralstatistik*, p. 421. (See footnote 9 for full reference.)
[13] Alexander von Oettingen, "Über die methodische Erhebung und Beurteilung kriminalstatistischer Daten," *Z. ges. Strafrechtswiss.* 1:414–438 (1881), p. 422.
[14] William Douglas Morrison, "The interpretation of criminal statistics," *J. Royal Statistical Soc.* 60:1–24 (March 1897), p. 3.

that should be employed in studies of the extent and the movement of criminality; indeed, they were the only ones available in nearly all countries that issued statistical reports. Statistics of offenses known to the police were being advocated by some scholars, but theirs were mostly voices crying in the wilderness. They were to be heard later, for as we shall see the last forty years have seen a startling change of opinion concerning the value of statistics of complaints to or offenses confirmed by the police.

The United States

In 1920, August Vollmer presented a plan for the organization of a bureau of criminal records and included among its duties the compilation of statistics of crimes known to the police.[15] Two years later, H. B. Chamberlain reported the defeat of a bill in the Illinois legislature, which would have empowered the Department of Public Welfare of the state to collect and publish criminal statistics, beginning with crimes known to the police.[16] A few years later, influential leaders of the International Association of Chiefs of Police began a concrete effort to secure police statistics of crimes that would accurately reflect the extent and trends of criminality. In 1927, a Committee on Uniform Crime Records was set up by the Association, funds were secured to permit the engagement of a professional staff of experts, and in 1929 the Committee published a manual,[17] which in great detail provided a blueprint for a system of collecting statistics from local police departments in the various states.

We are not concerned here with all the recommendations and arguments presented in this manual, but only with the objectives and the justifications advanced for the use of crimes known to the police for index purposes. The Committee regarded its efforts as

a natural development because all criminal statistics, whatever their scope and character, find their origin in police activity; in the investigation of crimes and the apprehension of offenders. It was a necessary development, because police represent the sole source of reliable information concerning the extent and distribution of criminal acts. . . . Most American crime

[15] "The Bureau of Criminal Records," *J. Amer. Inst. Crim. Law and Criminol.* **11**:171–180 (May 1920).
[16] "The proposed Illinois Bureau of Criminal Records and Statistics," *J. Amer. Inst. Crim. Law and Criminol.* **12**:418–520 (February 1922).
[17] *Uniform Crime Reporting, A Complete Manual for Police* (xvi, 464 pp. New York: Committee on Uniform Crime Records, International Association of Chiefs of Police, c. 1929).

statistics, as well as many of the foreign systems, begin with the number of persons arrested. Such as these entirely ignore those basic records which, properly compiled, may be made to show the number and nature of criminal offenses committed. Even the most elaborate systems for collecting and tabulating arrests, judicial dispositions, and prisoners cannot do that. The latter have their important uses in showing (1) the social characteristics of persons who are arrested, prosecuted, convicted or imprisoned, and (2) the manner in which the machinery of criminal justice actually functions. Lack of any constant relation between the number of arrests, convictions, and prisoners, on the one hand, and criminal acts on the other, must always prevent measurement of the extent of crime by any such changing standards. Frequent efforts to draw such comparisons and conclusions have yielded conflicting results and done the cause of criminal statistics incalculable harm.[18]

The result of the Committee's work was the establishment of the system of uniform crime reporting by police agencies, at first instituted by the Committee itself on an experimental basis and soon taken over by the Federal Bureau of Investigation and exemplified in the periodical *Uniform Crime Reports*,[19] still published by that agency.

The same year that the Committee published its report (1929) Mr. Bennet Mead, in charge of the section of prison statistics of the Bureau of the Census, wrote: "Statistics of the number of offenses known to the police form the best available means of measuring the extent of crime at a given time, and the changes from time to time in the prevalence of the more serious offenses against persons and against property."[20] Two years later, the National Commission on Law Observance and Enforcement, better known as the Wickersham Commission, in its extensive report on *Criminal Statistics* prepared by Sam Bass Warner, stated categorically that "the best index of the number and nature of offenses committed is police statistics showing offenses known to the police."[21] But it recommended great caution in the use of such data until police agencies had become fully aware of the duty of accurate reporting. An article published the same year analyzed in some detail the reasons for relying on police statistics for

---

[18] *Ibid.*, pp. 2–4.
[19] Beginning as a monthly in 1929, it later became a quarterly and then a semi-annual publication. Since 1957 it has been issued annually, supplemented by very brief quarterly reports.
[20] Bennet Mead, "Police statistics," *Ann. Amer. Acad. polit. and soc. Sci.* 194:74–85 (November 1929), p. 76.
[21] National Commission on Law Observance and Enforcement, *Report on Criminal Statistics* (v, 205 pp. Washington, D.C.: U.S. Government Printing Office, 1931), p. 25.

the construction of an index to crime.[22]   Since then, such statistics have been at least in theory accepted as the best source of data for measurement, as may be seen by an inspection of any one of the numerous textbooks on criminology published in the United States.

Some Other Countries

The same shift of opinion is observable in some other countries. Statistics of crimes known to the police began to be published in Great Britain in 1857, but as late as 1924 the official report on criminal statistics for England and Wales claimed that "the figures of persons tried for indictable offenses are usually considered to be the best index to the annual fluctuations of crime. . . . Owing to changes in procedure and practice, trustworthy conclusions as to the increase or decrease of crime cannot be based upon figures of persons convicted or of persons imprisoned."[23]   By 1928, the lengthy introduction to the report for that year relied heavily on crimes known to the police in its discussion of the nature of changes in criminality, and in 1930 the statement appeared that "in these introductions, the number of crimes known to the police is now regarded as the best index to the volume of crime."[24]   In later reports, however, a more cautious attitude could be seen.   The report for 1931 seemed to give equal weight to the figures of crimes known to the police and to the statistics of persons prosecuted, but by 1933 it was thought that offenses of violence against the person and sex offenses, as given in the police statistics, could be regarded "as a reliable indication."   In 1934, frauds and false pretences were added to this list.   Until 1945, the *Criminal Statistics: Scotland* always featured the statistics of persons proceeded against, but in 1946, the introduction to the report for that year began with a discussion of crimes known to the police, illustrated by 13 diagrams showing the trends of various offenses during the period 1937–1946.

This change of view on the part of the official compilers and interpreters of criminal statistics in the British Isles has been given the support of British criminologists, by and large.   Professor Leon Radzinowicz, now director of the Institute of Criminology at the University of Cambridge, wrote some twenty years ago that "it seems

---

[22] Thorsten Sellin, "The basis of a crime index," *J. Crim. Law and Criminol.* **22:**335–356 (September 1931); "Die Grundlagen eines Kriminalitätsindex," *Monats. f. Kriminalpsych. und Strafrechtsref.* **22:**477–497 (October 1931).

[23] *Criminal Statistics . . . for the Year 1924* (London: H. M. Stationery Office), p. 1.

[24] *Criminal Statistics . . . for the Year 1930,* footnote, p. iv.

to us that the tendency recently displayed in England to consider the number of crimes known to the police as the best index is the right one." More recently, he referred to police statistics as being "now regarded by virtually all criminologists as the most reliable and sensitive instrument for the assessment of trends in crime."[25] And, in 1951, Dr. M. Grünhut, Reader in Criminology at the University of Oxford, after considering various problems of assessing the value of judicial statistics, stated that "for these reasons the number of crimes known to the police, as the nearest possible approach to the source, has been generally recognized as the best available index of the volume of crime."[26]

Dr. Hermann Mannheim has taken a much more sceptical attitude toward English criminal statistics in general and has provided the most extensive analysis of their organization, content, and usefulness for measurement purposes.[27] Notwithstanding the doubts he expressed in that connection, his excellent study of *Social Aspects of Crime in England between the Wars* was based, to a considerable degree, on crimes known to the police. A pessimistic view was recently expressed by Barbara Wootton,[28] refuting, by implication, the statement in the most recent (or rather only) "textbook" of criminology in England, published a few years earlier, that "the generally accepted view nowadays is that stated by Sellin in the following general rule: 'The value of a crime rate for index purposes decreases as the distance from the crime itself in terms of procedure increases.'"[29]

Denmark was the first Scandinavian country to begin the collection and publication of statistics of crimes reported to the police. The system was established in 1921 and in 1933 data on offenses "cleared

---

[25] Leon Radzinowicz, "English criminal statistics," *Law Quart. Rev.* 46:384–503 (October 1940), p. 498; *In Search of Criminology* (vii, 254 pp. Cambridge: Harvard University Press, 1962), p. 59.

[26] M. Grünhut, "Statistics in criminology," *J. Royal Statistical Soc.* (Ser. A.) 114, pt. II: 139–162 (1951), p. 152.

[27] Hermann Mannheim, *Social Aspects of Crime in England between the Wars* (382 pp. London: Allen & Unwin, 1940). Part I, pp. 27–102, contains the discussion of the "structure and interpretation of the criminal statistics for England and Wales."

[28] Barbara Wootton, assisted by Vera G. Seal and Rosalind Chambers, *Social Science and Social Pathology* (400 pp. London: Allen & Unwin, 1959). "That we should reject the official criminal statistics as evidence of criminal trends is hard doctrine, because it means that we must be content to confess ourselves quite ignorant as to whether our population is becoming more, or less, addicted to crime. Nevertheless, such ignorance has to be admitted" (p. 25).

[29] Howard Jones, *Crime and the Penal System* (269 pp. London: University Tutorial Press, 1956), p. 18.

up" were added. In 1947, Professor Stephan Hurwitz, author of the leading textbook on criminology in Denmark, stated that "whereas formerly importance was attached to the court statistics, in recent literature prominence is given to the police statistics as the truest indication of actual criminality."[30]

In Finland, a decision by the Cabinet in 1926 instituted the collection of data on offenses known to the police; the first published report of this series covered the year 1927. One of its purposes was to exhibit the "visible criminality" or "the criminality that comes to the attention of the police authorities, whether the offenders have been prosecuted or not."[31] From the beginning and until the end of the Second World War, these statistics were gathered under the supervision of Dr. Veli Verkko, who strongly believed in their usefulness for measurement purposes.

Early in 1950, a Royal Proclamation in Sweden ordered police and prosecution agencies to report periodically to the Statistical Central Bureau the offenses made known to them. Quarterly and annual publications of such data began with the calendar year 1950. The annual report for that year included not only the offenses reported, classified in a rather detailed manner, but also the results of the police investigations of complaints and certain data on the persons charged with the offenses. In the introduction, the statement was made that "the data in the police statistics concerning the number of offenses known to the police furnish the best possible basis of a crime index, numerically speaking, showing variations in criminality from one period to another."[32] The same view has been repeatedly expressed, since then, by those in charge of the section of criminal statistics in the Statistical Bureau[33] and also by the special committee that studied and reported in 1954 on the reorganization of Swedish criminal statistics.[34]

Norway began the collection of police statistics in 1956. The

[30] Stephan Hurwitz, *Criminology* (442 pp. London: Allen & Unwin, 1952), p. 29.
[31] Finlands Officiella Statistik XXIII. Rättsstatistik, *Brottsligheten 1927*, I. *Brott som kommit till polisens kännedom* (43 pp. Helsinki, 1928), p. 1.
[32] Statistiska Centralbyrån, *Brott som kommit till polisens kännedom år 1950* (34 pp. Stockholm: Statistiska Centralbyrån, 1952), p. 1.
[33] For instance, Sverker Groth, "Polisstatistik," *Sociala Meddelanden* 1950: 344–352 and Sven Rengby, "Brottslighetsutvecklingen i Sverige under 1950-talet," *Svensk Juristtidning* 46:194–211 (March 1961), p. 104.
[34] Statens Offentliga Utredningar 1954:35. Justitiedepartementet, *Den Svenska Kriminalstatistiken*. Betänkande av Kriminalstatistikutredningen. (190 pp. Stockholm: Norstedt), 1954.

annual reports covering that and subsequent years contain information on offenses investigated by the police and on persons charged.[35]

In 1935, the Ministry of the Interior of Germany ordered that, beginning with 1936, police agencies would report statistics on offenses known, and a later order specifically stated that "the criminal statistics of the police is limited to giving information on the status of criminality . . . and is a numerical compilation of the offenses that have actually occurred and have been investigated by the police."[36]

Israel in 1949 and Italy in 1955 began to publish statistics of offenses known to the police. A systematic search would probably uncover additional countries that have instituted such statistics.

International

Attempts to make comparative studies of the criminality of different countries began as soon as the first judicial criminal statistics began to appear. The technical difficulties involved in such studies were also well understood. The lack of uniform definitions of offenses and the differences among countries in the administrative structure and procedures of the agencies dealing with crime and criminals appeared to present insurmountable hazards. The nine international statistical congresses, between 1853 and 1876, and the later organized International Statistical Institute periodically struggled with the problem. As a result of a communication made by Dr. J. R. B. DeRoos, associate director of the Netherlands Central Bureau of Statistics, at the meeting of the Institute at Cairo in 1927,[37] a new committee was appointed to make a study of how the criminal statistics of the various countries might be used in comparative researches. The committee made its report to the meeting held in Warsaw in 1930. Having noted that statistics of convicted persons or statistics of convictions "constituted the basis of most criminal statistics," the committee recommended that national statistics of "crimes known to the police" be collected as a supplement to already existing data.[38] In 1931, one

[35] The latest report examined is Norges Offisielle Statistikk XII 48, *Kriminalstatistikk 1959* (61 pp. Oslo: Statistisk Sentralbyrå), 1961.
[36] K. Krug, K. Schäfer, F. W. Stolzenburg, and O. Behrens, *Strafrechtliche Verwaltungsvorschriften* (3rd. rev. ed., xlvii, 1192 pp. Berlin: R. V. Deckers Verl., 1943), p. 1040.
[37] J. R. B. DeRoos, *Consonnes et voyelles; Communication sur la statistique criminelle* (7 pp. Cairo: Government Press), 1927.
[38] "Rapport de la Commission pour l'étude comparative des statistiques criminelles dans les divers pays," *Bull. de l'Institut intern. de Statistique* 24:567-568 (1930).

of the members of the committee, Professor Corrado Gini, and A. Spallanzani presented to the session of the Institute, held in Madrid, an international plan for the collection of uniform statistics of "crimes known to the police" strongly resembling the system of Uniform Crime Reporting instituted in the United States two years earlier.[39]

After World War II, interest in international criminal statistics was revived—this time by the United Nations. In 1948 the Social Commission and the Economic and Social Council requested the Secretariat to make some studies in the field of the prevention of crime and the treatment of offenders, and a topic chosen for immediate investigation was that of "criminal statistics, with a view to a report on the state of crime." As a matter of fact, the Secretariat had already begun such a study a year earlier, to cover the period 1937–1946. The results of the study were published early in 1950.[40]

Late in 1950 an international *ad hoc* expert committee was assembled by the Secretariat. One of the topics on its agenda was the matter of what step should be taken next to develop international uniform criminal statistics. The Committee recommended the collection of certain basic data on crimes known to the police as being most apt to yield a basis for indices to criminality.[41] The recommendation was accepted by the policy-making organs of the United Nations and the Secretariat was requested to institute the necessary measures to make the plan a reality. So far, however, this project is still in a preparatory stage. A report based on a comparative study of the criminal law of the member states of the United Nations and suggesting how comparative statistics of criminal homicides, aggravated assault, robbery, and burglary might be secured through uniform reporting of such offenses, has been submitted to governments for comments.

---

[39] C. Gini and A. Spallanzani, *Sulla comparazione dei dati di statistica criminale dei diversi Stati* (16 pp. plus 5 comp. tables. Madrid: 1931). The proposal was quite in line with the earlier plea of Georg von Mayr, not mentioned by the authors, who in his *Moralstatistik* urged the collection of international police statistics of murder and manslaughter, robbery, burglary and theft, at least, and considered it feasible to do so for comparative purposes. See the work mentioned, pp. 503–504.

[40] United Nations Economic and Social Council, Social Commission, Sixth Session, *Statistical Report on the State of Crime 1937–1946* (Prepared by the Secretariat. 72 pp. mimeo. New York: United Nations, 1950). (General. E/CN.5/204.23 February 1950. Original: English.)

[41] The committee consisted of Margery Fry, chairman, Marc Ancel, Ronald H. Beattie, Thorsten Sellin, and Veli Verkko.

In the meanwhile, the International Criminal Police Commission (Interpol) had been working on plans to gather comparable statistics on "known offenses." At a General Assembly of the Commission in Bern, in 1949, Dr. Harry Söderman made a report which caused the Commission to resolve to explore the possibility of establishing a system of police statistics on an international scale. Dr. Söderman was entrusted with the task, aided by a committee. Two years later, he presented a plan to the General Assembly of the Commission, meeting in Lisbon, a few months after the Economic and Social Council of the UN had instructed the Secretary General of the United Nations to undertake the study referred to in the preceding paragraph. Dr. Söderman outlined a plan, which the International Criminal Police Commission was urged to adopt and which would involve the transmission, by member states of the Commission, of certain uniform data on selected offenses known to the police authorities of those states and on the persons charged with these offenses. The statistics of offenses involved were defended because "the increase or the decline in criminality is seen from a continuous examination, over a period of time, of all punishable offenses brought to the knowledge of the criminal police."[42]

The plan was promptly put into effect. It has permitted the Commission to publish a series of statistical reports; a recent one dealing with the calendar years 1957 and 1958 contains reports on seven selected offenses reported to the police of 54 national jurisdictions.[43] It is of interest to note that the only criminal statistics included in the annual *Statistical Data* book, 1959 (Table 89–91) of the Council of Europe are data on the above-mentioned offenses reported to the police in thirteen European countries in 1955 and 1956, and the number of offenders charged with these crimes.

This very cursory and rapid review of opinions and developments concerning the sources that should be used in an attempt to locate the basic data for the measurement of criminality shows that although in earlier times it was commonly believed that statistics drawn from the registers of the criminal courts were the only ones that would serve the purpose, there has been a gradual shift of opinion during the last forty years or more. Today there is increasing reliance on police statistics, evidenced by the fact that a growing number of

[42] Harry Söderman, *Objet: Statistiques internationales de police criminelle* (7 pp. Paris: International Criminal Police Organization, 1951). (20th General Assembly, Lisbon, June 11–15, 1951. Report No. 9.)
[43] International Criminal Police Organization-Interpol, *International Crime Statistics, 1957–1958* (xii, 109 pp. Paris: Interpol, n.d).

nations have instituted more or less elaborate systems for their collection and that more and more research studies by official bodies or by individual researchers interested in demonstrating changes and trends in criminality make use of the data of offenses or offenders known to police authorities, sometimes together with certain data from judicial statistics and often in preference to the latter.[44]

[44] A few recent examples are: R. Rijksen, *Criminaliteit en bezetting* (175 pp. Assen: van Gorcum & Comp., 1957); Tadashi Uematsu, "Criminality in Japan observed from the point of view of age and sex," *Ann. Hitotsubashi Acad.* 9:76–90 (1958); Knut Sveri, *Kriminalitet og alder* (242 pp. Uppsala: Almquist & Wicksell, 1960); F. H. McClintock and Evelyn Gibson, *Robbery in London* (xix, 147 pp. London: Macmillan, 1961); Marvin E. Wolfgang, *Patterns in Criminal Homicide* (xiv, 413 pp. Philadelphia: University of Pennsylvania Press, 1958).

3

The Historical Background:
choice of data

The fact that the offenses coming to the notice of public authorities represent only a part of the offenses actually committed was fully realized, of course, by the early students of criminal statistics. Quetelet observed, in the earliest research which he conducted, that

our observations can only refer to a certain number of crimes known and adjudicated, out of a total number of unknown crimes committed. Since this total sum will probably always remain unknown, all conclusions based upon it will be more or less erroneous; I do not hesitate to say that all we possess of statistics of crimes and misdemeanors would have no utility if we did not tacitly assume that there is a nearly invariable relationship between offenses known and adjudicated and the total unknown sum of offenses committed. . . . One appreciates therefore how important it is to validate such a relationship and can only be astonished that no one has been occupied in dong so up to the present time.[1]

The relationship of which we are speaking [Quetelet continued] necessarily varies with the nature and the gravity of the crimes; in a well organized society, where the police is active and justice well administered, this relationship would, in the case of murders and voluntary homicides, almost reach unity . . .; it might not be the same for poisonings; when it is a question of thefts and offenses of minor importance, the relationship might become very weak and a large number of offenses remain unknown, either because their victims do not become cognizant of the crime or do not want to prosecute their perpetrators, or because justice lacks sufficient evidence to

[1] Adolphe Quetelet, *Recherches sur le penchant au crime aux différens ages*, pp. 18–19.

act. . . . If all the causes that influence the degree of the relationship remain the same, one can also say that the effects would remain invariable.[2]

In a later work, he returned to this problem. After noting that crimes can be divided into three classes: those that are known and whose perpetrators are also known; those that are known but committed by unknown persons; and those that remain completely hidden, and remarking that only statistics pertaining to the first of these classes existed, he wondered how such incomplete documents could be utilized. "If I were well convinced that the number of crimes brought before the courts always were ten per cent of all the crimes committed, I could determine, from year to year, if the number of crimes increased or decreased. We would then be led to conclude that there exists a constant ratio which gives a measure of the *activity of justice.*"[3] But is this relationship constant? Yes, if "judicial prosecutions continue to be made with the same activity, if the statistics register the facts with the same exactness, if reforms in the law do not change the punishments and do not tend to correctionalize crimes [i.e., reduce felonies to misdemeanors], and if the condition of the country does not undergo substantial changes."[4] Because he found a constant relationship between the number of crimes reported and those *prosecuted* in Belgium during each year, 1833–1839, when such data were published, he concluded that there must also exist a similar proportionality between the adjudicated offenses and those remaining unknown. He placed no reliance, however, on the number of crimes resulting in convictions. "When it is a question of morality, one must consider the number of crimes and the number of persons charged rather than the number convicted, for when a crime has been established but an acquittal occurs, the fact that a crime has been committed nevertheless remains established."[5]

Quetelet's belief that a constant ratio existed between adjudicated and hidden criminality led him to accept judicial statistics of *prosecuted* crimes as the proper basis for measuring criminality, but only if he could assume that penal law and administration and the social conditions of a country remained completely unchanged during the period studied. In the studies he conducted, all of which covered relatively short periods, he made that assumption.

[2] *Ibid.*, pp. 19–20.
[3] Adolphe Quetelet, *Lettres à S.A.R. le Duc Regnant de Saxe-Cobourg et Gotha sur la théorie des probabilités appliquée aux sciences morales et politiques* (iv., 450 pp. Brussels, 1846), p. 324.
[4] *Ibid.*, p. 324.
[5] *Ibid.*, p. 327.

The problems involved in measurement were given considerable attention in the 1860's in two remarkable studies by Angelo Messedaglia (1820–1901) and Georg Mayr. Messedaglia[6] noted that "the number of offenses reported do not suffice to define the criminality of a country, because a fair share of them (varying with the region and the circumstances) are discovered to be unfounded. Hence we must wait until they have been clarified and not accept any but those that have, so far as it is possible, been objectively confirmed."[7] Here, he said, is the basic element of criminality seen objectively, but how could one form a correct conception of its statistical value? The following observations, he thought, might help to do so.

First, it is certain that the offenses regarded as ascertained do not include the totality of crimes committed. Many escape being reported or becoming officially known and therefore escape prosecution. Some remain unknown to the victims or if known to them are not reported, are condoned or may become subject to some transaction that is sometimes acceptable to or favored by the law under certain circumstances. Offenses, for instance, that injure public order, greatly depend for their discovery on the relative vigilance and activity of the agents of public safety and on the relative cooperation or tolerance of the population. Such circumstances can cause, from one region or epoch to another, a more or less great variation in the ratio of offenses reported to the offenses actually committed. . . . There are regions where a universally diffused civic virtue and institutions that have firm and felt roots in the general consciousness of the people convert all persons into vigilant and inflexible cooperators with justice; there are other regions where the opposite conditions, in many cases, cause most people to be indifferent spectators or even indulgent admirers and moral accomplices of the crimes of others.

On the other hand, there are many reported offenses that have at a preliminary stage been accepted as true and then are during later stages of procedure discovered to be unfounded, either because they had not, in fact, been committed or were not imputable to those accused of them. . . . Generally it is true that no crime can be defined as such until the personal responsibility of the offender has been assessed. The subjective element is, so to speak, necessarily combined with the objective one and governs it. Therefore, the reality or the absence of the crime can only be determined

---

[6] Angelo Messedaglia, "Esposizione critica delle statistiche criminali dell'Impero austriaco, con particolare riguardo al Lombardo-Veneto, secondo i resoconti uffiziali del quadriennio 1856–1859 e col confronte dei dati posteriori," *Atti dell' I. R. Istituto Veneto di Scienze, Letteri ed Arti* (Ser. 3, 11:153–211, 331–409, 483–510, 601–652, 993–1051, 1237–1258, 1865–1866; 12:227–268, 1866–1867). All references are to vol. 11.

[7] *Ibid.*, pp. 185–186.

when a definitive judicial decision is pronounced. . . . *However, there are offenses, the objective existence of which can be established, in most cases, at the preliminary stage before any one has been prosecuted for them (as, for instance most thefts, robberies, homicides, etc.) and there are others in which the decision is rather difficult (e.g., frauds)* [our italics] and therefore the comment just made has a certain value. . . .

It is said that the rates of objective criminality cannot run parallel to those of subjective criminality, i.e., the rates of crimes are different from the rates of criminals. This is important especially in connection with *participation* and *concurrence* as well as for *recidivism* and the repetition of crimes by the same offenders. With regard to the first point . . . there is considerable variation from region to region (and this would be even greater for different types of crimes) in the relation of the number of offenses to the corresponding number of offenders (including principals and accomplices, or all offenders generally). Similarly, there are crimes that are more easily repeated than are others and in which criminal activity can sometimes degenerate into a kind of occupation. This, for instance, is the case of theft and robbery. If vigilance and penal repression are relaxed the result would be inevitable. Crimes would multiply at a rate that could be incomparably greater than the increase in the number of offenders. A gang of thieves, without increasing its membership, could, unless discovered and dealt with, enormously raise the number of thefts and robberies. In such cases, the criminality of a region, seen objectively, could deteriorate without any corresponding change or as great a change in the general morality of the region, and rather reflect more or less serious defects in the conditions and instrumentalities of public safety and penal repression. . . . Hence it would be desirable to have detailed statistics that would reveal the objective criminality clearly for each type of crime. The character of the crime is indeed decisive . . . in causing variations in the relationship of objective to subjective criminality, because some crimes are more likely than others to be repeated by the same persons or permit, by their character and the circumstances in which they ordinarily occur, the participation of many persons.[3]

Where Quetelet relied on statistics of crimes prosecuted, Messedaglia relied on the statistics of crimes that, having been reported to the public authorities, were confirmed by judicial investigation. This view is still reflected by the criminal statisticians of Italy. It must be recalled that in that country, as well as in many others, "the investigation of crimes is usually carried on by a regular judge called the *giudice istruttore,* with the help of the police;" he determines if a crime has occurred, even if no offender is found or known, and de- decides "whether or not a formal accusation will be made against a

[3] *Ibid.,* pp. 204–207.

suspect."[9] His function is, therefore, not unlike that which, in the case of most types of offenses, devolves upon the police in Anglo-Saxon jurisdiction, including the United States.[10]

Mayr's "Statistics of the Judicial Police in the Kingdom of Bavaria and in Some Other Countries"[11] was the first study to be based on police statistics, and it has often been cited because of its importance in demonstrating the relationship of economic conditions to criminality. A punishable act, he said, must become known to the police and the courts before it can be dealt with. It is reported either by a private individual or some government organ, or—if it is an offense which can only be prosecuted when the offended party demands it— by the victim. What relationship do these reports bear to real criminality? They obviously do not involve all crimes committed, because many offenses remain unknown, perhaps even to the victim, and some are reported out of mischief although they are not crimes. The probability of nonreporting increases as the offense becomes pettier and the damage slighter. Thefts of large sums are reported but not many petty thefts, and serious injuries to a person resulting in death are always reported but not simple assaults. It must be kept in mind that "the number of punishable acts brought to official notice is only a quota of the really committed offenses" and that "the more insignificant the injury to person or property is and the lighter the offense, the more does the divergence increase. . . ."[12]

Mayr was convinced that

the rise or fall of crimes reported permits a direct conclusion as to the rise or fall of real criminality. . . . When one wants an exact picture of the moral condition of a population [he said] the figures that lump all crimes together have no value, however. One should first of all ask how great is the number of known offenses of different kinds, before one asks how many persons have been convicted of the different crimes. The immorality of a people is not ascertained by the number of convicted persons but by the number of crimes committed.[13]

The reason for Mayr's reliance on police statistics was due to a

[9] John Clarke Adams and Paolo Barile, *The Government of Republican Italy* (x, 245 pp. Boston: Houghton Mifflin, 1961), p. 139.
[10] See Patrick Devlin, *The Criminal Prosecution in England* (viii, 118 pp. London: Oxford University Press, 1960).
[11] Georg Mayr, *Statistik der gerichtlichen Polizei im Königreich Bayern und in einigen anderen Ländern* (200 + 187 + 10 pp. Munich, 1867).
[12] *Ibid.*, p. 2.
[13] *Ibid.*, cf. Quetelet's view; see footnote 5.

conviction that, contrary to what he assumed to be Quetelet's claim, the statistics of prosecuted or convicted persons did not remain as constant proportions of real criminality. His own study had revealed, for instance, that in different regions of Bavaria, the percentage of detected offenders varied from 39 to 48 per cent.[14]

Messedaglia and Mayr were apparently the first scholars to hold that crime rates of a crude nature, based on total population, were indefensible. Both insisted that such rates should be computed only for the population "legally capable, by reason of age, of committing crime."[15]

All the researchers mentioned were aware of the fact that in different crimes there exist differences in the likelihood of their being reported to public authorities and differences in the ease with which they can be detected. They understood that these differences depended on public attitudes toward criminal conduct in its various manifestations and on the degree to which the public authorities themselves were active in the enforcement of the law. They also recognized, either explicitly or by inference, that measurement of crime had to be based on information secured at the earliest possible stage in the procedure of dealing with crime, even though they were not in complete agreement on what that stage was. They did not, however, give any intensive attention to the various factors that made measurement of real criminality difficult, and many years passed before these were to receive more than passing notice by statisticians.

We have noted in earlier pages that the belief that police statistics are best for measurement purposes has manifested itself in various ways in recent decades. Mayr's early claim has thus been vindicated. But what are the reasons for this belief? Briefly, they are that once an offense has come to the notice of the police and, upon investigation or direct observation, been found to have occurred, a whole series of factors of a procedural nature begin to operate. The objective determination of the existence of the offense may or may not result in an arrest because of circumstances or policies that may vary from place to place and year to year. When an arrest has made it possible to bring a suspect before a court, variable policies of prosecution may affect the outcome—witness, for instance, the custom in the United States of accepting pleas of guilty to an offense of less gravity than the principal one committed by the defendant, not to mention the prosecuting attorney's power to decide not to prosecute for some

---

[14] *Ibid.*, p. 3.
[15] Messedaglia, *op. cit.*, p. 211; Mayr, *Moralstatistik* . . . , pp. 22–23.

reason or other. Finally, adventitious circumstances, such as the skill of prosecution or defense and the nature of the trial jury may affect the verdict. The result is that rates of arrests, prosecutions, or convictions, or rather rates of crimes resulting in these actions, may misrepresent the extent and trends of real criminality. Therefore, the variables introduced by changes over periods of time in administrative efficiency and policies make the generalization possible that "the value of a crime rate for index purposes decreases as the distance from the crime itself, in terms of procedure, increases."[16]

The time element involved is another variable of importance, since delays in prosecution and the protracted length of some cases may cause a prosecution or conviction to be recorded in a given year for an offense committed in some previous year. Since the investigation by the police of a crime reported is most likely to coincide in time with the occurrence of the offense, this furnishes an additional reason for thinking that the data concerning such events are most likely to furnish the best basis for the measurement of criminality.

The choice of police statistics for the purpose just mentioned does not, however, eliminate all problems. The user of the data on crimes known to the police must know their limitations as well as their strengths. First of all, he must know *how* offenses come to the notice of the police. Some are of such a nature that they are practically never reported to the police; they are usually detected during routine patrol duty, which means that unless there is consistency and uniformity in the extent and intensity of patrolling, the number of such offenses detected will depend on the extent to which activity of the police changes from time to time, a fact which Messedaglia noted. Others would rarely be known unless victims or other private persons report them to the police and in this connection it would be important to know if such offenses are consistently reported. Here, too, the nature of the offense plays a role and determines the degree of its reportability. Some offenses are reported in what we may assume is a very high percentage of cases; others are rarely reported with the result that the recorded sample is very small. There are other factors that affect reportability. Attitudes toward the seriousness of an offense may vary from time to time and from place to place, depending on the specific composition of the population. In some social groups or areas in a community, a given type of offense may be more

---

[16] Thorsten Sellin, "The Basis of a Crime Index," *J. Crim. Law and Criminol.* 22:335–356 (September 1931), p. 346. A telling illustration of the validity of this generalization has recently been made by R. Ledent. See his "La criminalité impunie en Belgique," *Bull. de statistique,* nos. 7–9 (July-October, 1951).

lightly regarded than in others. If the offender is known to the victim, his relationship to the victim or his personal characteristics, such as his youth or his social status, may also affect the reportability of the offense.

Once the offense has become known to the police in any manner, we must know if the records of the event and the subsequent investigation or action by the police are consistently, accurately, and fully kept. This depends on administrative policies and on the conscientiousness of individual officers and is not unrelated to the standards of selection and training which govern the employment of police personnel. An important problem connected with the recording process is that of the classification or labeling of the offense. The question will always arise whether police officers on patrol or after an investigation can give the proper legal label to the offense, especially if the offender is unknown and before courts have examined it. Unless the judgment of the police as to the proper legal description of the offense is reasonably correct and is uniformly and consistently applied, the data would suffer from inaccuracies that would make comparisons difficult.

All the problems mentioned become more thorny when data from a large number of jurisdictions are combined, as happens when they cover entire states or all cities of certain sizes, for instance. They are less likely to cause difficulty when they pertain to a single community, where the researcher is able to study them and estimate their importance.

Complementary Sources of Data

In discussing the basis of the measurement of criminality, we have so far considered only official data derived from agencies whose duty it is to investigate, prosecute, and punish crimes on behalf of the state. These are undoubtedly the most important sources, but official data from other agencies may, for some specific purpose or other, be equally useful and sometimes more so in providing a basis for measurement. One such source is the statistics of deaths due to willful homicide contained in the reports on mortality issued by bureaus of vital statistics. These statistics are believed to furnish a good index of criminal homicide and have been used for that purpose for many decades by researchers in many countries.[17]

---

[17] When we consider that Italian criminal statistics used to include in statistics of homicides not only completed crimes but also attempted homicides, while the mortality statistics dealt only with completed homicides, it would seem clear that the latter would furnish superior data on the problem.

Most of what we have called complementary sources of data are, however, primarily useful in securing an indication of the extent and nature of various types of criminality that may or may not be brought to the attention of the police: losses to mercantile establishments through theft; similar losses by industrial concerns, hotels, railroads, etc.; losses to telephone companies, transportation services, etc., through the use of slugs in automatically operated telephones, turnstiles, vending machines, and such; and insurance losses due to theft. The study of unofficial data of this type is important for arriving at a better idea of the ratio of recorded to unrecorded offenses, and hence for determining the validity of recorded offenses as a basis for measurement.

THE CHOICE OF OFFENSES FOR MEASUREMENT PURPOSES

Mayr's claim that statistics of total offenses which do not distinguish different kinds of crimes have no value for index purposes is now universally admitted as true. Suppose, however, that we possess statistics of a detailed nature giving us the number of offenses known to the police separately for all the different kinds of crimes defined by law; could we use them as true indicators of the extent and trends of the real criminality of which these statistics present us only with samples in each category? To answer this question we must examine in more detail the traits of different crimes as these traits affect reportability.

Broadly speaking, crimes can be divided into three general classes. (1) There are crimes that cause some harm to persons directly. The harm may be physical, as in assaults, or it may be done to the person's property, as in thefts. There is, then, a personal victim, or someone close to or responsible for or to him, who may be expected under ordinary circumstances to seek the assistance of the police in finding and punishing the offender and possibly recovering the property. (2) There are other crimes, where one can hardly speak of victims, crimes of a conspiratorial or consensual character, where the participants are nearly always the only ones who know of the wrongdoing and do their best to conceal it. Criminal abortion, blackmail, narcotic violations, gambling, and most sex offenses fall in this category, for instance. (3) Finally, there are crimes that do not directly affect any person. These are offenses against the public order, such as vagrancy, public drunkenness, prostitution, and violations of ordinances of many kinds. The police is relied upon to enforce the laws governing these offenses, and private citizens rarely call them to the attention of the police, with the result that statistics concerning them depend almost entirely on the extent and changes of police activity rather than on the extent and changes in the frequency of the conduct involved.[18]

It is generally agreed today that criminal statistics, including police statistics, do not furnish a sound basis for the measurement of the extent and trends of almost all the real criminality that falls in the second or the third class above. In the third class the number of "known offenses" tends to be identical or nearly identical with the number of offenses "cleared by arrest," proving the dependence of the former figure on the extent to which the police are active in repression. In the second class, the "known offenses" form such a small sample of the universe they represent that they can hardly be assumed to be representative. The "hidden" proportion is too overwhelming to permit us to believe that increases or decreases in the size of the sample would correspond to changes in the real criminality involved.

These conclusions have been arrived at by various researchers in recent decades, although they were foreshadowed in statements made by some of the earliest of the criminal statisticians. Messedaglia had noted, for instance, that statistics of offenses against public order depended on the activity of the law enforcement authorities as well as on changing levels of tolerance of the population affected. Mayr had observed that the quota of hidden offenses was unknown, but that it undoubtedly bore a relation to the seriousness of the offense, being small in the most serious offenses, and to the relative ease or difficulty of detecting crimes.[19] And in 1910, Giovanni Mortara wrote:

Of the most serious crimes (homicides, aggravated assaults, arsons, robbery, burglary with theft, etc.)—except for some types of frauds and sex offenses— the quota that escapes the eye of justice is not very large. Of other crimes (escapes, resistance to and outrages against public authority, counterfeiting, bankruptcy, etc.) reports are rather incomplete for various reasons. But what enormous numbers of thefts, frauds, and document forgeries are unknown to their victims; what number of simple assaults, threats, sex offenses, abuses of parental discipline, receiving of stolen goods, defamation, insults and thefts that never become known to magistrates because of the tolerance of victims! In the case of certain offenses, too, that do not directly injure any person's interests, the quota becoming known is surely extremely

---

[18] See Thorsten Sellin, "The measurement of crime in geographic areas," *Proc. Amer. Philos. Soc.* 97:163–167 (April 1953) ; and "The significance of records of crime," *Law Quart. Rev.* 47:489–504 (October 1951), pp. 495–496.

[19] Messedaglia, *op. cit.,* p. 204; Mayr, *Moralstistik* . . . , p. 414. Even Quetelet referred to it; see his *Recherches.* . . . , p. 19.

small by comparison with that remaining unknown. It suffices to mention the offense of criminal abortion.[20]

In 1930, Verkko published an article on "Criminal statistics and real criminality,"[21] which discussed this problem of measurement. The question, he said, is whether criminal statistics can give an accurate picture of the real proportions of criminality. He denied such a possibility because different crimes vary greatly in their detectability. In 1912, for instance, 167 persons were prosecuted in France for assault and battery resulting in the death of the victim, but only 93 were prosecuted for criminal abortion, although the number of such abortions annually had been estimated at 200,000. He said that one must take into consideration both the conception which the population has of the punishable nature of the crime and its seriousness in general, as well as its detectability. "If the crime is of such a nature that it creates great indignation on the part of the public, both the law enforcement authorities and the citizens will do their best to detect the offense. But if . . . it does not sufficiently hurt the sense of justice of the people, the detection of the offense is made more difficult and the work of the police weakened."[22]

Verkko concluded, after an examination of various statistics from several countries, that well-organized statistics of crimes known to the police would make possible the determination of the trends of real criminality with respect to willful homicides, aggravated assaults resulting in serious injury to the victim, robbery, and perhaps thefts. He expressed doubts about the usefulness of the number of negligent manslaughters for measurement purposes, was sure that statistics of simple assaults, infanticide, criminal abortion, liquor law violations, and drunkenness were misleading in that respect. He added the following offenses to the list of crimes," the statistics of which cannot be used as a base for speculations regarding real criminality":[23] adultery, offenses against morals, rape, perjury, certain important offenses against property, such as fraud, forgery, embezzlement, and bankruptcy, as well as certain crimes of violence, such as disturbing the peace and assaults on an officer (!) or hindering an officer in the exercise of his duty. To the same category he added statistics of attempts and of "mental participation in all kinds of crimes," namely

[20] Giovanni Mortara, "Tavole di criminalità e di recidività," *Giorn. degli economisti e Riv. di statistica,* Ser. 3, **40**:75–97 (1910), p. 76.
[21] Veli Verkko, "Kriminalstatistiken och den verkliga brottsligheten," *Nordisk Tidsskrift for Strafferet* **8**:95–128, 1930.
[22] *Ibid.,* p. 101.
[23] *Ibid.,* p. 118.

incitement to crime and certain cases of complicity.   "The crimes, the statistical number of which can serve as basis for conclusions regarding the real trend of crime, are surely in a minority."[24]

Independently, the Committee on Uniform Crime Records of the International Association of Chiefs of Police had arrived at the same conclusion.   In its *Uniform Crime Reporting,* published in 1929, the Committee stated that

many offenses are purposely concealed and therefore cannot be known to the police, no matter how much effort might be exerted in uncovering them. There are a number of reasons for this concealment: (1) the offense may be known only to the person committing it; (2) relatives or friends of the offender may not report it; (3) fear of annoyance or publicity prevents others from reporting; (4) some people are too ignorant or indifferent to report—The extent to which offenses are concealed varies considerably.   It is very marked for carrying concealed weapons, forgeries, embezzlements, sex offenses, etc.   Statistics of such offenses are especially incomplete and hence unreliable as measures of the prevalence of crime.   On the other hand, felonious homicides, aggravated assaults, robberies, burglaries, and major larcenies are generally known and reported.   These offenses may serve as a reliable index of the extent, nature and fluctuation of crime.[25]

These conclusions were not supported by any careful statistical analysis; they were apparently based mostly on the experience of the police and logical inferences founded on them.

It is obvious that the opinions just quoted are based on the assumption that the sample of known instances of any given type of criminality must be sizeable if changes in the amplitude of that sample from one period to another are to permit us to infer that corresponding changes have occurred in the total volume of such criminality.   If the quota of committed offenses that escape being reported to the public authorities—the hidden criminality—is very large, and the sample of known offenses therefore correspondingly very small, that sample would presumably be useless for measuring purposes.   The need to determine, if possible, the proportionate relationship of the hidden to the known criminality is therefore clear.

References to this particular problem are found scattered in numerous studies but serious attempts to investigate it have been few, particularly in the United States where statistical researches on the phenomenology of specific types of crimes have been rare or have usually ignored the problem.   Elsewhere such researchers have been more numerous. Three of these will be given special attention.

---

[24] *Ibid.,* p. 119.
[25] *Uniform Crime Reporting,* p. 22.

The first of these studies, by Kurt Meyer, appeared in 1941 under the title, *The Unpunished Crimes. An Investigation of the so called Dark Number in German Criminal Statistics.*[26] The "dark number" in Meyer's study was the figure representing the difference between the number of crimes actually committed and the number resulting in the conviction of an offender. He proposed to investigate this problem in connection with different types of crimes and criminals.

Meyer considered police statistics as the most valuable source of information for his purpose.

The special value of police statistics lies in the recording of all reported offenses (according to the kinds of crimes and their circumstances) and the success of the law enforcement authorities in clearing them up. Since the report of the offense comes nearer in time to the crime committed than does the conviction, police statistics show the fluctuations of criminality much better than the statistics of convictions. They also come closer to the real criminality, because they are statistics of events and offenders. As all reported offenses are counted in police statistics, it must be kept in mind that among those reported there are some that are not punishable. Only the most recent police statistics based on the Dec. 20, 1935, circular of the Reich and Prussian Ministries of the Interior, count as a "case" solely an event which has been investigated and in which there is a strong suspicion, when the case is turned over to the prosecutor, that a punishable act has occurred. Ascertained offenders are all persons, who have been found, as a result of the police investigations, to have taken part in the crime. . . . Here there is a possibility of double counting but generally an attempt is made to avoid this error. Furthermore it must be remembered that offenses that after an investigation cannot be clearly classified are uniformly counted among other offenses. This is especially true of receiving stolen goods which generally is counted as theft unless the case is clear. Similarly, reported homicides are often counted as murders, even when the case may be one of manslaughter.[27]

Meyer examined in more detail the "dark number" in voluntary homicides, criminal abortion, homosexuality, thefts (especially thefts in factories and big industrial enterprises, shoplifting, pocket-picking, railroad thefts, simple thefts), robbery, burglary, fraud, and arson. After an intensive analysis of available data he concluded that for *each* offense of a given category leading to someone's conviction there were (the percentages in parentheses indicating the ratio of these offenses to the estimated total criminality):

[26] Kurt Meyer, *Die unbestraften Verbrechen. Eine Untersuchung über die sog. Dunkelziffer in der Deutschen Kriminalstatistik* (83 pp. Leipzig: Wiegandt, 1941).
[27] *Ibid.*, p. 10.

3 to 5 willful homicides (17–25%)
100 or more abortions (less than 1%)
100 or more homosexual acts (less than 1%)
30 instances of shoplifting (3%)
30 instances of railroad thefts (3%)
16 to 20 simple thefts (5–6%)
8 aggravated thefts (burglary, etc.) (9%)
4 to 5 robberies (17–20%)
20 frauds (5%)
8 arsons (9%).

In 1957, the director of the criminal police of Düsseldorf, Dr. Bernd Wehner, published a study on *The Latency of Criminal Acts (The undetected criminality)*.[28] "The point of departure for the observation of criminality," he stated, "must be the criminal statistics of the police. Its figures come nearer to the real criminality than do the statistics of convictions."[29] After an analysis of various types of crimes based on police experience as well as other sources, he concluded that the relationship of the number of offenses known to the police to the speculative number of hidden crimes of the same category is the following. For each known offense there are

3 to 6 homicides (14–25%)
100 to 500 abortions (less than 1%)
0.5 to 4 physical injuries to persons (20–67%)
5 to 10 rapes (9 to 17%)
6 to 10 instances of indecent conduct with children (9–14%)
100 to 500 instances of homosexuality (less than 1%)
10 to 20 cases of pimping (5–9%)
7 to 15 instances of other immoral offenses (6–13%)
0.25 to 1 case of thefts, aggravated and simple, robbery and extortion by threat (50–80%)
1 to 3 cases of embezzlement, larceny by bailee, and receiving stolen goods (25–50%)
8 to 12 cases of fraud (8–11%)
1 to 2 cases of document forgery, offenses by public servants, and narcotics offenses (33–50%).

These are regarded by the author as minimum estimates. Had he used Meyer's basis for calculation, his quotas of "hidden" criminality would, of course, have been much larger.

[28] Bernd Wehner, *Die Latenz der Straftaten (Die nicht entdeckte Kriminalität)* (100 pp. Wiesbaden: Bundeskriminalamt, 1957).
[29] *Ibid.*, p. 98.

In 1958, Mr. C. N. Peijster, a Dutch police official, published a work entitled *The Unknown Crime.*[30] The author was concerned mostly with a few types of offenses with large or very high quotas of unknown offenses, such as criminal abortion, adultery, prostitution, homosexuality, exhibitionism, perjury, fraud, and shoplifting. Passing notice was given to some other types. He did not try to compute the "crime quotient," as he called it, for all the offenses studied, i.e., the ratio of known to unknown offenses, but ventured the guess that this ratio was 1 to 250 (0.4%) for criminal abortion, 1 to 4 for shoplifting (20%), and 1 to 2 (33%) for pocket-picking. He expressed his belief that police statistics were the most useful source for his purpose and concluded that the number of homicides, aggravated assaults, robberies, and burglaries could be used for the measurement of these forms of criminality.

A comparison of the studies mentioned is difficult because they do not all deal with the same types of offenses; when they do, they often include offenses of different kinds under the same label. There is agreement on the fact that the known sample of consensual crimes, such as adultery, homosexuality, and criminal abortion is infinitesimally small. Their estimated samples of willful homicides, aggravated assault, and forcible rape range from 14 to 25 per cent in homicide, 20 to 67 per cent in physical injuries to persons, and 9 to 17 per cent in rape. As for thefts, there is no agreement; Wehner believes that at least 50 per cent becomes confirmed by the police, while Meyer places the figure at less than 10 per cent. Both these authors regard the sample of known robberies as being at least 17 per cent.

It is obvious from these and other studies examined that we are dealing with unknown quantities which in the nature of things can only be conjectured. However, the findings support in general the contention that for the measurement of criminality we have to rely on offenses that fall mostly in the first class in the classification suggested earlier in this chapter, namely those in which there is a personal victim who suffers in some way from the crime. This does not mean that all offenses in this class can supply equally valuable data for measurement purposes. Some of them are undoubtedly too trivial in nature or not sufficiently reportable for other reasons to yield an adequate basis for measurement.

In a paper published by the United Nations in 1954, we find the following statement:

[30] C. N. Peijster, *De onbekende misdaad* (xvi, 231 pp. The Hague: Martinus Nijhoff, 1958).

Attention has also been drawn to the fact that certain types of offenses are so severe, both in the eyes of public opinion and from the point of view of the victim and those near to him, that the great majority of these offenses, if not all of them, are likely to become known to the authorities. In regard to such offenses, it may be assumed that under normal conditions the number of offenses reported bears a reasonably constant relation to the total criminality of these types. It would also seem that actions of this kind are characterized as criminal by all legislations concerned and that they are relatively easy to recognize and classify both from a factual and a subjective point of view. Statistics concerning these specific types of crime are consequently of a particular value for the study of criminality within countries and, even more so, when countries are compared.[31]

It is regrettable that no really comprehensive investigation of the problem of hidden criminality has been made so far. In recent years especially, attempts have been made, by questionnaire studies, to discover the number and kinds of criminal acts not known to the public authorities which have been committed by a group of respondents during their lives. As would be expected, the investigations have revealed the existence of much hidden criminality, but otherwise their findings are not of any great value for measurement purposes, since the information gathered refers to no specific year, and therefore cannot be compared with any data on "known offenses" during that year in a given community. What they have demonstrated is that most of the hidden acts committed by the respondents were, although illegal, of a trivial nature and belonged mostly to the classes which we have already assumed to be unadapted for measurement purposes.[32]

---

[31] *Survey of Social Statistics.* Statistical Papers, Ser. K, no. 1 (46 pp. New York: United Nations, December 1954), p. 44.

[32] In a pioneer study, *Can Delinquency Be Measured?* (xxvi, 277, pp. New York: Columbia University Press, 1936), Sophia M. Robison discusses the differences between the statistics of juvenile offenses known to public authorities in New York City and those known to private welfare agencies; Edward E. Schwartz does the same for Washington, D.C., in "A community experiment in the measurement of juvenile delinquency," *N.P.P.A. Yearbook* (1945:157–181). Fred J. Murphy, Mary M. Shirley, and Helen L. Witmer, in "The incidence of hidden criminality," *Amer. J. Orthopsychiat.* 16:686–696 (1946), compare the frequency of delinquent acts among 114 boys known to a social agency with the number known to the juvenile court and attributed to these boys.

Several questionnaire studies have tried to discover the number and nature of offenses committed by specific groups of respondents during their past life and the extent to which such offenses remained unknown to the police. See Austin L. Porterfield's *Youth in Trouble* (vii, 132 pp. Fort Worth, Texas: Leo Potishman Foundation, 1946), (237 college students); James S. Wallerstein and Clement J. Wyle, "Our law-abiding law-breakers," *Probation* 25:107–112 (March-

The Classification of Offenses

Although a violation of the criminal law is the statistical unit used for the measurement of criminality, such units must be grouped into classes on the basis of some identical characteristic. As a whole, the classification scheme should be based on principles governed by the aim it is to serve. Suppose, then, that we wish to compute an index figure for the criminality of a given community and for a given period of time—a year, for instance—and to take into account not merely the number of offenses but also their various degrees of seriousness. Suppose, furthermore, that we would look for our basic data in official reports of criminal statistics, would we be able to produce such an index figure? The answer would be negative if we expected that figure to withstand critical examination. One reason lies in the crudity of the classification of offenses commonly used in criminal statistics.

Criminal statistics arose as an adjunct to the administration of justice. It is natural, therefore, that the legal definitions of offenses dealt with by public authorities and the brief labels attached to them by the law would furnish the basis for the classification of the offenses in the statistics. This has seemed so obvious that it is accepted as axiomatic. As a result we may be able to discover how many felonies or misdemeanors are handled during a year or the number of robberies, larcenies, burglaries, simple assaults, etc., so dealt with. Such a purely formal classification does not yield the information needed for the construction of a sensitive index. Legal labels are too deceptive. A few examples will suffice.

April, 1947), (1698 adults); James F. Short, Jr., "Extent of unrecorded juvenile delinquency. Tentative conclusions," *J. Crim. Law, Criminol. and Police Sci.* 49:296–309 (November-December 1958). Three similar studies have recently been made in the Scandinavian countries. Johs. Andenaes, Knut Sveri, and Ragnar Hauge, "Kriminalitetshyppigheten hos ustraffede. I. Norsk undersøkelse," *Nord. Tids. for Kriminalvidenskab* 48:97–112, (1960), (125 college students); Ola Nyquist and Ivar Strahl, "Kriminalitetshyppigheten hos ustraffede. II. Svensk undersökning," *op. cit.*, pp. 113–117 (94 college students). Hans Forssman and C. F. Gentz, "Kriminalitetsförekomsten hos presumptivt ostraffade," *op. cit.*, 50:318–324 (1962), (164 medical students). See also John M. Wise, *A Comparison of Sources of Data as Indexes of Delinquent Behavior*, M. A. thesis, University of Chicago (1962). Maynard L. Erickson and LeMar T. Empey, "Court records, undetected delinquency and decision-making," *J. Crim. Law, Criminol. and Police Sci.* 54:456–469 (December 1963). Two extensive studies are in progress in Norway and Finland, and in the United States Dr. Sophia M. Robison is engaged in a Kinsey-type research on hidden criminality.

Larceny is theft, whether the property stolen is worth a penny, fifty dollars, or a million. First-degree murder may mean a deliberately planned and extremely violent and brutal murder or a killing in self-defense by a person engaged in a burglary. Robbery may mean the holdup of an adult by another adult at the point of a gun or the threat of a pummeling made by one schoolboy to a younger one, if the latter does not hand over his lunch money. The theft of an automobile may mean its removal by a professional thief for alteration and resale or the temporary borrowing of a car for a joyride. Burglary may mean the breaking and entering of a bank or of an abandoned house marked for demolition. Considering the variety of acts that are given the same label in statistics we must conclude that a classification of offenses using the legal label as the sole identifying trait is bound to disguise much criminality and, therefore, be misleading, even if we were to consider only the relatively serious crimes which were mentioned earlier as the only ones that probably would yield sufficiently large and constant samples of offenses known to the police. A classification that permits the grouping together under one heading of offenses of the disparate content indicated in the above illustrations is analogous to one in which the word "house," defined as a structure with walls and a roof, would permit the combining together of single occupancy dwellings, apartment houses, doll houses, dog houses, the Empire State Building, and the Library of Congress.

That the legal label alone is an inadequate designation to show the relative seriousness of an offense is seen from the fact that judges, in sentencing offenders guilty of the same crime, impose punishments of different kinds and severity, depending on the circumstances of the crime, thereby recognizing qualitative differences among offenses bearing the same designation even when the subjective characteristics of the perpetrators do not influence the sentence.

A more useful classification of offenses for the purpose of measurement would be one based on their relative seriousness in terms of injury caused to the victim's person or property[33] and on the degree of public disapproval of an offense, as determined by a sampling of public opinion or by a grading of official measures taken for its repres-

---

[33] This view is also defended in Gunnar Fredriksson's *Kriminalstatistiken och Kriminologien* (385 pp. Stockholm: Almquist & Wicksell, 1962), a work that contains the most exhaustive analysis in recent decades of the premises of criminal statistics, the classification of offenses, the classification of offenders, the measurement of crime, criminals, and criminality, the problem of hidden criminality, and the organization of criminal statistics.

sion. This idea was adumbrated by von Mayr in 1898 and repeated in his *Moralstatistik* (p. 439) where he wrote:

Another manner of grouping offenses and their offenders into materially important classes of offense gravity is a worthy future task for moral statistics. One would, then, have to differentiate the officially labeled crimes into those, on the one hand, that are regarded by public social ethics as very serious and serious attacks on the social equilibrium from, on the other hand, those that are from expedience defined by the state but are less serious from a socio-ethical point of view. The number of gradations must not be too great but such a classification of the mass of criminal statistical data is obviously essential.

Lately, and in the same vein, Ronald H. Beattie called attention to the need for a more careful inspection, evaluation, and classification of the events described in the offense reports prepared by police officers so that a classification could be made that would "classify offenses into those which—from the public point of view—are most serious, those that are more or less the expected behavior in such an offense, and those that are of a relatively minor level of consequence."[34]

It must be acknowledged that even if such a classification could be developed, it would, to the extent that it would ignore strict legal labels, meet opposition for various reasons from administrative agencies accustomed to traditional ways of producing criminal statistics. Without such a classification, however, a qualitative (weighted) index of criminality would be difficult to construct.

Those who have claimed that police data could not be utilized for measurement purposes have accepted the data of judicial agencies because they believe that until an offense has been investigated by such agencies, its real nature cannot be determined nor can an accurate label be attached to it. The police, they say, do not possess the legal knowledge required for an accurate legal description of the offense.

There is obviously some truth in this assertion, but to estimate its importance for measurement purposes we must consider a number of factors. (1) Insofar as the correct designation of an offense depends on an investigation of the motives and mental state of the offender or the presence of certain aggravating or mitigating circumstances of his conduct, neither the police nor a judicial agency can, with any absolute certainty, give an accurate legal label to an offense committed by an unknown person, which is the case in a high proportion

[34] Ronald H. Beattie, "Criminal statistics in the United States—1960," *J. Crim. Law, Criminol. and Police Sci.* **51**:49–65 (May-June, 1960), p. 56.

of offenses.   A corpse, let us say, is found riddled with bullets under circumstances precluding accident or suicide.   The death is due to a criminal act and may properly be listed as a criminal homicide, but so long as the offender is not found and examined, no one can tell whether it is murder or manslaughter in this or that degree.   Even if the offender is found and tried, he may be deemed insane and, therefore, not punishable, or various considerations may so influence the court that it returns a verdict not in full accord with the facts and, thereby, gives an incorrect label to the homicide.   For various purposes, it would be valuable to have accurate statistics of the various kinds of criminal homicide, but all such classifications must be considered as approximations.   In localities where expert medical examiners are lacking, the determination of the cause of death may be based on erroneous conclusions, but where such services exist, we may assume that the police authorities' classification of a death as due to *criminal homicide* is satisfactory whether the killer is known or unknown.

What has been said of homicide applies, of course, also to other offenses.   It must be remembered, however, that at the investigatory stage the police is concerned chiefly with discovering how a given event, reported to them as a crime or observed by them, occurred. A reading of offense reports prepared by the police reveals that the investigation is focused on the objective character of the event, how and when it occurred, who the victims are and what harm, injury, or discomfort was suffered by them or by the community at large. Generally speaking, these descriptions of events can be given broad legal labels by the police with considerable accuracy.   This is especially true of the more serious offenses which might yield an index to criminality.

The entire problem of accurate legal labels would dissolve, however, if we were to ignore them and instead use police descriptions of events to develop a classification of offenses evolved entirely from these descriptions.   The manner in which an offense was committed, the nature and degree of the harm caused by the offense, the kind of victimization involved, and other similar characteristics of the offense, rather than the generic labels used by the law, would then be of importance.   We believe that the offense reports prepared by the police in our large cities are or could be made adequate for such a classification and that the result would yield a more accurate basis for measuring serious criminality than we now have.   We shall return to this problem of definition and classification of offenses in later chapters.

4
Historical Background:
the qualitative element

If criminality is to be measured by an index constructed of data pertaining to a variety of selected offenses known to the police—or known to other official agencies, such as courts, for that matter—the mere sum of these offenses or a rate computed by using that sum would give no indication of the relative gravity of the offenses composing the rate. Suppose, for example, that the actual number of the offenses remained unchanged during a decade in a certain region and that the population base used in the computation of a rate also remained unchanged, the crime index would remain stabilized. But, suppose that during that decade there was a considerable change in the relative proportions of the crimes committed and that serious offenses against the person had increased and petty offenses against property decreased, would it not be true to say that criminality had grown worse? And should not a measure of criminality take into account and reflect qualitative as well as quantitative changes in time and space?

Early criminal statisticians were not unaware of this problem, even though they struggled with it on the basis of statistics of convictions rather than those of offenses known to the police. Messedaglia,[1] for instance, proposed a method for arriving at a kind of punishment index that would presumably indicate, from year to year, qualitative changes in the crimes leading to the conviction of offenders. This index could be achieved by computing the arithmetic mean of the shortest and the longest sentences imposed on criminals for each

[1] Angelo Messedaglia, *op. cit.*, full reference in footnote 6, Chapter 3.

separate class of punishments, multiplying this figure for each class by the number of criminals in that class, giving the average number of years, months, and days to which these offenders were sentenced, adding this figure to the corresponding figures of the other classes, and dividing by the total number of individuals sentenced. The product would represent the weighted mean punishment suffered by an offender.

Mayr, who was apparently unaware of his contemporary's suggestion since he believed himself to be the first to attack the problem, experimented with the idea in a study of the administration of justice in Bavaria, 1862–1866.[2] After having compared the rates of various crimes in the different districts of the country, he said:

> These relative figures are of capital importance for judging the criminality of the various districts, because they give insight into the qualitative strength of the tendency to crime, quite apart from numerical frequency. In order to be able to compare the total criminality of the different districts in a precise manner it is, however, necessary to establish a definite estimate of the criminal *value*—if this term is allowed—of felonies (*Verbrechen*) and misdemeanors (*Vergehen*). This problem offers great difficulties, but a contribution to its solution will be made based on the length of prison terms (p. xx).

For each district, Mayr added together the length of all prison sentences imposed for felonies and divided the total by the number of felons sentenced. He used an analogous procedure for misdemeanors; where fines alone had been imposed he took the prison sentence that according to law could have been imposed for nonpayment. He discovered that the average felony sentence was 72 months and the average misdemeanor sentence 4 months. This figure of 4 he called an offense unit. There were consequently 18 offense units in a felony sentence, but because he had found it impossible to reduce life or death sentences to any usable figure and include them in his computations, he arbitrarily assigned 20 units to a felony sentence.

He found that in the Kingdom of Bavaria, during 1862–1866, the annual average number of felony sentences was 15.71 and the corresponding number of misdemeanor sentences was 256.04. Multiplying the number of felony sentences by 20 and adding the result to the average number of misdemeanor sentences he arrived at the figure of 570.24 offense units, a figure "which must be regarded as the most nearly correct representation of the criminality" (p. xlvii).

---

[2] Georg Mayr, *Ergebnisse des Strafrechtspflege im Königreich Bayern* (lxxxi, 296 pp. Munich: K. Statist. Bureau, 1868). (Heft xix, *Beiträge zur Statistik des Königreichs Bayern*).

Mayr knew that the index figure he had produced represented only what he called the "penal quantum" of a given period and area. "Total criminality cannot be measured by sentences," he said, "[such measurement] must be based on the known offenses." But, he also believed that "the sentence statistics, especially when they consider the length of the sentences, provide an essential supplement to the statistics of known offenses," because he assumed that "the offenses that do not reach the point of sentence are proportionally of the same gravity as those that eventuate in a sentence" (p. xlvi).[3]

So far as we know, no one tried to improve on these early efforts until Diego De Castro became interested in it in the early 1930's. His first work on the subject, *Methods for Calculating Indexes to Criminality*, appeared in 1934.[4] Its aim was stated to be the construction, by the use of weighted categories, of an index to criminality similar to a price index.

A careful examination of the Italian penal code of 1889 and of the Commercial Code disclosed that if all the possible penal dispositions available to courts were taken into account, and the maximum punishment that could be imposed in each instance were noted, there were 1647 variates. De Castro grouped the offenses defined in the codes into five classes: (1) petty offenses against the person; (2) offenses aginst property and those defined in the Commercial Code; (3) offenses against morals and the family; (4) serious offenses against the person; and (5) other offenses. The last category comprised offenses against public order, etc., that threatened no specific individual's person or property.

Taking each class separately, the number of variates in maximum punishments possible within the class was counted and the sum of their length, in days, was produced. This sum was divided by the number of variates in the class; the result represented the mean maximum punishment provided for offenses in that class. Having repeated this procedure for each of the five classes, he gave a value

[3] The scope of the understanding of this problem and the naiveté exhibited in the suggestion for its solution by American students may be seen in the appendix to Louis N. Robinson's *History and Organization of Criminal Statistics in the United States* (104 pp. Boston: Houghton Mifflin 1911).

[4] Diego De Castro, *Metodi per calcolare gli indici della criminalità* (119 pp. Turin: Istituto Giuridicho della R. Università, 1934). (R. Univ. de Torino, *Memorie dell'Istituto Giuridicho.* Ser. II, vol. 25.) Since then, Professor De Castro has also published the following articles: "Di un indice di criminalità e di un indice di criminosità," *Riv. italiana di demografia e statistica* 1:211–222, (October 1947); "Statistica della criminalità," *Dizionario di Criminologia* 2:945–948 (1949); "Indici di criminalità e indici di criminosità," *Delitto e personalità* (vii, 666 pp. Milan: A. Giuffré, 1955), pp. 181–191.

TABLE 1. *Mean Maximum Punishments, Code of 1889*

OFFENSE CLASS	TOTAL NO. OF DAYS IN EACH CLASS	NO. OF VARIATES WITHIN EACH CLASS	MEAN MAX. PUN. IN EACH CLASS IN DAYS	RELATIONSHIPS OF MEAN MAX. PUNISHMENT WHEN LOWEST MEAN EQUALS 1.0
Petty offenses against persons	21,875	80	273	1.0
Offenses ag. prop. and offenses defined in Commercial Code	195,007	248	786	2.87
Offenses against morals and family	254,150	79	3217	11.78
Serious offenses against persons	220,329	155	3337	12.30
Other offenses	3,191,699	1085	2942	10.78

of 1.0 to the lowest mean and proportionate values to the means of the other four classes. The classification is illustrated in Table 1.

The last column of the table gave De Castro a scale of values that permitted him to assign different weights to the five classes of offenses. Expressed in round numbers, these weights were 1-3-12-13 and 10. The reasons for increasing somewhat the weight of serious offenses against persons and decreasing that of the last offense class need not concern us here. De Castro was aware that the scale was, as he expressed it, theoretical, in that it was based on possible rather than on actual punishments. He believed that a more accurate scale of the relative seriousness of offenses should be based on sentences actually imposed by courts.

Having determined the qualitative differences of the offenses punishable by law, a qualitative index of criminality could now be constructed. It would first have to be decided what source of data should be used. De Castro believed that for a purely quantitative index, i.e., one which took no account of the relative gravity of different crimes, data on offenses ascertained by investigatory authorities as having been committed would be the best. For a qualitative index, however, he believed that the data on definitive and irrevocable sentences would have to be employed, because he assumed that such verdicts and sentences gave the most precise definition of the offense involved and the most accurate measure of its degree of gravity.

In order to construct the index number for a given period—a year, for instance—it would be necessary to know (a) the number of persons sentenced for the offenses in such subcategory (variate) of the five classes and (b) the mean length, in days, of sentences within each of the subcategories. Where fines were imposed, the length of time into which they could be converted might be used. The basic figure for each class would be arrived at by multiplying the sum of the means with the number of persons sentenced and, as a next step, multiplying the result with the weight assigned to the class. The sum of the basic figures for the five classes would then be divided by the sum of the equally weighted numbers of the persons sentenced in each class. The result would be the qualitative criminality index number for the period.

De Castro's index cannot be regarded as a measure of criminality. Since it is based on all offenses, regardless of their quotas of hidden criminality, and furthermore is based only on those resulting in the conviction of their perpetrators, it is rather a formula for transforming conventional statistics of convictions and punishments in such a manner that the composition of the criminality they represent can be qualitatively appraised. It becomes then a weighted index of punished crimes which, if calculated year after year for a period of time, would portray changes in what Mayr called the "penal quantum" and therefore indicate whether in their totality crimes leading to conviction inflict greater or less injury on the social values of the nation as time passes.

The interesting feature of De Castro's work is its focus on the degree of public disapproval of criminal acts, as reflected in maximum punishments and the placing of these acts within five larger classes and, within each class, regardless of the label attached to the offenses, into variate groups according to the size of the maximum punishment that distinguishes each such group. By doing so, he abandoned, in a sense, the formal legal definitions of crimes for a classification of criminal conduct based on a kind of scale of the social attitudes reflected by the administrators of justice.

Only one illustration of a different method of weighing the relative gravity of offenses will be mentioned here, from the American literature. In 1951, Robert C. Angell published a study in which he attempted to measure the degree of "moral integration" of American cities, a condition which he defined as "the degree to which there is a set of common ends and values toward which all are oriented and in terms of which the life of the group is organized."[5]   He first developed a "welfare effort index" for each of the 28 cities studied. This index was based on welfare expenditures from local public funds, private contributions, and income from endowments on the assumption that the more citizens sacrifice their private interests for the public interest, the greater would be the moral integration of the city. Unable to find any other positive index he turned, like the moral statisticians of old, to crime data and constructed a crime index for comparison with the welfare effort index.   Taking figures from *Uniform Crime Reports*, showing the number of willful homicides (murder and non-negligent manslaughter), robbery, and burglary in his cities during 1936–1940, he computed the annual average rate per thousand population for each of these offenses.   He then divided the burglary rate by each of the homicide and robbery rates and extracted the square roots of the quotients; he multiplied the homicide square root with the number of homicides in each city separately, did the same for the robbery square root and the number of robberies, added the number of burglaries and divided the total by the 1940 population of each city, in thousands, and thus arrived at his "crime index." The procedure gave the crimes of homicide and robbery weights proportional to the square roots of their frequency.   Thus, one homicide equalled 7.75 burglaries and one robbery equalled 2.44 burglaries. The same procedure could, of course, have been applied to all classes of crimes in *Uniform Crime Reports*, thereby providing a more complete scale.

There have been other American researches that have explored the problem of constructing a weighted index, but since they have dealt with juvenile delinquency they will be discussed later.

A Note on Rates

No matter what agency, police or judicial, in a given jurisdiction or area, is selected as the source of statistics of criminality, and no matter what types of criminal conduct are chosen and their relative gravity weighted, the composite figures arrived at, year after year, would only indicate whether criminality changed in an absolute sense, without reference to possible changes in the population.   Even though it could be shown that more or fewer persons had committed the offense involved, it would be impossible to claim that criminality

[5] Robert Cooley Angell, *The Moral Integration of American Cities* (viii, 140 pp. Chicago: University of Chicago Press, 1951). *Amer. J. Sociol.* 57, no. 1, pt. 2 (July, 1951), p. 2.

had increased or decreased relatively, since no account would have been taken of the size of the population that could have committed crimes. We must, therefore, relate the crime figures to the population at risk and reduce them to rates.

But, what is the population that should be charged in this manner with the criminality that occurs in a given area? When rates are presented in official reports in the United States, they are as a rule computed per 100,000 population. This is referred to as a *crude* rate. It is based on an unstated assumption that all humans are equally capable of conmmitting crimes. This assumption is obviously erroneous, for criminal conduct is not evenly distributed over all segments of the population. By definition it cannot occur among children under 7 years of age and is rare among children up to 10 years, at least. It appears predominantly in males who are between, let us say, 12 and 50 years of age. The custom in some foreign countries of computing rates on the basis of the population "of punishable age" or "capable of committing a crime," as recommended nearly a hundred years ago by Messedaglia and Mayr, therefore represents a slight refinement. What is actually needed, however, are rates calculated on a population standardized for age and sex, at least, and perhaps for other factors, depending on the availability of properly subclassified and accurate statistics of the population concerned.

There are other disturbing factors. Available population statistics count people who reside within specific geographic areas, whether this is an administrative district such as a state or a city, or a census tract within a city. Suppose that we possessed all the requisite information on crimes for calculating a crime index figure for a given large city and knew certain basic facts about its resident population. The city is surrounded by many satellite communities, most of whose residents work in the city. Travelers and other transients come and go daily. If it has a seaport, nonresident sailors spend brief periods ashore; if large military installations are found nearby, it becomes a rest area for their personnel, etc. The number of persons during the year who are capable of committing a crime in the city is then very much larger than the resident population about which we have some fairly accurate information. Now, since a high proportion of crimes committed are due to *undetected* offenders,[6] we have no means of separating crimes committed by residents from the others, *unless they*

---

[6] In Philadelphia, out of 40,067 crimes of homicide, aggravated assault, forcible rape, robbery, burglary, larceny, and automobile theft in 1960, the perpetrators of 24,695 were undetected.

result in an arrest. The result would be an index figure which burdens the resident population with some crimes committed by outsiders and conversely eases the figure for the communities where the nonresident offenders belong. No satisfactory way has been found to rectify this error which will continue to plague statisticians who work with data on crimes known to the police. It may not be a very serious problem when the data apply to the population of an entire state or country, but it is another matter when one has to deal with cities that are centers of large metropolitan districts. Whatever may be its deficiencies, information on offenses that lead to the arrest and/or prosecution of specific offenders, whether adults or juveniles, has at least the advantage of enabling us to separate the offenses committed by residents from the rest. Even so, only a highly developed system of statistical recording, covering entire states, would furnish full data on the offenses committed by members of the resident population of any given community, since some of them will be apprehended in other communities for crimes committed there.

There is only one study known to us which deals specifically with the criminality of a large city and throws light on this problem. Covering the period of 1923–1927 it deals with resident and nonresident offenders found guilty of crimes in Amsterdam and of residents of ‘ Amsterdam who were found guilty elsewhere in the Netherlands for crimes committed outside the city.[7] The offenses involved were sufficiently serious to require registration in the national penal register, a common institution in continental countries, which possessed the necessary data. The study is of particular interest to us because it compares juveniles under 18 years of age with those 18 years and older.

We shall examine here, for the sake of brevity, only the data pertaining to males in the two age groups mentioned and limit ourselves to two classes of offenses, those against the person and those against property. The appended table[8] shows some interesting things.

In the case of offenses against the person, no nonresident juvenile was found guilty of having committed such an offense in Amsterdam, and in offenses against property all but 3.6 per cent of the male juveniles involved were residents. The situation was different in the case of adults; 7.7 per cent of males found guilty of offenses against the person and 17 per cent of those involved in property offenses were

---

[7] *Criminaliteit in Amsterdam en van Amsterdammers* (xlii, 87 pp. Amsterdam: J. M. Meulenhoff, February, 1932). (Statistische Mededeelingen uitgegeven door het Bureau van Statistiek der Gemeente Amsterdam, no. 94.)

[8] Based on data in tables 1 and 67 of the study cited.

TABLE 2.   Males Found Guilty in The Netherlands, 1923–1927, of Offenses Against Person or Property, by Age and Residence

OFFENSES	−18 No.	−18 %	18+ No.	18+ %	TOTAL No.	TOTAL %
I. Against person						
a. Committed by residents						
in Amsterdam	13	92.9	877	92.0	890	92.0
outside	1	7.1	76	8.0	77	8.0
Total	14	100.0	953	100.0	967	100.0
b. In Amsterdam						
by residents	13	100.0	877	92.3	890	92.4
by nonresidents	...	...	73	7.7	73	7.6
Total	13	100.0	950	100.0	963	100.0
II. Against property						
a. Committed by residents						
in Amsterdam	346	96.6	2431	85.3	2777	86.6
outside Amsterdam	12	3.4	419	14.7	431	13.4
Total	358	100.0	2850	100.0	3208	100.0
b. In Amsterdam						
by residents	346	96.3	2431	83.0	2777	84.6
by nonresidents	13	3.6	494	17.0	507	15.4
Total	359	100.0	2925	100.0	3284	100.0

nonresidents. We do not know exactly how many offenses were actually committed by these age or residence groups, since in each of the five years covered an offender was counted only for the offense carrying potentially the heaviest penalty, regardless of the number of offenses he may have had to answer for during the year. However, it would appear that all juvenile offenses against the person and nearly all such offenses against property resulting in conviction in Amsterdam were chargeable to resident juveniles.

Now, let us see what the data presented in the table mean in terms of over-all crime rates in Amsterdam. If the number of persons convicted of offenses against the person in Amsterdam were used to construct a rate based on the Amsterdam census population of punishable age, that population would be charged with 8 per cent of the convictions of nonresidents for offenses against the person; in the case of offenses against property, with 15.4 per cent. If inferences regarding

TABLE 3. Number of Males Found Guilty in The Netherlands, 1923–1927, by Age and Residence

OFFENSES	−18	18+	TOTAL
Against the person			
Committed in Amsterdam by residents and nonresidents	13	950	963
Committed by Amsterdamers outside	14	953	967
Against property			
Committed in Amsterdam	359	2925	3284
Committed by Amsterdamers	358	2850	3208

the extent of criminality of Amsterdamers were drawn from these conviction rates, the possibility of erroneous conclusions would appear to be substantial.

There is a curious fact that emerges from the table however, one that would seem to make superfluous the warnings presented earlier in this note. There was, in fact, very little difference between the number of Amsterdamers found guilty, whether they committed their offenses inside or outside the city, and the number of residents and nonresidents found guilty of offenses committed in Amsterdam, especially in the case of the juveniles as is shown in Table 3.

If this relationship were generally constant, local rates based on the resident census population would reflect quite closely the actual criminality of that population, since the offenses committed outside the city by residents would balance those committed in the city by nonresidents. No additional research that would substantiate such a conclusion has ever been engaged in as far as we know, but the assumption it contains has often been stated and, even more frequently, just taken for granted.

5

The Historical Background: the measurement of juvenile delinquency

In the foregoing chapters we have raised and discussed many of the problems involved in the measurement of conduct that violates the criminal law, whether the offender is known or unknown and hence, in a high proportion of cases, is not assignable to any specific population segment or social group. The *raison d'être* of our research, however, is to investigate the possibility of measuring the delinquency of the *juvenile* population, which means that it becomes necessary to identify, within the total of known offenses, those committed by juveniles. Objectively ascertained conduct in violation of law, which we have defended as furnishing the best basis for the measurement of criminality in general, now has to be ignored, unless it is possible to determine that at least certain kinds of objective illegal acts are always or almost always committed by juveniles. But identification of such acts is usually impossible unless the offenders have been apprehended and examined and their exact ages learned. The important question, then, is whether—and under what circumstances—the fraction of the total offenses of juveniles that results in the apprehension of offenders can offer a reasonably firm basis for an index of delinquency. In other words, when, if at all, can we assume that known juvenile offenses are a constant proportion of all offenses committed by juveniles?

In attempting to answer this question, we shall follow the same general outline used in previous chapters and first examine the sources of data about juvenile delinquency and their relative usefulness for our purpose; second, the kinds of delinquency that should be selected for the construction of an index; and finally the problem of weighting.

But something should be said to begin with about the definition of what we are about to study, juvenile delinquency.

As now defined by American statutes, varying as they do in details from one state jurisdiction to another, juvenile delinquency is illegal conduct by a child within a certain age bracket, conduct which may, as its most serious consequence, lead to that child's commitment to an institution until he reaches the age of majority.

The kinds of conduct labeled delinquent fall into two broad classes. In the one we find conduct which, if engaged in by an adult, would be a violation of the criminal law, including ordinances. In the other we find conduct which an adult cannot engage in at all or which is not punishable if he does engage in it. This class of offenses might be called *juvenile status offenses.* An adult cannot be guilty of truancy if no law requires him to attend school, but a juvenile may be punished for it, and although both juveniles and adults are capable of frequenting pool rooms, for instance, only juveniles may be forbidden from doing so. This broad classification is not invalidated by the fact that in many states some forms of juvenile delinquency can be committed by persons beyond the "juvenile" age but still "minors" because they have not yet reached the age of twenty-one— the purchasing or possession of alcoholic beverages, for instance, or even incorrigibility, as may be seen from statutes dealing with wayward minors. For the sake of brevity, we refer to the offenses of the second class as status offenses and to those of the first class, which are analogous to adult crimes, as nonstatus offenses.

Sources of Data

The most important sources of data concerning juvenile offenses and offenders are the police and the juvenile courts. This is particularly true for data on nonstatus offenses. We shall examine these sources briefly as to their relative value for measurement purposes. We are not concerned with the manner in which data on juvenile offenses extracted from these sources are commonly presented in local, state, or national annual reports. Published reports frequently make little effort to distinguish the various kinds of delinquent conduct involved and often lump them all together under the single heading "juvenile delinquency," thereby rendering them useless for our purposes. The only national statistical report on this problem, now issued by the Children's Bureau under the title *Juvenile Court Statistics*, is of this character. What we are concerned with is the fact that both police and juvenile court agencies possess recorded information about known delinquencies and delinquents. This information is often quite complete and could be extracted, classified, and manipulated in various ways for different ends. They could be employed perhaps to develop proper indices of delinquency. If they are not so used, it is usually not the lack of raw data that is responsible for that or for the paucity of information often noted in the reports.

The wealth of information buried in the records of juvenile courts is much greater than that found in the records of the police, because of the more extensive investigation into the background of the delinquents carried out by the court, but important as this may be for some types of research, it is not an argument for using court data for measurement purposes. The gap between the offenses actually committed by juveniles as known to the police authorities and the offenses attributed to juveniles dealt with by the court is considerable. In the city of Philadelphia, for instance, only a third of the juvenile offenses known to the police in 1960 led to referral to the court, and of these more than a fifth were, in turn, "adjusted" without a court hearing. For these and other reasons, students of juvenile delinquency today are wary of using court data for the construction of an index of delinquency, as may be seen from the following comments.

In 1946, Helen L. Witmer, now research director in the federal Children's Bureau, said:

. . . court statistics are wholly inadequate as the measure of the amount of youthful illegal behavior in the community. In fact, so frequent are the misdeeds of youth that even a moderate increase in the amount of attention paid to it by law enforcement authorities could create the semblance of a "delinquency wave" without there being the slightest change in adolescent behavior. The same considerations throw doubt on the validity of court statistics as an index to change in the amount of juvenile misconduct from time to time for it is doubtful that such figures bear a constant relationship to the unascertainable total.[1]

More recently, Harry M. Shulman stated that "we lack a satisfactory index to the volume of delinquency, i.e., a measure that theoretically should vary concomitantly with the volume. Juvenile court statistics do not constitute a good index. . . ."[2] Similar views have been expressed by others. This problem has not been subjected to the critical analysis it deserves as may be seen in Peter P. Lejins' strange conclusion that juvenile court statistics must be used "for

[1] Fred J. Murphy, Mary M. Shirley, and Helen L. Witmer, "The incidence of hidden criminality," *Amer. J. Orthopsychiat.* **16**:686–696 (1946), Discussion, p. 696.
[2] Harry M. Shulman, *Juvenile Delinquency in American Society*, New York: Harper (1961), p. 62. Quoted by permission of publisher.

the purpose of an index to juvenile delinquency" on the assumption that statistics of delinquency "are most certainly not concerned with the identification of specific offenses committed by juveniles and therefore cannot be relied upon for precision in this respect."[3] Even after his categorical rejection of juvenile court statistics for index purposes, Professor Shulman feels that if it could be assumed that the role of the juvenile court "does not markedly change from decade to decade" in a given community, "its admission volume may *perhaps* be used as a sort of local delinquency index, *albeit a dubious one.*"[4]

It is difficult to understand why any index recognized from the start as dubious should be advocated. In fact, the primary usefulness of juvenile court statistics, as stated in the national report referred to earlier, is not to furnish an index to delinquency but "to indicate how frequently one important community resource, the juvenile court, is utilized for dealing with such cases."[5]

Compared with the juvenile court, the police of a community have much more extensive information about juvenile delinquency in its various forms, especially in larger urban areas. This information reaches the police in various ways. Reports of crimes committed may, upon investigation, result in the discovery that a juvenile was the perpetrator; or the one reporting the event may indicate that a juvenile, or even one or more specific juveniles, should be sought as offenders. In other instances, the police observe juveniles in the act of committing an offense. In their reports on all these incidents the police tend to follow the pattern used in dealing with adults. Offenses are not called "juvenile delinquency" but are given the labels of the criminal law, if they are definable as such, or the labels of the specific status offenses known to the juvenile court law. At the reporting and investigatory stage, then, there is little to differentiate juvenile from adult offenses, so far as police data are concerned.

The differentiation occurs when the police have to decide how to dispose of the delinquents taken into custody. Here the influence of the special nature of juvenile court legislation is felt. In dealing with adult offenders the police no doubt exercise some discretion by avoiding an arrest under certain circumstances,[6] just as they do in

---

[3] Peter P. Lejins, "Measurement of juvenile delinquency," American Statistical Association, *Proc. Social Statistics Section 1960,* pp. 47–49, p. 48.
[4] *Ibid.,* p. 52. Our italics.
[5] *Juvenile Court Statistics 1960* (18 pp. Washington, D.C.: Children's Bureau, 1961), Preface.
[6] See Joseph Goldstein, "Police discretion not to involve the criminal process:

some cases when juveniles are involved; but once an adult is arrested, the police can leave to a court of preliminary hearing the job of selecting the offenders who should be punished from those who might be discharged with a warning or otherwise discharged because of the petty nature of the offense or for some other reason. In the case of juveniles, the law prevents the use of such a screening device. The police are then faced with the requirement that a child who has violated the law be delivered directly to a juvenile court. Perhaps this is the reason that the police, not in the United States alone but elsewhere too, have come to assume quasi-judicial functions, extralegal though they may be, and to create a technical administrative distinction between the taking of a child into custodial care and his arrest. In the United States only about half of the children taken into custody for delinquent acts are "arrested" and referred by the police to the juvenile court. Others are severely lectured, warned in the presence of their parents, dismissed for want of any desire on the part of the victim to have the child prosecuted, or referred to some social agency for help and guidance. The proportion referred to the court varies, no doubt, with the kind of offense involved and the characteristics of the delinquent. The more insignificant the delinquency, the younger the child, and the fewer his previous contacts with the police, the greater the likelihood of his being "unofficially" disposed of without a court referral. The result of this process is, of course, that the delinquents referred to the court represent a selected group, and that their delinquencies give an inadequate picture of even the known instances of delinquency in the community.

If we consider these facts, the conclusion seems inescapable that data about juvenile delinquency known to the police would be superior to the data possessed by the juvenile court, when the measurement of delinquency is contemplated. They are closest, from a procedural point of view, to the events needed for measurement.

One objection that may be raised to relying exclusively on police data is that there are forms of delinquency or individual delinquent acts that do not come to the attention of the police at all because

---

low-visibility decisions in the administration of justice," *Yale Law Rev.* **69**:543–594 (March, 1960). This is an interesting discussion of the use of such discretion, especially in narcotics cases (full or partial immunity given to informer-addict), felonious assaults (no prosecution unless victim signs complaint), and gambling cases (harassment, not full enforcement of law). See also S. H. Kadish, "Legal norm and discretion in the police and sentencing processes," *Harvard Law Rev.* **75**:904–931 (March, 1962).

they are reported directly to the juvenile court. This is true. Parents or relatives may take that action, as well as the school authorities, or some social agency, or even the police agencies of private corporations, etc. However, most of the delinquencies involved in such cases fall in the class of the status offenses: truancy, incorrigibility, running away, etc. The tendency today is to advocate the removal of all such conduct from the delinquency category.[7]

Choice of Data

When the problem of the choice of the kind of delinquent conduct that might be used for measurement purposes is considered, police data are or can be made sufficiently inclusive. There is no strong reason to believe that central registries of juvenile delinquents, set up in some cities and advocated in others, would furnish more adequate data. Such registries should be of great value in avoiding duplication of effort by social agencies and in bringing juveniles in need of guidance to the attention of the proper agency, but a more complete enumeration of delinquency will not necessarily furnish a better basis for an index unless it could be shown that delinquency, useful for index purposes and known to other agencies but not to the police, does not vary concomitantly with that known to the police. No clear demonstration of such a condition has been made either for delinquency as a whole or for the specific classes of delinquency that would be usable for index purposes.

The fact that, in order to further the correction or treatment of juvenile offenders, legislators have chosen to avoid any invidious classification and description of most of the kinds of conduct embraced by the term juvenile delinquency, does not hide the fact that the nonstatus offenses committed by juveniles vary in their nature and gravity just as do analogous crimes committed by adults. Since all are agreed that no index of real criminality can be based on the totality of crimes regardless of their nature or gravity, it must be assumed that no index of juvenile delinquency can be based on the totality of delinquency. If consensual offenses among adults do not furnish a usable sample for measurement, then similar offenses among juveniles do not. If there are certain types of violations that are dependent for their discovery on the extent of police activity, it makes no difference whether they are committed by adults or juveniles, for in either case they measure fluctuations in police activity rather

[7] See pp. 76–78.

than fluctuations in the frequency of such violations. We are then largely left with offenses in which there are personal victims or their representatives to bring the offenses to the attention of police authorities. In other words, *the same principles that govern the choice of offenses for the purpose of measuring criminality in general apply to the measurement of juvenile delinquency.* This does not mean that criminal law labels must be attached to delinquency, but it does mean that different kinds of delinquency must be identified, classified, and graded in a manner analogous—if not identical—to the manner in which crimes are classified and graded by the criminal law; and it means that index offenses must be sought among those offenses by juveniles which seriously injure accepted social values, are not of a consensual nature or dependent on the activity of the police for their discovery, and induce the greatest desire on the part of the victims or other aroused citizens to bring the offenses to the notice of public authorities. In a general way, this was recognized by Ronald H. Beattie, a leading statistician in this field in the United States, when he stated recently that

. . . if we are even to have an index of juvenile crime or delinquency . . . we will have to establish a uniform reporting system relating to offenses above a certain level of seriousness. These would include offenses that for adults are considered felonies plus some of the misdemeanors, such as theft and assault, against which society demands protection. It would seem utterly impossible to obtain uniform information on all children contacted by law enforcement agencies or even arrested by law enforcement officers for a host of activities which are generally described as waywardness, incorrigibility, truancy, lack of parental control, etc. Very little has been accomplished to date in narrowing the reporting to specific offenses, but it would appear that this is the direction that must be taken if we are ever to have statistics on juvenile delinquency that have real comparability.[8]

Even if we assume that data gathered by the police on offenses committed by known juveniles are superior to the data recorded by courts or other agencies, we have not answered some questions that are fundamental for the establishment of a measure of delinquency. Can we assume that the number of offenses committed by juveniles taken into custody form a constant proportion of all juvenile offenses?

If all offenses by juveniles were to be considered, it is obvious that the answer would be negative. If we confine ourselves to the types

[8] "Summary statement," *Proc. Social Statistics Section 1960* (Washington: American Statistical Association, n.d.), pp. 50–52.

of conduct previously discussed as being suitable for measurement purposes, we have to assume that the proportionality exists. If that is an untenable assumption, an index to *real* delinquency cannot be constructed. In that case, all that could be done would be the development of an index to the nature and degree of harm to social values by acts attributable to juveniles. It may well be that from a community point of view it is enough to know that the harm done by such acts is increasing or lessening. In any case, it is necessary to take into account the quality of delinquency and not its frequency alone, since changes in a mere frequency index may hide important variations among its components. A weighted index is therefore indicated.

The Qualitative Element

The first attempt to construct a qualitative "delinquency index" was made in 1922 by Willis W. Clark, staff member of the California Bureau of Juvenile Research at the Whittier State School.[9] Clark believed that "in studying the behavior of delinquent boys one of the requisites for satisfactory analysis and intercorrelation of the problems involved is a manner of measuring the quality and quantity of the offenses committed." The delinquency index he wished to construct was to be a measure of the offenses committed by specific individuals, a kind of personal conduct assessment not to be confused with the measurement of delinquency discussed in previous chapters of this report. It was to provide "a numerical valuation . . . of the social consequence of delinquent acts, which may be useful to indicate the extent of delinquency in a given case and to afford statistical data for correlation with other factors showing their respective interrelation and importance."

Clark prepared 148 cards, each with a brief description of one of many different offenses. These cards were submitted to fifty university teachers and graduate students and fifty persons engaged in various social and educational activities. They were asked to sort the cards into ten groups ranging from the least to the most serious from the point of view of the consequences of the act to society and to the individual. The arithmetic mean of the values given by the various raters to each offense was then computed and taken as the

---

[9] State of California, Department of Institutions, Whittier State School, California Bureau of Juvenile Res. Bul. no. 11. *Whittier Scale for Grading Juvenile Offenses* (8 pp., April, 1922).

numerical value of the degree of seriousness of the offense. The 148 offenses were then grouped into fourteen classes, as defined by the law—truancy, incorrigibility, vagrancy, malicious mischief, drunkenness, stealing, burglary, larceny, forgery, assault, immorality, arson, highway robbery, and murder—and the median score, range of scores, and average of quartile deviation of ratings computed for each class. A standard score sheet, which listed the 148 offenses in each of the ten score groups was prepared. Offenses given a mean value under 1.5 were given a score of one, those with mean values of 1.5–2.4 were given a score of 2, etc. Within each group the exact value obtained for each offense by the ratings was also indicated. Applying this scheme to an individual delinquent, Clark would examine that person's record of known offenses, note the score value of each such offense, and arrive at a total that would constitute that individual's "delinquency index."

The same problem was attacked in 1933 by Mervin A. Durea.[10] His objection to Clark's study was that its method assumed that increments in score values from 1 to 10 proceeded by equal steps. He, on the other hand, was concerned with "the construction of an instrument which will give differential weightings to the different types of delinquent offenses on the principle that the scale separation between some offenses is greater than the distance between others.[11] Using the fourteen offenses from Clark's study, he arranged them in 91 pairs and asked four groups of professional people, a total of 192, to look at each pair and underscore which of the two offenses the rater regarded as the more serious one. Each rater was furnished a list of definitions of offenses drawn also from Clark's study. Of the raters, 119 (62 per cent) responded. The processing of the data permitted Durea to arrive at a scale of values illustrated by the table below. For purposes of comparison, Clark's median scores have been transformed into values approximately comparable with Durea's. It will be noted that the degrees of seriousness do not completely coincide and that the California raters gave considerably lower values to incorrigibility, forgery, and burglary. However, while Clark's score sheet would lead to an index based on equidistant score values, his median scores illustrate the very problem that Durea set out to solve by a different procedure.

[10] Mervin A. Durea, "An experimental study of attitudes toward juvenile delinquency," *J. appl. Psychol.* 17:522–534 (1933).
[11] *Ibid.,* p. 524.

OFFENSE	DUREA	CLARK
Murder	68	83
Highway robbery	45	64
Arson	44	60
Burglary	39	41
Forgery	36	47
Immorality	33	56
Assault	32	52
Larceny	30	46
Stealing	27	29
Drunkenness	21	26
Incorrigibility	20	11
Malicious mischief	18	15
Vagrancy	16	15
Truancy	10	10

In the Cambridge-Somerville study an attempt was made to develop a scale of seriousness of offenses. The Clark-Durea scale was found to be inapplicable because it contained only 14 offenses, four of which were not found in the Massachusetts study, which in turn used 69. The term seriousness was used "as it is ordinarily understood by . . . police and probation officers."[12] Four police officers and four probation officers were asked to rate each offense on a scale of four steps: least serious, fairly serious, serious, and most serious, giving corresponding scores of 1 to 4. The values given to an offense by the eight judges were totaled and divided by eight, resulting in a score for that offense. Offenses with score values of 1.00–1.74 were classed as least serious and those with values from 3.25–4.00 as most serious. The "seriousness index" was used in the study for the purpose of comparing the delinquencies of the treatment group of boys with those of a control group.

The studies just mentioned suffice to indicate that the qualitative element in delinquent conduct has been taken into consideration by some researchers who have clearly recognized the need for something more than a frequency measurement of delinquency. They were primarily concerned with a qualitative measure of an *individual's* involvement in delinquency, but the problem they have sought to solve also faces anyone who wants to measure the changes that occur

[12] Edwin Powers and Helen Witmer, *An Experiment in the Prevention of Delinquency* (xliii, 649 pp. New York: Columbia University Press, 1951), p. 329.

in delinquency within a geographic area or in a juvenile population.

So far we have assumed that measurement involves the establishment of an index to the delinquencies committed by known juveniles, but arguments might be made for another basis. It might be claimed that although a community is interested in seeing a reduction in delinquencies, objectively ascertained, it may be even more interested in seeing a reduction in the number of children who commit them. At first glance, it might appear that these bases for measurement are not much different, but it is possible to reduce the number of delinquencies while the number of delinquents is increasing and vice versa; this is a problem which hinges on the extent to which offenses are committed by groups or by repeaters. If, from one year to the next, more offenses are committed by groups, causing each participant to become an offender, fewer offenses may involve more participants, and if there is an increase in the number of juveniles who commit two or more offenses, more offenses could be due to fewer juveniles. It is these facts that have caused criminal statisticians, from Messedaglia to the committee that prepared the system of Uniform Crime Reporting, to claim that no constant relationship may be expected to exist between the number of known offenses and the number of known offenders. This would mean, then, that an index based on known *offenders* would not be acceptable as an index to *real* criminality or delinquency. This conclusion is undoubtedly accurate.

But, would it be possible to assume that the number of known delinquents stays constant in relation to the number of all those who commit offenses but remain unknown? Since we know that, technically speaking, most juveniles are delinquent in the sense that they at times do things which, were they caught, could lead to their being taken into custody and since many kinds of such delinquent conduct would depend for their discovery on the policies and activities of the police, the answer to that question would have to be negative. If, however, we consider only those forms of conduct which are of sufficiently serious nature to cause their victims to bring them to the attention of the police, it may be that the delinquents charged with them represent a constant quota of all juveniles who commit such offenses. If this hypothesis is correct—and we know of no way to prove it—an index to the number of serious *delinquents* could be based on information about such offenders apprehended by the police.

It is commonly assumed that whatever index is used, it would be computed for specific time periods—a year or a month, for instance—and that if the effect of a preventive policy or action program were to be measured it would be done by examining the index figures before

and after the introduction of such a policy or program for the purpose of determining changes in these figures as they apply to an area
or a population presumably affected. The logical principle involved
in this procedure is commonly accepted and applied in all fields of
investigation.

Many students of juvenile delinquency have raised objections, however, to the use of periodic (monthly, annual) statistics for the
measurement of delinquency. They believe that a true index of delinquency or delinquents must be based on an assessment of conduct
during the entire time that juveniles are subject to the law. They say
that indices based on annual data give no hint of the number of
juveniles who become delinquents before they reach adulthood. "It
is suggested," says Savitz, "that the most accurate measure of the
'real' delinquency of any section of the city would be a rate based
on that probability of any child in the area ultimately becoming
delinquent if he remains in the area for the full period of delinquency
exposure (from ages 7 through 17)."[13] In the selected areas of
Philadelphia which he studied, he found, for instance, that while only
5 per cent of the children were brought to the juvenile court on delinquency charges during a year, 59 per cent of the boys living in these
areas had acquired a court record before they reached the age of 18.

Another author recently stated:

The United States Children's Bureau estimated in 1956 that roughly 2.2
per cent of children of juvenile court age . . . were known in that year to
juvenile courts . . . [but] the use of annual arraignment rates as the basis
of calculation of the size of our delinquent child population is downright
misleading. Not only are court arraignment rates markedly incomplete as
a delinquency measure . . . but when issued annually markedly under-
estimate the percentage of delinquents in the court-age child population.[14]

If the implications of these statements were to be acknowledged as
valid, a measure of the total past delinquency or the most significant
part thereof, attributed to each age cohort leaving the "juvenile" age
bracket should be constructed. Based on the principles employed by
Clark in his construction of the "delinquency index" of an individual
delinquent, such a measure would indeed rest on a summarization of
such individual indices for members of the cohort. It could be done

[13] Leonard D. Savitz, *Delinquency and Migration* (159 pp. Ph.D. dissertation,
University of Pennsylvania, 1960); also in Marvin E. Wolfgang, Leonard Savitz,
and Norman Johnston, comps., *The Sociology of Crime and Delinquency* (xiv,
423 pp. New York: Wiley, 1962), p. 205.
[14] Shulman, *op. cit.*, pp. 44–45.

if, during the requisite span of years, the information necessary for the classification and weighting of the known offenses of members of the cohort is recorded by the police and if account were taken both of the attrition by death and out-migration of cohort members, since they entered the age bracket, and of changes in their numbers due to in-migration; both of these are considerations that increase in significance as the geographic area decreases in which the studied population lives. If a preventive action program is introduced in a community, let us say, it would be expected that its beneficent effects would be shown by a progressive drop in the delinquency index in successive cohorts exposed to the program.

If the information available in police records would permit the retrospective construction of an age cohort index, it would equally permit the construction of measures of the delinquency of each age cohort entering the juvenile age bracket as it grows to adulthood. We could then discover at what age different members of the cohort first became delinquent, and the extent and nature of their recidivism during their juvenile years. If this were done for each successive age cohort, the relative value of preventive action programs aimed at juveniles could be tested by investigating changes in patterns of delinquent conduct, reduction of recidivism, etc., in successive age cohorts as they progressively come under the influence of such programs. For instance, would the cohort that had reached the age of 16 when a certain program was established show a history of delinquency different from that of the cohort which was 7 or 10 years old at the time and was therefore presumably influenced by the program during many more years?

The value of such cohort studies has been recognized for a long time. In 1890, the director of the National Statistical Bureau of Germany, H. von Scheel, wrote:

Ideal criminal statistics that would want to follow carefully the evolution of criminal tendencies in a given population should not work with crude annual contingents but with generations. They would start with the first offenders of a given year and continue to observe these persons, showing their later convictions, instead of counting them as new individuals each time they are convicted.[15]

Not long afterwards, Otto Köbner observed that "correct statistics of offenders can be developed only by a study of the total life history

---

[15] H. von Scheel, "Zur Einführung in die Kriminalstatistik, insbesondere diejenige des Deutschen Reichs," *Allg. Stat. Archiv* 1:185–211 (1890), p. 191.

of individuals."[16]   Twenty-five years later, in his *Moralstatistik* (pp. 425–426), Georg von Mayr defended this idea in the following words:

A deeper insight into the statistics of criminality is made possible by the disclosure of developmental regularities which must be sought through a study of the manner in which criminality develops in the course of a human lifetime. To do this it is necessary to identify the offender and his offense in the population and keep him under constant statistical control so that it is possible, for each cohort entering punishable age and until all its members are dead, to study statistically its participation or non-participation in criminality and the intensity of such participation in its various forms. . . .

[16] O. Köbner, "Die Methode einer wissenschaftlichen Rückfallsstatistik als Grundlage einer Reform der Kriminalstatistik," *Z. ges Strafrechtswiss.* 13:615–740 (1893), p. 670. Köbner's monograph stated the principles that should govern the development of statistics of recidivism. The statement has not been improved upon, nor have the principles been applied in official publications of criminal statistics. Many professional criminal statisticians are apparently unacquainted with them. The monograph stimulated a number of studies, however, beginning with those, still unsurpassed in many respects, by R. Böckh, director of the Municipal Statistical Bureau of Berlin: "Arbeiten des Statistischen Amts der Stadt, die Criminalität der Bevölkerung betreffend." I. "Methodische Behandlung des Gegenstandes," *Statistisches Jahrbuch der Stadt Berlin.* 22 *Statistik des Jahres 1895,* pp. 433–453, II. "Statistische Messung der Bestrafung der Bevölkerung von Berlin insbesondere mit Gefängniss und Zuchthaus," *Ibid.,* 23 *Statistik des Jahres 1896,* pp. 435–457, III. "Die mit Gefängniss Bestraften in der Berliner Bevölkerung," *Ibid.,* 24 *Statistik des Jahres 1897,* pp. 605–621). Like Köbner, Böckh was interested in how statistics of recidivism might be best used to test the effectiveness of different penal and correctional policies. The statistical methodology of such studies was also presented by Giovanni Mortara in 1910, "Tavole di criminalità e di recidività," *Gior. degli economisti e Riv. di statistica,* 3d Ser., 21st year, 40:75–97 (1910). During the last two decades interest in the construction and use of crime expectancy tables has been revived, especially in the Scandinavian countries, beginning with Gunnar Dahlberg's paper on the risk of being convicted of a serious crime for the first time during one's lifetime ("Risken att dömas för svårare brott," *Nord. Tids. f. Strafferet* 31:145–201, 1943; In English, "A new method in crime statistics applied to the population of Sweden," *J. Crim. Law and Criminol.* 39:327–341, September–October 1948), and ending, for the present, with a Danish study of the risk of criminality in Denmark before and after the war (Karl O. Christiansen, Lise Møller, and Arne Nielsen, "Kriminaliktsrisikoen i Danmark før og efter krigen," *Nord. Tids. f. Kriminalvidenskab* 48:300–313, 1960; 49:73–78, 1961). In the United States Thomas P. Monahan, statistician of the County Court of Philadelphia, recently applied the technique in an investigation of the risk of a child's being brought before the juvenile court of that city on a delinquency charge before reaching the age of eighteen. ("On the incidence of delinquency," *Social Forces* 39:66–72, October 1960. See also the annual reports of the Municipal Court of Philadelphia for 1959, pp. 163–175, and of the County Court of Philadelphia for 1960, pp. 49–54.)

This is the task of the "criminality table" of the future, as one might call it, in analogy with the "mortality table" or the "marriage table," etc. This also has significance for the important problem of recidivism.

Three recent studies of the offenses of age cohorts are especially worthy of notice because their authors have not been satisfied with the mere determination of the nature and extent of each cohort's delinquency but have correlated this information with other phenomena. In 1960 the young Norwegian criminologist, Nils Christie, published the results of an investigation of the delinquency of all boys born in Norway in 1933 until they reached their twenty-fifth year in 1957, comparing the offenders with the nonoffenders with respect to a variety of traits and factors.[17]

The other two studies compare successive age cohorts with a view to observe the impact of changing social conditions on their delinquency. The first was carried out by Leslie T. Wilkins for the British Home Office. Its main object was "to examine and test the theory that children born in certain years (for example during war time) are more likely to commit offenses than others, and that this tendency remains from childhood to early adult life."[18] The investigation covered all children born each year during 1938–1949 in England and Wales and male children born in Scotland. The official statistics of the indictable offenses during 1946–1957 of each cohort entering punishable age were studied. The general conclusion reached by Wilkins was that the greatest proneness to crime was found to be associated with those age cohorts

who passed through their fifth year during the war. This is the year immediately preceding school attendance except for the small percentage who attend nursery school prior to compulsory primary school attendance. Whether this means that disturbed social conditions have their major impact on children between the age of four and five is not proved, but this is a likely hypothesis. It is not clear how any hypothesis which related the greatest impact of disturbed social conditions to a much earlier age could be consistent with these results.[19]

The second study was made by Karl O. Christiansen on Danish material for the purpose of comparison with the one by Wilkins.

[17] Nils Christie, *Unge norske lovovertredere* (xx, 311 pp. Oslo: Universitetsforlaget, 1960). English summary, pp. 297–308.
[18] Leslie T. Wilkins, *Delinquent Generations* (iv, 19 pp. London: H. M. Stationery Office, 1960). Home Office Studies in the Causes of Delinquency and the Treatment of Offenders 3, p. 1.
[19] *Ibid.*, p. 8.

Although he found that children who passed through their fifth year during the post-war period (1945–1948) later had higher rates of delinquency than did other generations, he concluded that his findings supported the general hypothesis that was tested by Wilkins.[20]

It is obvious that if, instead of being concerned with the impact of presumably deleterious social forces on children, the researchers mentioned had been interested in knowing what impact some specific policy or action program designed to prevent or reduce delinquency had had, their procedure would have been equally applicable. An index or measure of delinquency that, in contrast with a periodic annual index, might be called an age cohort index, would be especially useful for this type of research.

This concludes our brief survey of the history of ideas concerning the measurement of criminality and delinquency and of some of the most important researches that have touched this problem. Before proceeding to the discussion of our specific study, however, a closer look at a matter is needed, since it has an important bearing on the issue of measurement, namely the definitions of the conduct which brings juveniles into conflict with the law and, insofar as it results in the apprehension of the offenders, permits the recording of information needed for the construction of indices of delinquency.

[20] Karl O. Christiansen, "Kriminalitetstruede generationer," *Nord. Tids. f. Kriminalvidenskab* 49:268–274 (1961).

6

The Legal Basis of Delinquency

A clear definition of fundamental concepts is a prime requisite for all research. Therefore, any study of delinquency must first establish the meaning of this term. This task has often been neglected by criminologists who have spent more time on examining the terms and concepts of the independent variables than of the dependent one—delinquency—which they have hoped to explain. As Mack has written: "It is impossible to undertake any such [etiological] research without having to decide first of all what you mean by delinquency. This is a condition which most textbooks and research papers acknowledge in their first paragraph and then go on to ignore."[1] The need for a definition of delinquency is equally stressed by Tappan, who states:

Certainly there is no more central question in this study and probably none more difficult to answer. Yet it is important to see the nature of delinquency as clearly as possible and to understand the problems that have impeded efforts at definition . . . , because on the interpretation of the term depend all those vital differences which set off the juvenile delinquent from the adult criminal at the one extreme and from the non-offender at the other.[2]

These quotations may appear strange in view of the fact that definitions of delinquency exist in laws that provide the basis for

[1] J. A. Mack, "Juvenile delinquency research: A criticism," *Sociol. Rev.* N.S. 3:47–64 (July 1955), p. 56.
[2] Paul W. Tappan, *Juvenile Delinquency* (613 pp. New York: McGraw Hill, 1949), p. 3. Quoted by permission of publisher.

dealing with juvenile offenders. It is these definitions that have been used in the compilation of official statistics about delinquency and delinquents, on which so many studies have relied, or in classifying delinquents, when the researcher has had access to the original records of public agencies. Indeed, innumerable variables have been statistically correlated with the events covered by the legal terms "crime" and "delinquency" and provocative theories about these phenomena have been formulated, but even in the most sophisticated researches little or no account has been taken of the great diversity of conduct represented, not only by the inclusive designation of "delinquency" but even by such legal categories as "offenses against the person," "offenses against property," criminal homicide, rape, robbery, burglary, larceny, and others. This, we think, is a cogent reason for the dissatisfaction with present definitions of juvenile delinquency and for the demand that something be done about it. But first, let us look at what the law calls delinquency.

This involves not only an examination of the specific statutes, which in creating juvenile courts also prescribed the scope of their jurisdiction in terms of the kinds of conduct and classes of juveniles affected, but also of the criminal law, since all juvenile court statutes in the United States provide that a child is a juvenile delinquent if he commits any act which would be a crime if done by an adult. Were delinquency limited to such conduct, our task would be simpler, but all jurisdictions, except the federal, label a variety of other forms of conduct as delinquency. Sussmann has listed all of them in the order of their frequency and has shown, for each state, which ones are specified.[3] They number thirty-four, varying from truancy, incorrigibility, and running away from home to using tobacco in any form. No state has adopted all of them, but Indiana leads with seventeen; Maine, at the other extreme, names but one—"growing up in idleness and crime." Some of them could equally well come under the heading of dependency or neglect because the distinctions are often difficult to draw. As a matter of fact, some states classify as delinquency a condition which other states define as dependency or neglect.

The problem is not limited to the United States, as is seen from the following statement:

In many countries the meaning of juvenile delinquency is so broad that it embraces practically all manifestations of juvenile behavior. Under the

---

[3] Frederick B. Sussmann, *Law of Juvenile Delinquency* (96 pp. New York: Oceana Publications, 1959), pp. 21–22.

influence of certain theories, juvenile delinquency is identified either with maladjustment or with forms of juvenile behavior which actually are more a reflection of poor living conditions or inadequate laws and regulations than a delinquent inclination. Thus, disobedience, stubbornness, lack of respect, being incorrigible, smoking without permission, collecting cigarette butts, hawking and the like are considered juvenile delinquency. Very often these "forms of delinquency" are hidden in statistical data under the vague term "other offenses." More often than would be desirable, these "offenders" are lumped together with real ones not only because services and institutions for them are not available but also because, according to some policies and practices, all of them are considered "maladjusted" and sent to the same institutions. The result is an artificial inflation of the juvenile delinquency problem and its "forms."[4]

Confusion results from these legal definitions of delinquency.

It is reasonable to believe [says Tappan] that all, or at least a vast majority of, normal children sometimes indulge in forms of behavior that might come within the purview of the juvenile court. Whether a given child will get into trouble depends largely on the interpretation that is attached to his conduct and the willingness or ability of the parent to deal with it. Considering the broad scope of legal provisions on insubordination, "questionable behavior," "injuring or endangering the morals or health of himself or others," truancy, running away, trespassing, and petty theft, it would be difficult to find any paragons of virtue who would be wholly exonerated of delinquency, save through parental understanding and leniency.[5]

The lack of uniformity among jurisdictions makes comparative studies especially difficult. Although violations of criminal laws and ordinances are generally considered "delinquency" when committed by a juvenile, many states give exclusive jurisdiction to the criminal court if the violation is of a certain kind. This holds true for capital crimes in the federal code and in the laws of eleven states (Colorado, Georgia, Iowa, Maryland, Massachusetts, Minnesota, South Carolina, Tennessee, Delaware, Vermont, and West Virginia) and for crimes punishable by life imprisonment in the first eight of these mentioned; for murder in five states (Kansas, Louisiana, Montana, New Jersey, and Pennsylvania); for homicide (Texas); for manslaughter (Montana); for rape (Louisiana, Tennessee); for attempted rape (Louisi-

---

[4] The Second United Nations Congress on The Prevention of Crime and the Treatment of Offenders (London, August 8–20, 1960). *New Forms of Juvenile Delinquency: Their Origin, Prevention and Treatment*. Report prepared by the Secretariat, A/Conf. 17/7.
[5] Paul W. Tappan, *op. cit.*, p. 32.

ana); for crimes of violence (Illinois); for crimes punishable by more than ten years imprisonment (North Carolina); for infamous crimes (Maine); for traffic law (Indiana, New Jersey) or motor vehicle law offenses (Rhode Island); and for "any crime" (Florida).[6] Juveniles prosecuted for these offenses in the jurisdictions just mentioned fall outside of "delinquency" properly speaking. In studies of the illegal conduct of juveniles, they would, of course, have to be included, but if they have not been processed by juvenile courts they do not figure in the records of these courts which have so often been the chief source of data for delinquency studies.

Comparative analysis of such studies is complicated by still another problem, namely the lack of a standard definition of who is capable of engaging in "delinquency," both as to age and sex. Considering the fifty-two jurisdictions—constituted of fifty states, the District of Columbia, and the federal government—anyone under 21 years of age can commit a "delinquency" and therefore be adjudged a juvenile delinquent in 4 of the jurisdictions; under 19 in 2; under 18 in 28; under 17 in 10; and under 16 in 8. This is true for both sexes, but in one state that has a maximum limit of 19 for males, the limit is 21 for females; in two states these maxima are respectively 16 and 18, and in five states, 17 and 18. The effect of these diverse age limits on interstate research is easy to imagine, unless comparable age and sex groups have been used.

Except for the jurisdictions mentioned earlier, no state has given criminal courts exclusive jurisdiction over juveniles, but most have given them concurrent jurisdiction, which means that a juvenile in these states may, under certain circumstances, be adjudged a criminal rather than a delinquent. The scope of this power varies greatly among the jurisdictions, as may be seen from the tabulation on page 75, which takes only juvenile males into consideration.[7]

Although it can be seen that more than half of the jurisdictions (28) limit delinquency to illegal conduct by those under 18 years of age, there could be substantial errors made, for instance, in comparing the results of studies made in the eleven states, in which any juvenile may be prosecuted for crime, with those made in the two states (New Hampshire and Virginia) where criminal courts have no jurisdiction at all over those under 18.

In most states there is no lower age limit set for the adjudication

---

[6] Based on Sussman, *op. cit.*, pp. 65–77, as adapted from Paul W. Tappan, "Children and youth in the criminal court," *Ann. Amer. Acad. polit. and soc. Sci.* **261**:128–136 (January 1949), pp. 129–130.

[7] Compiled from Sussman, *ibid.*

Where the original jurisdiction of the Juvenile Court extends to age	The Criminal Court has overlapping or concurrent jurisdiction over juveniles above the age of	in ____ jurisdictions
21	11	1
	17	3
19	all ages	1
	14	1
18	all ages	11
	19–21	1
	11–21	1
	13	5
	15	8
	none	2
17	all ages	2
	9	1
	11	1
	15	1
	16	1
	none	4
16	all ages	2
	14	1
	none	5

of a child as delinquent; Mississippi and Texas place that limit at ten and New York at seven.[8]

Our brief discussion of how diversely "delinquency" and "delinquents" are defined in American statutes and how judicial administration may affect the assignment of an offense or an offender to the criminal or the delinquency area has been pursued to indicate one aspect of the difficulties involved in securing uniform and reliable data for the measurement of delinquency. Although these difficulties are especially great when data from different jurisdictions are involved, they are not absent in studies dealing with a single state or community. So long as the definition of delinquency in law in any jurisdiction includes so many ill-defined kinds of conduct and admits of the exercise of wide administrative discretion at all levels in handling juvenile offenders, the problem of standardization of data needed for measurement purposes will always face the student. Indeed, it has forced us, in the present research to develop a system of classify-

[8] Sol Rubin, "The legal character of juvenile delinquency," *Ann. Amer. Acad. polit. and soc. Sci.,* **261**:1–8 (January 1949), p. 6.

ing delinquent acts which is in a sense independent of the labels attached to them by the law.

THE PENNSYLVANIA JUVENILE COURT ACT

The source documents used in our study are records of various kinds, compiled by the police of Philadelphia in connection with their routine enforcement of the law. So far as juveniles are concerned, such enforcement is circumscribed by what is considered to be delinquent conduct by the legislature of the Commonwealth of Pennsylvania and recorded in an act of June 2, 1933, Public Law 1433, with amendments of 1937, 1939, 1953. Section I, Subsection 2 and 4, contains the following definitions.

> (2) The word "child," as used in this act, means a minor under the age of eighteen years.
> (4) The words "delinquent child" include:
>> (a) A child who has violated any law of the Commonwealth or ordinance of any city, borough or township;
>> (b) A child who, by reason of being wayward or habitually disobedient, is uncontrolled by his or her parent, guardian, custodian, or legal representative;
>> (c) A child who is habitually truant from school or home;
>> (d) A child who habitually so deports himself or herself as to injure or endanger the morals or health of himself, herself, or others.

As can be seen, Section 1, Subsection 4a, defines delinquency as any act, which if committed by an adult would be a crime; and Subsections 4b, c, and d define delinquency in terms of an age status and constituting acts or conditions that could not be attributed to an adult.

THE STANDARD JUVENILE COURT ACT

The definition of delinquency, such as the one used in the Pennsylvania statute, is no longer supported by leading authorities. It is challenged, in particular, by the drafters of the Standard Juvenile Court Act. The first edition of this Act was published by the National Probation Association in 1925. It was revised and reissued in 1928, 1933, 1943, 1949, and 1959. Prepared by the Committee on Standard Juvenile Court Act of the National Probation and Parole Association, in cooperation with the National Council of Juvenile Court Judges and the United States Children's Bureau, the new act emphasizes the basic concept in *parens patriae*. Under the act, Article 1, Sections 2e and 2f, a "child" is defined as a person under

18 years of age and a "minor" as any person under 21 years of age. As in the 1943 and 1949 editions of the Act, the terms "delinquency" and "neglect" are avoided. Article 2, Section 8, Subsection 1 reads:

[Except as otherwise provided herein, the court shall have exclusive original jurisdiction in proceedings]

1. Concerning any child who is alleged to have violated any federal, state, or local law or municipal ordinance, regardless of where the violation occurred; or any minor alleged to have violated any federal, state, or local law or municipal ordinance prior to having become 18 years of age. Such minor shall be dealt with under the provisions of this act relating to children. Jurisdiction may be taken by the court of the district where the minor is living or found, or where the offense is alleged to have occurred. When a minor 18 years of age or over already under the jurisdiction of the court is alleged to have violated any federal, state, or local law or municipal ordinance, the juvenile court shall have concurrent jurisdiction with the criminal court.[9]

This delimitation of the scope of juvenile delinquency has received recent support from two sources. The Second United Nations Congress on the Prevention of Crime and the Treatment of Offenders, London 1960, passed a resolution that stated: "The Congress considers that the scope of the problem of juvenile delinquency should not be unnecessarily inflated . . . it recommends that the meaning of the term juvenile delinquency should be restricted as far as possible to violations of the criminal law."[10]

The New York Joint Legislative Committee on Court Reorganization, in its draft of a Family Court Act, has taken a similar stand:

"Juvenile delinquent" is defined in the proposed legislation as "a person over seven and less than sixteen years of age who does any act which, if done by an adult would constitute a crime, and requires supervision, treatment or confinement." This definition, considerably narrower than the current definition, accords with the common understanding.[11]

We believe that statistical collections and analyses in terms of the definitions of delinquency must adopt this delimitation if they are to provide a useful measurement or index of the volume, character or trend of delinquency.

Although the present research has had to depend on the definition

[9] "Standard Juvenile Court Act," *National Probation and Parole Assoc. J.* 5:323–391 (October 1959), p. 344.
[10] See *Report Prepared by the Secretariat* (iv, 95 pp., New York: United Nations, 1961), p. 61.
[11] Joint Legislative Committee on Court Reorganization, II, "The Family Court Act," New York State, Daniel G. Albert, Chairman (Albany, N.Y., 1962), p. 6.

of delinquency found in the Juvenile Court Act of Pennsylvania in selecting an appropriate sample of delinquent acts for analysis, we decided that it would be impossible to utilize the data on the "juvenile status" offenses in the construction of an index to delinquency. Such offenses are viewed by most writers only as predelinquent behavior or symptomatic of potential delinquent behavior. That is why it is often argued that they should not be labeled delinquency, and that is the chief reason behind the recommendations of the Standard Juvenile Court Act.

Truancy, for example, is a violation of a regulation requiring compulsory school attendance, but the explanation for truancy involves parental influence or lack of it or the failure of educational facilities and authorities to solve purely educational problems. To call the absence from classes delinquency places the truant in the same category with more serious violators of substantive legal codes. Shulman suggests: "Since chronic truancy often antedates serious delinquency by several years and may serve as a valuable warning signal of impending serious behavior disorder, we may raise the question of whether its formal handling as an aspect of juvenile delinquency is a proper one."[12]

The law presumes that children belong at home, and consequently a child who runs away from home is considered delinquent. But as in the case of incorrigibility and ungovernable behavior, the problems of family neglect are the important issues to be considered by the juvenile court in handling these children rather than behavior that constitutes serious and injurious threats to other members of the community.

Excluding these and similar acts from use in the measurement of delinquency and concentrating only on violations by juveniles of the law and ordinances that, were they committed by adults, would be considered crimes, reduce but do not eliminate the problem of legal definitions and classifications. The substantive content of the definitions of these offenses in the criminal law therefore has to be considered since it is common practice in official statistics of delinquency, especially in police statistics, to classify delinquents and their conduct in categories designated by labels derived from the criminal law.

The Labels of the Criminal Law

Since police agencies are entrusted with the enforcement of the criminal law, it is both obvious and natural that, in the investigation

---

[12] Harry M. Shulman, *Juvenile Delinquency in American Society* (New York: Harper, 1961), p. 33.

of offenses, they think in terms of the specific definitions of crime contained in the law. When a complaint is made and they investigate the incident, or when they observe an offense being committed, its objective characteristics lead them to call it burglary, robbery, larceny, etc. And when they prepare reports on the incidents on some standard forms, these labels are recorded and furnish the basis for later periodic tabulations of the number of different offenses the police have dealt with whether or not an offender is taken into custody. The result is that when juveniles are apprehended by the police, their offenses are not labeled "delinquency" but are given appropriate criminal designations or, in the case of juvenile status offenses, a specific designation supplied by the juvenile court law, such as truancy, runaway, incorrigibility, etc.

No police department, to our knowledge, publishes any statistics of juvenile *offenses*. Since most offenses are committed by unknown persons, those committed by juveniles can be segregated only when an apprehension is made. Even then, however, the practice is to publish only statistics of juvenile *delinquents* without reference to the number of offenses of different legal categories that have been "cleared" by their apprehension. In any event, such statistics are commonly relied on today as indicators of the movement and character of juvenile delinquency. Therefore, it becomes necessary to ask if (a) the criminal law labels best characterize delinquency and (b) if customary practices of statistical classification of juvenile offenses present the best picture of such delinquency.

Answers to these questions are complicated by the fact that the problems they involve are not independent of one another. The criminal law of a state may contain a very large number of distinctive crime designations, several hundreds of them, but when police departments record offenses with a view to their later inclusion in statistics, they are accustomed to use relatively few such designations and give the same label to a variety of offenses that resemble one another in some way. This practice has become more and more common and has been greatly stimulated by the formulation of the Uniform Classification of Offenses in the early 1930's. This classification is used in national statistics of offenses known to the police and of persons charged with offenses and published in *Uniform Crime Reports* issued by the FBI and based on reports now submitted by most civil police agencies in the United States. The classification, as slightly revised in 1958, contains 26 offense categories. Police agencies periodically submit reports to the FBI on standard forms containing these categories; and to facilitate the preparation of these reports the police now tend to label offenses not according to the more specific designations in the criminal law but by the code numbers and titles used in the Uniform Classification.

UNIFORM CLASSIFICATION OF OFFENSES

Part 1

1. Criminal homicide
   a. Murder and non-negligent manslaughter
   b. Manslaughter by negligence
2. Forcible rape
3. Robbery
4. Aggravated assault
5. Burglary—breaking or entering
6. Larceny-theft (except auto theft)
   a. $50 and over in value
   b. Under $50 in value
7. Auto theft

Part 2

8. Other assaults
9. Forgery and counterfeiting
10. Embezzlement and fraud
11. Stolen property: Buying, receiving, possessing
12. Weapons: Carrying, possessing, etc.
13. Prostitution and commercialized vice
14. Sex offenses (except forcible rape, prostitution, and commercialized vice)
15. Offenses against the family and children
16. Narcotic drug laws
17. Liquor laws (except drunkenness)
18. Drunkenness
19. Disorderly conduct
20. Vagrancy
21. Gambling
22. Driving while intoxicated
23. Violation of road and driving laws
24. Parking violations
25. Other violations of traffic and motor vehicle laws
26. All other offenses

Each of the titles in the above classification is derived from the criminal law but of necessity each covers a considerable variety of illegal conduct. When juvenile delinquency which violates the criminal law is subsumed under them, the result is a highly simplified and considerably distorted picture of that delinquency. A few illustrations will suffice. They will be limited largely to some of the titles of offenses which in *Uniform Crime Reports* are considered as "index crimes," that is, susceptible of use as a measurement of criminality. These are murder and non-negligent manslaughter, forcible rape, robbery, aggravated assault, burglary-breaking and entering, larceny or theft of property valued at 50 dollars or more, and auto theft (motor vehicle theft). It should be recalled that so far as juveniles are concerned, these titles are applicable only in descriptions of *offenses* attributable to juveniles or to *apprehended juveniles* charged with their commission.

Robbery

This title implies to most people that there is only one kind of robbery, that it is terrible and that it connotes taking something of value from a person, usually with violence. Yet, evidence points to significant differences in the quality of these acts.[13] As Beattie points out,

. . . there is no knowledge of the variation that has occurred in different types of robbery. Such increases or decreases as have been observed may be due to variations in armed robbery or in strong-arm robbery, which in some instances amounts to no more than drunk rolls. Reports are often received today that children have been engaged in highjacking coins from each other. These incidents have been reported as robberies.[14]

The victim-offender relationship is also important, by sex, age, and other variables. There is certainly a vast difference between a 16-year-old boy's forcing a gas station attendant at the point of a gun to give up money from the cash register and an eight-year-old boy's twisting the arm of another eight-year-old boy in the school corridor in order to take his lunch money. Both acts are classified legally and statistically as robbery. This same kind of situation was referred to in the 1956 Annual Report of the Crime Prevention Association of Philadelphia:

And again, what is "highway robbery"? In the thinking of the American people, this indeed is a serious offense. Yet we know of a case last year in

---

[13] These differences in adult robberies have recently been examined in some detail by F. H. McClintock and Evelyn Gibson, *Robbery in London* (xix, 147 pp. London: Macmillan, 1961).

[14] *Crime in California 1958*, p. 18. See also Nochem S. Winnet, *Twenty-Five Years of Crime Prevention* (Philadelphia: Philadelphia Crime Association) *Annual Report 1956*, p. 1: "Hundreds of robberies were reported. An analysis showed many of them involved petty sums, one as low as ten cents, a tribute exacted by one school child from another."

which a 14-year-old approached another boy of similar age and demanded 15 cents; the boy accosted stated he had only a quarter. The "highway robber" took the quarter, had it changed and returned to the other boy 10 cents. *This offense is listed as highway robbery.* Another instance involved two boys who extorted 20 cents daily for a week from another boy as he went to and from school. This youthful highjacking was reported by the victim's parents to the police; charge against the two offenders—highway robbery. Now we must admit that such extortion and highjacking is nasty behavior but to call this highway robbery and still keep a straight face is naive.[15]

Burglary

Burglary is another example of the need for subclassifications, for while it is an offense that has shown a steady increase over the past years, we are never sure what kind of burglary has been increasing. The California Report has raised this same question: "Is the increase in safe burglary, large-scale residential and commercial burglary, or in just smallscale pilferings that are technically burglary? A large part of the latter could be the result of juvenile behavior. Under present classification methods, this question cannot be answered."[16] There are wide variations in the state statutes that define burglary. Although breaking into a locked car is defined as burglary in California and is reported thus in many instances, it is an offense that is often reported by many law enforcement agencies as petty theft and classified as larceny.

Some of these problems were raised in papers presented in 1960 before the Social Statistics Section of the American Statistical Association. It was pointed out, for example, that broad crime groupings are used to tally major offenses which differ according to some element in definition. The following cases were given as illustrations:

(A) Two juveniles while on school vacation break into a neighbor's barn, steal some nails, a hammer, and a saw in order to build a treehouse nearby; (B) a prowler sneaks into an unoccupied bedroom and rummages for money or jewelry while the occupants are having dinner downstairs; (C) a team of thugs, armed and with heavy burglar tools force entrance into an office and attack a safe. Each of these cases is classified ordinarily as a "burglary" according to police statistical practices.[17]

---

[15] *Ibid.,* p. 11.
[16] *Crime in California 1958,* p. 18.
[17] Edward V. Comber, "Discussion," *Proc. Social Statistics Section 1960.* (viii, 211 pp., Washington, D.C.: American Statistical Association, n.d., mimeo.); pp. 36–37.

Both from the viewpoint of police protective services and of threats of danger to life or property, these acts are clearly distinguishable, but the differential variables are hidden in formal statistical tabulations that use legal categories. Such factors as the presence or absence of violence to obtain entry, the legal or illegal presence of the offender at the scene of the crime, the amount of property loss or damage, etc., are totally neglected.

Assaults

The legal definitions of aggravated assaults, sexual assaults, rape, and similar offenses against the person each cover a variety of forms of conduct. The 1958 California report again suggests:

. . . because of the relationship of the parties or the conditions under which the assaults occurred, many altercations, largely domestic quarrels, characterized in reports as aggravated assault, do not seem to fall in the general area of felonious assault. There is need to sub-classify this type of offense in order to arrive at a true picture of assault.[18]

A New Jersey analysis of juvenile court cases a decade ago alluded to the same problem: "Personal injury, while having a higher percentage of dismissals as malicious mischief, does not carry comparable value under analysis. A majority of personal injury complaints were not assault cases per se—proper classification would be street fighting."[19] Moreover, the differences between a simple assault and battery and aggravated assault and battery are such that not only police variations but statutory provisions as well lend confusion rather than clarity to the classification problems. The legal nomenclature often distorts the true character of an attack on the person because of the difficulties of determining "grievous bodily harm" or extent of the injury and because suspects are often willing to confess to a simple assault or the police and courts are willing to accept a plea of guilty to a simple assault in order to obtain a conviction even when the more serious aggravated assault occurred.[20]

Rape

The categories of rape—even forcible rape—assault with attempt to ravish, sexual license, and sexual offenses generally fail to provide

[18] *Crime in California 1958*, p. 18.
[19] *Children in New Jersey Courts 1953*, p. 24.
[20] See Donald J. Newman, "Pleading guilty for considerations: A study of bargain justice," *J. Crim. Law, Criminol., and Police Sci.*, **46**:780–790, March-April, 1956.

qualitative information on the broad range of activities and on the dimensions of seriousness or injury that may be involved in these acts. Forcible rape can range from violent and unprovoked attacks on women by strangers to a common pickup in a barroom that ends in greater sexual intimacy than the woman intended. The lines between forcible rape, statutory rape, fornication, and contributing to the delinquency of a minor are never clear from statistical tabulations that merely use these legal terms. Without examination of the detailed descriptions in police reports, the compilation of data in tabular form usually fail to represent important distinctions in the facts. As the United Nations Congress in 1960 reported on an attempt to collect international data on sex offenses: " 'Sexual license' was too vague. The replies do not always make clear what kind of offenses are referred to: Full sexual relations or sexual games between children? Relations between lovers, sexual promiscuity, dissolute behavior, prostitution?"[21]

Certainly there are vast differences in the types of offenses that are listed as "assault with intent to ravish." The conduct of a 16-year-old boy, who attacks a 30-year-old woman, drags her into a dark alley to assault her sexually but is thwarted by screams and the appearance of a police officer, is surely different from a 9-year-old boy's exploratory sexual curiosity with a neighbor girl aged 8. When she innocently tells her mother about the afternoon's adventure, and when the mother imagines horrendous things, calls the police, and has the boy arrested, this case like the previous one is listed as "assault with intent to ravish." Once again, Beattie has remarked:

Much has been said in recent years of the apparent growth of viciousness in certain types of crime. There is no basis upon which to determine whether or not there has been such a growth. There have been many cases that have received a great deal of publicity, but without careful classification, it cannot be known whether the impression of increase is backed by fact.[22]

We believe that these illustrations suffice to show that the use of the broad titles of offenses derived from the Uniform Classification of Offenses for a description of delinquency chargeable to juveniles would be an unsatisfactory procedure that cannot provide sensitive measures of delinquency.

A second problem arises out of certain arbitrary practices of classifying and ordering offenses in official statistics of delinquency. These

[21] United Nations Congress, London, August 8–20, 1960, A/Conf. 17/6, p. 64.
[22] *Crime in California 1958*, p. 19.

practices are directly attributable to the manner in which the Uniform Classification is applied in accord with the instructions governing its use. There are, of course, many ways of presenting offense statistics. The offenses involved could be listed alphabetically, or grouped in broad classes—for instance, offenses against the person, offenses against property, etc.—with appropriate subclasses, or grouped according to the Uniform Classification, to mention but a few patterns. For reasons already stated the last mentioned method is the most common one in American police statistics.

There are two built-in features of the use of this classification which reduce its value. First, an implicit hypothesis underlies it, namely that its 26 classes are arranged in decreasing order of seriousness. This hypothesis is not completely invalid. Certainly most offenses in Part 1 of the classification are more injurious than most of those in Part 2, but arson, kidnapping, abortion, blackmail and extortion, and malicious mischief now falling into the last class of "all other offenses," and simple assault and battery (item 8) and embezzlement and fraud (item 10) may in fact involve more personal injury or loss of property, for instance, than many of the offenses listed among the "index crimes" under rape, aggravated assault, burglary and larceny. Therefore, the present grouping of the offenses by the broad legal labels employed does not provide the best typology of offenses based on an hypothesis of degree of seriousness, not to mention the fact that it does not provide for differential weighting of the classes, nor of the great number of variants among the offenses included in any single class. One theft of fifty dollars is given as much weight as one homicide, and one such theft as much weight as one of $5000.[23]

Second, the manner in which the classification is used conceals a great deal of delinquency known to the police because it offers no possibility of counting all the *components* of a delinquent event. The problem does not arise in the case of uncomplicated events. A mere breaking and entering can be classified as burglary, but suppose that in committing this offense a juvenile also steals property of great value, and on being surprised, assaults and wounds the owner with a dangerous weapon. The instructions for classifying this total event require that only the offense highest in the order of the Uniform Classification be counted—in this instance, the aggravated assault

---

[23] For a more detailed discussion of these and related problems, see Marvin E. Wolfgang, "Uniform crime reports: A critical appraisal," *University of Pennsylvania Law Rev.* 111:708–738 (April 1963).

and battery. This conceals both the burglary and the theft. If a juvenile holds up the occupants of an automobile, kills the driver, rapes his female companion, and steals her pocket book, jewelry, and the car, this complex event must be counted as one non-negligent criminal homicide (item 1) and the rape and the thefts will be concealed. All kinds of other complex events could be cited to show that the manner in which offenses are commonly tabulated for statistical presentation results in an incomplete picture even of the delinquency known to the police.

The conclusion seems inescapable that when an offense is given, in official police statistics, a broad legal label which does not allow for adequate discriminatory separation and weighting of the variants covered by it, and when all but the hypothetically most serious component of a delinquency event are concealed by the procedure followed in scoring offenses, the resulting statistics are not adequate for the measurement of delinquency.

The Philadelphia Police Department faithfully applies the Uniform Classification of Offenses and the instructions for its use, except that it regards item 12 of the classification as applying only to guns. In addition, it has extracted several distinct classes from "other offenses," thereby reducing the size of that residue. These classes are: arson, corner lounging, malicious mischief, trespassing, incorrigible, runaway, and weapons other than guns. Furthermore, it has defined a total of 267 subclasses in order to secure statistics useful for internal administrative purposes.

Important as are the qualitative differences among the types of conduct now indiscriminately grouped statistically with the aid of a legal nomenclature, criminologists have taken little or no cognizance of them in researches dependent on such sources of data. Unlike scholars in most other fields of scientific research, they have, in such instances, relied upon terms, concepts, and definitions of units of investigation that they themselves did not establish. In the present research we have tried to solve this problem by an operational definition and classification of delinquent acts which cuts across legal categories. However, since we have relied upon data compiled by the police during their investigation of such acts, a preliminary description of the organization and functioning of the Philadelphia Police Department's Juvenile Aid Division, which is the repository of the data we have used, is desirable.

7

The Juvenile Aid Division
of the Philadelphia Police

In 1932, when the Crime Prevention Association of Philadelphia (C.P.A.), a private citizens' organization, was formed, a Crime Prevention Unit in the police department was also created, consisting of two plainclothes officers and a lieutenant who were to work with the detective divisions. Now called the Juvenile Aid Division (J.A.D.) this unit had a total strength of 220 in 1960 when Inspector Joseph Max was appointed its Commanding Officer and consisted of several squads with widely different functions, some only peripherally concerned with juveniles.

LINE SQUADS

Most of the personnel of the Division are in line squads comprised (in 1960) of two lieutenants, 12 sergeants, and 83 plainclothes officers. Assigned to police divisions composed of several contiguous police districts, squad members work in three shifts. Whether alone or as two-man teams, these officers have unmarked police cars for their use. It is their duty to investigate all cases of juveniles referred to them by the uniformed police. They also cooperate with the detective divisions in investigating cases in which juveniles are the victims, and they may be given special assignments at such places as school or city athletic events, parades, and other public gatherings attended by young people. Several men from these line squads may be assigned to subway duty, which involves riding subway trains and patrolling underground concourses as preventive measures. In addition, line squad personnel are expected to make routine checks of "hoagie shops" and other hangouts considered trouble spots, and to make routine patrols to look out for truants and curfew violators. These duties are discussed in more detail in a subsequent section of this report.

GANG CONTROL

The Gang Control Squad, consisting of a sergeant and 14 plainclothes officers (in 1960), is responsible for the observation and attempted control of identifiable delinquent groups in the city. The personnel of this squad, like those of the line squads, are assigned on a divisional basis but have considerably more freedom to function in a preventive capacity in other parts of the city. Officers ride in unmarked, radio-equipped cars. They patrol areas where gang activities have previously been evident, and, in order to familiarize themselves with all the delinquent groups, their locations, and membership, they observe corner gangs and other identifiable groups congregating in known hangouts. They keep notebooks listing gang members, their nicknames, and addresses so that offenses committed by these groups can be more readily solved. Information on new gang members, rival groups, and probable gang conflicts is elicited during frequent visits to recreation centers, schools, and church affairs and through contacts with area youth workers and conversations with gang members themselves. Sometimes a variety of nicknames, discovered in conversations with rival gang members, provides the first lead in a case. The Gang Control Squad is active in confiscating weapons and in cooperating with other agencies and interested persons who are trying to redirect gang activities. The presence in an area of Squad members who have intimate acquaintances with various gangs and their operations is believed to operate as a deterrent to the more flagrant and violent forms of gang activity.

The line squads and the Gang Control Squad are concerned exclusively with juveniles. For historical or administrative reasons the Morals Squad, the Policewomen's Squad, and the Police Community Relations Squad deal with both adults and juveniles.

MORALS SQUAD

The Morals Squad consists of a lieutenant, two sergeants, and 16 officers. They work on the same shifts as the line squads. The Morals Squad has sole responsibility for investigating sex offenses committed by juveniles: all cases of incest, statutory rape, and sex relations of juveniles with "adult friends, neighbors or employers," and cases in which both adults and juveniles are involved.[1] Cases involving prostitution or homosexual activities in which all persons are adults may be handled by either the Morals Squad or by district plainclothesmen. On a few occasions the relative burden of work of the detective divisions or of the J.A.D. Morals Squad will determine which group assumes responsibility for the investigation. Morals Squad men are assigned cases from their operations room in J.A.D. headquarters, with the exception that men assigned to the investigation of prostitution and homosexual activities circulate in areas of the city where they are most likely to make arrests, or in neighborhoods from which complaints have been received.

POLICEWOMEN

The Policewomen's Squad, with an authorized strength of a lieutenant, three sergeants, and 50 policewomen, is the second largest section of the J.A.D. Division. Assigned to shifts and to police divisions in the same manner as the line squads, policewomen have responsibility for all cases involving female juvenile offenders or victims and for investigating cases of neglected, abandoned, or missing children. The detective divisions and the uniformed police usually call in policewomen to make searches and to assume hospital guard duties when female offenders are involved, and the Morals Squad frequently uses their services to interrogate female victims or offenders. Occasionally policewomen are assigned to attend public events, sometimes in uniform, and, on a temporary basis, to aid special investigative squads in an undercover capacity.

POLICE COMMUNITY RELATIONS OFFICERS

In the J.A.D. there are 20 members of the "Police Community Relations Officers" (P.C.R.O.) Unit under a sergeant. An officer of this unit attached to a particular police district is assigned to attend meetings of various business and professional organizations, civic organizations, schools, and churches in order to explain the facilities, services, and functions of the police and other social agencies that are available to the community. Because of the nature of their duties these officers rarely make arrests.

Two Human Relations Officers, attached to the Gang Control Unit,

---

[1] In an emergency, when all Morals Squad personnel are busy, the above-mentioned type case may be handled by a member of the J.A.D. line squad.

are expected to investigate complaints involving discrimination, possible racial or religious conflict, or vandalism in churches, synagogues, etc.

HEADQUARTERS SQUAD

In addition to a sergeant and eight officers assigned to headquarters, court cases, and duties at the Youth Study Center, there is a small Referral Unit consisting of one policeman and one policewomen. This Referral Unit processes all Juvenile Information Cards (see Appendix A-3) submitted on cases handled by the J.A.D. and make referrals to the appropriate section of the Youth Conservation Services of the Department of Welfare.[2]

RELATIONS WITH OTHER AGENCIES

Far from being an isolated and independent organization, the J.A.D. cooperates and works closely with community organizations, both governmental and private, which are similarly concerned with juveniles. One of the main agencies involved is the Youth Conservation Services, just mentioned. The J.A.D. also has contact with the County Court (formerly the Municipal Court) in several ways. First, officers in the field must make arrangements for the detention of all juveniles they arrest. This process involves checking with the Youth Study Center, which is the detention facility under the supervision of the County Court, in order to make proper arrangements for holding a child overnight or until his parents can be notified to come to the Y.S.C. to pick him up. In addition, three J.A.D. officers under the headquarters sergeant are assigned full time to the Y.S.C. Two of these men appear at the "intake interviews" which are held on the morning following the child's arrest. Each morning they pick up at headquarters the appropriate police reports on the juveniles who are to have preliminary hearings that day and thus provide information to the probation officer conducting the hearing, present any items of evidence taken by the police, and make notations of the case disposition for the police records. The County Court provides ten officers under a supervisor for these intake and screening duties and for counselling work. On the basis of the preliminary hearing, all cases of police arrest or other cases brought in directly to the Center by private petition from parents, railway police, and sometimes the

[2] This function was taken over from the C.P.A. in 1957.

school authorities, are screened to determine which merit court hearings and which do not. At this time the hearing officer determines whether a juvenile will be detained in the Center until the hearing or remain with his parents. A transcript of the hearing is prepared and added to the data being accumulated by court personnel for the guidance of the judge. In minor matters with parents, victims, and offender present, a case may be "adjusted," that is, satisfactorily terminated so that it need not further burden the court.

A third J.A.D. officer is assigned to reinterview juveniles in cases in which he feels that additional offenses, which were not discovered during the preliminary interrogations, may have been committed by the juvenile. He scans the offense reports on the juveniles admitted to the Center and notes cases in which additional stolen property may have been mentioned or been taken into possession by the police. He has lists of stolen motor vehicles and keeps in touch with developments in the districts so that, for example, if he notes a boy brought in for purse snatching in the twenty-third district, he will want to question the boy if there are many unsolved offenses of this sort in that area. Or, he may call a given district and make inquiries if he should pick up a lead during the preliminary hearings he attends. Sometimes a police captain calls to ask that a particular individual be interviewed or that the officer be on the lookout for a particular type of burglar or other offender. Although a string of burglaries may carry a distinctive *modus operandi* which can be linked to a known offense and offender, there are also cases such as runaways in which it is likely that, with an extended absence from home, other offenses may have been committed. In determining which offenders to interview, the officer often is guided by his own "hunch" based on past experience. When a juvenile has confessed to additional offenses, contact is made with the detective division in the area involved to determine the exact offenses so that appropriate clearance for these cases can be made.

In addition to the three men assigned to the Youth Study Center, two men are assigned from J.A.D. headquarters to attend the hearing in the juvenile court concerning all children referred there from the intake interviews. These men attend court on alternate days and spend the rest of their time preparing cases and doing reinterviewing.

INITIAL CONTACTS

The J.A.D. officer, whether line squad or special squad member, is brought in contact with the offender in one of two ways: (1) through a referral by the district after a case is discovered or an offender is taken into custody by a patrolman or a detective; or (2) directly in the course of his duties.[3]

Relative to the former, the patrolman makes out an Incident Report and gives it to the desk officer upon returning to the station. If a juvenile is taken into custody, the officer in charge calls the J.A.D. Operations Room in the Board of Education Building. If no suspect is taken into custody and no descriptions are available the case will normally remain with the detective divisions. If a description or the offense itself suggests that the offender is probably a juvenile—bicycle thefts and school vandalism, for example—the case will be turned over to the J.A.D. as well. The J.A.D. dispatcher checks his log indicating which men in that division have been assigned cases and, after locating a J.A.D. officer by phone, indicates other details and jots these on his log.[4]

If the case involves a group of boys who might belong to an organized gang or if the offense was committed by a single gang member, the case will be assigned to a member of the Gang Control Unit who is familiar with the area where the offense originated. If the offense is a sex crime involving a juvenile offender or victim or involving certain family offenses, the Morals Squad is assigned to the case. In offenses involving girls under 18, the officer in charge of the Police-women's Section is called. All of these officers are equipped with unmarked cars, some of which have two-way radios.

The cases thus far mentioned are those referred by uniformed police or detectives. There are other situations, however, in which J.A.D. personnel initiate the investigation, apprehend an offender, or observe an offense while pursuing an investigation of a case previously assigned to them. In these situations the J.A.D. officer makes up the Incident Report, telephones to get C.C. and D.C. numbers, and then proceeds in the same manner as with the referred cases. Such cases would arise, for instance, out of routine duties involving education laws and municipal curfew ordinances. Although the Board of Education maintains "attendance officers," the brunt of initial enforcement now seems to fall on the J.A.D., who check streets and hangouts during school hours.[5] Since 1955 Philadelphia has had a curfew ordinance

---

[3] See Appendix B for a description of the crime-reporting system in Philadelphia.
[4] From time to time an officer in Central Communications Room will call, giving C.C. numbers to the districts for their cases. This number along with the D.C. number is secured by the J.A.D. officer. See Appendix B.
[5] Investigation of specific students with excessive absences is still handled by the school authorities as is any counselling which might be required.

which prohibits children under 17 from being on the streets unescorted by an adult after 10:30 P.M. during the period from Sunday through Thursday and after 12 midnight on Friday and Saturday nights. All personnel are expected to turn in some curfew violations each week.[6] Another routine duty connected with curfew check involves the "Preventive Patrol Checks," which consist of stops at "hoagie shops," cafes, skating rinks, and other places where juveniles congregate and which are either considered a problem by the police or in which the proprietor himself has earlier complained of disorderly behavior. Individual Incident Reports are made out for these checks and sometimes a curfew violator is found or an adult is charged with an offense against a pertinent ordinance.

In addition to these cases where the J.A.D. has exclusive responsibility for investigation and reporting and for decisions regarding custody, there are other cases in which they share responsibility. This might occur in cases in which some but not all of the offenders are juveniles or in which the J.A.D. provide only supplementary reports if a juvenile is a victim or a witness but is not an offender. In a case of homicide, regardless of the age of the offender, the Homicide Squad has primary responsibility.

INTERVIEWING AND FOLLOW-UPS

When the officer receives a case from J.A.D. headquarters he proceeds to the police station in the district where the offense originated, picks up the Incident Report and, in order to obtain additional details, talks with the police officer or his lieutenant. If no offender is yet in custody he makes a series of investigative interviews, during which he occasionally jots down a few notes. He may bring a suspect into the station for interrogation or one may already have been taken into custody by a uniformed officer. Juveniles under 16 are not permitted to be placed in a cell with adults, and observation indicates that the rule is scrupulously obeyed. In newer stations there may be a special detention room, but in older structures the juvenile is either kept in an improvised cubicle or simply seated near the desk sergeant so that he is kept in reasonable safety until the J.A.D. officer arrives. In some stations there are special J.A.D. interviewing rooms; in others, detective division rooms are used. There is seldom any privacy. The parents may be present, other juvenile offenders may be in the

---

[6] Because of the nature of their duties Morals Squad personnel rarely become involved in curfew offenses.

room, and, in fact, detectives and adult offenders may also be involved in some other interrogation. If the investigation has been initiated by the J.A.D., for example by a member of the Gang Control, some part of this preliminary interrogation may take place in the squad car, in a recreation center, or in the child's home.

On the basis of these contacts, an Offense Report (see Appendix A-1) will be typed by the J.A.D. officer, probably before he completes his shift. This process sometimes takes as long as the investigation itself, particularly if the case involves the arrest of several offenders. The Offense Report will contain a more accurate classification of the offense, information about the complainant, a description of the current offense, a list of contacts made and details of these interviews, a paragraph devoted to attributes of the offender such as age, sex, and race, the part the offender played in the offense, his version and the version of others, action taken, and the current status of the case. This report would include these kinds of information whether or not the case was "founded" (a true case of delinquency), "active" (i.e., not solved and with a further report to follow), "inactive" (not "cleared" and with little likelihood that an offender will be discovered), "cleared by arrest" (meaning that an offender has been taken into custody), or "exceptionally cleared" (if the child is released with a warning, has died, escaped jurisdiction, is already confined in a correctional institution, or is about to have a hearing on another offense). If the report is long enough to require an additional page, a Continuation Report is used.

If the case is not closed by the Offense Report and if further developments occur, subsequent reports will be made on Investigation Report forms. The order of these reports cannot be uniform as in the other reports, and except for minimal identifying information in blocks at the top and the manner of case clearance at the bottom, these reports are simply narratives of new developments.

DECISION ON ARREST

With few exceptions juvenile aid police in the United States are empowered with a quasi-judicial choice of whether formally to arrest an offender or to rely on alternatives such as a reprimand, referral to a social agency, etc. Since the early days of the J.A.D. in Philadelphia such a choice has been available between arrest and what used to be termed "referral." This latter alternative, now termed "remedial," is actually subsumed by the Philadelphia J.A.D.

under the category of "exceptionally cleared" cases. In the case of juveniles, the bulk of the "exceptionally cleared" cases are "remedials."

CRITERIA FOR JUDGMENT

The J.A.D. officer's decision to make an "arrest" or a "remedial" is governed by five criteria, as set forth in training posters, informal talks by Commanding Officers during roll calls, and other forms of indoctrination: (1) the juvenile's previous contacts with the police; (2) the type of offense resulting in his current custody; (3) the attitude of the complainant; (4) the offender's family situation; and (5) potential community resources. In addition, there are a number of informal considerations which may enter into the decision. Let us consider these in some detail as they seem to be very influential.[7]

(1) A careful consideration is given to the current offense and the juvenile's role in it as instigator, follower, or bystander. Theoretically any case, no matter how serious, may be handled as "non-arrest," but for serious offenses permission for such a clearance must be secured by phone from the sergeant or the lieutenant. An arrest on a minor charge is generally handled in the same way, but for some minor cases the J.A.D. officer may feel that an arrest is not merited or he may suspect from past experience that intake interviewers or judges of the County Court will send the offender home anyway. He may also "remedial" a case when the evidence does not strongly suggest guilt, when there are extremely mitigating or extenuating circumstances (such as voluntary participation by the "victim"), or when the nature of the offense suggests the need for immediate psychiatric care.

Before the initial disposition of a case is made, the officer calls headquarters and requests a check on the previous record of the offender. This check is made by consulting an alphabetical Master File (see Appendix A-2) which lists, among other pertinent data, address, birthdate, and previous police contacts by date, charge, and disposition. The information is subsequently listed in the Offense or Investigation Reports submitted by the officer and has an important effect on his decision. Even if the instant offense is minor a series of five previous petty offenses, none of which resulted in arrest, com-

---

[7] This description is based on numerous interviews, informal conversations, and contacts with past and present J.A.D. Commanding Officers, lieutenants, and sergeants, as well as conversations with and observation of the officers in their routine duties in the field over a period of several months.

mitted during a relatively brief period of time, may cause the J.A.D. officer to decide that an arrest should be made for the benefit of the child and the community. Because parents are often brought into these cases, it is difficult, although possible, to avoid the discovery of a previous record by giving a false name. Occasional mistakes due to misspelling or to careless checking without seeking alternative spellings may result in a child's being considered a first offender when he actually has a previous record.

Occasionally, upon reviewing a case of a persistent offender who has been repeatedly "remedialed," the Youth Conservation Staff or the J.A.D. Inspector will decide that there are to be no more remedial dispositions. In such a case, a "remedial stop" card is attached to the juvenile's record card in the Master File with the result that the next officer handling the juvenile will be so informed when he requests a record check and will make an arrest.

The effect on the disposition of a case of incomplete knowledge by the disposing officer of a juvenile offender's past contacts with the police, arising out of errors in checking the Master File, is evidenced by an experiment made in the course of our research. Because some of the offense reports in our sample made no mention of any previous contacts with the police on the part of the juvenile involved or merely made mention, without further specification, of a given number of previous arrests and/or remedial actions, we checked the appropriate cards in the Master File. In the process we noticed other discrepancies and ended by checking the records of all juveniles in our sample. Most errors uncovered were inconsequential but in 20 cases it seemed to us that the decision to arrest or "remedial" the juvenile would have been different had the disposing officer known all the facts of the juvenile's past history of delinquency. In some of these cases only one offender was involved, in others two or more. When there were multiple offenders we decided to select the one whose record in the Master File showed the greatest discrepancy with that known to the disposing officer, and by arrangement with the Inspector of the Juvenile Aid Division conducted a test that would reveal the effect that a knowledge of the true record could have had on the disposition of the offender. Of the 20 offenders chosen, 19 had originally been "remedialed" and one arrested.

The police reports on offenses in which the offenders had figured were copied in two versions—one with the record of the offender as it appeared in the original offense report and one with the corrected record as shown in the Master File. Both reports were typed on regular police forms and were identical save for an identifying number and fictitious names and addresses. Ten J.A.D. officers were selected by the Inspector and each was given a kit consisting of 20 cases, 10 with the original information and 10 with the corrected record. No officer read both versions of any case. Moreover, the cases were arranged so that there was a random selection according to the seriousness of the offense. The officers were asked not to identify themselves on the documents but simply to read the cases in sequence, circle the word "arrest" or "remedial" on the face sheet appended to each case and not to discuss dispositions with each other until all decisions had been so recorded. Since no officer read both versions of a case, five of them read the original and five the "true" version. Each group had to make a total of 100 decisions as to the proper disposition of the 20 offenders. Of those who read the original versions, all agreed with the original disposition in 7 instances, but in 8 other cases an arrest would have been made by some one in the test group, 2 of them would have made that disposition in 1 case, 3 in 1, 4 in 2, and all 5 in 1 case.

The five officers who read the documents containing the corrected record would have "remedialed" only three of the offenders. Some one of the officers voted for arrest in 3 cases, 2 in 6 cases, 3 in 4, and 4 in 4. Altogether the 26 decisions to arrest, based on the original report, rose to 43 when the correct information was known. Conversely, 74 per cent of the decisions based on the original record and 57 per cent of those based on the corrected record were the same as those actually made by the original disposing officer.

The above results suggest, of course, that the disposition in a given case depends in some degree on what officer makes the decision and that if he is not in full possession of accurate data on known previous contacts of the juvenile with the police, his disposition of the offender will be affected in most such instances.

(2) The attitude of the victim or the prosecutor is another very important criterion for assessing the situation. Particularly for serious property offenses or for crimes against the person, strong feelings by the victim for prosecution are likely to result in a decision to arrest. However, if the officer decides otherwise, in spite of the victim's attitude, he will generally suggest that the victim submit a direct petition to the juvenile court. Experienced officers are often able to change a complainant's attitude for prosecution if a nonarrest apears to be beneficial to the child's welfare. Should the complainant definitely refuse to prosecute or to appear at hearings, the officer may drop all but a minor general charge, such as "disorderly conduct," or he may simply "remedial" the case. On the other hand, he may

decide that an arrest should be made and list himself as the complainant. On the basis of our contacts with officers during their tours of duty and of reading a large number of reports, it seems evident that cases which probably would have been "cleared by arrest" are instead "exceptionally cleared" ("remedialed") because the victim, for one reason or another, does not want to prosecute.

(3) Two additional factors officially recognized as important in the arrest versus remedial decision are closely interrelated: the home condition, the attitudes of the parents, and their resources and ability to help the child; and the availability of other community agencies which might be useful in helping the offender. The same rationale used by the County Court to prefer probation and related services to institutionalization enters into the evaluation of these two factors. The J.A.D. officer makes a judgment about the home of the offender, parental responsibility for the boy, and (perhaps with emphasis) parental attitudes toward the police in general and himself in particular. With apparent justification these officers believe that uncooperative or hostile parents are likely to promote in the boy a rationalization for his offense, thus making his future adjustment more difficult. However, if the parents appear sincerely interested in the boy and have a good relationship with him, the advantages of a remedial action are obvious. Constructive or destructive factors outside the home, and the likelihood that religious, fraternal, or governmental organizations may become interested in helping the juvenile can also influence a decision to arrest or remedial an offender.

(4) In addition to the nature of the offense, previous record, and other "official" and stated criteria for making decisions about disposition, the officer sometimes is guided by the behavior, attitude, and appearance of the offender himself. If the offender is very young, immature, or naive, the officer may feel sympathy for him or may reason that he will be constructively impressed by merely being brought into the police station for questioning. An arrest decision may be based partly on the fact that the juvenile is dressed in a particular style, has a peculiar hairdo, or is wearing a gang jacket, or that a girl appears to be oversophisticated and excessively made up. Sometimes in writing their Offense Reports officers have noted that the "offender was nicely dressed and gave a neat appearance," etc. More important than clothes, however, is the presence or absence of cooperation and respect shown the investigator in the current contact and possibly in the past as well. It is important that the officer evaluate the sincerity of a cooperative attitude to determine whether it is feigned and whether the suspect is telling the truth. If the officer

senses strong hostility toward the police, or if there had been any obscene language or resistance used during the initial police contact, the officer weighs these factors in his decision. A juvenile may threaten to use his influence, or pressure to release the boy may be applied by local politicians at the police station. When these things occur, the J.A.D. officer is more likely to make an arrest than if such pressure had not been applied.

(5) Officers are influenced in their decision not to arrest a juvenile when the Youth Study Center is overcrowded. Occasionally this reason is stated in the report. Moreover, some J.A.D. officers claim that the Y.S.C. does not like to accept juveniles with severe mental disturbances because parents often will not call for their children, who must consequently be detained at the Center while waiting for a court appearance.[8] The Y.S.C. may refuse to accept an intoxicated offender and this policy has an influence on the decision to arrest or remedial. It might also be noted here that some officers may send a child to the Y.S.C. as an arrest case although through experience they anticipate that he will not be held for court by the intake interview officer. This latter procedure is regarded by the J.A.D. officer as somewhat more inconvenient for the offender, i.e., a slightly greater punishment than a mere remedial disposition that involves only momentary detention in a police station. He hopes that the trip to the Y.S.C. and the preliminary hearing will impress the child and thus act as a greater deterrent than would a simple and direct release to the custody of his parents. In very minor cases, "exceptional clearance" may be made by the officer instead of an arrest so that he can avoid giving the child a more damaging record. Actually, unless regulations were violated and referral cards not made out, the juvenile will have, in the Master File in the J.A.D., the same "record" with a remedial that he would have with an arrest. It is true, however, that he will have no Juvenile Court or Y.S.C. notation. Should a juvenile confess to additional crimes, which had earlier been or are not identified with C.C. and D.C. numbers, he usually will be "exceptionally cleared" on those cases because he is arrested only for the instant offense. By regulation, curfew cases cannot result in arrest.

(6) Finally, officers are affected in their judgment of disposition by what they know to be the practice of court references at the Y.S.C. The J.A.D. officer may believe that although a particular boy has had

---

[8] The validity of this observation of Center policy is open to question, but the fact that some officers are guided by it suggests that such informal criteria cannot be neglected in any realistic discussion of the ingredients of decisions.

many previous remedials and presently feels cocky and unscathed, the intake interviewer will not hold the boy for a court appearance or the judge will not sentence him because the charge is minor, residential facilities are crowded, and probation case loads are too high. The J.A.D. officer, therefore, may feel that he is wasting his time in making an arrest. It should be noted, however, that men in the Morals Squad cannot make these decisions independently but must obtain permission from the sergeant or lieutenant to "remedial" any case.

In summary then, the decision to arrest or "remedial" is based upon the following criteria, some official and others informal: (1) previous police contacts as determined by a record check; (2) type of offense and the role which the juvenile has played in it; (3) attitude of the victim or complainant; (4) the family situation of the offender; (5) the potential community resources which might be utilized; (6) the general appearance and attitude of the offender towards the police; (7) possible overcrowding at the Youth Study Center; and (8) the police officer's anticipation of juvenile court action should an arrest be made.

ARREST PROCEDURE

When an officer decides that an offender should be arrested, he contacts his sergeant to clear the disposition of the case, calls the Youth Study Center to make arrangements for the boy's admission, and then contacts the parents so that they can, except under unusual circumstances, go to the Y.S.C. to take the boy home until the preliminary intake hearing the following morning. The boy is then transported by district personnel to the Y.S.C. As has been noted earlier, the court probation officer during the intake interview the following day will determine whether (a) the case should be "adjusted," (b) the juvenile should be held in the Center until his court appearance, or (c) the juvenile should be released into the custody of his parents. When an arrest is made the officer fills out the upper portion of an Arrest Report giving the same facts that are contained in the Offense and Investigation Reports concerning age, sex, race, crime code classification and brief description of the offense.

A Juvenile Information Card (Appendix A-3) is also prepared giving the name and address, school, church affiliation, date, time, and nature of the complaint. Although these cards are identical to those filled out in remedial cases, a referral is not indicated by the officer, for the assumption is that such action will now be made, if necessary, by the County Court. These cards are used for statistical purposes and to compile master record cards and files by district of residence. On arrests, the J.A.D., Y.C.S., County Court and C.P.A. receive copies of this form. When "remedial" action is taken on a case, a copy goes to General Services (which is returned), Y.C.S., County Court, and C.P.A. In cases of truancy the C.P.A. copy is sent to the Board of Education, and with curfews the copy which would otherwise go to the County Court is retained at J.A.D.

REMEDIAL PROCEDURE

If a decision to "remedial" a case is made, the child, or the child and his parents, will be given a reprimand or advice and then dismissed. No special form corresponding to the arrest form is filled out, but the case is "closed" on the Offense or Investigation Report form and a Juvenile Information Card is filled out as in the case of an arrest.[9] The card indicates whether the officer believes a referral is necessary. According to a command letter, dated 9/1/60, the decision to refer a case is based on the following reasons:

(1) Offense is Part 1, remedial.
(2) The previous behavior pattern on J.A.D. record card of the offender so indicated.
(3) The offense, currently being investigated, is serious.
(4) In your judgment, the parents have no control of the juvenile.

A decision not to refer a case is made when:

(1) Offense is so minor that further contact might lead to resentment on the part of the parents and child.
(2) Offense Report is the result of a "crank complaint."
(3) When J.A.D. investigator's adjustment [of the case] is extremely satisfactory to all parties concerned (the parents, children and complainant) and any further follow-up with a home visit could be detrimental.

The case is now concluded so far as the line officer is concerned, and all the cards are sent to the J.A.D. headquarters. One copy is sent to the Referral Unit. About 23,000 cases are processed each year by the Unit. Approximately 5800 cases are marked by the line officer for referral, including about 700 arrest cases. The officer in the Unit reads the cards and sometimes reverses the judgment of the squad officer by deciding to make a referral even if not recommended,

[9] In truancy and curfew cases only Juvenile Information Cards are made out in addition to the initial Incident Reports.

or not to make a referral when recommended. In cases slated for some sort of referral, a Parent-Youth Aid Program form is begun by the officer, with information supplied from the Juvenile Information Card. These forms are sent to the Youth Conservation Services, whose personnel examine their records to determine whether there are several delinquents in the same family. If there are, the case is assigned to the intensive counseling section. If not, the case will be sent to the appropriate school counselor for his consideration and attention. If the school counselor does not take the case, he generally fills in more pertinent information on the referral form and then sends the case to the local Parent-Youth Aid Committee in the area from which the child comes. This committee investigates and decides upon the appropriate agency to handle the case.

RECORD KEEPING AND STATISTICS

Although most records are now kept in the Central Records section at City Hall, some are independently maintained in J.A.D. headquarters. Offense Reports and Investigation Reports are arranged in two main files for the current year: one contains all offenses cleared by arrest; the other has all cases "exceptionally cleared" by remedial action, active cases and inactive cases. Cases in both of these files are separated by police district, and within each district by offense category and D.C. number. Separate files for the current year and the preceding year are also kept at J.A.D. headquarters. Earlier records are in a storeroom elsewhere and not easily available. All cases handled by the Morals Squad are kept in a separate morals file arranged by offense category and D.C. number, with open (unsolved) cases separated from the cases closed by arrest or remedial action. Most of these cases represent arrests. Separate files for the two previous years are also maintained here, but earlier records are stored.

In addition to these basic source documents several other records are maintained and filed by the J.A.D. Most important of these is the active Master File. This file consists of cards which contain the name and nickname, the address, the birthdate, the father's and mother's names, race, school, and church affiliation. Below this information all known offenses are listed chronologically with D.C. numbers, date of occurrence, disposition by the police, and usually the disposition by the court. Two separate "over-age" files for those between the ages of 18 and 21 and those over 21 years of age are also maintained, consisting of cards which have been removed periodically from the active file. Aside from the Master File, a file of Juvenile Information Cards for the past two years, arranged by district of residence but in no other order, is also maintained. From this last file the offense category can be determined if the D.C. number is known. Ledger books which have the written record of offenses occurring each day and their D.C. numbers are useful when an officer knows only the date an offense occurred. From these ledgers a "district-of-occurrence" file of 3 x 5 cards was kept until 1961, arranged according to D.C. numbers but also containing C.C. numbers and a notation giving the status of the case. There has also been a separate curfew file for the past three years, arranged alphabetically by name of the offender.

Besides the source document files in the Morals Squad, a file of complainants' names is maintained, alphabetically arranged on 3 x 5 cards dating from about 1952. This Squad also has an offenders' file, by name and by race and a file of photographs of adult offenders. A *modus operandi* file is kept by offense category and by race for "probable repeaters" who are involved in acts such as indecent exposure. An arrest book, containing a day-to-day record of cases handled by the Morals Squad personnel, and a "wanted" card file are kept in the same office.

The Gang Control Unit maintains at headquarters a modest file consisting of two parts: (1) an alphabetical 3 x 5 index by name and nickname of gang boys with addresses and gang affiliations; and (2) a file of names of gangs, with names and addresses of the members of each gang. These files are more or less cumulative but sometimes cards of those over 21 years of age are removed. More recent lists, kept by the sergeant in charge, indicate under various gang names, membership (including nicknames), age, sex, and race. Cards for the members of each gang are arranged roughly in the order of the boys' cooperativeness and service in giving information to police about gang activities. This information is current and corresponds roughly to the information kept individually in notebooks by the members of the Gang Control Squad.

Besides the statistical reports published by General Services, dealing with adults and juveniles, certain reports concerned *only* with juveniles are prepared on a monthly and yearly basis. These latter usually do not originate in the J.A.D. but are often based upon their compilations and on data from General Services. The basic juvenile statistical report appears each month and contains cumulative figures so that the issue for December constitutes a yearly summary. The first tables contain, by sex, data on arrest and remedial dispositions, on Part 1 and Part 2 offenses, with monthly and yearly totals and comparisons with the corresponding period of the previous year. The same breakdown is made for curfew violations. The rest of the report consists of tables containing a more detailed breakdown by district of residence and district of occurrence for boys and girls, remedials and arrests, and with the same Part 1 and 2 breakdowns and comparisons with the previous year.

Each month single-sheet tables appear giving age, sex, and race of juveniles arrested or "remedialed" for 35 offense categories. Similar monthly reports are issued on curfew violations by district, day of the week or time of the day, with a breakdown by age and sex.

An annual "Juvenile Statistics Report" is released by the Research and Planning Section of General Services. The report for 1960 presents: 13 tables or graphs covering J.A.D. assignments; the number of arrests and remedials by offense categories, district of occurrence, residence of offenders, and sex of offenders; arrests by offense categories and sex by age group; remedials by offense categories and sex; and curfew violations each month by disposition and sex.

APPRAISAL OF SYSTEM

In order to utilize realistically current police statistics dealing with juveniles in a research design and to evaluate their adequacies and weaknesses, it was necessary to become thoroughly familiar with the manner in which J.A.D. personnel operated in the field, made judgments, and filled out reports, and with the way these reports were handled at J.A.D. headquarters and Central Records Division. An understanding of changes in policy and procedure over time was necessary too. Toward these ends, our inquiry was directed along three lines: (1) participant observation of field operations; (2) interviews with key personnel outside the J.A.D.; and (3) familiarization with the activities at J.A.D. headquarters and the Central Records Division.

One member of the research staff spent well over 200 hours and two others worked a total of about 75 hours accompanying J.A.D. officers in the various squads on all shifts in every part of the city. These experiences provided intimate knowledge of the official reporting procedure and the use of various reporting forms. Of even greater importance, unusual opportunities arose to observe the routine work of the police, not as "outsiders" but as more or less neutral "insiders." This favored status obviously was not granted immediately; it came about as the result of being continually present in all sorts of situations. Through informal conversations during which our opinions were overtly or covertly sought on a variety of issues, by intonation or a facial gesture which might give a clue to our feelings, and by showing no obvious interest in such matters as corruption, efficiency, police brutality, or morals cases, we eventually were accepted. The fact that no personnel shifts, work changes, increased duties, etc., resulted from our presence, helped to allay earlier anxiety and concern about us on the part of some officers. Eventually we were exposed to the everyday, usual activities of the officers, who seemed to be relatively unaffected by our presence. Consequently, it was possible to evaluate realistically the reporting procedures and the source documents as to their validity, defects, and manipulations and in so doing, to get answers to questions which even completely candid supervisors could not always provide. During this participant observation of J.A.D. personnel we also had the opportunity to observe incidentally some of the work of detectives and uniformed officers and to engage in informal conversations with both groups concerning their attitudes and practices. This phase of our experiences proved valuable in clarifying some of the relationships between the J.A.D. and the Police Department as a whole.

Aside from the tours of duty with J.A.D. officers, it was necessary to have individual interviews with persons who work in other branches of the Police Department and some who do not. In attempting to learn something of earlier operations we interviewed a former Commanding Officer, Inspector Harry Fox, now Superintendent of the Police Academy. To learn how "remedial" and other cases eventually come to the attention of community agencies, we visited the Referral Unit and talked with officials connected with the Youth Conservation Services in the Department of Public Welfare. The Youth Study Center was also visited and the J.A.D. personnel assigned there were interviewed as were certain County Court officials, including the head of the petition section, intake interviewers, et al.

Through (a) conferences with the Inspector of the J.A.D., (b) time spent in familiarizing ourselves with the various files and in drawing a ten per cent sample from arrest and remedial files, (c) a series of in-service training lectures given by one of the staff, and (d) numerous other activities, various members of our staff probably spent more time at J.A.D. Headquarters than the hours with officers in the field. These operations afforded opportunities for formal interviews with the lieutenants in charge of policewomen and the Morals Squad and with the sergeants in charge of the Gang Control Squad and the office records. During lunch and office visits many informal conversations were held with personnel, from the Inspector to the civilian file clerks, and a thorough working knowledge of the files was thereby secured. Work done in selecting the sample cases provided the best knowledge of these files. Complete cooperation and candor continued to mark these contacts.

Initially it was desirable that the whole staff tour the General Services Division in City Hall in order to become familiar with the over-all operation of police reporting and recording, the types of files, IBM operations, the Central Radio Room, etc. Special interviews with Captain Doran and Inspector Faust were conducted many times during the study. Even old J.A.D. records, stored in a police station basement, were examined to determine what material would be available for previous years. On a number of occasions, copies of forms, maps, etc., were supplied by General Services for our use.

SOURCES OF ERROR

Any errors that exist in J.A.D. reports and statistics are most likely to occur in five critical areas: (1) initial reporting; (2) source documents; (3) crime classification; (4) enforcement policies; and (5) the Master File. Before discussing these sources of error in detail it is important to emphasize that generally these reports appear to be reasonably accurate, conscientiously written, and carefully compiled by Central Records and J.A.D. personnel.

INITIAL REPORTING FLUCTUATIONS

The number of cases eventually referred to J.A.D. are not identical with all offenses committed by juveniles and known by the police or the public. The readiness of the public to report and of uniformed patrolmen and detectives to refer cases to J.A.D. show some variation from district to district and over periods of time. Generally, with an increase in the number of J.A.D. officers, a new Youth Study Center, Police Community Relations Officers speaking in schools and public gatherings, and widespread publicity given in the community to child problems, each year the public shows greater willingness to refer cases of petty misdemeanors and violations, such as incorrigibility and truancy, to the police. This is characteristic of school authorities, church officials, and representatives of social welfare agencies. However, in high delinquency areas there seem to be two conflicting tendencies: (1) a tendency to "live and let live" characterized by traditional toleration of some forms of theft and vice and by anti-police attitudes and general hostility toward constituted authority—all of which militate against complete reporting of all offenses and offenders; and (2) a counter-tendency to become increasingly dependent upon agencies outside the family to solve family problems of income, medical care, and discipline and training of children. In some cases, without making any effort themselves, families rely on the police to find runaway children or expect the J.A.D. officer to discipline their children; if so, the reporting of a juvenile offender may sometimes represent parental indifference for the welfare of the child. This condition seems to be evident each fall when school opens and when many parents, fearing a fine from the Board of Education because their children are absent, report them as "runaways," which may head off punitive action by the Board. Reliance on police services in these areas is perhaps a part of a larger pattern of increasing dependency upon governmental and private social agencies to solve problems, especially when the family is broken, weak, or impoverished. Moreover, school officials may make a police referral so that the school will have a more substantial reason for transferring the student to a disciplinary school.

On the other hand, in some delinquency areas where subcultural values are hostile to law enforcement generally, many victims prefer to settle matters informally rather than by contacting the police or they may refuse to prosecute or bear witness if the offense is reported. A minor fight or theft, which most certainly would be reported in some districts, is considered too common an occurrence in high delinquency areas to bring to the attention of the police. In such areas there is little psychological identification with the law and a policeman is considered an adversary or potential source of trouble rather than a protector.

Aside from the public's readiness to report, inaccuracies may creep into juvenile statistics because of over- or underreferral by the uniformed and detective divisions. A certain small number of cases of juveniles known to be involved in offenses never officially come to the attention of the J.A.D. because they are disposed of by uniformed officers in the district. This practice used to be more widespread, but because of the efficiency of the present reporting procedure, especially with the use of C.C. and D.C. numbers, it has been greatly curtailed. There are several types of situations, however, in which it may still occur. If, for example, a uniformed officer encounters a group of unruly boys playing ball and annoying the neighbors or perhaps engaging in even more serious incidents he may simply lecture the boys and send or take them home to their parents. Sometimes the officer will check with the lieutenant who agrees that the case is petty and that, as the J.A.D. is busy, the matter should be handled informally. Should a complaint be made to the Central Radio Room or should the child actually be brought into the station, then the J.A.D. is notified and the regular procedure is followed. Occasionally, if the J.A.D. officer has close, friendly relationships with district personnel or detectives, a case may be handled informally without being reported to Central Records in order to save the time and effort involved in report writing. One officer estimated that he handles about five cases a month this way, including street fights. Another officer, who also has good relations with the detectives, regards younger J.A.D. men who bring in groups of corner loungers and charge them with disorderly conduct as "silly." He says he tries to handle such matters "sensibly," i.e., by avoiding reports that would "give the boys a record" through C.C. or D.C. numbers. Some of his friends in the districts will hold on to their Incident Reports so that no C.C. numbers are acquired and the case will then be handled without additional paper work. He may actually bring parents in and lecture them, for example, in connection with a school fight. It should be noted that this officer is a particularly skillful and conscientious investigator whose intentions are honorable and not deceptive. Sometimes cases are handled in the district through a classification on the Incident Report form known as "Investigation of Persons," which then makes it possible to close the case without further handling. Such a procedure may be used for corner lounging if the officer feels that the boys were not really creating a disturbance. At any rate, these are all cases that are likely to result in underreporting. In relationship to the total number of cases, however, they comprise a very small number.

Overreporting only happens when unsolved cases are "fobbed off" on the J.A.D. by the various detective divisions. Sometimes a victim wrongly assumes that a given juvenile was responsible for a particular offense. A case was referred to the J.A.D. in which a woman claimed that jewelry and $20 in cash were taken from her bedroom. She accused three neighborhood youths who had been in her house that day supposedly when she stepped out of her bedroom for a brief period. No one saw the children take the money and the parents saw no evidence of unusual spending or of newly purchased items that would lead them to think that the children had taken the money.

The testimony of some victims regarding the probable age of fleeing offenders is often revealed as highly inaccurate or is recorded inaccurately on the Incident Report because of carelessness by the officer or because of the vagueness in the informant's description. For example, an Incident Report on aggravated assault and battery indicated that a man had his jaw broken by a group of 17-year-old youths. The case was referred to the J.A.D. When interviewed, the man described his assailants as 35, 30, and 19 years of age. The case was returned to the detective division. Because each detective division is evaluated on the basis of its rate of clearance by arrest, there is a temptation to route cases to the J.A.D. when no suspect is immediately available and none is likely to be found. Certain officers seem only too ready to assume that the offender is a juvenile in such cases.

Other cases are invariably referred to the J.A.D. because the character of the offenses strongly supports the assumption that the offender is a juvenile. Offenses of this kind include breaking into schools, bicycle thefts, and certain motor vehicle thefts. Some, but probably few of these cases, are later revealed to be adult cases. Recently a private high school had money taken from a cash box in the school cafeteria. A student who had on several occasions entered the school through a window early in the morning was the prime suspect, but further investigation revealed that he was not involved and that the theft was committed with greater skill than commonly attributed to juveniles: no disarray was evident in the vicinity of the cash box, bills but not change were taken, and a set of keys had been used to open doors and the cash box. This case was referred back to the detectives.

ERRORS ON REPORTING FORMS

The basic descriptive data on the Offense Reports and the Investigation Reports may not always be completely accurate. Inaccurate observations by the victim or the witnesses account for some of these errors. The police can reduce such inaccuracies only by careful and persistent interrogations. In a recent case of auto larceny, the victim said that a Negro woman in a third-floor apartment opposite his store had seen boys who were 12 years of age drive away in the stolen car. After great difficulty the police located the witness who was in fact a *white* woman who had been on the *first* floor, and who said that the boys were *15* or *16* years of age. The police are also aware of the fact that victims often inflate the value of stolen property. Through no fault of the police officer, information about the value of such property is often of limited accuracy.

Other inaccuracies occur through carelessness in entering information for certain items routinely required on the Offense Report: filling in "time of reporting the offense," where actually "time of occurrence" is requested; using meaningless phrases, such as "criminal traits" where *"modus operandi"* is requested; or failing to supply data on age, race, or nativity of the complainant. Sometimes incomplete listing is made of an offender's previous record. An officer may write that the offender had "five remedials" and "two arrests," without indicating, as is expected, prior charges and dates. A more frequent error occurs in checking the method of disposition of the case in the block at the bottom of the Offense Report. The body of the report may make statements indicating that the case was "exceptionally cleared," and giving the officer's reasons, but the "arrest" box may be checked by mistake, or vice versa. Occasionally a case is marked "cleared" when, for one reason or another, no offender was actually taken into custody. This latter situation may not always be an error, however, for if a 17-year-old juvenile, for example, runs away from home, goes to New York, and has his 18th birthday, his case may be "cleared" without his having been apprehended by the police.

OFFENSE CLASSIFICATION ERRORS

A third major area of error involves the decision on crime classification, which at times presents a complicated problem of judgment. Although the Uniform Crime Reports Manual and various directives are used as a guide, and although the supervisory personnel are conscientious and careful in their attempts to conform to accepted usage and classificatory procedure, errors occasionally occur.[10] Some decisions involve independent individual judgment and although these are likely to lack uniformity they probably should not be considered strictly as errors. An officer commenting on a schoolyard fight involving two nine-year-old boys said that he would have used "disorderly conduct" rather than "assault and battery," the latter of which his fellow officer had employed in classifying the offense. Some errors made in crime classification are, of course, caught by the supervisor and corrected.

[10] Many years ago, even after the U.C.R. system came in use, there was apparently flagrant tampering with crime classifications. A district captain sometimes passed the word along to "down-grade" Part 1 offenses such as burglary in order to place them in Part 2 categories. Especially did this occur in the case of crimes that were unlikely to be cleared by arrest; a particular district might then "look good" in comparative statistics.

Although not an error in terms of U.C.R. reporting or Police Department directives, the strict application of adult offense categories to juvenile offenses results in an impression of more serious juvenile crime than the actual facts warrant and includes in final totals cases which in former years would never have resulted in a police report. A large number of juvenile "assaults and batteries" and "aggravated assault and batteries" are in fact relatively petty schoolyard fights, normal childhood scrapes, and unruly behavior that in past years were handled by parents or school officials without police notice. Two boys, 11 and 12 years of age, had a fight on their way to school, in the course of which one bit the other on the arm. Neither had a previous record. Result: a reported "aggravated assault and battery." Two four-year-old boys left alone in their house, began playing with matches and accidently set the house on fire. Offense category: "arson." Some very petty offenses receive full police investigation and reporting. A boy stole a lemon from a fruit cart and when the proprietor tried to stop him the boy threw the lemon at the adult. Classification: "larceny." A 17-year-old youth coming home from a wedding party where he had been drinking beer, stopped en route, fell asleep on a park bench and was seen by the officer who noted alcohol on his breath. Classification: "intoxication."

EFFECT OF ENFORCEMENT

In the literature dealing with police statistics and reporting it is commonly said that some fluctuations in offenses simply reflect variations in police enforcement and policy. Obviously, in offenses such as intoxication, illegal possession of weapons, and corner lounging, the more squad cars and foot personnel there are, the greater will be the number of offenses reported. In this section, however, we are only considering variations brought about by the operation of the J.A.D. itself.

One reason for artificial increases and decreases in the number of juvenile offenses and offenders is the activity of the J.A.D. officer at the Youth Study Center who re-interviews offenders in his attempt to clear up cases which were not given to the J.A.D. previously because no juvenile offender was under suspicion. If two men were assigned to this job instead of one, presumably the number of offenses discovered in this way would rise considerably, for the present officer has time to follow only a limited number of leads.

In some cases, such as truancy, curfew violations, and corner lounging, which are most likely to originate with the J.A.D., variations in policy as determined by the inspector, captain, or sergeants will affect the number reported. Reporting truancies and curfew violations is a time-consuming task for the officers who sometimes feel that they could better spend their time investigating or making out reports for more serious offenses. Very few minor offenses like the ones just mentioned would be reported were it not for administrative pressure. Officers feel that they are to some extent judged by the tally made of such activities by their superiors. Consequently, "going out and getting a few curfews" is viewed almost as a fishing expedition. Some officers even "save up" curfews from one night to be turned in later when they are too busy to go out or when the weather is so inclement that few juveniles are likely to be on the street. Certain sex crimes, such as solicitation, although rarely a juvenile offense, are also a function of the degree of enforcement and the size of the staff. The number of offenses of corner lounging and disorderly conduct, especially those originating with the Gang Control Unit, will be determined largely by the amount of time available for cruising about the streets in their cars. The volume of these offenses is also contingent upon the attitudes of the officers towards this kind of activity, for some have sympathy for the slum boys who have no place to go and therefore will simply disperse the group with a warning.

THE MASTER FILE

The Master File has already been mentioned. The decision to arrest or "remedial" a juvenile depends greatly on the File's accuracy and completeness of recorded information regarding previous delinquency. Occasionally some names are not found in the File because some officer has neglected to submit a Juvenile Information Card, which is used to construct the file. In a few cases the officer deliberately avoided submitting such a referral form because he felt that the juvenile "should not have a record," even though such unilateral decisions are not permitted; the juvenile will then appear to have had no previous police contacts. In other cases a given juvenile's record of past contacts cannot be located because his name was misspelled either originally or at the time of the search. The juvenile may intentionally misspell his name, or an unusual or "foreign" name may have been inaccurately reported by the officer in the field or received over the telephone by the clerk at headquarters. Surprisingly few offenders give false names and addresses although some give a brother's name and a few lie about their age. Children whose mothers have lived with a series of "husbands" may have had several last names over a number of years. If no cross references appear in the File, proper location and identification become extremely difficult in such cases. Although errors due to deliberate falsification are usually detected, different spellings of last names or different names due to step-father changes, may result in the presence of two or more cards in the file for the same offender. As only one card is likely to be consulted, an incomplete record of previous police contacts will be reported to the officer in the field. Conscientious searching for alternate spellings, and checking on other identifying data can prevent some of these inaccuracies from occurring, but clerical and officer personnel do not always take the time to make such checks. In still other cases, two offenders with the same name or very similar names may be assumed to be one person, and the record will be undeservedly long.

8

Assumptions Underlying
the Research Design

All research begins with some set of notions about the phenomenon
to be studied. In this respect, establishing a device for measuring
delinquency is no different; it is basic research inherently including
some number of *a priori* assumptions. Dependent on what is present,
the researcher seeks to rearrange, manipulate, and recreate until he
has erected his own perspective in a communicable and permanent
form. The traditional canons of science are at his disposal but
intuitive judgment and insight must also be part of his equipment
for investigation. He must proceed knowing that mistakes will be
made, sometimes corrected in time but often transmitted to others.
Errors of the past have the excuse of history. The present creates
its own.

We are not testing hypotheses in the ordinary sense but we are
building upon accumulated experience and logic. The mechanics
of constructing a procedure for sifting information, the raw tools of
the workman, and the tedious tasks of transcription are all part of
the structure and function of scientific research. Often these procedures are undisclosed or inadequately relayed to others. We feel that
the nature of this research requires more than the usual sharing of
the thought processes that were involved in construction of the
particular forms we used for collecting data. The present chapter,
therefore, discusses some of the fundamental assumptions underlying
our project and the decisions to use certain kinds of information that
were transcribed from police reports to our own specially designed
Offense and Offender Cards, described in a later chapter.

Some of these assumptions grew out of our earlier thinking about the problem we were examining, and others emerged from our reading of volumes of police reports on juvenile offenses.

Our basic belief that police sources of data are best for the purpose of measuring delinquency, and the reasons for this belief, have been substantiated in earlier chapters. We have obviously assumed also that delinquency is measurable by an appropriate instrument and that such an instrument can be devised. In addition we have assumed:

1. *That the problem of measurement, of index construction per se, is not directly related to etiology or treatment.* Obviously, causation research must ultimately depend upon adequate tools of measuring delinquency, but formation of the tools does not require analysis of factors that cause that phenomenon. An index of delinquency may be expected to describe changes that occur in the amount and type of delinquency but not the reasons for these changes. Without such an index, however, changes in delinquent activity are inadequately known and therefore cannot adequately be explained.

2. *That primary focus should be placed on the delinquent event.* We refer to "event" when discussing delinquency in order to distinguish the variables in the act from the offense. The term "offense" connotes a legal category in the traditional sense of robbery, rape, burglary, etc. The term "event" refers to a configuration of objectively observable and describable elements of the law violation. We have assumed, in line with our previous argument about deficiencies in the use of purely legal categories of offenses, that constituents of the act, rather than its legal label and the actors committing it, are the important variables to be considered.

3. *That the community is interested, for measuring purposes, in serious delinquent events rather than symptomatic or predelinquent behavior.* Not until later in the analysis of data did we determine what behavior forms should be considered as symptomatic of delinquent behavior rather than as serious conduct to be included in an index. Therefore, at this stage of the study design, almost all kinds of acts presently labeled delinquent were described on our fact sheets (Offense and Offender Cards). We considered this process necessary for examining later the differences between serious and nonserious acts. "Serious" is defined in subsequent sections of this report. Our original assumptions about seriousness were based upon the infliction of physical injury or harm to the person, or damage or loss of property, or both. Early in the study we viewed truancy, running away from home, or having the status of incorrigible as acts that are not serious. That each of these latter types of conduct may be preludes

to subsequently serious violations of the law may be true, but as reflections of serious delinquency in the community they are merely portents.

4. *That it is necessary to use an empirically derived measuring device.* The presence or absence of physical harm or of damage or loss of property were assumed to be the kinds of data that could yield an instrument with an empirical derivation. Moreover, we wanted a device that would measure, rather than be affected by, changes in the volume of delinquent activities. The mere frequency of an act should not cause its inclusion or exclusion from an index. It is well known that the amount of juvenile homicide is numerically small, but this would not be a good reason for eliminating it from an index. Furthermore, the measuring device should not be affected by changes in legal classifications, categories, or terminology. (We assumed that injury to body or property would not be eliminated by administrative policy or legislative action from the definitions of crime and delinquency.)

These assumptions were initially made not simply to insure uniformity of reporting delinquency over time or space, for uniform crime reporting can conceivably be accomplished by administrative decision no matter how involved or otherwise poorly constructed an index may be. Instead, they were made because the process of collecting data for the administration of the law by the police does not (and perhaps cannot) involve collecting complete information about the psychological motivations or intentions of the juvenile offender. A child who hopes, wishes, or intends to burn down the school building but accomplishes no more than burning the wastepaper basket may be a potentially dangerous threat and from the viewpoint of judicial disposition should be carefully diagnosed and treated. To measure *potential* damage or threat of danger or injury involves, however, the utilization of data beyond those available from the police. We must, therefore, rely on objective items in a delinquent event— the result and manifestations that can be described within present practice and procedure and that allow an empirically derived tool for measuring to emerge from a detailed analysis of these items.

5. *That if the presence or absence of physical injury and of property loss or damage are important factors in constructing an index, some variable related to the degree of harm or loss is also important information.* An extremely refined itemization of physical harm was not possible because descriptions in offense reports generally do not possess sufficient details. Moreover, such refinement was assumed to be unnecessary. That no harm occurred in a vis-à-vis encounter

between victim and offender was an important piece of information. But equally important was the fact that in other encounters there was at least a push, shove, or slap; in still others a cut or stab needed some brief medical attention; in others, the wound required hospitalization of the victim. Some qualitative aspect of the harm was early selected as a meaningful datum. Property loss or damage could be handled for the moment, it was assumed, by the monetary value. The designated or estimated value, based on 1960 prices and recorded in the source document, was used for this kind of degree of loss. How to collapse or compress the specific values and their wide range was a problem we did not have to face at this stage of the study.

6. *That the type of victimization is meaningfully related to a variety of factors important to a delinquency index.* Not all conceivable characteristics of victims could be gleaned from police reports, nor would all be necessary or useful, but we assumed at the outset of the design that certain broad groupings would yield information that could be related to seriousness of the delinquency event and perhaps to reportability. For example, an assault on a person or the burglary of a private house results in a kind of victimization different from disorderly conduct or running away from home. Moreover, the victim in most shoplifting offenses is a large commercial establishment, while in most public drunkenness the community as a whole is a generalized impersonal and diffused "victim." In offenses like fornication, statutory rape, and sodomy, the victim is usually a willing participant in the act, so that the victimization may be considered mutual. Such consensual relationships, as we have noted, are private and not likely to be reported to the police by the voluntary partners. Some acts, like truancy, incorrigibility, and running away from home involve only the person of the offender (save for the unmeasurable mental anguish of parents and teachers), and consequently there is no victim or other person to be injured in any way. We assumed that the type of victimization would be related to how an offense was first discovered and became known to the police and hence part of any set of delinquency statistics. We further assumed that victimization type might correlate with whatever standard of seriousness would eventually emerge.

7. *That the victim-offender relationship may be an important variable in the determination of seriousness of a delinquent act, and that a variety of victim-offender disparities should be examined as possibly relevant to the construction of an index.* Cases involving personal victims usually include data on the age, sex, and race of each victim. Because a segment of the community is threatened and

injured by these offenses, we wanted to know by what types of such acts members of the community were so injured. Moreover, there is practically no information available in the literature on the number and types of delinquent acts that involve the mixed participation of juvenile and adult offenders. From the beginning we felt that juvenile acts involving harm to an adult victim might be either more serious or at least qualitatively different from acts involving the same degree of harm to juveniles only.

We also assumed that certain kinds of disparate relationships between victims and offenders constituted another qualitative dimension of importance to a delinquency index. A male attacking a female puts the latter in a disadvantageous condition because of assumed differentials in physical size and strength. Similarly, the 17-year-old boy attacking a 9-year-old boy or an aged victim in his 70's renders the victim more unlikely to counter the attack because of the physical advantage which the offender enjoys. Disparity, or offender advantage, also occurs when two offenders attack one victim, when the offender is in possession of a deadly weapon, and so forth. The law on robbery in Pennsylvania, for example recognizes this kind of disparity advantage:

Section 704. (Pennsylvania Penal Code) Robbery and Robbery by Assault and Force.—Whoever robs another, or steals any property from the person of another, or assaults any person with intent to rob him, or by menace or force, demands any property of another, with intent to steal the same, is guilty of a felony, and upon conviction thereof, shall be sentenced to pay a fine not exceeding five thousand dollars ($5000), or undergo imprisonment, by separate or solitary confinement, not exceeding ten (10) years, or both.
Section 705. Robbery with Accomplice or while Armed or by Violence. —Whoever, being armed with an offensive weapon or instrument, robs or assaults with intent to rob another; or, together with one or more person or persons, robs or assaults with intent to rob; or robs any person, and at the same time, or immediately before or immediately after such robbery, beats, strikes, or ill-uses any person, or does violence to such person, is guilty of felony, and upon conviction, shall be sentenced to pay a fine not exceeding ten thousand dollars ($10,000), or undergo imprisonment by separate or solitary confinement at labor, not exceeding twenty (20) years, or both.[1]

The extent to which these disparities should be included in index construction was difficult to determine initially, but because we

[1] *Laws of the General Assembly of the Commonwealth of Pennsylvania . . . Session of 1939* (1323 pp. Harrisburg, 1939), p. 955.

assumed their relevance, we transcribed data that would allow for analytical evaluation. Most disparities were not exclusive because most cases in which disparity appeared involved double or triple disparity, i.e., sex, number and age, or age, number and weapon, etc. The combinations, including no disparity or absence of a particular disparity, amounted to sixteen and are analyzed in a later chapter.

8. *That the presence of intimidation, the means of intimidating a victim, and the method used to inflict harm are variables of importance in establishing a scale of seriousness of delinquency.* Our assumptions were that the presence of intimidation makes for a more serious act than its absence and that verbal intimidation is less serious than threats supported by a knife, gun, or some other physical instrument connoting potential immediacy of action and the likelihood of bodily harm. Moreover, the infliction of harm by means of a cutting or stabbing tool or of a gun were presumed to have some relationship to the degree of harm. The presence of a deadly weapon implies a stronger degree of threat or intimidation than the absence of such a weapon, whether one or more offenders are present in the same criminal situation.

9. *That not all offenses against property have the same dimensions and that the critical variables are whether:* (a) *the presence of the offender at the place where the offense occurred was legal;* (b) *force was used to obtain presence;* (c) *the offense involved theft from a place or a person;* (d) *violence was used to accomplish the offense.* As with other types of offenses bearing legal nomenclatures, the dimensions involved in property offenses may cut across the specifically titled acts of robbery, burglary, larceny, etc. Some robberies are performed without violence; some larcenies are performed with violence or damage to some property (parking meter thefts, for example); many automobiles are stolen without forcible entry into the automobile, and so forth. Disorderly conduct often involves damage to property as does malicious mischief, but not *all* of these offense types cause damage. The amount of property stolen or damaged and the amount of recovery of any property loss were additional factors, in offenses involving property, that were assumed useful in judging the seriousness of a delinquent act. Is a theft of fifty cents less serious than a theft of fifty dollars? Or is it only the act of theft that is important for index purposes? These were the types of questions, unanswerable at the outset, that were assumed to be of sufficient value to require the collection of data. If the factor of seriousness were to provide a unidimensional scale, the refinements of the degree of property loss or damage and the

modus operandi by which those degrees were performed were assumed to be points along the scale and could offer significant details for weighting.

10. *That sexual violations occur in a variety of acts classified under the label of a delinquent offense which in itself does not necessarily imply sex behavior.* For this reason we transcribed data under the heading of "subsidiary sex activity." It is not uncommon for police and other agencies to use "runaway," "incorrigible," and similar terms to mask sexual violations in which the juvenile participated but for which direct evidence may be difficult or nearly impossible to obtain. However, even when confessions of unlawful sex conduct appear in police reports, the offense for which the juvenile is taken into custody is often listed as running away from home because the juvenile was in fact away without consent or intention of returning.

11. *That the police sometimes incorrectly classify offenses; that the written description of an offense does not always coincide with the Uniform Classification of Offenses used for criminal and delinquency statistics.*[2] Under this assumption, it would be necessary to examine the offense reports in order to determine how often this kind of discrepancy occurs and what types of offenses are officially underreported and overreported by being erroneously recorded. It may be that offenses are randomly recorded incorrectly and that their true distribution is thereby unaffected. However, an equally plausible hypothesis is that only certain types of offenses are improperly classified and that this process occurs sufficiently often to produce significant differences between the real and recorded frequency of these offenses. We decided, therefore, to check the accuracy of the offense classification recorded by the police.

The validity of our assumption was ultimately verified in cases such as the following:

(a) One type of offense is described in the Offense Report but another is used for the classification of the offense. For example, if breaking and entering a private residence at night and the stealing of property therein were classified as a larceny, this error would require correction. It is the legal title of the offense that is punched on IBM cards by the police department, used in statistics tabulated by type of offense, and recorded for inclusion in Uniform Crime

---

[2] Franco Ferracuti, Rosita Perez Hernandez, and Marvin E. Wolfgang, "A study of police errors in crime classification," *J. Crim. Law, Criminol., and Police Sci.* 53:113–119 (March 1962).

Reports. Another example of misclassification, less serious because only the degree of the UCR offense is involved, occurs when a larceny of over $50 in value is classified as a larceny of between $5 and $50.

(b) One offense is described for a juvenile, another for an adult in the same event, but the crime classification used by the police for tabulation refers only to the offense of the adult. This is not an administrative misclassification or an error made by the police officer filling out the report, for his instructions require this procedure, but for our purposes the juvenile offense constitutes the important unit. The most obvious example of this type involves a male 18 years of age having had consensual sex relations with a female under 16 years of age. The male is an adult and his offense is statutory rape, the offense tabulated by the police. For our purposes, of course, the girl has committed fornication. Or, an adult may be arrested for the offense of selling liquor to a minor and the juvenile for intoxication.

(c) Several offenses are charged against the juvenile in the offense report, but the incorrect one is used for classifying the event. "Incorrect" here means that the officer did not use the offense highest in the hierarchical ordering of offenses according to the Uniform Classification of Offenses and the more refined Philadelphia Crime Code. If a juvenile who is charged with being a runaway, with having committed an assault and battery, and disorderly conduct is classified under disorderly conduct, this would be an error to be corrected to assault and battery.

12. *That all delinquent events known to the police should be counted and described, no matter how the police may dispose of them.* In almost every city the police have considerable discretion in the handling of juvenile delinquents. Of course we cannot account for police action that does not become part of the written record. Should an officer observe some boys engaging in a technically labeled malicious mischief and merely warn them to desist and send them on their way, no record is made and consequently this action never becomes subject to a measurement process. But most communities permit the police to dispose of some juvenile offenders by warning them rather than arresting them and turning them over to the Juvenile Court. Such "nonarrest" or "remedialed" juveniles would not be counted in delinquency statistics if only juvenile court data were used for measuring delinquency in the community. In Philadelphia, in 1960, this would have meant that over two-thirds of all delinquent children known to the police would not have been counted.

13. *That there are differences in the reportability of delinquent*

events and in the apprehensibility of delinquent offenders. Previous theoretical analysis suggested that certain acts are presumed to have high, and others low, probability of being reported to public authorities. Several additional corollary assumptions have been made: (*a*) that reportability is a function of the presence of injury to a victim; (*b*) that cases involving a conspiracy of silence or a consensual relationship between a willing "victim" and an offender or which involve a private dyadic responsibility for law violation and do not contain any other victim will have low reportability; and (*c*) that some acts come to the attention of the police only or principally because of police decisions to take action and that these acts fluctuate numerically as a function of such activity.[3]

To keep clear the extent of the gap between assumption and evidence we must emphasize that no data are available to test empirically and directly ideas about high and low reportability of different offenses. The experiences of police and criminal statisticians over the years have engendered these assumptions which are supported by logic and reason. We have had no data for testing these hypotheses which would permit us to affirm that certain offenses have high reportability and others have low reportability. Consequently, the *degree* of reportability, is not measured in this study.

Among those offenses that have come to the attention of the police, however, we sought to determine the persons through whom the information was received. Thus we decided in reading the original source documents to record who first discovered the offense. In some cases the discovery was made by the police; in others it was made by the victims or persons who, like store managers, represented the owner-victim, and in still others by unrelated passers-by who were strangers to the victim. We were also interested in whether the discovery occurred during or after commission of the delinquent act. In combination, data on who made the discovery of the offense, and when, would provide some interesting material that should, we thought, support or reject our other notions about reportability. The police

---

[3] Relative to these corollary assumptions, see Isidor Chein, *Some Epidemilogical Vectors of Delinquency and Its Control: Outline of a Project* (v, 130 pp. New York: Research Center for Human Relations, New York University, 1963, mimeographed), especially pp. 87–100; Maynard L. Erickson and LaMar T. Empey, "Court records, undetected delinquency and decision-making," *J. Crim. Law, Criminol., and Police Sci.* **54**:456–469 (December 1963); Arthur L. Stinchcombe, "Institutions of privacy in the determination of police administrative practice," *Amer. J. Sociol.* **69**:150–160 (September 1963); John I. Kitsuse and Aaron V. Cicourel, "A note on the uses of official statistics," *Social Problems* **11**:131–139 (Fall 1963).

sometimes observe an offender committing an illegal act, but most frequently they discover a violation only after it has occurred; or they find it quite indirectly, as, for example, when they find an offender in possession of an unlicensed firearm. The personal victim of a burglary is often unaware of the act until hours or even long vacation days have passed. But if he was the first to discover the burglary and bring it to the attention of the public authority, we recorded this kind of information, considering it important for learning something, albeit indirectly, about reportability. At least, we assumed, we may learn empirically that some offenses, when discovered, are almost always discovered only by the police. These would be offenses whose volume over time, therefore, would be a function of police activity and should be excluded from any index.

Another thing to keep in mind is that we have information only about offenses that resulted in the apprehension, or taking into custody, of an offender who happened to be defined as a juvenile, or under eighteen years of age. The relationship between reportability and apprehensibility is not entirely clear; nonetheless, it may be an important if unmeasurable variable in the problem of measuring delinquency. Although we do not know definitely which offenses have high and low reportability we can be reasonably sure of our extremes, the parameters of assumption. It is the middle group of offenses, those that logic suggests may or may not be of a certain level of likelihood of being reported, that remain in ambiguous categories. But we can isolate and analyze this group on other bases, as will be shown later. However, in some offenses that may have a high probability of being reported to the police, the probability of apprehending the offender may be low. Does apprehensibility remain a constant over time? If so, perhaps its low level should be considered inconsequential.

In order to formalize some assumptions about reportability, we can classify offenses into the following groups and attributes.

A. *Consensual (Mutual) Offenses* (low reportability)
1. The offenses are shareable; i.e., they require the presence and either active or passive participation of at least two persons.
2. Privacy is an important condition of these offenses. They are secret and hidden from public view because the participants, whether or not they recognize that what they are doing is illegal, do not want others to know of their behavior. The behavior may be known to them to be illegal but it may not be considered "immoral" or a violation of communal norms.

Actually, both kinds of situations may occur: (a) the participants know the act is illegal but their mores support it; (b) the participants do not know it is illegal and the mores do not support it. In both cases the participants will want to engage in the behavior in privacy.

3. The conduct by both (or all) parties is volitional.

4. Only the participants in the offenses are directly involved in either an offender or "victim" capacity.

5. The following offenses, according to traditional legal categories, would fit into this category.

    (a) Abortion.

    (b) Adultery.

    (c) Fornication.

    (d) Incest.

    (e) Receiving stolen goods.

    (f) Sodomy.

    (g) Statutory Rape.

B. *Conspiratorial Offenses* (low reportability)

1. These offenses contain almost all the characteristics attributed to consensual offenses, except that some may be performed out of fear rather than pleasure and, therefore, the behavior may not always be volitional. However, most conspiratorial offenses are shareable, private, and motivated by pleasure, with attempts to restrict visibility beyond the moment of perpetration.

2. The offenses include

    (a) Bawdy house (proprietor, inmate, frequenter).

    (b) Blackmail (when successful).

    (c) Bribery (when successful).

    (d) Conspiracy.

    (e) Frequenter of unlawful drinking place.

    (f) Gambling (proprietor, frequenter, on highway, etc.).

    (g) Horse racing (proprietor, frequenter, handbook).

    (h) Lottery (numbers, others).

    (i) Selling liquor to minors.

    (j) Selling narcotics.

C. *Hidden Individual Offenses* (low reportability)

1. These are nonshareable offenses in the sense that no one else participates in the act or mutually enjoys any benefits from the violation. The offender alone commits the violation.

2. Only the offender has knowledge of the offense and concealment is essential; that is, concealment not merely of his

identity of involvement (as any burglar would try to do, for example) but observation of the offense itself. *Both* act and actor must be kept secret. Evidence of commission of the act is not even potentially available for observation by any persons in the pursuit of their normal life activities or by police officers in carrying out their expected roles and duties except when they stop the offender for investigation and questioning.

3. The offenses generally have an element of continuation, of relatively longer duration than the more momentary acts of assault, theft, etc. The act in most cases is one of possession rather than a typical transitory act of commission or omission.

4. Offenses in this classification are

   (*a*) Carrying and concealing deadly weapons.

   (*b*) Illegal possession of liquor.

   (*c*) Narcotics user.

   (*d*) Operating motor vehicle after license has been suspended.

   (*e*) Possession of burglary tools.

   (*f*) Possession of narcotics.

   (*g*) Possession of stolen property.

   (*h*) Transporting liquor illegally.

D. *Offenses Whose Reportability Is Affected by Police Activity*

1. As previously described, experience and reason have suggested that a considerable number of offenses are discovered by or become known to the police mostly, if not exclusively, because of police activity. The more search and seizure the police pursue, legally or illegally, the more raids they make on houses of prostitution or of gambling establishments, the greater will be the volume of these offenses. As administrative policy changes from an emphasis on reducing bookmaking to curbing commercial sex, so does the recorded incidence of the offense type change. An increase in the police squad assigned to investigate these offenses will increase their volume. These were the assumptions we made about this set of criminal activities, and we assumed that the data collected under "discovered by" would reveal high proportions of these offenses discovered by the police.

2. The offenses in this class overlap with those found in previous classes of (A) Consensual, (B) Conspiratorial, (C) Hidden Individual; and, as a rule, many of those offenses in A, B and C come, or can come, to the attention of the police through what administrators somewhat zealously describe

as aggressive police action. Up to this point the groups have been exclusive; this one necessarily interlocks with some of the others. The offenses include

(a) Bawdy house (inmate, proprietor, frequenter).

(b) Breach of peace.

(c) Carrying and concealing deadly weapons.

(d) Corner lounging.

(e) Defacing manufacturer serial number of automobile.

(f) Disorderly conduct.

(g) Disorderly house (proprietor, frequenter).

(h) Disorderly street walker.

(i) False reports to or requests for police services.

(j) Fortunetelling.

(k) Frequenting an unlawful drinking place.

(l) Indecent publications.

(m) Intoxication (or drunkenness).

(n) Loitering and prowling.

(o) Male bawd.

(p) Narcotics (user, seller, possession of).

(q) Operating motor vehicle after license has been suspended or revoked or after registration has been suspended.

(r) Pandering.

(s) Panhandling.

(t) Professional thieves, status of.

(u) Public indecency (indecent exposure, obscene shows).

(v) Solicitation for immoral purposes.

(w) Sodomy (buggery, including solicitation).

(x) Turning off lights (of motor vehicle) to avoid identity.

(y) Vagrancy.

E. *Offenses with Serious Bodily Injury; Loss of, or Damage to Property* (high reportability)

Because our assumptions about the relevance of this class of delinquent events were carried throughout the entire research, we will defer until later a fuller discussion of this group and the rationale underlying their utilization. Assuming that personalized victims seriously injured or suffering considerable loss of property through theft or damage will report the events, we thought the following would fall into this class: criminal homicide, forcible rapes, attempts to rape if physical harm occurred, attempts to kill if harm occurred, aggravated assault, robbery, larceny if the victim considered the property of a certain value, auto theft, damage to city property, arson, some malicious mischief, and some disorderly conduct.

Our *a priori* assumptions were generally confirmed by the kinds of evidence available, but, as will be noted, many refinements of them and of the collected data were necessary to produce a meaningful measurement based upon the seriousness of the event.

Briefly summarizing, high reportability means that an offense has a great likelihood of being reported to the police. Again we must recall that our measurement of delinquency functions within the universe of offenses that result in juveniles being taken into custody by the police. Given these variables, the extent of our assertion is as follows: In offenses with high reportability there is greater likelihood that offenses known to the police and cleared by police custody will come closer to the reality of delinquency than do offenses with low reportability.

14. *That the measurement of delinquency can validly be based upon offenses known by the police to have been committed by juveniles.*

Most offenses ascertained by the police are committed by persons who are not captured. The proportion of such "uncleared" offenses varies with the detectability and reportability of the offense. Some of them have been committed by adults, others by juveniles. The question is: Is it valid to assume that a constant ratio exists between the number of offenses cleared by the apprehension of juveniles and the total number of offenses, cleared and uncleared, committed by them? If this were true, variations in the size of the former would be indicative of corresponding variations in the size of the universe of which it is a part and would, therefore, provide the basis for an index of delinquency.

Some years ago, O. W. Wilson[4] asserted that such an index could be arrived at for serious offenses by (*a*) counting all crimes or separate categories of crimes in Part 1 of the Uniform Classification of Offenses; (*b*) finding the number cleared by the arrest of juveniles; (*c*) expressing this number as a percentage of the total of such cleared offenses; and (*d*) using this percentage as an index. If, for instance, 40 per cent of cleared automobile thefts were cleared by the arrest of juveniles it could be assumed that 40 per cent of all automobile thefts, whether cleared or not, could be charged to juveniles. It would follow that, in such case, (*a*) 60 per cent of all automobile thefts could be charged to adults and (*b*) the "uncleared" automobile thefts would be attributable to juveniles and adults in the same proportions.

[4] O. W. Wilson, "How to measure the extent of juvenile delinquency," *J. Crim. Law, Criminol., and Police Sci.* 41:435–438 (December 1950).

It is the general principle contained in Wilson's assertion that interests us, for the specific method he suggests raises a number of problems. First, although police departments no doubt record information that would enable them to count the *offenses* that have been cleared by the arrest of one or more juveniles, they publish only statistics of the number of juvenile offenders charged with various offenses.

Second, the meaning of "offenses cleared by arrest" is not obvious. So far as uniform statistical tabulation and reporting are concerned, the police are supposed to record as cleared any offense committed by a juvenile, no matter how it was disposed of by the police, if he could have been arrested had he been an adult. Therefore, certain juvenile offenses cleared by "remedial" or "non-arrest" action would be reported as cleared by arrest, while offenses by adults resulting only in a similar warning by the police, would not be so reported, because no policy requires it.

Third, there is the vexing problem of offenses committed jointly by juveniles and adults, which has not been solved nor even fully analyzed anywhere, so far as we know. All these problems, however, arise no matter what method of measurement is used and are, therefore, not specific to the one suggested by Wilson.

It would presumably be possible to find means of dealing with the issues raised above, but even if this could be done we would be compelled to reject Wilson's general principle. We do not believe it a correct assertion that the proportion of serious juvenile offenses cleared is the same as the proportion of juvenile offenses among all offenses, cleared or uncleared. The primary reason for this belief is that it is generally claimed that juvenile offenses are easier to clear. "Juveniles are more truthful and less hardened than many would have us believe. They generally commit crimes in groups, are easier to catch than adults, and are more apt to 'talk'."[5] If this is so, the more this raises the proportion of juvenile offenses among all offenses cleared, the more it depresses the proportion of juvenile offenses among the uncleared ones. The ratios held to be constant by Wilson, then, could never be equal. Hence, we could not assume that, let us say, if juveniles committed 40 per cent of cleared automobile thefts, they also committed 40 per cent of all automobile thefts known to the police. That percentage would be smaller if juvenile automobile thieves are easier to catch; the same would hold true for other serious offenses.

[5] Arthur C. Meyers, Jr., "Statistical contacts of a police department," *J. Natl. Council on Crime and Delinquency* 8:58–64 (January 1962).

The operational assumption we are making is somewhat different. *Among properly selected index offenses whose reportability are least affected by changes in police activity, we assume that from one time period to another the number of offenses cleared by the apprehension of juveniles is in constant proportion to the number of all offenses committed by juveniles.* The same assumption may, of course, be applied to adults, with logical and mathematical consistency maintained when both assumptions are made simultaneously.

A symbolic model may clarify these assumptions and their meaning for index purposes. In the most simple form for illustration we shall omit the relatively few offenses that involve both juveniles and adults in the same event.

Let N = all index offenses known to the police.
a = offenses cleared by the apprehension of juveniles.
b = uncleared juvenile offenses.
c = offenses cleared by the apprehension of adults.
d = uncleared adult offenses.

TIME 1   Index Offenses Known to the Police

	CLEARED	NOT CLEARED	TOTAL
Juvenile offenses	a	b	$a + b$
Adult offenses	c	d	$c + d$
Total	$a + c$	$b + d$	$N_1 = a + b + c + d$

In two cells, a and c, two marginal totals, $a + c$ and $b + d$, and the total, N, figures recorded by the police can be inserted. Let us call this model Time 1 and construct a similar one, a later period, Time 2.

TIME 2   Index Offenses Known to the Police

	CLEARED	NOT CLEARED	TOTAL
Juvenile offenses	e	f	$e + f$
Adult offenses	g	h	$g + h$
Total	$e + g$	$f + h$	$N_2 = e + f + g + h$

We assume that for index offenses

$$\frac{a}{a + b} = \frac{e}{e + f} \text{ and } \frac{c}{c + d} = \frac{g}{g + h}$$

These assumptions are consistent with one another and are not disturbed by the contention that juvenile offenses are easier to clear than are adult offenses.

Wilson assumes, on the other hand, that

$$\frac{a}{a+c} = \frac{b}{b+d} = \frac{a+b}{N_1} \text{ and } \frac{e}{e+g} = \frac{f}{f+h} = \frac{e+f}{N_2}$$

This does not require that

$$\frac{a}{a+c} = \frac{e}{e+g}$$

nor an assertion that

$$\frac{a}{a+b} = \frac{e}{e+f}$$

It does require that juvenile and adult offenses be equally easy to clear, and this we contend is not the case.

There is no way to test our assumption of constancy in the clearance rate of juvenile offenses. Furthermore, the model requires properly selected index offenses and consistency in the investigatory and patrol functions of the police. Increases of police personnel generally or of personnel assigned to juvenile work would probably affect clearance rates, but it could be expected that index offenses would be least affected by such changes.

We reiterate that we have been considering proportions of cleared offenses among known offenses and not delinquency or crime rates in populations. These rates may rise or decline without affecting our assumption that the ratio of cleared to uncleared juvenile offenses is constant. We would expect, however, that if juvenile offenses are easier to clear, delinquency rates would, due to this fact, be consistently higher than they would be if the case of clearance were the same for juveniles and adult offenses.

9

The Sample

It will be recalled that one of our major assumptions viewed delinquent *events*, not delinquent juveniles, as the major focal point for establishing an index. Although the configuration of variables included in the definition of a delinquent event does not strictly coincide with the legal label assigned to a delinquent act, the Uniform Crime Reports Classification system provides a set of offense categories from which these events may be derived and described if intensively examined. The Juvenile Aid Division files of offense reports are classified according to this system. The decision to use the universe of offense reports was, therefore, made early but not hastily. Although we shall later make recommendations about statistical reporting of delinquency, based on our inductively emerging model, we are not suggesting that police operating files be maintained in a manner different from what now exists in Philadelphia. Record keeping for research and for administrative purposes are usually different. Therefore, unless a model of index items were already established, research designed to construct such a model must utilize existing filing procedures when choosing a sample. Because 1960 cases were needed for the present study, we relied upon the existing record system.

Nowhere in published police reports is there information about the size of the universe of known juvenile *offenses*. Moreover, the file of offense reports in the Juvenile Aid Division did not supply this kind of information directly, even though each offense report was a separate document. As we have indicated elsewhere, two persons may be apprehended for two different offenses that are coded, classified and filed under only one of these offenses (such as statutory

131

rape for the male and fornication for the female, but coded only as statutory rape). Thus the size of the universe was *a priori* undetermined, as is common in such social science research. The offense files are administratively maintained by the broad uniform crime classification ranging from the assumed most serious offense of criminal homicide to petty violations of city ordinances. Even so, the broad research objectives and the manner of labeling variant offenses under one title made the use of stratified sampling impractical. Moreover, we could not decide *a priori* which strata were relevant for the purpose of our study because one of the objectives was to discover the most important variables which might make sampling efficient and meaningful in future studies. Attempting to decide the strata beforehand would have meant an encroachment upon the research objective itself.[1]

Because examination in complete detail of a multitude of phenomena about juvenile delinquency recorded in the offense reports would have involved such a mass of data that analysis would have been inordinately tedious and slow, selecting a sample was necessary. A random sampling was chosen as the technique and there was no reason to believe that a bias could result. Actually a systematic (random) sampling method was employed, every tenth case being selected. It was felt that this process would yield a representative sample because the basis of the arrangement of the universe was unbiased with reference to the purpose for which the sampling was conducted. We made certain that no records were missing, that each case as defined by the police was represented by only one folder, and that each case had an equal chance of appearing in the sample. Because of the arrangement of offense reports in the police files, taking every tenth case yielded a sample which approximated stratification.

DESCRIPTION OF THE FILES

The various source documents we used are kept in three different files in the Juvenile Aid Division headquarters:

1. The *arrest file* which includes all arrests made by the Juvenile Aid Division, exclusive of the Morals Squad.

2. The *remedial file* which contains all cases of offenders handled by the Juvenile Aid Division (exclusive of the Morals Squad) who

---

[1] For a detailed description of similar problems in a quite different kind of research, i.e., one concerned with the social and cultural structure and process in a bulb-growing region in The Netherlands, see I. Gadourek, *A Dutch Community* (xvi, 555 pp. Leiden: H. E. Stenfert Kroese, 1956), pp. 293–301.

were released without an arrest, cases which were unfounded, and those for which no offender was taken into custody.

3. The *Morals Squad file* which includes all morals offenses handled by that squad, regardless of the type of disposition.

The Arrest Sample

The arrest file for 1960 is arranged by the police district which was responsible for making the arrest. Within each district, cases are arranged by the Uniform Crime Classification system, and within each offense category they are arranged by district complaint numbers, with the most recent cases in front.

A randomly selected digit (9) between one and ten served as the starting point, after which each tenth case was selected. This process yielded 489 cases for the arrest sample.

Some cases appearing in this arrest file are also found in the Morals Squad file. This duplication arises from three different situations. First, some offenses not involving morals, many of which originated as morals complaints, are handled by the Morals Squad. The records for these cases appear in the Morals Squad file, but single copies of the various investigative reports are sometimes supplied for the arrest file. None of these cases appeared in the arrest sample, and only an insignificant few were present in the arrest universe.

Second, actual morals cases handled by the Morals Squad occasionally appear as duplicates when copies of the reports kept in the Morals Squad file are also placed in the arrest file. Four such cases appeared in the arrest sample, but because they were later counted in the sample of the Morals Squad file, they were simply replaced in the arrest file and not used again. If our sampling is unbiased, probably no more and perhaps fewer than 40 of these duplicate cases appear in the entire arrest file. Consequently, the 40 cases that were included in the universe from which the arrest sample was drawn could not have seriously affected the arrest sample.

The third type of duplication occurs in cases involving morals offenses that are handled by the Line Squad when no personnel from the Morals Squad are available. These cases were easily spotted and eliminated from the Morals Squad file because they contain no carbon copies of source documents.

In the arrest file from which this sample was selected, some offenses involved adult offenders only, i.e., certain liquor law violations, neglect of children, and corrupting the morals of a minor. In addition, some cases in the arrest file consisted of juveniles arrested by the Juvenile Aid Division for jurisdictions other than Philadelphia. Both types of cases, when appearing in the arrest sample, were eliminated and were not replaced or substituted for they are not considered in the analysis of the sample. It is assumed that both the purely adult cases and the juvenile arrests for other jurisdictions that originally appeared in the sample adequately represented, respectively, the number of each type in the file. The final arrest sample, then, consists only of the universe of these juvenile cases in the arrest file.

The Remedial Sample

The remedial file for 1960 is arranged in the same way as the arrest file, i.e., by district complaint number within each offense category and within the district responsible for handling the case.

In order to obtain a universe of actual or "founded" cases in which at least one juvenile was taken into custody and released without arrest, some cases were initially eliminated from this file. These were

(a) Adult cases (i.e., cases in which only adults were taken into custody).

(b) Unfounded cases (i.e., cases in which no offense was committed).

(c) Active cases (i.e., cases for which no offender was taken into custody but for which one is still being sought).

(d) Inactive cases (i.e., cases in which no offender was taken into custody and none was being sought).

(e) Curfew cases.

(f) Investigation of persons.

(g) Miscellaneous police service cases.

The active and inactive cases (c and d in the above list) for which no juvenile offenders were taken into custody were not included in the universe from which the sample was selected because the police had not established the existence of a juvenile offense. Actually, at the time the samples were drawn (February–March 1961) none of the cases originally labeled "active" had resulted or were expected to result in the apprehension of the offenders. To all intents and purposes, the Juvenile Aid Division dismissed these cases and they remained thereafter as "not cleared." In another section of this chapter we shall describe the process of selecting a sample of these cases and shall later briefly analyze them. For the present, they are excluded.

Curfew cases (e, above) were excluded from the universe because they constituted very petty violations of a regulatory and administrative municipal decree rather than violations of substantive law or even of juvenile court law. Consequently, they are not delinquent events.

The police occasionally take juveniles into custody under the rubric of "Investigation of Persons" (*f*, above). These cases do not involve delinquent acts but are instead part of the general social welfare functions of the police. Material witnesses, children in need of some kind of care outside the home, and neglected children are included under "investigation." Finally police service cases, which appear in the remedial file, do not involve delinquencies and consequently were excluded from the remedial sampling frame.

A digit (5) between one and ten was randomly selected, and starting with this case every tenth case was selected. This process yielded 824 cases for the remedial sample.

If a case was selected by mistake (that is, if one of the cases mentioned above from *a* to *g* were selected) it was returned and the first proper case before it was substituted.

The Morals Sample

The files for 1960 include all cases, a few of which are not sex offenses, handled by the Morals Squad. The cases are filed by offense category, and within each category by central complaint number, the most recent being in front.

To obtain a sample from a universe of actual or founded morals offenses in which at least one juvenile offender was taken into custody, certain other cases originally appearing in the files were excluded. These were

(*a*) Adult cases.

(*b*) Unfounded cases.

(*c*) Active cases.

(*d*) Inactive cases.

(*e*) Duplicate cases. These are morals cases originally handled by the Line Squad which appear occasionally in both files. These cases were counted in the arrest file but not in the Morals Squad file.

(*f*) Special cases. Sometimes a juvenile victim or complainant is also an offender. Such cases involving juvenile victim-offenders were included in our sampling, except when a female involved in a sex offense was taken into custody only for the purpose of being medically examined. In the past, an additional charge such as disorderly conduct or incorrigibility might be added in conjunction with the real charge, "investigation and medical examination." However, if valid offenses such as prostitution, fornication, or sodomy were present in cases of this kind, they constituted part of the universe from which the sample was selected, and consequently they appear in the sample.

A digit (5) between one and ten was randomly selected as a starting point, after which every tenth case was selected with the qualifications noted above. This process yielded 30 cases for the morals sample.

Additional Sample Units Discovered during Examination of the Preceding Samples

Some source documents of juvenile offenses contained two or more different Central Complaint Numbers which meant that more than the one offense in the folder was involved in the instant case. If these numbers were accompanied by their original source documents, the cases were considered part of the sample. If the Central Complaint Numbers were *not* accompanied by their original source documents, it was necessary to check the three Juvenile Aid Division files to determine whether these source documents were located in them. If they were in one of the Juvenile Aid Division files, the cases were not included in the sample because they already were part of the universe from which the sample was drawn. If they were not located in one of the Juvenile Aid Division files, they were found only in Central Records (of the Police Department) and therefore had had no opportunity for being selected in a sample. Consequently, these latter cases were then included as part of the sample. Specifically, the cases used represented a portion of the larger universe of all juvenile offenses located in the Police Department's Central Records but not located in any of the Juvenile Aid Division files. They were often cases involving both juveniles and adults and were handled by district officers or detectives who were not part of the Juvenile Aid Division.

Why the Master Record File of Juvenile Delinquents Was Not Used as the Sampling Frame

The Master Record File, consistently maintained since 1953, consists of a series of cards (see Appendix A-2) arranged alphabetically for all juveniles who have had a Juvenile Aid Division police contact that resulted in a report. The cards contain the juvenile's name and nicknames, his past and present addresses, father's and mother's names, current school attended, church affiliation, birthdate, race, and a chronological listing of police contacts with date, charge, arrest or nonarrest, District Complaint Number, and sometimes the final court disposition. Cards of offenders under 18 years of age are in the main portion of the Master Record File; an 18- to 21-year-old section and an over-21-year-old section are in separate files.

Information for the original Master Record File card for a given offender, as well as subsequent items of information noted on that card, come from Juvenile Information Cards (see Appendix A-3) submitted for each offender by the Juvenile Aid Division officer when he closes a case. Data from these Juvenile Information Cards are transferred to the Master Record File card by a clerk.

Theoretically it would have been possible to have used the Master Record File to select a sample. There are several major reasons why this was not done:

1. The assumptions underlying the research design placed an emphasis on delinquent events, not delinquents, for purposes of measuring the amount and type of harm to the community committed by juveniles. Therefore, it was necessary to secure a universe of juvenile acts rather than juvenile actors.

2. Because the District Complaint Number of each offense appears on the juvenile's card in the Master Record File, it would have been possible to have indirectly obtained a sample of juvenile offenses by having selected a sample of juvenile offenders. In order to do so, however, it would have been necessary to have checked every Offense Report corresponding to each 1960 District Complaint Number on every juvenile card to determine, for example, that Joe Adams with a D.C. 5-3106 (burglary) was involved in an offense with Joe Williams, also D.C. 5-3106 (burglary). Such information was readily available by our taking a sample of juvenile offenses, but the labor involved in discovering this same information by a sample of offenders would have been enormous.

3. Another tedious task would have been the necessity of examining visually every one of the 45,000 juvenile cards in the active file and each of 65,000 cards in the over-age file (18 to 25 years) in order to pick up juveniles who committed delinquencies in 1960, the year for our analysis.

4. Finally, we discovered early that police officers usually but do not always submit a referral form, or Juvenile Information Card, in remedial cases. Consequently, although the offense reports used for

our sample of delinquent acts constituted a valid universe of all acts, the Master Record File as a universe of all delinquent juveniles had some omissions.

Sample of Unsolved Cases

In an attempt to learn something about the characteristics of 1960 offenses for which juveniles were suspected but no one taken into custody, two 5 per cent samples were drawn from the unsolved cases which were referred to the Juvenile Aid Division. An unknown number of uncleared offenses remain in the various detective divisions but are not given over to the Juvenile Aid Division because there is no evidence to indicate that the offender was a juvenile. Some of these latter offenses, of course, are committed by juveniles, so that no accurate estimate of unsolved juvenile offenses can be projected from those which are referred to the Juvenile Aid Division.

Cases are given to the Juvenile Aid Division when they involve: (1) school burglaries and thefts, bicycle thefts, and a few less common offenses in which it is assumed, even with no details, that the offender was a juvenile because of the nature of the offense; or (2) some description of the offender by bystanders or victims is available which suggests that he is likely to be under 18.[2]

All cases referred to the Juvenile Aid Division, whether or not they result in the apprehension of an offender, are recorded in a daily log, which lists the District Complaint Number, the Central Complaint Number, type of offense (burglary, larceny, etc.), the officer assigned to the case, disposition and date of occurrence. Disposition is indicated as "active," "inactive," "remedial," "exceptionally cleared-closed" (used when no offense occurred, "unfounded"), "arrest," and "Morals Squad case." Cases are listed chronologically as they come in, although the final disposition may be entered some time later.

The two 5 per cent samples were selected from the universe of unsolved offenses (active or inactive cases), excluding Morals Squad cases.[3] A randomly selected digit between one and ten served as the

[2] Some detectives may send cases to the Juvenile Aid Division because these officers see little chance of solving them. Some erroneous referrals are due to inaccurate preliminary information; others are due to the gratuitous assumption that the offender is a juvenile.
[3] There was no notation indicating the ultimate disposition of these Morals Squad cases. Because this lack of information would have necessitated examining the Morals Squad file of source documents, and because that file included adults as well as juveniles, the tremendous labor involved did not justify the inclusion of such Morals Squad cases.

starting point, after which every tenth unsolved case was selected, numbered alternately "1" or "2," with the identifying District Complaint and Central Complaint Numbers on our Study Offense Cards. The notation "1" or "2" indicated in which 5 per cent sample the case fell. When the samples were drawn, the source documents were secured and attached to the face sheets (Study Offense Cards) of the sample with number "1" or "2" on the cards. When a tabulation of offense categories in the two samples indicated an extremely high degree of similarity in the distributions, only a single 5 per cent sample was used, thus reducing labor and time without loss or bias. Offense Cards were then filled out for this final 5 per cent sample of 280 cases.

Drawn in the sample but not used and not replaced were the following cases: three "religious incidents" in which it was clear that no actual offense such as malicious mischief had occurred; a "bomb scare" case; a case which had actually resulted in a boy being taken into custody but which was not properly noted in the log; and nine cases involving adult offenders (which were later referred back to the detective divisions by the Juvenile Aid Division). None of these cases was replaced, for these inappropriate cases in the sample reflected their proportion in the entire universe; consequently, replacing them would have resulted in more than a 5 per cent sample of valid unsolved offenses involving juvenile suspects.

This sample of uncleared (i.e., unsolved, or not cleared by arrest) cases from the files of the Juvenile Aid Division will be briefly analyzed in a special section of this study. We have not included them in our general descriptive analysis of delinquency, nor have we included them in the measurement of delinquency primarily because too many unknown variables preclude the certainty that all or even most of these acts were committed by persons under 18 years of age.

Representative Character of Sample

The 10 per cent sample drawn yielded 1313 offenses involving 2094 delinquents, some of whom were involved in more than one offense during the year. Whether the sampling procedure was proper had, of course, to be determined. This could be done by comparing the sample with 10 per cent of the total universe of offenses attributed to juveniles during the year. It was possible to derive this information from the IBM cards in the Central Records Office of the Police Department. These cards are maintained by calendar year, and although they refer to *juveniles* arrested or remedialed, the fact that the same complaint number appears on the cards of two or more juveniles participating in an offense made it possible to count the total number of offenses as well as the total number of (duplicated) juveniles who were involved in them.

The sample was divided into four groups based on the Uniform Classification of Offenses used by the police (see p. 80, *supra*), Part 1 and Part 2 offenses, each part divided into those leading to arrests and those leading to remedial action. The results were compared with the data from the police universe, similarly classified, and divided by ten. The same procedure was followed for the offenders.

Certain adjustments had to be made in order to achieve comparability.

1. Some offense groups had to be removed from the police figures because they were not sampled by the study.

2. The police count it one offense when two or more truants, or runaways, or incorrigible children are apprehended together, whereas in the study we recorded as many cases of truancy, etc., as there were truants, runaways, or incorrigibles.

3. Some offenses or offenders which were counted by the study had no punch cards in the police files. In a few cases no card was punched at all and sometimes, when a case would be cleared by, for example, the arrest of one juvenile, a card for him would be punched but none for his partner(s) in the offense.

4. A few cases were included in the study by mistake. It was sometimes difficult to tell if a juvenile mentioned in the Offense Report had been simply released or had been subject to official remedial disposition.

5. In a few cases the police had punched two cards for the same offender in the same case.

6. Some police cards were found to refer to adults who had lied about their age; no correction on the card had been made after the true facts had become known.

7. The study had excluded out-of-state runaways, but cards had been punched by the police in such cases.

8. The study had overlooked a few offenses or offenders who should have been included and were counted by the police.

9. In some cases, the offense, erroneously recorded by the police, had been corrected in the study. It was necessary in such cases to use the original offense classification for comparisons, since this was the one punched on the card.

The net number of adjustments made to the sample to insure comparability and the difference between the expected and observed number of offenses and offenders are shown in Table 4 and in sum-

TABLE 4. *Net Number of Adjustments to Sample for Comparison with Police Universe*

ADJUSTMENTS		OFFENSE					OFFENDER				
		Arrest		Remedial		Σ	Arrest		Remedial		Σ
		I	II	I	II		I	II	I	II	
SAMPLE TOTAL BEFORE ADJUSTMENT		221	223	153	720	1317*	422	346	287	1039	2094
Adjustment for count — Counted by study not by police	Missed by police	−16	−7	−9	−35	−67	−39	−18	−33	−62	−152
	Included in error	0	0	0	0	0	−1	0	−4	−2	−7
	Repeats	0	0	0	0	0	+7	0	+3	+4	+14
	Adults	0	0	0	0	0	+2	0	0	+1	+3
Counted by police not by study	Omitted on purpose	0	+17	+1	0	+18	0	+22	+2	+3	+27
	Omitted in error	0	+1	0	+1	+2	+2	+1	+2	+3	+8
Adjustment for charge		0	−1	0	+1	0	−11	+11	0	−6	−6
Sample total after adjustment		205	233	145	687	1270	382	362	257	980	1981
10% of police total		203	243	142	702	1290	392	365	242	1030	2029
Number off (adjusted sample minus 10% of police total)		+2	−10	+3	−15	−20	−10	−3	+15	−50	−48

* The sum here is 1317 instead of 1313 because all figures in the table are adjusted to the Police procedures. There were four offenses in which mixed disposition occurred, i.e., some offenders in the same case were arrested and some were disposed of through remedial action. The Police counted these cases twice.

TABLE 5. *Study Sample Compared with Police Universe (in per cent)*

	OFFENSES						OFFENDERS					
	Arrest		Remedial		Total		Arrest		Remedial		Total	
	Study	Police	Study	Police	Study	Police	Study	Police	Study	Police	Study	Police
Part 1 Offenses	16.1	15.8	11.4	11.0	27.5	26.8	19.3	19.3	13.0	11.9	32.3	31.2
Part 2 Offenses	18.4	18.8	54.1	54.4	72.5	73.2	18.2	18.0	49.5	50.8	67.7	68.8
Total	34.5	34.6	65.5	65.4	100.0	100.0	37.5	37.3	62.5	62.7	100.0	100.0

mary form in Table 5. The similarity of the percentage distributions of the data from the sample and from the universe is clear; a statistical test[4] revealed that the differences were definitely within the range expected by chance variation. The sample appears, therefore, to be reasonably representative of the universe from which it was drawn, at least when broken down in the manner shown.

UTILIZING THE OFFENSE REPORTS

One of the most important elements in constructing a research design is the provision of clearly defined empirical referents, so that accuracy in recording and transcribing data will be achieved. We have already discussed the importance of using objective, empirical criteria for measuring delinquency. But unless the data used to describe these criteria are carefully and consistently recorded, empiricism loses its value and what is communicated to other scholars is invalid. The importance of establishing operational definitions for many terms loosely used in the vernacular but also needed in a research project is therefore obvious. The meaning of terms must be stated as precisely as possible; they should be mutually exclusive, permit no doubtful inclusions, be communicable without further explanation and allow replications with the assurance that no confusion of terminology will exist to render comparisons impossible or invalid. Similar clarity is needed for all units of analysis and all concepts used in analysis. After drawing the sample of offense reports, we therefore devised an Offense Card and an Offender Card onto which data from the reports were transcribed. We knew what information was available and had decided what might be useful and potentially significant for our purpose. It was important, however, that the categories and terms placed on these cards have the same meaning for all staff members engaged in the transcription process, in order to avoid subjective interpretations. Complete agreement on terminology was acquired only after weeks of staff conferences during which the meanings of our empirical referents were discussed and debated. More than semantics was involved. The small group experience of mutual criti-

---

[4] The test used was chi-square and the expected n was formed by redistributing the police proportions as if they totaled the sample n. The formula used employed the Continuity Correction. Chi-square was .509; d.f. = 1; P between .75 and .50. No chi-square was computed on the offender sample since all offenders were used if an offense was in the sample. This means that the offenders were a cluster sample and not a random or systematic sample and hence violates the requirement of independence demanded by chi-square.

cism was itself a valuable creative intellectual process. Out of these discussions grew the instructions to be followed by the transcribers to ensure uniformity, and as the work progressed and some unexpected or new problem arose the directives were clarified. Reproductions of the study cards and the instructions to be followed in completing them are found in Appendix C.

10
Classification of Delinquency

Science is concerned with discovering and describing uniformities in large numbers of phenomena. The process of determining these uniformities consists in breaking down the mass of the phenomena into categories on the basis of likenesses and differences. Items that possess characteristics significant for certain purposes are classified together. However, the end sought for any classification must always determine which characteristics will be used. Scientists in all disciplines assert that a classification is valid only for a specific purpose and that an extensive knowledge of the properties of objects is necessary for a good classification.

Because classification is important for science, any classification is to some degree superior to an array of disconnected knowledge, for "without classification there would never be the knowledge of the resemblances and uniformities in nature which is so fundamental in the discovery and formulation of scientific laws."[1] Thus, classification is never an end in itself but always serves some function. In our case, it should function to give social relevance to the forms of delinquency, facilitate efficiency in statistical compilation, and promote analytical theory that can be tied to empirical data.

Logicians and scientists have provided many rules for valid classifications. Paraphrasing George Lundberg:

1. Classifications must be mutually exclusive. A classification certainly loses its usefulness if any of the data to be classified can prop-

[1] Morris R. Cohen and Ernest Nagel, *An Introduction to Logic and Scientific Method* (xii, 467 pp. New York: Harcourt, Brace 1939), pp. 224–225.

erly be placed in more than one category. This means that there must be only one basis for division at a time, and that the basis must be as objective as possible.

2. Closely related to the principle of exclusiveness is the principle that a valid classification must be exhaustive, that is, include all the data studied.

3. Finally, a classification must be appropriate, that is, suited to the end sought.[2]

We have emphasized previously that there are many deficiencies in the use of legal categories and classifications of delinquency and crime for purposes of measuring delinquency.[3] Most research in causation and correction have made use of these legal labels for determining the volume and quality of delinquency; but as Kahn has remarked, "We often blur potential research findings by acting as though a legal designation in a court room or commitment to an institution creates a group with the kind of homogeneity which will yield significant findings in basic research."[4]

Many years ago, one of the authors of this report suggested[5] that research on deviant conduct should evolve definitions of such conduct that would be independent of legal definitions, and that, when crime or delinquency become the object of research, these be analyzed and redefined in a manner to enable the researcher to group them into sociologically (or ethologically) more meaningful categories.

---

[2] George A. Lundberg, *Social Research* (2nd ed., xx, 426 pp. New York: Longmans, Green, 1942), p. 106. See also for good examples of formal classification and discussions of its uses, Karl Menger, "An exact theory of social groups and relations," *Amer. J. Sociol.* 43:797–798 (1938); George A. Lundberg, "Some problems of group classification in measurement," *Amer. Sociol. Rev.* 5:351–360 (1940); and Wilson Gee, *Social Science Research Methods* (New York: Appleton-Century-Crofts, 1950), pp. 222–223.

[3] We are not unaware of the great interest and valuable efforts made by many legal scholars and philosophers in modern times to develop a proper classification of offenses in penal codes, from Jeremy Bentham's to that of the American Law Institute's Model Penal Code. There is no doubt that some of these schemes, more than others, would furnish a basis for more meaningful criminal statistics, but this has not been their aim. Even the best of them would be subject to some of the criticisms of legal definitions made in an earlier chapter.

[4] Alfred J. Kahn, "Sociology and social work—challenge and invitation," *J. soc. Problems* 4:220–228 (January 1957), as cited by Sol Rubin, "Legal definitions of offenses by children and youths," reprinted from University of Illinois *Law Forum*, "Current problems in criminal law" (I) (Vol. 1960, Winter number, 512–523), p. 517.

[5] Thorsten Sellin, *Culture Conflict and Crime* (116 pp. New York: Social Science Research Council, 1938), Ch. 2.

We already noted that the legal definition of juvenile delinquency not only covers, without further specification, all offenses that would be criminal, if committed by an adult, but also various forms of conduct that advanced thinking today would not label delinquency, such as incorrigibility, truancy, running away, etc. This encourages researchers on juvenile delinquency, whether it is broadly or narrowly defined, to develop any definition and classification of delinquent acts which may suit their purpose.[6]

In our research, we were not unmindful of the specific legal labels attached by police to the conduct of delinquent juveniles, but we sought descriptive elements of such conduct that would permit us to develop a classification which would not depend on those labels. We assumed that what is of concern to a community is not that a juvenile commits what in an adult would be called "burglary," "robbery," or "larceny" for instance; that such general labels alone do not adequately portray what such conduct involves; that it is the degree and kind of harm to persons or their property inflicted by juvenile offenders which arouses concern; that constancy in the reporting of such offenses begins when harm exceeds a certain level of tolerance, depending on the seriousness of that harm; and that certain classes of offenses are of such a nature that their fluctuations are dependent on adventitious factors, such as the extent of police activity or the accidental discovery of a consensual offense, and therefore not indicative of changes in the *real* delinquency they represent.

The classification used in the present study may be called a sociological one and has been specifically designed to permit our developing a mathematical model and/or statistical basis for establishing a

[6] A recent example of such an effort is found in Joseph W. Eaton and Kenneth Polk, *Measuring Delinquency: A Study of Probation Department Referrals* (xv, 102 pp. Pittsburgh: University of Pittsburgh Press, 1961), p. 9, a statistical study of delinquents which does not deal with "measurement" in the sense of a delinquency index. Since about five out of six juvenile offenders apprehended by the police were not referred to the Probation Department, the universe of delinquent acts studied by the authors was greatly restricted. Some of the five "analytic categories" of offenses (minor violations, property violations, major traffic violations, human addiction, and bodily harm) contain a strange assortment of offenses, hit-and-run driving and automobile manslaughter, for instance, being classified with automobile theft under "major traffic violations" and fornication being considered a "human addiction." As David Bordua wrote in a review of the book (*J. Crim. Law, Criminol., and Police Sci.* **53**:242, June 1962) "The grouping of offenses serves no purpose well and is the result of confusing several dimensions of classifications. Legal definitions, ideas of objective social harm, and presumptions about causal process are combined in a way which is unclear logically and probably without practical use."

delinquency index. Our major focus has been on the presence of physical or property harm to the victim. "The emphasis on harms," as Jerome Hall has suggested in a slightly different context, "is not intended to exclude other approaches but to indicate that the problems confronting us compel a choice between rigorously described criteria, which narrow the field but promise an organization of knowledge within those limits, and wide criteria, which may be very important with regard to the functions of lawyers but do not lead to organized knowledge."[7]

For the above reasons we grouped the offenses committed by the juveniles in our sample into two main classes with appropriate subdivisions. In the first class we placed offenses that involved the infliction of some physical harm on the victim or caused the loss or destruction of property. In the second class we placed offenses against persons that did not result in any harm to them or to their property, offenses that disturbed public order, the "juvenile status" offenses, and those of a consensual or conspiratorial nature. All the forms of juvenile conduct that led to police intervention are thus included in the two classes except curfew law violations, which were excluded from our study from the beginning. The main part of our analysis of the data will deal with the offenses in the first class; they are assumed to be the only ones that might yield some kind of index to the frequency and seriousness of the conduct of which they are a sample.

The suggestion that, for measurement purposes, juvenile delinquency be narrowly defined to cover only offenses which would be punishable if an adult committed them does not imply that, for purposes of social control and treatment, only the juveniles involved in such offenses should be dealt with by the juvenile court or similar agencies. All children with problems of personal or social maladjustment that cannot be adequately dealt with by their families may require the intervention of a public agency such as the juvenile court. In some countries, all such children, even those who have committed offenses, are merely referred to as "minors" or "maladjusted" juveniles in need of care. We have no quarrel with such designations, but when it comes to measuring the frequency and seriousness of juvenile misconduct, it becomes necessary to segregate conduct that inflicts measurable harm on persons and their property from conduct which, no matter how much concern it may arouse, causes no such measurable harm.

[7] Jerome Hall, "Some basic questions regarding legal classification for professional and scientific purposes," *J. Legal Educ.* 5:329–343 (1953), p. 339.

Although the rationale for dichotomizing delinquency into Class I and Class II events is based principally upon the presence of some degree of objectively recordable harm, it is possible that not all Class I events should be considered index offenses. Ultimately, the selection of index events from the universe of all acts recorded should be based upon the assumption that the former are considered serious by the victims or their representatives and consequently possess a high probability of being reported to the public authorities. The presence or absence of other attributes and variables are merely analytic addenda that do not affect their inclusion among index events. Non-index events, therefore, will not involve bodily injury, property loss or damage, but may involve a greater variety of other conditions, including a belief by the police and other members of the community who are not victims that some of these acts are serious ones.

The classification scheme is based upon a process of continuous elimination of all preceding major variables once the first category is established. After a variable is selected for determining a category, the category is derived by dividing all the delinquency events which do not possess the major variable of (i.e., rejects from) the preceding category into those in which the new variable is present and those in which it is absent.[8] Although some characteristics of one category may be found in another category, each category fully defined and described includes all cases which possess its major variable and consequently is exclusive of all other categories. This process also eliminates "catch-all groups" or any congerie commonly listed in studies elsewhere as "all other offenses" or "miscellaneous offenses." Our classification scheme includes ten major categories; subcategories will be described later. The classification model on page 150 shows the process by which they were derived.

Class I offenses include Categories A, B, and C. Class II offenses include Categories D, E, F, G, H, I, and J. All categories share the following characteristics:

1. They are derived from police data.
2. They are based upon data that are empirically verifiable.
3. They are mutually exclusive, for no acts embraced by one category can be classified under any other category.

---

[8] It is interesting to note that Jeremy Bentham applied this procedure in his attempt at a "scientific" classification of offenses. "The procedure of classification to which Bentham tried to conform is the 'dichotomic procedure,' called by him the 'exhaustive method.' This method consists in first defining the logical domain which one proposes to study, and then dividing this into two parts, and so on until the domain is used up or exhausted." Elie Halévy, *The Growth of Philosophical Radicalism* (554 pp. Boston: The Beacon Press, 1955), p. 60.

4. The description of each category permits objective and reliable classification so that different observers can place the same acts in the same categories.

MODEL FOR THE CLASSIFICATION OF DELINQUENCY

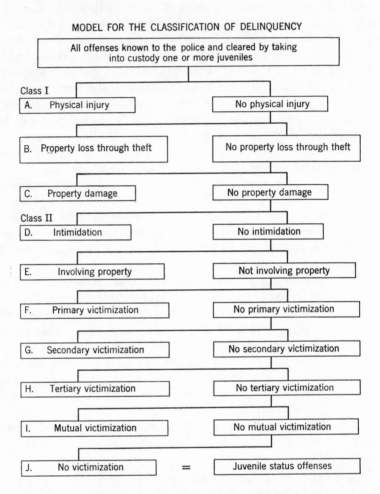

All offenses known to the police and cleared by taking into custody one or more juveniles

Class I
A.   Physical injury | No physical injury

B.   Property loss through theft | No property loss through theft

C.   Property damage | No property damage

Class II
D.   Intimidation | No intimidation

E.   Involving property | Not involving property

F.   Primary victimization | No primary victimization

G.   Secondary victimization | No secondary victimization

H.   Tertiary victimization | No tertiary victimization

I.   Mutual victimization | No mutual victimization

J.   No victimization   =   Juvenile status offenses

A Class I offense contains either physical injury, property theft, or property damage but could conceivably possess all these characteristics. An offense that contains none of these variables is subsumed under Class II. Thus, within Class I there are seven possible combinations in a delinquency event. It appeared to be both theoretically logical and empirically efficient to reduce these seven possible combinations to three—Injury, Theft, and Damage—because:

(a) Some of the combinations have no or very few cases in our sample; (*b*) we made *a priori* assumptions that the community in general, the police, and the courts consider physical injury more serious than theft or damage; (*c*) criminal statutes provide more severe penalties for most offenses against the person than for most offenses against property; (*d*) judicial sentencing practices reflect this same attitude; (*e*) preliminary runs of the scaling analysis of seriousness showed significantly higher weights applied to injury cases than theft and damage, in that order; and (*f*) none of the subsidiary dimensions of any priority allocation would be lost in the final scoring of an offense regardless of the sequential ordering of the classification.

The procedure adopted is shown in Table 6 which indicates that if an offense possessed any bodily injury, regardless of the presence of other characteristics, it was assigned to Category A. If an offense lacked bodily harm but contained theft it was assigned to Category B, and if an offense lacked both harm and theft but caused damage it was assigned to Category C. Although this classificatory procedure does not statistically eliminate the scoring of combinations, because any weights applied to a delinquency event should be additive, certain facts are masked by the titles in the classification. It is still true that Category A offenses may or may not contain theft, or they may or may not contain damage, and that Category B offenses may or may not contain damage. Despite the fact that our choice of ordering offenses by allocating priority to Injury, then to Theft, and then Damage is logical and efficient, we also sought to determine the optimum procedure, where optimum is defined as masking the least amount of information in the classification.

TABLE 6. Classification Procedure

Number of Combinations	CHARACTERISTICS OF THE OFFENSE			CATEGORY PLACEMENT	
	Physical Injury	Property Theft	Property Damage	Category	Title
1	Injury	Theft	Damage	A	Injury
2	Injury	Theft	No damage	A	Injury
3	Injury	No theft	Damage	A	Injury
4	Injury	No theft	No damage	A	Injury
5	No injury	Theft	Damage	B	Theft
6	No injury	Theft	No damage	B	Theft
7	No injury	No theft	Damage	C	Damage
8	No injury	No theft	No damage	D–J	Not index categories

To illustrate the process of arriving at the best sorting sequence, we shall use the following abbreviations:

I = offense with injury,
T = offense with theft,
D = offense with damage.

A sequence is a triple of letters separated by colons. I:T:D, therefore, denotes the fact that the sorting sequence should be first for injury, then for theft, then for damage. Although this is the sequence actually used in the present study, there are six different ones that could have been used:

I:T:D
I:D:T:
T:I:D
T:D:I
D:T:I
D:I:T

Each of these sorting sequences could mask certain information in a classification. If an offense has only one characteristic no masking

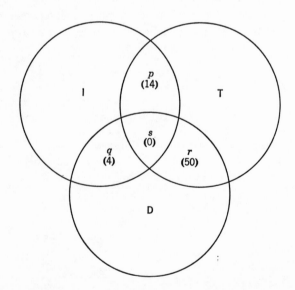

FIGURE 1.   *The overlap in a classification by bodily injury, property loss, and property damage.*

TABLE 7. *Optional Assignments of Masked Characteristics of Offenses*

SETS OF SORTING SEQUENCES	NUMBER OF OPTIONAL ASSIGNMENTS		
	I (Injury)	T (Theft)	D (Damage)
I:T:D	$\cdots$	$p + s$	$q + r + s$
I:D:T	$\cdots$	$p + r + s$	$q + s$
T:I:D	$p + s$	$\cdots$	$q + r + s$
T:D:I	$p + q + s$	$\cdots$	$r + s$
D:T:I	$p + q + s$	$r + s$	$\cdots$
D:I:T	$q + s$	$p + r + s$	$\cdots$

arises; but if an offense has multiple characteristics masking is bound to arise. Figure 1 and Table 7 show the number of characteristics concealed by each sorting sequence, where in each event grouping

p = injury and theft,
q = injury and damage,
r = theft and damage,
s = injury, theft, and damage.

If we accept the assumption that it is worse to mask an injury, next worse to mask a theft, and least serious to mask damage, then it is possible to apply any kind of weight to the number of masked characteristics which are shown on Table 7. The weighted number would represent the judged seriousness of the masked characteristic. Thus, if weights a, b, c are applied to the characteristic concealed by the classification sequence, damage = a, theft = $a + b$, and injury = $a + b + c$ (where a, b, c are all greater than zero), injury is not only considered the most serious offense but its being masked causes the most serious loss of information. The formula used for determining the total amount of concealment relative to any weighing scheme that accepts these assumptions is

$$\sum_{i=1}^{k} W_i N_i.$$

This procedure, applied to the sorting sequence possibilities in Table 7 yields the following results:

I:T:D   Optimum sorting sequence

I:D:T   Adequate sorting sequences
T:I:D
T:D:I
D:I:T

D:T:I   Poorest sorting sequence

To extend the example to the present study, we may note that $p =$ 14 cases, $q = 4$, $r = 50$, and $s = 0$. If, for purposes of illustration, we suppose that $a = b = c = 1$, the following results emerge from application of the formula to the various sets:

SETS OF SORTING SEQUENCE		HYPOTHETICAL WEIGHTED NUMBER OF MASKED CHARACTERISTICS
I:T:D	=	118
I:D:T	=	122
T:I:D	=	132
T:D:I	=	150
D:I:T	=	190
D:T:I	=	204

The conclusion, therefore, is that the sorting sequence finally adopted is the optimum of the six considered. It is important to emphasize that this sort does not depend on exact weights chosen, for all that is required is a system for ranking the weights, and that the I:T:D sort is best, independent of the actual number of multiple characteristics.

Finally, as we have indicated, seven categories are possible for offenses involving injury, theft, and damage. In Chapter 18 we refer to these possibilities as providing subindices that might be useful to police departments and researchers. It should be noted that the A, B, C categories can always be obtained by grouping of the seven categories according to the priority allocation of the model employed in the present analysis.

In order to illustrate the principles of our classification the following descriptions are given.

CLASS I OFFENSES

Category A. Bodily Injury. Any offense, regardless of its legal title, that produces bodily injury to one or more victims is included in this category. The amount of injury may vary from "minor" to "treated and discharged," "hospitalization," and death. (For definitions of these and other terms, see Appendix C.) There must be some victim in these cases. Almost all the offenses involve primary victimization although mutual victimization is possible. Secondary or tertiary victimization is not possible; property may or may not be stolen or damaged; there may or may not be intimidation preceding the physical injury; and there may or may not be a sex violation.

Category B. Property Theft. Any offense, regardless of its legal title, that does not produce physical injury to the victim, but which involves the loss of property through theft, is included in this category. The value of the amount stolen may vary from less than one dollar to an undesignated upper limit. Most of the offenses have primary or secondary victimization, although some are tertiary. There must be some victim; mutual victimization is not possible. The property stolen may or may not be damaged, and there may or may not be intimidation.

Category C. Property Damage. Any offense, regardless of its legal label, that does not produce (a) physical injury to the victim or (b) loss of property through theft, but does include damage to property, is included in this category. The amount of the damage may vary from less than one dollar to any upper limit. Victimization may be primary, secondary, or tertiary, but not mutual; there must be some victim and there may or may not be intimidation.

CLASS II OFFENSES

Category D. Intimidation. Regardless of its legal title, any offense that does not produce (a) physical injury to the victim, (b) property theft, or (c) property damage, but does involve some form of intimidation, is included in this category. Intimidation may be by verbal threats, the display of a fist or weapon as an instrument of potential harm, or the use of physical restraint. Victimization is usually primary but could be secondary or tertiary.

Category E. With Property Loss Threatened. Regardless of its legal title, any offense that does not produce (a) physical injury to the victim, (b) property theft, (c) property damage, or (d) intimidation, but does involve the threatened loss of property, is included in this category. Victimization may be primary, secondary, or tertiary.

Category F. Primary Victimization Only. Any offense that does not involve (a) physical injury to the victim, (b) property theft, (c) property damage, (d) intimidation, or (e) threatened loss of property, but does involve a personalized victim, is included in this category. By definition all other types of victimization are excluded.

Category G. Secondary Victimization Only. Any offense that does not involve (a) physical injury to the victim, (b) property theft, (c) property damage, (d) intimidation, (e) threatened loss of property, or (f) a personalized victim but does involve secondary victimization is included in this category. Secondary victimization generally refers to commercial establishments, such as department stores, railroads, theaters, chain stores, and churches. The victim is impersonalized but not so diffusive as to include the community at large.

Category H. Tertiary Victimization Only. Any offense that does not involve (a) physical injury to the victim, (b) property theft, (c) property damage, (d) intimidation, (e) threatened loss of property, (f) a personalized victim, or (g) secondary victimization, but does involve tertiary victimization, is included in this category. Tertiary refers to a very diffusive victimization that extends to the community at large and includes offenses against the public order, social harmony, or the administration of government. Regulatory offenses and violations of city ordinances are typical.

Category I. Mutual Victimization Only. Any offense that does not involve (a) physical injury to the victim, (b) property theft, (c) property damage, (d) intimidation, (e) threatened loss of property, (f) a personalized victim, (g) secondary victimization, or (h) tertiary victimization. The category refers to those cases in which the participants engage in mutually consensual acts that are violations of the law, for example, fornication, adultery, or statutory rape.

Category J. No Victimization Only. Any offense that does not involve (a) physical injury to the victim, (b) property theft, (c) property damage, (d) intimidation, (e) threatened loss of property, (f) a personalized victim, (g) secondary victimization, (h) tertiary victimization, or (i) mutual victimization, but does involve what is designated as no victimization, is included in this category. These are offenses that cannot be committed by an adult and to which we have previously referred as "juvenile status" offenses.

UNIFORM CRIME CLASSIFICATION COMPARED

In view of earlier comments on the index value of the classification of offenses used in the tabulations in Uniform Crime Reports it may be of interest to see how it compares with the one used in this research. Tables 8 and 9 show the results of this comparison. Classes I and

TABLE 8. Number, Per Cent, and Rate of Offenses by Uniform Crime Code and Class I (Categories A, B, C) Offenses

| | CATEGORY | | | | | |
	A Bodily Injury N	B Theft N	C Damage N	Total N	%	Rate* per 10,000 × 10
UNIFORM CRIME CODE						
Part 1 Offenses						
Criminal homicide	2	...	...	2	0.4	0.6
Rape	5	...	...	5	1.0	1.5
Robbery	17	10	...	27	5.4	7.9
Aggravated assault	30	...	...	30	5.9	8.8
Burglary	...	66	7	73	14.5	21.3
Larceny	1	174	2	177	35.1	51.7
Auto theft	...	35	...	35	6.9	10.2
Total Part 1 Offenses	55	285	9	349	69.2	
Rate	16.1	83.3	2.6			102.0
Part 2 Offenses						
Other assaults	83	...	1	84	16.7	24.5
Forgery & counterfeiting	...	1	...	1	0.2	0.3
Embezzlement & fraud	...	1	...	1	0.2	0.3
Stolen property	...	1	...	1	0.2	0.3
Sex offenses	4	...	...	4	0.8	1.2
Disorderly conduct	1	...	1	2	0.4	0.6
Other traffic & motor vehicle law violations	...	...	1	1	0.2	0.3
Trespassing	...	...	2	2	0.4	0.6
Malicious mischief	...	...	51	51	10.1	14.9
Other offenses	2	...	6	8	1.6	2.3
Total Part 2 Offenses	90	3	62	155	30.8	
Rate	26.3	0.9	18.1			45.3
Total						
N	145	288	71	504		
%	28.8	57.1	14.1		100.0	
Rate	42.4	84.1	20.8			147.3

* Rates based on 342,254 juvenile population 7–17 years in Philadelphia, 1960.

TABLE 9. *Number, Per Cent, and Rate of Offenses by Uniform Crime Code and Class II (Categories D to J) Offenses*

CATEGORY

UNIFORM CRIME CODE	D Intimidation N	E Property Loss Threatened N	F Primary Victimization N	G Secondary Victimization N	H Tertiary Victimization N	I Mutual Victimization N	J Juvenile Status Offenses N	Total N	Total %	Rate* per 10,000 × 10
Part 1 Offenses										
Rape	3	...	...	...	...	...	...	3	0.4	0.9
Robbery	2	...	...	...	...	...	...	2	0.2	0.6
Burglary	...	7	...	...	...	...	...	7	0.9	2.0
Larceny-theft	...	7	...	...	...	...	...	7	0.9	2.0
Auto theft	...	3	...	...	...	...	...	3	0.4	0.9
Total Part 1 Offenses	5	17						22	2.8	
Rate	1.5	4.9								6.4
Part 2 Offenses										
Other assaults	3	...	2	...	...	...	...	5	0.6	1.5
Weapons	...	...	...	...	33	...	...	33	4.0	9.6
Sex offenses	3	...	14	...	...	19	...	36	4.4	10.5
Liquor law violations	...	...	...	...	29	...	...	29	3.6	8.5
Drunkenness	...	...	...	...	32	...	...	32	4.0	9.3
Disorderly conduct	7	1	16	11	63	...	...	98	12.1	28.6
Vagrancy	...	...	2	...	...	...	...	2	0.2	0.6

TABLE 9. Number, Per Cent, and Rate of Offenses by Uniform Crime Code and Class II (Categories D to J) Offenses (Continued)

	CATEGORY							Total		Rate* per
	D	E Prop-erty Loss Threat-ened	F Primary Victimi-zation	G Second-ary Victimi-zation	H Tertiary Victimi-zation	I Mutual Victimi-zation	J Juvenile Status Offenses			
UNIFORM CRIME CODE	Intimi-dation N	N	N	N	N	N	N	N	%	10,000 × 10
Gambling	...	...	...	...	8	...	...	8	1.0	2.3
Violations of road & driving laws	...	...	...	...	1	...	...	1	0.1	0.3
Other traffic & motor vehicle law violations	...	...	...	...	1	...	...	1	0.1	0.3
Truancy	...	...	...	...	...	...	168	168	20.8	49.1
Trespassing	...	...	8	24	10	...	...	42	5.2	12.3
Incorrigible	...	...	...	...	...	...	41	41	5.1	12.0
Runaway	...	...	...	...	...	...	245	245	30.3	71.6
Malicious mischief	...	3	3	2	5	...	...	13	1.6	3.8
Other offenses	11	1	...	...	20	...	...	33	4.1	9.6
Total Part 2 Offenses	24	5	46	37	202	19	454	787	97.2	229.9
Rate	7.0	1.5	13.4	10.8	59.0	5.6	132.6			229.9
Total										
N	29	22	46	37	202	19	454	809	100.0	236.3
%	3.6	2.7	5.7	4.6	25.0	2.3	56.1			
Rate	8.5	6.4	13.4	10.8	59.0	5.6	132.6			236.3

* Rates based on 342,254 juvenile population 7–17 years in Philadelphia, 1960.

159

II refer to our classification and Parts 1 and 2 to the one used in Uniform Crime Reports before 1958.

There is considerable overlap of course. Of the 371 Part 1 offenses, 349 (94%) fall into our Class I and of the 942 Part 2 offenses, 787 (83%) fall into our Class II. But, 155 of our Class I offenses are in the Part 2 categories, and 22 Part 1 offenses are in our Class II. These 22 include 3 assaults with intent to rape; 2 attempted robberies, accompanied by verbal threats only; 7 attempted burglaries; 7 attempted larcenies; and 3 attempted motor vehicle thefts. In none of them did physical harm or even temporary property loss occur. The 155 Part 2 offenses found in our Class I are mostly assaults and batteries (84, or 54%) and malicious mischief (51, or 33%). As will be noted in later chapters, a large number of these simple assaults resulted in as serious or more serious bodily injury to victims than did some aggravated assaults among Part 1 offenses, and many of the cases of malicious mischief caused as much or more property loss through damage than did some robberies, burglaries, and larcenies in the Part 1 classes.

Beginning with 1958, certain classes and subclasses of the Part 1 offenses known to the police were selected as "index crimes" by Uniform Crime Reports. Manslaughters by negligence and larcenies of values under 50 dollars were excluded, as was statutory rape, the last of which was transferred to Part 2. Of the 177 larcenies in our Class I, 166 were of values under 50 dollars. The following table shows in summary fashion how our classification differs from the UCR one.

TABLE 10. *The Study Classification and the Uniform Classification Compared*

UNIFORM CRIME CLASSIFICATION	CLASS I	CLASS II	TOTAL
Part 1 All offenses	349	22	371
(Of these, "Index crimes")	(183)	(22)	(205)
Part 2	155	787	942
	504	809	1313

In brief, where our classification places 504 offenses in a class that we operationally assumed to contain offenses useful for index purposes, the Uniform Crime Classification system would place only 349 of the offenses in that class, and only 183, if its "index crimes" were alone considered.

Offense rates per 10,000 juveniles in the 1960 population of Philadelphia are also given in the tables. The over-all rate for the

TABLE 11. *Number, Per Cent, and Rate of Juvenile Offenders by Uniform Code and Class I (Categories A, B, C) Offenses*

| | CATEGORY | | | | | |
UNIFORM CRIME CODE	A Bodily Injury *N*	B Theft *N*	C Damage *N*	 Total *N*	 %	Rate* per 10,000 × 10
Part 1 Offenses						
Criminal homicide	6	...	...	6	0.6	1.8
Rape	7	...	...	7	0.7	2.0
Robbery	37	18	...	55	5.8	16.1
Aggravated assault	53	...	...	53	5.6	15.5
Burglary	...	130	12	142	15.0	41.5
Larceny	1	341	2	344	36.2	100.5
Auto theft	...	76	...	76	8.0	22.2
Total Part 1 Offenses	104	565	14	683	71.9	
Rate	30.4	165.1	4.1			199.6
Part 2 Offenses						
Other assaults	141	...	6	147	15.5	43.0
Forgery & counterfeiting	...	1	...	1	0.1	0.3
Embezzlement & fraud	...	2	...	2	0.2	0.6
Stolen property	...	1	...	1	0.1	0.3
Sex offenses	5	...	...	5	0.5	1.4
Disorderly conduct	2	...	3	5	0.5	1.4
Other traffic & motor vehicle law violations	...	...	1	1	0.1	0.3
Trespassing	...	...	4	4	0.4	1.2
Malicious mischief	...	...	90	90	9.5	26.3
Other offenses	2	...	9	11	1.2	3.2
Total Part 2 Offenses	150	4	113	267	28.1	
Rate	43.8	1.2	33.0			78.0
Total						
N	254	569	127	950		
%	26.7	59.9	13.4		100.0	
Rate	74.2	166.3	37.1			277.6

* Rates based on 342,254 juvenile population 7–17 years in Philadelphia, 1960.

TABLE 12. *Number, Per Cent, and Rate of Juvenile Offenders by Uniform Crime Code and Class II (Categories D to J) Offenses*

UNIFORM CRIME CODE	CATEGORY							Total		Rate* per
	D Intimidation N	E Property Loss Threatened N	F Primary Victimization N	G Secondary Victimization N	H Tertiary Victimization N	I Mutual Victimization N	J Juvenile Status Offenses N	N	%	10,000 × 10
Part 1 Offenses										
Rape	4	...	...	...	...	...	...	4	0.3	1.2
Robbery	7	...	...	...	...	...	...	7	0.6	2.0
Burglary	...	12	...	...	...	...	...	12	1.0	3.5
Larceny-theft	...	9	...	...	...	...	...	9	0.8	2.6
Auto theft	...	3	...	...	...	...	...	3	0.3	0.9
Total Part 1 Offenses	11	24	...	...	...	...	...	35	3.0	10.2
Rate	3.2	7.0								10.2
Part 2 Offenses										
Other assaults	5	...	2	...	...	...	...	7	0.6	2.0
Weapons	...	...	...	...	44	...	...	44	3.8	12.9
Sex offenses	4	...	15	...	...	29	...	48	4.2	14.0
Liquor law violations	...	...	...	...	45	...	...	45	3.9	13.1
Drunkenness	...	...	...	...	38	...	...	38	3.3	11.1
Disorderly conduct	9	1	50	22	197	...	...	279	24.4	81.5
Vagrancy	...	...	2	...	...	...	...	2	0.2	0.6
Gambling	...	...	...	...	18	...	...	18	1.6	5.3

TABLE 12. *Number, Per Cent, and Rate of Juvenile Offenders by Uniform Crime Code and Class II (Categories D to J) Offenses (Continued)*

UNIFORM CRIME CODE	CATEGORY							Total		Rate* per
	D Intimidation N	E Property Loss Threatened N	F Primary Victimization N	G Secondary Victimization N	H Tertiary Victimization N	I Mutual Victimization N	J Juvenile Status Offenses N	N	%	10,000 × 10
Violations of road & driving laws	...	...	...	...	1	...	...	1	0.1	0.3
Other traffic & motor vehicle law violations	...	...	...	...	1	...	...	1	0.1	0.3
Truancy	...	...	...	...	...	...	168	168	14.7	49.1
Trespassing	...	...	13	47	30	...	...	90	7.9	26.3
Incorrigible	...	...	...	...	...	...	41	41	3.6	12.0
Runaway	...	...	...	...	...	...	245	245	21.4	71.6
Malicious mischief	...	6	8	7	9	...	...	30	2.6	8.8
Other offenses	18	1	1	...	32	...	...	52	4.6	15.2
Total Part 2 Offenses	36	8	91	76	415	29	454	1109	97.0	
Rate	10.5	2.3	26.6	22.2	121.3	8.5	132.7			324.1
Total *N*	47	32	91	76	415	29	454	1144		
%	4.1	2.8	8.0	6.6	36.3	2.5	39.7		100.0	
Rate	13.7	9.3	26.6	22.2	121.3	8.5	132.7			334.3

* Rates based on 342,254 juvenile population 7–17 years in Philadelphia, 1960.

163

1313 offenses is 383.6. If we had used the old UCR system, the Part 1 rate would have been 108.4 and the Part 2 rate 275.2. Had the present UCR system been used, the Part 1 rate would have been 59.8 and the Part 2 rate 324.0.

The number, rate, and percentage of juvenile offenders are not of primary concern in the present volume and will be analyzed later in detail. But as Tables 11 and 12 show, the relative distributions of Parts 1 and 2 and of Classes I and II offenders are not significantly different from the same distributions for offenses. The total rate for the 2094 offenders is 611.9 and the subclass rates are in the same proportions greater than the rates for offenses.

11

The Discovery of Offenses

The preceding chapters have, we believe, sufficiently described the background of our research, its design and the nature of our data. In this and subsequent chapters, these data will be analyzed in some detail in the light of the assumptions that are basic to our study.

CLASSES AND CATEGORIES OF OFFENSES

One of our underlying assumptions has been that offenses involving bodily injury, property loss, or damage have greater likelihood of being entered in official police statistics than offenses not having these attributes. As noted previously, there are no absolutely reliable data on the differential reportability of offenses.[1] We have been able, however, to obtain information on who discovered offenses that initially or ultimately became known to the police. Sometimes the victim reports the offense, or a family member, friend, or neighbor reports it for him. If the police do not discover the offenses, it is obvious that someone else discovers and reports it and thus makes it

---

[1] In addition to the previous references on "hidden delinquency," an interesting effort has been made to compare official police data with information about delinquent offenses recorded by detached workers in Chicago. See John M. Wise, "A Comparison of Sources of Data as Indexes of Delinquent Behavior," M.A. thesis, University of Chicago, 1962, Unpublished. Relative to our classification of delinquency, it is especially interesting to note from this Chicago study that, with the exception of "creating a disturbance" and rape (including statutory rape), "generally, it is the more serious offenses which have the higher [police] detection rates . . ." (p. 44).

known to the public authorities. On the other hand, some offenses become known principally through police action. Some of these, such as burglary, robbery, and other relatively serious offenses, would most likely have been reported to the police anyway, at some later time; others, such as carrying concealed and deadly weapons, become known to the authorities almost entirely through police activity. Because we have assumed that offenses which become known to the police chiefly through police action are unreliable for index purposes, we have hypothesized the following: *A significantly higher proportion of Class I offenses than of Class II offenses are discovered by persons other than the police.* If the data confirm this hypothesis, they will also provide empirical justification for part of the theoretical rationale underlying the classificatory scheme which we have adopted. Tables 13, 14, and 15 show the distribution of Class I and Class II offenses according to the groups which discovered them. In chi-square analyses of 2 x 2 tables showing Class I and Class II offenses by police and nonpolice discovery, significant differences emerge ($\chi^2 = 65.55$; d.f. $= 1$; $P < .001$), for a higher proportion of Class II offenses (37%) compared to Class I offenses (16%) are discovered by the police. Contrariwise, 84 per cent of Class I offenses and only 63 per

TABLE 13.   Number of Class I and Class II Offenses by Category and Discovering Group

| | DISCOVERING GROUP | | | | | | | |
| | Police | | | Nonpolice | | | | |
CLASS AND CATEGORY OF OFFENSE	Direct	Indi-rect	Total	Vic-tim	Repre-sentative	Other	Total	TOTAL
Class I								
A. Phys. injury	6	1	7	86	1	51	138	145
B. Prop. loss	20	45	65	122	61	40	223	288
C. Prop. damage	4	6	10	35	10	16	61	71
Class I Total	30	52	82	243	72	107	422	504
Class II								
D. Intimidation	. . .	. . .	. . .	23	. . .	6	29	29
E. Involving prop.	7	. . .	7	7	4	4	15	22
F. Prim. vict.	7	. . .	7	36	. . .	3	39	46
G. Second. vict.	5	. . .	5	. . .	21	11	32	37
H. Tert. vict.	84	33	117	. . .	6	79	85	202
I. Mutual vict.	3	1	4	. . .	. . .	15	15	19
J. Juv. status	5	157	162	. . .	. . .	292	292	454
Class II Total	111	191	302	66	31	410	507	809
Total	141	243	384	309	103	517	929	1313

TABLE 14. Per Cent of Class I and Class II Offenses by Category and Discovering Group

	DISCOVERING GROUP							
	Police			Nonpolice				
CLASS AND CATEGORY OF OFFENSE	Direct	Indirect	Total	Vic-tim	Repre-sentative	Other	Total	TOTAL
Class I								
A. Phys. injury	4.1	0.7	4.8	59.3	0.7	35.2	95.2	100.0
B. Prop. loss	6.9	15.6	22.5	42.4	21.2	13.9	77.5	100.0
C. Prop. damage	5.6	8.5	14.1	49.3	14.1	22.5	85.9	100.0
Class I Total	6.0	10.3	16.3	48.2	14.3	21.2	83.7	100.0
Class II								
D. Intimidation	...	...	...	79.3	...	20.7	100.0	100.0
E. Involving prop.	31.8	...	31.8	31.8	18.2	18.2	68.2	100.0
F. Prim. vict.	15.2	...	15.2	78.3	...	6.5	84.8	100.0
G. Second vict.	13.5	...	13.5	...	56.8	29.7	86.5	100.0
H. Tert. vict.	41.6	16.3	57.9	...	3.0	39.1	42.1	100.0
I. Mutual vict.	15.8	5.3	21.1	...	...	78.9	78.9	100.0
J. Juv. status	1.1	34.6	35.7	...	...	64.3	64.3	100.0
Class II Total	13.7	23.6	37.3	8.2	3.8	50.7	62.7	100.0
Total	10.7	18.6	29.3	23.5	7.8	39.4	70.7	10.00

TABLE 15. Number and Per Cent of Offenses by Class and Discovering Group

	DISCOVERING GROUP					
	Police		Nonpolice		TOTAL	
OFFENSES	N	%	N	%	N	%
Class I	82	21.4 (16.3)	422	45.4 (83.7)	504	38.4 (100.0)
Class II	302	78.6 (37.3)	507	54.6 (62.7)	809	61.6 (100.0)
Total	384	100.0 (29.3)	929	100.0 (70.7)	1313	100.0

$\chi^2 = 65.55$; d.f. $= 1$; $P < .001$.

TABLE 16. Number of Juveniles in Class I and Class II Offenses, by Category and Discovering Group

| | DISCOVERING GROUP | | | | | | | |
| | Police | | | Nonpolice | | | | |
CLASS AND CATEGORY OF OFFENSE	Direct	Indirect	Total	Victim	Repre-sentative	Other	Total	TOTAL
Class I								
A. Phys. injury	7	1	8	162	4	80	246	254
B. Prop. loss	37	102	139	224	121	85	430	569
C. Prop. damage	11	8	19	61	14	33	108	127
Class I Total	55	111	166	447	139	198	784	950
Class II								
D. Intimidation	...	...	...	37	...	10	47	47
E. Involving prop.	11	...	11	8	7	6	21	32
F. Prim. vict.	8	...	8	78	...	5	83	91
G. Second. vict.	11	...	11	...	38	27	65	76
H. Tert. vict.	155	43	198	...	12	205	217	415
I. Mutual vict.	5	1	6	...	...	23	23	29
J. Juv. status	5	157	162	...	...	292	292	454
Class II Total	195	201	396	123	57	568	748	1144
Grand Total	250	312	562	570	196	766	1532	2094

TABLE 17. Per Cent of Juveniles in Class I and Class II Offenses, by Category and Discovering Group

| | DISCOVERING GROUP | | | | | | | |
| | Police | | | Nonpolice | | | | |
CLASS AND CATEGORY OF OFFENSE	Direct	Indirect	Total	Victim	Repre-sentative	Other	Total	TOTAL
Class I								
A. Phys. injury	2.8	0.4	3.2	63.7	1.6	31.5	96.8	100.0
B. Prop. loss	6.5	17.9	24.4	39.4	21.3	14.9	75.6	100.0
C. Prop. damage	8.7	6.3	15.0	48.0	11.0	26.0	85.0	100.0
Class I Total	5.8	11.7	17.5	47.1	14.6	20.8	82.5	100.0
Class II								
D. Intimidation	...	...	...	78.7	...	21.3	100.0	100.0
E. Involving prop.	34.4	...	34.4	25.0	21.9	18.7	65.6	100.0
F. Prim. vict.	8.8	...	8.8	85.7	...	5.5	91.2	100.0
G. Second. vict.	14.5	...	14.5	...	50.0	35.5	85.5	100.0
H. Tert. vict.	37.3	10.4	47.7	...	2.9	49.4	52.3	100.0
I. Mutual vict.	17.2	3.5	20.7	...	...	79.3	79.3	100.0
J. Juv. status	1.1	34.6	35.7	...	...	64.3	64.3	100.0
Class II Total	17.0	17.6	34.6	10.8	5.0	49.6	65.4	100.0
Total	11.9	14.9	26.8	27.2	9.4	36.6	73.2	100.0

TABLE 18. Number and Per Cent of Offenses by Class and Discovering Group

| | DISCOVERING GROUP | | | | | |
| | Police | | Nonpolice | | TOTAL | |
OFFENDERS	N	$\%$	N	$\%$	N	$\%$
Class I	166	29.5 (17.5)	784	51.2 (82.5)	950	45.4 (100.0)
Class II	396	70.5 (34.6)	748	48.8 (65.4)	1144	54.6 (100.0)
Total	562	100.0 (26.8)	1532	100.0 (73.2)	2094	100.0

$\chi^2 = 77.68$; d.f. $= 1$; $P < .001$.

cent of Class II offenses are discovered by groups other than the police. The hypothesis is confirmed and thereby strengthens the *a priori* division of offenses into two classes. Table 16, 17, and 18 show the same kinds of distributions of offense classes and discovering groups for the number or percentage of the 2094 juveniles who were involved in the 1313 offenses. Frequency distributions for the number of offenders are similar to those for the number of offenses, and chi-

TABLE 19. Number and Per Cent of Class I Offenses, by Discovering Group and Number of Offenders per Offense

	DISCOVERING GROUP														
	Police						Nonpolice								
NUMBER OF OFFENDERS	Direct		Indirect		Total		Victim		Victim Representative		Other		Total		TOTAL	
	N	$\%$	N	$\%$	N	$\%$	N	$\%$	N	$\%$	N	$\%$	N	$\%$	N	$\%$
One	8	3.3	16	6.6	24	9.9	126	52.3	33	13.7	58	24.1	217	90.1	241	100.0
Two	15	11.0	18	13.1	33	24.1	61	44.5	19	13.9	24	17.5	104	75.9	137	100.0
Three	5	8.5	8	13.5	13	22.0	30	50.9	9	15.2	7	11.9	46	78.0	59	100.0
Four	1	2.5	5	12.5	6	15.0	11	27.5	8	20.0	15	37.5	34	85.0	40	100.0
Five or more	1	3.7	5	18.5	6	22.2	15	55.6	3	11.1	3	11.1	21	77.8	27	100.0
Total	30	6.0	52	10.3	82	16.3	243	48.2	72	14.3	107	21.2	422	83.7	504	100.0

TABLE 20. *Number and Per Cent of Class II Offenses, by Discovering Group and Number of Offenders per Offense*

DISCOVERING GROUP

	Police			Nonpolice				TOTAL
NUMBER OF OFFENDERS	Direct	Indirect	Total	Victim	Victim Repre- sentative	Other	Total	
	N %	N %	N %	N %	N %	N %	N %	N %
One	44 7.1	180 29.2	224 36.3	37 6.0	14 2.3	342 55.4	393 63.7	617 100.0
Two	32 32.7	6 6.1	38 38.8	16 16.3	11 11.2	33 33.7	60 61.2	98 100.0
Three	16 36.4	3 6.8	19 43.2	6 13.6	4 9.1	15 34.1	25 56.8	44 100.0
Four	13 68.4	1 5.3	14 73.7	1 5.3	1 5.3	3 15.7	5 26.3	19 100.0
Five or more	6 19.4	1 3.2	7 22.6	6 19.4	1 3.2	17 54.8	24 77.4	31 100.0
Total	111 13.7	191 23.6	302 37.3	66 8.2	31 3.8	410 50.7	507 62.7	809 100.0

square analyses reveal similar significant differences ($\chi^2 = 77.68$; d.f. $= 1$; $P < .001$).

The number of juveniles involved in an offense does not appear to vary between groups. Tables 19, 20, and 21 show these distributions by Class I and Class II offenses. Nonpolice discovery groups have

TABLE 21. *Number and Per Cent of Offenders Discovered by Police and Nonpolice, by Class of Offense*

	POLICE DISCOVERY		NONPOLICE DISCOVERY	
NUMBER OF OFFENDERS	Class I (A)	Class II (B)	Class I (C)	Class II (D)
	N %	N %	N %	N %
1	24 29.3	224 74.2	217 51.4	393 77.6
2	33 40.2	38 12.6	104 24.6	60 11.8
3	13 15.9	19 6.3	46 10.9	25 4.9
4	6 7.3	14 4.6	34 8.1	5 1.0
5 or more	6 7.3	7 2.3	21 5.0	24 4.7
Total	82 100.0	302 100.0	422 100.0	507 100.0

For columns A × B: $\chi^2 = 59.54$; d.f. $= 4$; $P < .001$.
For columns A × C: $\chi^2 = 15.36$; d.f. $= 4$; $P < .001$.
For columns C × D: $\chi^2 = 83.43$; d.f. $= 4$; $P < .01$.
For columns B × D: $\chi^2 = 14.61$; d.f. $= 4$; $P < .01$.

higher frequency of discovery than the police for both Class I and Class II offenses when the number of offenders in an offense is one, two, three, five, or more.[2] However, regardless of the number of offenders participating in an offense, nonpolice discovery remains significantly higher for Class I offenses compared to Class II offenses ($\chi^2 = 83.43$; d.f. $= 4$; $P < .01$). Except when five or more offenders appear in Class I offenses, the percentage of offenses discovered by the police is consistently and significantly higher in Class II offenses no matter how many offenders participate in an offense. Police discovery in Class I offenses (16%) occurs with less than half the frequency that it does in Class II offenses (37%). This ratio remains constant when we examine direct and indirect police discovery, for 6 per cent of Class I offenses compared to 14 per cent of Class II offenses are discovered by direct police activity, and 10 per cent of Class I compared to 24 per cent of Class II are discovered by indirect police activity. Thus, it seems to make no difference how the police discover an offense, for Class I offenses will in any case be less frequently discovered by them than will Class II offenses. Moreover, for both classes, the ratio of indirect police discovery remains consistently twice as great as direct police discovery.

Several particular subgroups are interesting. Police discovery is lowest when only one offender is involved in a Class I offense (10%) and highest when four offenders participate in a Class II offense (74%). Thus, for the largest group of Class I offenses, which have only one offender (241, or 47% of the 504 in Class I), 90 per cent are discovered by nonpolice groups. This is what we expected, and the finding adds empirical confirmation to the argument that most Class I offenses are unaffected by police activity. Furthermore, the difference in police compared to nonpolice discovery between Class I and Class II one-offender delinquency is significant. In Class II one-offender cases, the police make discovery in 36 per cent and nonpolice in 64 per cent. Victims discover Class I offenses in 48 per cent of the cases compared to only 8 per cent in Class II offenses. Discovery by the victim is especially striking in cases involving only one offender: Class I has 52 per cent and Class II only 6 per cent.

Examination of the distribution of discovery groups within offense categories reveals some additional variations that require interpretation. For example, of all groups, Category A (Offenses with Bodily

---

[2] Only when there are four offenders in Class II offenses do the police have a higher frequency of discovery. The number of Class II offenses with four offenders is smaller (19) than for any other group and appears to reflect a spurious condition.

Injury) shows the lowest frequency discovered by the police (5%), and consequently the highest percentage discovered by nonpolice groups (95%). The offense category with the highest proportion of offenses discovered by the police is Category H with 58 per cent. Most of these are cases of disorderly conduct and account for 38 per cent (157 of 415) of Category H. No offenses involving only intimidation, Category D, were discovered by the police; however, it must be noted that only 29 offenses are included in this category.

Offense Category B in Class I has a relatively high proportion of offenses discovered by the police (23%) compared to the other two offense categories, A (5%) and C (14%) in this class. As a matter of fact, there are two offense categories, F (15%) and G (14%), in Class II, which have substantially lower proportions than in Category B (23%) discovered by the police. Category B is made up of offenses involving property loss through robberies, larcenies, burglaries, and automobile thefts. It is not unexpected that the police discover some of these offenses while patrolling the streets late at night at times when the victims would not ordinarily become aware of them until the next morning or even sometime later. Through police activity, automobiles are frequently first found to be stolen. A brief analysis of Categories B and C combined reveals that 60 per cent of these theft or damage offenses occurred between 6 P. M. and 9 A. M.; that 85 per cent were committed either on the street (42%) or in commercial establishments (43%), thus leaving only 15 per cent in private dwellings; that victims or their representatives were absent from the scene in 93 per cent of the events discovered by the police and that in nearly two-thirds the victims were still unaware of the offenses when notified by the police.

If police activity alone were responsible for the discovery and consequently the appearance of these offenses in official statistics, we would have to argue, to be consistent with prior contentions, that these offenses should not be included in Class I. However, the mere fact that property losses of substantial value occurred is sufficient reason to retain them in that class, despite the fact that over one-fifth of them are discovered by the police. There is every reason to believe that the offenses would have been discovered by the victims eventually, and that because property has been stolen or damaged they would have reported them. Consequently, the slightly higher proportion of offenses in Category B discovered by the police does not nullify the importance of this category for index purposes. Moreover, it should be kept in mind that nearly 80 per cent of the offenses in Category B were discovered by groups other than the police.

Four-fifths (79%) of the offenses in Category D (Intimidation) are "discovered" by the victim, the rest by other persons in the non-police group. Once again, we must qualify the reasons for not including this group in Class I. The mere fact that certain types of offenses become known to the public authorities only through complaints from groups other than the police is not in itself sufficient justification for inclusion in an index. As we have previously noted, certain types of acts have low degrees of reportability. The fact that only 29 of these offenses appear in our entire sample (2% of the total of 1313 offenses) is sufficient reason to query this group's usefulness for index purposes. When one thinks of the innumerable times that persons are verbally intimidated especially among juveniles, without the presence of any weapon or without harm or loss of property, it would surprise no one that few become known to the police. Intimidation, therefore, without any subsequent physical restraint of liberty, without even the most minor harm through a push or shove and without theft or damage to property, must be a very common occurrence among the juveniles of any community. The small number of such events reported and the multitude of variables that might enter into the willingness or unwillingness to report these offenses are almost totally unpredictable and therefore can hardly be considered useful or valid for index purposes. The character of this type of offense is such that it is obvious that the police could not know of their occurrence either directly or indirectly as initial discoverers.

Offense Categories F and G also have reasonably high proportions discovered by nonpolice groups (85% and 86%, respectively). These, too, are numerically relatively small offense categories totaling 46 and 37 respectively, or 4 per cent and 3 per cent of the total offenses in our sample. The modal group, about one-fourth of Category F, is made up of disorderly conduct cases, and the majority (65%) of offenses in Category G are trespassing. Offenses in these two categories involve no property loss or damage, and it is difficult to determine why and under what circumstances such offenses would be reported to the police at all. The victims' levels of tolerance of annoyance and disturbance presumably would be a clue to understanding the level of reportability, but without the kind of information necessary to establish a tolerance level, we cannot include them in an index. The number of times that juveniles make disturbing noises or trespass on property without the victims' knowing it or reporting it must be extremely high. The small number of these offenses reported to the police may be interpreted as an indication of the infrequency of reporting.

Category I, which comprises only 19, or 1.45 per cent of the total cases, is the only other category in Class II offenses that has a proportion discovered by nonpolice groups (79%) as high as any category in Class I. All Category I cases are sex offenses involving incest, sodomy, fornication, or statutory rape. The consensual or conspiratorial nature of these offenses is confirmed by the fact that none of them was reported to the authorities by the participants. The police discovered a little over one-third of the cases (36%) during the act or through questioning afterwards; and in nearly two-thirds (64%), parents or other relatives were mostly the discoverers and responsible for reporting them to the police. The fact that only 19, or a little over 1 per cent, of such acts appeared in our sample is evidence either that few fornications, statutory rapes, incests, and sodomies occur in our population, or that few are made known to the public authorities. It is the latter interpretation which, in the light of other knowledge about sexual behavior, seems most plausible. The vicissitudes governing the reportability of these offenses make them useless for index purposes.

Offense Category H contains the highest proportion of offenses discovered by the police (58%). All the offenses of carrying or possessing weapons, illegal possession of liquor, and intoxication are found in this category, comprising over two-fifths (42%) of its 202 offenses. These are acts that are most likely to be discovered directly by the police or indirectly through investigatory questioning that follows apprehension of an offender for some other offense. The largest single offense in Category H is disorderly conduct (47, or 23%) and involves disturbing the peace without directly affecting individual victims or commercial establishments. These cases as well as corner lounging (an additional 7%) have a relatively fluid character and their discovery by the police is somewhat adventitious. With no change in the frequency of their real occurrence in a community, an increase in the number of police or in the intensity of their patrols would undoubtedly increase the number of officially recorded offenses of these types.

Offenses in Category E, mostly attempts to commit property offenses, and Category J, runaways, truancies, and incorrigibilities, have relatively high proportions discovered by the police (32% and 36%, respectively). They discover attempted property offenses entirely by direct action. The offenses with no victimization detected by the police are almost entirely discovered through patrol activity or indirectly through questioning. Once again, the small number of cases (22 or 2%) of offenses involving property without loss or damage attests to the fact that either (1) there are few attempts made, or (2) few attempted property offenses are reported by or to the police. It might be argued that if these acts had been completed they would have been reported to the police and that as potential property thefts they should be included in an index. On the other hand, there is equal reason to argue that because no theft or damage actually occurred, either the police or the intended victims would be reluctant to record the violation against a juvenile. This would be true particularly in cases of malicious mischief and larceny. Because there are few cases in Category E, and because one-third of these are discovered by the police, we are led to conclude that most attempts at committing property offenses are not discovered at all, and that of those which are discovered, a high proportion become known as the result of police activity. Consequently, we exclude them on both counts from our index offenses.

The large number, 454 or 35 per cent of Offense Category J, is a different matter. First, we have excluded these offenses from our index class because juvenile status events do not constitute a criminal violation in the ordinary sense. This is the major reason for exclusion. Moreover, next to Category H, this category has the highest proportion of offenses discovered by the police, mostly indirectly.

In general, we have seen that by combining theory regarding discovery of particular offense categories with the hypotheses the theory generates and that are empirically confirmed, Class I offenses emerge as that group least vulnerable to unpredictable, fortuitous discovery and reporting. Class I offenses remain, then, as the most valid and reliable for purposes of constructing a delinquency index. To pursue this argument further, we must examine more details of the process by which both classes of offenses are discovered and officially recorded.

12

Sequence and Locus of Discovery

In order to analyze more fully the relationship between offense categories and how they come to the attention of public authorities, we have divided offense categories and discovering groups into events discovered during and those discovered after the commission of the act. Our assumptions and previous data have led us to hypothesize the following:

(1) *A higher proportion of offenses discovered during the act than after the act are discovered by the police.* We have already established that more offenses are discovered by private persons (929, or 71% of the 1313 cases) than by the police (384, or 29%); and that a significantly higher proportion of Class I (84%) than of Class II offenses (63%) are discovered by private persons.

(2) *A higher proportion of offenses discovered by the police are discovered during rather than after the act.* This hypothesis is a corollary of (1). While recognizing that less than three-tenths of all offenses are discovered by the police, it asserts that most of these are the result of direct police discovery during the act and that relatively few acts will be discovered by the police after their occurrence.

(3) *A higher proportion of offenses discovered by the police than of offenses discovered by nonpolice groups become known during the commission of the act rather than after the act.* This hypothesis follows as a corollary of (2) and suggests that not only are most offenses discovered during the act and by nonpolice groups, but also that when the police discover offenses, it is more likely to occur during the act than when nonpolice groups discover offenses. All three of

these hypotheses emphasize that when offenses become known through police activity the reason is the presence of the police when these acts are committed.

Tables 22–25 permit us to test these hypotheses statistically. Chi-square analyses indicate that all three of the hypotheses are confirmed and that significant variations exist between the time when the offenses are discovered (during/after) and the groups (police/nonpolice) which are responsible for the discoveries. Relative to the first hypothesis, 31 per cent of the 1064 offenses discovered during the act are discovered by the police, compared to 22 per cent discovered by the police among the 249 offenses discovered after the act (Table 26). The difference is significant ($\chi^2 = 7.60$; d.f. = 1; $P < .01$). Findings relative to the second hypothesis strengthen the first for 86 per cent of the 384 offenses discovered by the police were discovered *during* their commission, while only 14 per cent of all offenses discovered by the police were discovered *after* their commission. The third and correlative hypothesis is further confirmed when the proportion of police discovery during the act (86% of the 384) is

TABLE 22. Number of Offenses Discovered during the Act, by Class, Category, and Discovering Group

CLASS AND CATEGORY OF OFFENSES	DISCOVERING GROUP							
	Police			Nonpolice				
	Direct	Indirect	Total	Victim	Victim Repre-sentative	Other	Total	TOTAL
Class I								
A. Phys. injury	6	...	6	86	...	17	103	109
B. Prop. loss	14	3	17	39	44	20	103	120
C. Prop. damage	4	5	9	31	8	12	51	60
Class I Total	24	8	32	156	52	49	257	289
Class II								
D. Intimidation	...	...	...	22	...	....	22	22
E. Involving prop.	7	...	7	7	4	3	14	21
F. Prim. vict.	7	...	7	36	...	...	36	43
G. Second. vict.	5	...	5	...	20	11	31	36
H. Tert. Vict.	82	33	115	...	6	76	82	197
I. Mutual vict.	3	...	3	...	...	2	2	5
J. Juv. status	5	155	160	...	...	291	291	451
Class II Total	109	188	297	65	30	383	478	775
Total	133	196	329	221	82	432	735	1064

TABLE 23. Per Cent of Offenses Discovered during the Act, by Class, Category, and Discovering Group

| | DISCOVERING GROUP | | | | | | | |
| | Police | | | Nonpolice | | | | |
CLASS AND CATEGORY OF OFFENSES	Direct	Indirect	Total	Victim	Victim Representative	Other	Total	TOTAL
Class I								
A. Phys. injury	5.5	...	5.5	78.9	...	15.6	94.5	100.0
B. Prop. loss	11.7	2.5	14.2	32.5	36.7	16.6	85.8	100.0
C. Prop. damage	6.7	8.3	15.0	51.7	13.3	20.0	85.0	100.0
Class I Total	8.3	2.8	11.1	54.0	18.0	16.9	88.9	100.0
Class II								
D. Intimidation	...	...	...	100.0	...	...	100.0	100.0
E. Involving prop.	33.3	...	33.3	33.3	19.1	14.3	66.7	100.0
F. Prim. vict.	16.3	...	16.3	83.7	...	...	83.7	100.0
G. Second. vict.	13.9	...	13.9	...	55.5	30.6	86.1	100.0
H. Tert. vict.	41.6	16.8	58.4	...	3.0	38.6	41.6	100.0
I. Mutual vict.	60.0	...	60.0	...	...	40.0	40.0	100.0
J. Juv. status	1.1	34.4	35.5	...	..:	64.5	64.5	100.0
Class II Total	14.1	24.2	38.3	8.4	3.9	49.4	61.7	100.0
Total	12.5	18.4	30.9	20.8	7.7	40.6	69.1	100.0

TABLE 24. Number of Offenses Discovered After the Act, by Class, Category, and Discovering Group

| | DISCOVERING GROUP | | | | | | | |
| | Police | | | Nonpolice | | | | |
CLASS AND CATEGORY OF OFFENSES	Direct	Indirect	Total	Victim	Victim Representative	Other	Total	TOTAL
Class I								
A. Phys. injury	...	1	1	...	1	34	35	36
B. Prop. loss	6	42	48	83	17	20	120	168
C. Prop. damage	...	1	1	4	2	4	10	11
Class I Total	6	44	50	87	20	58	165	215
Class II								
D. Intimidation	...	...	...	1	...	6	7	7
E. Involving prop.	...	...	...	...	...	1	1	1
F. Prim. vict.	...	...	...	...	...	3	3	3
G. Second. vict.	...	...	...	...	1	...	1	1
H. Tert. vict.	2	...	2	...	...	3	3	5
I. Mutual vict.	...	1	1	...	...	13	13	14
J. Juv. status	...	2	2	...	...	1	1	3
Class II Total	2	3	5	1	1	27	29	34
Total	8	47	55	88	21	85	194	249

TABLE 25. Per Cent of Offenses, by Class, Category, and Discovering Group

DISCOVERING GROUP

CLASS AND CATEGORY OF OFFENSES	Police			Nonpolice				TOTAL
	Direct	Indirect	Total	Victim	Victim Representative	Other	Total	
Class I								
A. Phys. injury	...	2.8	2.8	...	2.8	94.4	97.2	100.0
B. Prop. loss	3.6	25.0	28.6	49.4	10.1	11.9	71.4	100.0
C. Prop. damage	...	9.1	9.1	36.4	18.1	36.4	90.9	100.0
Class I Total	2.8	20.5	23.3	40.4	9.3	27.0	76.7	100.0
Class II								
D. Intimidation	...	...	...	14.3	...	85.7	100.0	100.0
E. Involving prop.	...	...	...	...	...	100.0	100.0	100.0
F. Prim. vict.	...	...	...	...	...	100.0	100.0	100.0
G. Second. vict.	...	...	...	...	100.0	...	100.0	100.0
H. Tert. vict.	40.0	...	40.0	...	...	60.0	60.0	100.0
I. Mutual vict.	...	7.1	7.1	...	...	92.9	92.9	100.0
J. Juv. status	...	66.7	66.7	...	...	33.3	33.3	100.0
Class II Total	5.9	8.8	14.7	2.9	2.9	79.5	85.3	100.0
Total	3.2	18.9	22.1	35.3	8.4	34.2	77.9	100.0

TABLE 26. Number and Per Cent of Offenses by Discovering Group and When Discovered

WHEN DISCOVERED

DISCOVERING GROUP	During Act		After Act		TOTAL	
	N	%	N	%	N	%
Police	329	30.9 (85.7)	55	22.1 (14.3)	384	29.2 (100.0)
Nonpolice	735	69.1 (79.1)	194	77.9 (20.9)	929	70.8 (100.0)
Total	1064	100.0 (81.0)	249	100.0 (19.0)	1313	100.0

$\chi^2 = 7.60$; d.f. $= 1$; $P < .01$.

compared to the proportion of nonpolice discovery during the act (79% of the 929).

Having determined the relatively greater importance of police discovery of offenses during the act, we can turn attention to a comparison of Class I and Class II offenses. Our assumptions would lead us to assert that even the 82, or 16 per cent of the offenses discovered by the police among the 504 offenses in Class I, would probably have been reported by the victims, the victims' representatives, or by other nonpolice groups and thus have become part of official police statistics. Clearly, our assumption does not involve a large number of cases, but the direction of the empirical findings could strengthen or weaken some of the prior assertions about the validity of using Class I offenses for index construction. In order to close in on the assumptions as much as possible, we have hypothesized the following regarding Class I and Class II offenses relative to discovery group and moment of discovery:

(1) *Among police-discovered offenses, a smaller proportion of Class I than of Class II offenses are discovered during the act.* Our contention is that Class I offenses discovered by the police during the act should constitute a relatively small proportion of all offenses discovered by the police, while Class II offenses are not useful for index purposes and mostly discovered by the police during the act, should constitute a relatively large proportion of all offenses discovered by the police. Our *a priori* assumption, which cannot be directly confirmed empirically, still remains, namely, that even these Class I offenses discovered by the police during the act, which are small in number, would eventually have been discovered and reported by the victims or some victim group. The empirical verification which we are seeking is, first of all, that this group is numerically small and that it is significantly different from the Class II offenses that are discovered by the police during the act. If this hypothesis, derived from the assumption, is true, then the importance of stressing a wide range of variation in the probability of Class II offenses being discovered through police activity is strengthened.

(2) *There is a smaller proportion of Class I offenses among those discovered by the police during the act than of Class I offenses among those discovered by the police after the act.* This hypothesis is a corollary to (1) above and suggests that when the police discover a delinquency during its commission it is rare that the offense is of the kind that would be useful for index purposes, and that, therefore, police activity directly involved in discovery during their commis-

sion must be limited. It further asserts that when the police discover a Class I offense the discovery usually occurs after the act. If the victim did not discover the offense immediately, and if the police most commonly discover these offenses *after* they have occurred, we would suspect that most of these offenses would have been discovered by a victim group and reported to the police later. Inference suggests that if these assertions are true, most Class I offenses discovered by the police after the act would be property offenses.

The findings confirm both of these hypotheses as indicated by chi-square analysis of Tables 27 and 28. There is in fact a very strong association between police-discovered offenses occurring in Class II during the act and in Class I after the act. Of the 82 Class I offenses discovered by the police, 32 (39%) were discovered during the act; of the 302 Class II offenses so discovered, 297 (98%) were discovered during the act. The difference is significant ($\chi^2 = 180.20$; d.f. -1; $P < .001$) and confirms our earlier argument about the types of offenses most commonly affected by police activity. Furthermore, of the 329 offenses discovered by the police *during* the act, only 32 (10%) are Class I offenses. This is a significantly small proportion, for of the 55 offenses discovered by the police *after* the act, 50 (91%) are Class I offenses. These findings again mean that when the police discover delinquent acts, these acts are, in most instances, of a kind which our a priori assumption has excluded from index

TABLE 27. *Number and Per Cent of Offenses Discovered by Police, by Class and When Discovered*

| | WHEN DISCOVERED | | | | | |
| | During Act | | After Act | | TOTAL | |
OFFENSES	N	%	N	%	N	%
Class I	32	9.7 (39.0)	50	90.9 (61.0)	82	21.4 (100.0)
Class II	297	90.3 (98.3)	5	9.1 (1.7)	302	78.6 (100.0)
Total	329	100.0 (85.7)	55	100.0 (14.3)	384	100.0

$\chi^2 = 180.20$; d.f. $= 1$; $P < .001$.

TABLE 28.   Number and Per Cent of Offenses Discovered by Nonpolice, by Class and When Discovered

| | WHEN DISCOVERED | | | | | |
| | During Act | | After Act | | TOTAL | |
OFFENSES	N	%	N	%	N	%
Class I	257	35.0	165	85.0	422	45.4
		(60.9)		(39.1)		(100.0)
Class II	478	65.0	29	15.0	507	54.6
		(94.3)		(5.7)		(100.0)
Total	735	100.0	194	100.0	929	100.0
		(79.1)		(20.9)		

$\chi^2 = 174.94$; d.f. $= 1$; $P < .001$.

offenses. Class I offenses discovered by the police during the commission of the act constitute only 8.3 per cent of *all* 384 acts discovered by the police, whereas Class II offenses discovered by the police during their commission constitute 77.3 per cent of all offenses discovered by the police. And of the total of 384 offenses discovered by the police, 329 (86%) were discovered during the act. It is therefore upon this group that we must focus attention.

Class I offenses discovered by the police during their commission represent an extremely small number. Knowing that these offenses cannot have their volume much affected by police activity, we feel more confident empirically about using them for index purposes. Neither a change in the number of police in a given area of the community nor variations in the investigatory intensity of the same number of police operating within the same area would have much, if any, effect upon changing the amount of these Class I offenses. However, because 98 per cent of Class II offenses discovered by the police are discovered during their commission, it is obvious that a change in police policy would have a serious effect upon the frequency by which these offenses become part of official delinquency statistics.

There is another point to be made about the 50 offenses which are in Class I and discovered by the police after the act. We have said in our argument above that most of these offenses would probably have been discovered by the victim or some victim group and reported to the public authorities after the act if the police had not discovered them, and that these would most likely be property offenses that occurred in the absence of the victim. As a matter of fact, of these 50 offenses, 48 (96%) fall in Category B of Class I, a category made up of property theft without bodily injury to the victim. These are mostly burglaries and larcenies, and except for some unknown variables, there is little reason to believe that they would not have eventually been discovered by the victim and reported to the police. This assertion is further strengthened by the fact that of the 194 offenses discovered after the act by nonpolice groups, 165 or 85 per cent are in Class I; and that of the 165 Class I offenses discovered by nonpolice groups after the act 120, or 73 per cent, are in Category B (cf. Table 24).

This analysis lends further empirical validity to the claim that Class I offenses are important for purposes of index construction. Moreover, as can be observed from Tables 29 to 32 the frequency distribution of juveniles, instead of offenses, by Class I and Class II, by discovery group and when discovered, does not differ significantly from the prior tables that relate these same variables to offenses. Most traditional delinquency statistics, as we have elsewhere noted,

TABLE 29. Number of Juveniles in Class I and Class II Offenses Discovered during the Act, by Category of Offense and Discovering Group

| | DISCOVERING GROUP | | | | | | | |
| | Police | | | Nonpolice | | | | |
CLASS AND CATEGORY OF OFFENSES	Direct	Indirect	Total	Victim	Victim Representative	Other	Total	TOTAL
Class I								
A. Phys. injury	7	...	7	162	...	36	198	205
B. Prop. loss	26	6	32	77	83	41	201	233
C. Prop. damage	11	7	18	52	10	23	85	103
Class I Total	44	13	57	291	93	100	484	541
Class II								
D. Intimidation	...	...	...	35	...	...	35	35
E. Involving prop.	11	...	11	8	7	5	20	31
F. Prim. vict.	8	...	8	78	...	...	78	86
G. Second. vict.	11	...	11	...	36	27	63	74
H. Tert. vict.	152	43	195	...	12	201	213	408
I. Mutual vict.	5	...	5	...	...	6	6	11
J. Juv. status	5	155	160	...	...	291	291	451
Class II Total	192	198	390	121	55	530	706	1096
Total	236	211	447	412	148	630	1190	1637

TABLE 30. Per Cent of Juveniles in Class I and Class II Offenses Discovered during the Act, by Category of Offense and Discovering Group

| | DISCOVERING GROUP | | | | | | | |
| CLASS AND CATEGORY OF OFFENSES | Police | | | Nonpolice | | | | |
	Direct	Indirect	Total	Victim	Victim Representative	Other	Total	TOTAL
Class I								
A. Phys. injury	3.4	...	3.4	79.0	...	17.6	96.6	100.0
B. Prop. loss	11.1	2.6	13.7	33.1	35.6	17.6	86.3	100.0
C. Prop. damage	10.7	6.8	17.5	50.5	9.7	22.3	82.5	100.0
Class I Total	8.1	2.4	10.5	53.8	17.2	18.5	89.5	100.0
Class II								
D. Intimidation	...	...	...	100.0	...	...	100.0	100.0
E. Involving prop.	35.5	...	35.5	25.8	22.6	16.1	64.5	100.0
F. Prim. vict.	9.3	...	9.3	90.7	...	...	90.7	100.0
G. Second. vict.	14.9	...	14.9	...	48.6	36.5	85.1	100.0
H. Tert. vict.	37.3	10.5	47.8	...	2.9	49.3	52.2	100.0
I. Mutual vict.	45.4	...	45.4	...	...	54.6	54.6	100.0
J. Juv. status	1.1	34.4	35.5	...	...	64.5	64.5	100.0
Class II Total	17.5	18.1	35.6	11.0	5.0	48.4	64.4	100.0
Total	14.4	12.9	27.3	25.2	9.0	38.5	72.7	100.0

TABLE 31. Number of Juveniles in Class I and Class II Offenses Discovered After the Act, by Category of Offense and Discovering Group

| | DISCOVERING GROUP | | | | | | | |
| CLASS AND CATEGORY OF OFFENSES | Police | | | Nonpolice | | | | |
	Direct	Indirect	Total	Victim	Victim Representative	Other	Total	TOTAL
Class I								
A. Phys. injury	...	1	1	...	4	44	48	49
B. Prop. loss	11	96	107	147	38	44	229	336
C. Prop. damage	...	1	1	9	4	10	23	24
Class I Total	11	98	109	156	46	98	300	409
Class II								
D. Intimidation	...	...	...	2	...	10	12	12
E. Involving prop.	...	...	...	...	...	1	1	1
F. Prim. vict.	...	...	...	...	...	5	5	5
G. Second. vict.	...	...	...	...	2	...	2	2
H. Tert. vict.	3	...	3	...	...	4	4	7
I. Mutual vict.	...	1	1	...	...	17	17	18
J. Juv. status	...	2	2	...	...	1	1	3
Class II Total	3	3	6	2	2	38	42	48
Total	14	101	115	158	48	136	342	457

TABLE 32. *Per Cent of Juveniles in Class I and Class II Offenses Discovered After the Act, by Category of Offense and Discovering Group*

	DISCOVERING GROUP							
	Police			Nonpolice				
CLASS AND CATEGORY OF OFFENSES	Direct	Indirect	Total	Victim	Victim Representative	Other	Total	TOTAL
Class I								
A. Phys. injury	...	2.0	2.0	...	8.2	89.8	98.0	100.0
B. Prop. loss	3.3	28.6	31.9	43.7	11.3	13.1	68.1	100.0
C. Prop. damage	...	4.2	4.2	37.5	16.7	41.6	95.8	100.0
Class I Total	2.7	24.0	26.7	38.1	11.2	24.0	73.3	100.0
Class II								
D. Intimidation	...	...	...	16.7	...	83.3	100.0	100.0
E. Involving prop.	...	...	...	...	...	100.0	100.0	100.0
F. Prim. vict.	...	...	...	...	...	100.0	100.0	100.0
G. Second. vict.	...	...	...	...	100.0	...	100.0	100.0
H. Tert. vict.	42.9	...	42.9	...	...	57.1	57.1	100.0
I. Mutual vict.	...	5.6	5.6	...	...	94.4	94.4	100.0
J. Juv. status	...	66.7	66.7	...	...	33.3	33.3	100.0
Class II Total	6.2	6.2	12.5	4.2	4.2	79.1	87.5	100.0
Total	3.1	22.1	25.2	34.6	10.5	29.7	74.8	100.0

present only the number of juveniles arrested or taken into custody by the police for various kinds of delinquency. In the analyses thus far, there are no proportional differences to be noted between juvenile offenses and juvenile offenders. More refined analyses in subsequent chapters, however, will point to significant differences when delinquency is studied by these two dimensions.

INSIDE/OUTSIDE

It can be seen from Table 23 that the difference in the number of offenses in Class I committed inside a building (217) compared with the number committed outside (286) is not very large; whereas in Class II over four times as many offenses occur outside (656) as inside (152) (see Table 33). We have noted that the police are much more likely to discover Class II than Class I offenses. Of the 286 Class I offenses outside, only 47 (16%) are discovered by the police. But of the 656 Class II offenses outside, 279 (43%) are discovered by the police (Table 33, columns $d \times e$; $\chi^2 = 58.80$; d.f. = 1; $P < .01$).

Perhaps most important is that among Class I offenses it makes

TABLE 33. *Number and Per Cent of Offenses Occurring Inside and Outside,* by Class and Discovering Group*

	WHERE OCCURRING						
	INSIDE			OUTSIDE			
	DISCOVERING GROUP						
	Police (a)	Nonpolice (b)	Total (c)	Police (d)	Nonpolice (e)	Total (f)	GRAND TOTAL
OFFENSE CLASS	N %	N %	N %	N %	N %	N %	N %
Class I	34 59.6	183 58.6	217 58.8	47 14.4	239 38.8	286 30.4	503 38.4
Class II	23 40.4	129 41.4	152 41.2	279 85.6	377 61.2	656 69.6	808 61.6
Total	57 100.0	312 100.0	369 100.0	326 100.0	616 100.0	942 100.0	1311* 100.0

* Place of occurrence unknown in two cases.
For $c \times f$: $\chi^2 = 89.52$; d.f. $= 1$; $P < .001$
$\quad c \times e$: $\chi^2 = 36.34$; d.f. $= 1$; $P < .001$
$\quad a \times b$: $\chi^2 = 0$;$\quad$ d.f. $= 1$; $P < .90$
$\quad d \times e$: $\chi^2 = 58.80$; d.f. $= 1$; $P < .01$

TABLE 34. *Number and Per Cent of Class I Offenses, by Discovering Group and Where Occurring*

	DISCOVERING GROUP					
	Police		Nonpolice		TOTAL	
WHERE OCCURRING	N	%	N	%	N	%
Inside	34	42.0 (15.7)	183	43.4 (84.3)	217	43.1 (100.0)
Outside	47	58.0 (16.4)	239	56.6 (83.6)	286	56.9 (100.0)
Total	81	100.0 (16.1)	422	100.0 (83.9)	503	100.0

$\chi^2 = .01$; d.f. $= 1$; $P < .90$.

TABLE 35. *Number and Per Cent of Class II Offenses by Discovering Group and Where Occurring*

WHERE OCCURRING	DISCOVERING GROUP				TOTAL	
	Police		Nonpolice			
	N	%	N	%	N	%
Inside	23	7.6	129	25.5	152	18.8
		(15.1)		(84.9)		(100.0)
Outside	279	92.4	377	74.5	656	81.2
		(42.5)		(57.5)		(100.0)
Total	302	100.0	506	100.0	808	100.0
		(37.4)		(62.6)		

$\chi^2 = 38.42$; d.f. $= 1$; $P < .001$.

no difference whether an act occurred inside or outside, for the two major discovery groups (police/nonpolice) have about the same proportionate involvement in discovery, with the police making discovery in 16 per cent, the nonpolice group in 84 per cent of inside offenses, and the police discovering 16 per cent, the nonpolice groups 84 per cent of outside offenses (see Table 34). Among Class II offenses, however (see Table 35), significant differences may be seen. Of those committed inside, 15 per cent are discovered by the police and 85 per cent by nonpolice; but of those committed outside, 43 per cent are discovered by the police and 58 per cent by nonpolice ($\chi^2 = 38.42$; d.f. $= 1$; $P < .001$).

Therefore, it is not just that an offense is committed outside that renders it more likely to be discovered by police officers. The important factor is the character of the offense. The major group of offenses that deviate from the pattern of around 14 to 15 per cent being discovered by the police is found in Class II offenses committed outside, of which 43 per cent are discovered by the police. The principal categories contributing to this deviation (see Table 37) are Categories H, Tertiary Victimization Offenses (68%), and E, Threat of Property Loss (54%). It is especially interesting to note that Category A, Bodily Harm, which has the greatest proportion of offenses discovered by nonpolice groups, has about as many discovered by these groups when committed outside (95%) as when committed inside (96%).

TABLE 36. Number of Offenses by Class, Category, Place of Occurrence* and Discovering Group

CLASS AND CATEGORY OF OFFENSES	INSIDE					OUTSIDE				
	Police			Non-police	Total	Police			Non-police	Total
	Direct	Indirect	Total	Total		Direct	Indirect	Total	Total	
Class I										
A. Phys. injury	...	1	1	26	27	6	...	6	112	118
B. Prop. loss	10	20	30	138	168	10	24	34	85	119
C. Prop. damage	1	2	3	19	22	3	4	7	42	49
Class I Total	11	23	34	183	217	19	28	47	239	286
Class II										
D. Intimidation	...	...	...	11	11	...	...	...	17	17
E. Involving prop.	...	...	...	9	9	7	...	7	6	13
F. Prim. vict.	3	...	3	7	10	4	...	4	32	36
G. Second. vict.	3	...	3	19	22	2	...	2	13	15
H. Tert. vict.	4	6	10	34	44	80	27	107	51	158
I. Mutual vict.	2	1	3	15	18	1	...	1	...	1
J. Juv. status	...	4	4	34	38	5	153	158	258	416
Class II Total	12	11	23	129	152	99	180	279	377	656
Total	23	34	57	312	369	118	208	326	616	942

* There are two (2) cases with place of occurrence unknown.

TABLE 37. *Per Cent of Offenses by Class, Category, Place of Occurrence,* and Discovering Group*

CLASS AND CATEGORY OF OFFENSES	INSIDE					OUTSIDE				
	Police			Non-police	Total	Police			Non-police	Total
	Direct	Indirect	Total			Direct	Indirect	Total		
Class I										
A. Phys. injury	...	3.7	3.7	96.3	100.0	5.1	...	5.1	94.9	100.0
B. Prop. loss	6.0	11.9	17.9	82.1	100.0	8.4	20.2	28.6	71.4	100.0
C. Prop. damage	4.5	9.1	13.6	86.4	100.0	6.1	8.2	14.3	85.7	100.0
Class I Total	5.1	10.6	15.7	84.3	100.0	6.6	9.8	16.4	83.6	100.0
Class II										
D. Intimidation	...	...	...	100.0	100.0	...	...	...	100.0	100.0
E. Involving prop.	...	...	...	100.0	100.0	53.8	...	53.8	46.2	100.0
F. Prim. vict.	30.0	...	30.0	70.0	100.0	11.1	...	11.1	88.9	100.0
G. Second. vict.	13.6	...	13.6	86.4	100.0	13.3	...	13.3	86.7	100.0
H. Tert. vict.	9.1	13.6	22.7	77.3	100.0	50.6	17.1	67.7	32.3	100.0
I. Mutual vict.	11.1	5.6	16.7	83.3	100.0	100.0	...	100.0	...	100.0
J. Juv. status	...	10.5	10.5	89.5	100.0	1.2	36.8	38.0	62.0	100.0
Class II Total	7.9	7.2	15.1	84.9	100.0	15.1	27.4	42.5	57.5	100.0
Total	6.2	9.2	15.4	84.6	100.0	12.5	22.1	34.6	65.4	100.0

* There are two (2) cases with place of occurrence unknown.

13

Offenses Involving Bodily Injury

The first of our categories contains offenses that cause bodily injury to some person. We shall inspect them more closely in this chapter. They number 145, or 11 per cent of the 1313 offenses in our sample, and they represent nearly 30 per cent of the 504 offenses in Class I. Although the rate of delinquency per 10,000 juveniles in the city was 383.6 in 1960, the rate in the category under discussion was only 42.5. Juveniles participating in these 145 offenses numbered 254, or about 12 per cent of the 2094 juveniles in our sample. This means that 74 per 10,000 juveniles engaged in them, compared with 612, when all delinquents are considered. It should be noted that except for Categories E and J in Class II, the lone offender is most likely to be found committing delinquencies causing bodily injury (61%) (see Table 19).

We have previously observed that these offenses are not always identifiable by a legal classification. In 115, or 79 per cent, of our cases, the police called the offense homicide, aggravated assault, or assault, all of which obviously imply physical injury to a person, but 30 of our cases were found among other offenses. Only 38 per cent (Codes 111–633; Table 38) of the offenses causing bodily injury fall within the classes that in Uniform Crime Reports are included in their "crime index." This index, then, ignores the majority of offenses causing bodily injury that often are as serious or more serious than those caused by "aggravated assault and battery," and fails to take into account bodily harm resulting from offenses that, by their legal label, do not invariably imply such harm. If physical harm to a victim is important for measuring the seriousness of a delinquent act, a classificatory scheme must take account of it.

Table 38 also indicates the type of harm that is involved in these 145 offenses. "Minor" harm, it will be recalled, refers to any bodily injury, however slight, which does not require medical treatment and may include pushing, shoving, knocking down, even cutting. "Treated and discharged" includes any physical violence done to the victim that requires and receives medical care but does not require detention of the victim for further treatment. "Hospitalization" means that the victim received in-patient care for any duration in a medical institution but also includes those cases for which the victim required repeated out-patient care for three or more visits.

TABLE 38. Bodily Injury Offenses, by Philadelphia (UCR) Code and Type of Harm

| | TYPE OF HARM | | | | | | | | | |
| | Minor | | Treated | | Hospi-talized | | Death | | Total | |
PHILADELPHIA CODE TITLE AND NUMBER	N	$\%$	N	$\%$	N	$\%$	N	$\%$	N	$\%$
Murder & non-negligent homicide 111	...	...	...	...	...	...	2	100.0	2	1.4
Forcible rape 211	1	1.2	4	8.3	...	...	...	...	5	3.4
Highway robbery—no gun 310	7	8.6	1	2.1	...	...	...	...	8	5.5
Highway robbery—attempt 312	2	2.5	2	4.2	...	...	...	...	4	2.8
Purse snatching 315	2	2.5	1	2.1	...	...	...	...	3	2.1
Robbery—commercial house, gun 321	1	1.2	...	...	...	...	...	...	1	0.7
Robbery—misc., no gun 370	1	1.2	...	...	...	...	...	...	1	0.7
Assault with intent to kill 401	...	...	1	2.1	2	14.3	...	...	3	2.1
Aggr. A & B 404	1	1.2	21	43.7	5	35.7	...	...	27	18.6
Shoplifting 633	1	1.2	...	...	...	...	...	...	1	0.7
A & B 801	55	67.9	16	33.3	6	42.9	...	...	77	53.1
A & B on police 802	3	3.7	...	...	...	...	...	...	3	2.1
Resisting arrest 803	2	2.5	1	2.1	...	...	...	...	3	2.1
Indecent assault 1402	1	1.2	...	...	...	...	...	...	1	0.7
Sodomy 1405	3	3.7	...	...	...	...	...	...	3	2.1
Disorderly conduct 1904	1	1.2	...	...	...	...	...	...	1	0.7
Viol. ordinance 2605	...	...	1	2.1	...	...	...	...	1	0.7
Arson 2628	...	...	...	...	1	7.1	...	...	1	0.7
Total	81	100.0	48	100.0	14	100.0	2	100.0	145	100.2

These criteria have been used because (a) they are systematically recorded on the police offense reports, (b) they are objective data that require no impressionistic judgment for classification, (c) the variance in medical technology would be slight from one area of the city to another and during a single year.

Most of the offenses resulted in minor injuries (81, or 56%), one third in treatment and discharge (48, or 33%), about one-tenth (14, or 10%) in hospitalization, and only two (1.4%) in deaths. Rates per 10,000 juvenile population are: minor, 23.8; treated, 14.0; hospitalized, 4.1; death .6.

As might be expected from the legal labels, the modal type of harm in cases of aggravated assault was more serious than in simple assaults. Nearly three-quarters (73%) of the victims of aggravated assaults required medical treatment compared to one-fifth (21%) in simple assaults. Only 3 per cent of aggravated assaults compared to 72 per cent of simple assaults brought minor injuries; and in 23 per cent of the former compared to but 7 per cent of the latter was hospitalization required. Yet, it is significant that as many as 28 per cent of bodily injury cases classified by the police as simple assaults were as serious as or more serious, in terms of the resultant harm, than three quarters of the cases classified as aggravated assaults.

Robbery always involves a confrontation of victim and offender. Physical violence may or may not occur. Among those in which violence was present, however, 76 per cent resulted in minor harm, and the remaining 24 per cent were injuries resulting in treatment and discharge. No cases of greater harm occurred in robbery. As a matter of fact, offenses classified as simple assaults resulted in proportionately more serious injurious consequences to victims than did robberies with personal violence.

The remaining cases that involved bodily injury were small in number. There were only five cases of rape, one having minor harm and the other four requiring medical treatment but no hospitalization. Only minor harm resulted from one indecent assault, three sodomies, and one disorderly conduct. In an unusual case of violation of a city ordinance medical treatment was required, and in one arson case hospitalization was necessary.

Little analytic value is gained from examining type of harm according to who discovered the offense. Except for the two homicides, one of which was discovered directly by the police, more than 95 per cent of bodily injury offenses, regardless of type of harm, were discovered by nonpolice groups. It is interesting that in as many as 51 (35%) of the cases nonpolice persons other than the victim dis-

TABLE 39. *Number and Per Cent Bodily Injury Offenses, by Type of Injury and Discovering Group*

	DISCOVERED BY													
	Police		Nonpolice									TOTAL		
	Total* Direct		Victim		Victim Repre- sentative		Other		Total					
TYPE OF HARM	N	%	N	%	N	%	N	%	N	%	N	%	N	(%)	%
Minor	4	4.9	48	59.2	1	1.1	28	34.8	77	95.1	81	(55.9)	100.0
Treated	2	4.2	32	66.6	...	...	14	29.2	46	95.8	48	(33.1)	100.0
Hospitalized	...	...	6	42.9	...	...	8	57.1	14	100.0	14	(9.6)	100.0
Death	1	50.0	...	...	...	...	1	50.0	1	50.0	2	(1.4)	100.0
Total	7	4.8	86	59.3	1	0.7	51	35.2	138	95.2	145	(100.0)	100.0

* Police discovered none indirectly.

193

TABLE 40.   Number and Per Cent of Offenses Involving Bodily Injury, by Disposition and Type of Harm

| | DISPOSITION OF CASE | | | | | |
| | Arrest | | Remedial | | TOTAL | |
TYPE OF HARM	N	%	N	%	N	%
Minor	39	50.6	42	61.8	81	55.9
		(48.2)		(51.8)		(100.0)
Treated and discharged	29	37.7	19	27.9	48	33.1
		(60.4)		(39.6)		(100.0)
Hospitalized or death (2 cases)	9	11.7	7	10.3	16	11.0
		(56.2)		(43.8)		(100.0)
Total	77	100.0	68	100.0	145	100.0
		(53.1)		(46.9)		

$\chi^2 = 1.88$; d.f. $= 2$; $P < .50$.

covered the offenses.[1]   Sixty per cent were made known to the police by the victims (see Table 39).

As we have made clear elsewhere, only offenses resulting in an arrest disposition find their way to the juvenile court.   This point is especially cogent for offenses that might be included in an index. Of the 145 offenses involving bodily injury, 68 or 47 per cent were cleared by remedials (see Table 40).   But the loss to court statistics is compounded by the fact that 38 per cent of these cases were relatively serious injuries resulting in treatment and discharge or hospitalization of the victims.   While it is true that this figure is not so high as the 49 per cent of arrest cases for the same levels of serious harm, still it is obvious that a remedial disposition of the offender does not consistently mean that the injury to the victim was slight; the determination of disposition is made on more criteria than degree of harm.   Half of the arrests were for minor injuries requiring no medical treatment.   Knowledge of the degree of harm alone would make extremely difficult any prediction of police disposition among these cases of physical injury.   The death of a victim certainly pro-

[1] Of these, 30 were discovered by relatives of the victim, 3 by neighbors, 7 by employers, employees, school, church, or institutional personnel, and 6 by strangers.   In 5 cases the relationship was unknown.

vokes an arrest, but in cases resulting in hospitalization half were followed by arrests and half by remedials; the split for cases of minor harm is again nearly fifty-fifty; cases with remedial treatment show a higher proportion of arrests (60%) than remedials (40%). A chi-square analysis of degree of harm in hospitalization and death cases combined, by disposition, reveals no significant difference in the distributions ($\chi^2 = 1.88$; d.f. = 2; $P < .50$). Even when reduced to a 2 x 2 table of minor versus all other harm, by arrest and remedial disposition, differences are not significant ($\chi^2 = 1.80$; d.f. = 1; $P < .20$).

Shifting analysis from offenses to offenders does not much improve predictability of disposition from degree of harm. As Table 41 shows, offenders causing minor harm are remedialed only slightly more often (52%) than they are arrested (48%); offenders causing harm needing medical treatment are significantly more likely to be arrested (75%) than remedialed (25%). Quite unexpectedly, more offenders causing victims to be hospitalized are remedialed (62%) than are arrested (38%). The over-all percentages of offenses and offenders resulting in arrest (53%; 59%) or remedial action (47%; 41%) are not strikingly different. Chi-square test of type of harm, by disposition of offender, does show a significant difference ($\chi^2 = 18.68$; d.f. = 3; $P < .001$).

TABLE 41. *Number and Per Cent of Offenders Inflicting Bodily Injury, by Disposition and Type of Harm*

| | DISPOSITION OF CASE | | | | | |
| | Arrest | | Remedial | | TOTAL | |
TYPE OF HARM	N	%	N	%	N	%
Minor	58	38.4	64	62.1	122	48.0
		(47.5)		(52.5)		(100.0)
Treated and discharged	79	52.3	26	25.3	105	41.4
		(75.2)		(24.8)		(100.0)
Hospitalized or death	14	9.3	13	12.6	27	10.6
(6 offenders)		(51.8)		(48.2)		(100.0)
Total	151	100.0	103	100.0	254	100.0
		(59.4)		(40.6)		

$\chi^2 = 18.68$; d.f. = 2; $P < .001$.

VICTIM-OFFENDER DISPARITY AND BODILY INJURY

In some criminal offenses the law recognizes as an aggravating circumstance the use of a deadly weapon by the offender, or some kind of age, sex, or number disparity between victims and offenders. In our own concern about the degree of seriousness of offenses and the problem of scaling offenses for index construction, the presence of such aggravating factors became an obvious area for further investigation.

If an association is found to exist between any one or a combination of disparities and the degree of bodily harm in certain offenses, such disparities might be useful in (a) weighing offenses by seriousness and (b) differentiating offenses which might otherwise fall under the same legal category but could vary widely in their seriousness.

The term "disparity" is used to refer to a condition which would be expected to confer on either the victim or the offender an advantage and consequently a greater capacity of the offender to inflict an injury on the victim or of the victim to resist attack.

Suitable disparities (age, sex, number of participants in offense, and presence of weapon) were selected using two criteria.

1. Disparities should be based on *observable data*. This limited the selection to disparities that could be established on the basis of information routinely recorded by the police.

2. They should be based on *relational, not individual, factors*. As an example, age disparity should be based on the *difference* between the ages of victim and offender.

Age Disparity

Age disparity refers to the difference between the ages of the offender and the victim. More specifically, it is based on the mean age of the offenders minus the mean age of the victims. Thus, if there are two offenders aged 12 and 14 and one victim aged 10, the mean age of the offenders is 13. The age disparity, therefore, is 3 years. If all persons in a delinquent event are of the same age, disparity will be zero.

HYPOTHESIS 1. When the offender is much older than the victim or when the victim is of advanced years, bodily injury to the victim will be more serious than when there is little or no age disparity. We assumed that an older juvenile would be stronger than his younger victim, and that a juvenile would generally avoid committing serious injury in a criminal assault on a young adult but would be both able

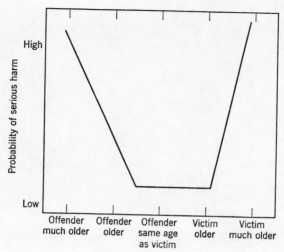

FIGURE 2. Hypothetical relation between age disparity and degree of harm.

and more likely to injure an aged adult, or one of advanced years. Some relation like the one pictured in Figure 2 was suspected.

Sex Disparity

There were only six cases in which males and females participated, either as offenders or victims; because these cases were too few in number to discuss in detail they were excluded from all analysis of sex disparity.

HYPOTHESIS 2. More serious harm is likely to result when the offender is a male and the victim a female than when the offender is a female and the victim is a male. We assumed that the male offender, because of his normally greater strength, size, and aggressive potential, would be both able and more likely to inflict greater injury on a female victim. Some result like the following was suspected:

	VICTIM	
OFFENDER	Male	Female
Male	No or Minor Harm	Serious Harm
Female	No or Minor Harm	No or Minor Harm

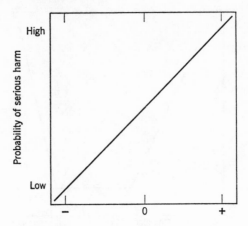

FIGURE 3. Hypothetical relation between number disparity and degree of harm.

Number Disparity

A number disparity exists when the number of offenders is different from the number of victims.

HYPOTHESIS 3.   More serious injury is likely to result when offenders outnumber victims than when they do not.   A relationship similar to the one pictured in Figure 3 was suspected, with the minus sign meaning that victims outnumber offenders, the plus sign meaning that offenders outnumber victims, and zero referring to equal numbers.

Weapon Disparity

A weapon disparity exists when the offender is armed and the victim is not.   No victim in this study was armed.   Weapons include, for example, stones, knives, guns, and clubs.

HYPOTHESIS 4.   More serious injury is likely to occur to the victim when the offender is armed than when he is not armed.   Some result like the following was suspected:

WEAPON DISPARITY	DEGREE OF HARM
Present	
(Offender armed)	Serious Harm
Absent	No or
(Neither armed)	Minor Harm

Testing the Hypotheses

In order to determine whether the disparities really correlated with serious injury for a relevant group of offenses, it was necessary (*a*) to define clearly the meaning of serious injury or harm and (*b*) to select relevant cases.

Serious harm was defined as the infliction of bodily injury, upon a victim, so severe that the victim received medical care, was hospitalized, or killed. No or minor harm occurred if the victim was merely pushed, shoved, knocked down, or otherwise injured but required no medical treatment, or received only a routine medical examination (as in cases of prostitution). Therefore, all cases could be sorted into two classes: those with serious harm and those with minor or no injury.

The 177 cases selected for analysis were those in which physical injury *could* have occurred, whether or not it actually did occur. The following criteria were established for selection:

(1) *There must be a victim.* Certain offenses, such as running away from home or truancy, have no victim.

(2) *The victim must be a person.* This means that the victimization must be primary and not secondary or tertiary as we have defined these terms elsewhere.

(3) *The offender and victim must meet face to face.* The two must have direct contact with one another.

(4) *The victim may not also be an offender.* In statutory rape or fornication, there is mutual consent, and as a willing partner the victim also commits an offense. Such cases were excluded from the analysis.

The Findings

The relation between each type of disparity and the type of harm was determined by using the chi-square test. All χ^2's with one degree of freedom were computed using Yates correction for continuity. The level of significance was chosen as $P < .05$.

Age Disparity

Table 42 shows the frequency distribution of eleven age-disparity groups by type of physical harm and reveals that age disparity is not related to serious harm in the way anticipated. Hypothesis 1, then, is rejected. The relation appears to be nearly reversed; i.e., serious harm seems to occur when the victim and offender are close to one another in age. The frequency of all 167 cases with serious harm is 34 per cent, and most of the age-disparity groups with a higher percentage of serious harm cluster near the center where no age disparity exists.

No significant differences occur when the proportion of offenses

TABLE 42. *Age Disparity and Degree of Harm*[a]

AGE DISPARITY IN YEARS[b]

DEGREE OF HARM	Victim Older than Offender % V > 0							Victim and Offender Same Age	Offender Older than Victim % 0 > V					Total
	+32	16–31	8–15	4–7	2–3	1	Total	%	1	2–3	4–7	8–15	Total	%
No or minor harm	69	56	75	50	50	50	60	59	58	64	74	100	59	66
Serious harm	31	44	25	50	50	50	40	41	42	36	26	...	41	34
Total number of cases	16	9	12	6	7	8	58	22	26	36	23	2	87	167

[a] Excluding 10 cases in which some or all ages were missing.
[b] Difference in years between the mean age of offenders and the mean age of victims.

resulting in serious harm among $V > 0$ (40%) is compared to $V = 0$ (41%) and $0 > V(41\%)$. If the number of cases in group cells were larger, perhaps it would be more safe to assert, should the same ratios be maintained, that the direction of the disparity makes little or no difference when compared to degree of injury. If anything, the present data suggest that as age disparity increases among $0 > V$ offenses, the proportion of these offenses with severe injury decreases; and that with greatest disparity in $V > 0$ offenses, the proportion with severe injuries is least. Similarity in age between victim and offender results in the highest probability of severe injury. Forty-three per cent of these vis-à-vis offenses in which the offender was the same age as, or one year older or younger than, the victim (56) involved serious harm; whereas only 31 per cent of the remaining 111 cases, or those in which there was more than one year age difference in either direction between victim and offender, involved serious harm. This percentage difference is significant, thus indicating the strong association between similarity in victim-offender ages and the probability of serious harm.

It may be that when assaultive, or potentially assaultive, offenses occur between persons of similar age, the striking power of the offender and the resistance potential of the victim are more likely to be of similar quality. And because this similarity results in a more intense struggle of matched groups or individuals, the amount of injury finally inflicted on the victim will be greater, for a greater amount of violence is needed by the offender to subdue or overcome the victim. The analysis reveals, in any case, that victim-offender age differentials are empirically of little value in determining seriousness of physical harm. The degree of harm is still assumed to be of importance in judging seriousness of an offense, but age disparity is not important as a variable in relation to harm.

Sex Disparity

Table 43 shows the sex of offenders and victims in vis-à-vis offenses. There is a similarity between the two in 76 per cent of the cases. Thus, intrasex offenses are significantly more common than intersex offenses within this universe of vis-à-vis cases.

Table 44 reveals by inspection that there is obviously no relationship between seriousness of harm and sex disparity. Indeed, it is surprising that there is no more chance variation than the close percentages indicate. Male offenders encountered male victims in 71 per cent of cases involving serious bodily injury compared to 68 per cent of cases involving no or minor harm. Male offenders attacked

TABLE 43. *Sex of Offender and of Victim in All Vis-à-Vis Offenses*[a]

	VICTIM					
	Male		Female		Total	
OFFENDER	N	% of Total	N	% of Total	N	%
Male	118	69	37	22	155	91
Female	4	2	12	7	16	9
Total	122	71	49	29	171	100.0

$\chi^2 = 16.16$; d.f. $= 1$; $P < .01$.
[a] In six cases, either there were both male and female offenders or male and female victims. These mixed cases are excluded from the table.

female victims in only four out of the 171 vis-à-vis offenses, the result being serious harm in two cases and no or minor harm in two cases. There are other ways in which to examine the data on sex disparity and harm, but they all express the same general conclusion—a lack of significant association between type of harm and any possible combination of sexes as victims and offenders.

Numbers Disparity

We had hypothesized that more serious harm would occur if offenders outnumbered victims, but as Table 45 shows, the relationship is not statistically significant. However, the pattern of percentage changes as number disparity changes is in the expected direction. With a larger number of vis-à-vis offenses it is conceivable that a number disparity giving an advantage to offenders would be related to the greater probability of serious harm for the victims. As it is, we predicted that the proportion of cases with serious harm would increase as number disparity increased in favor of the offender.

Weapon Disparity

A weapon disparity occurs when an offender has a blunt instrument, a knife or a gun, and the victim has none. The offender's lack of use of the weapon affects the presence or absence of harm, but the disparity remains. Because no victims in these cases were armed, we need not be concerned about possible cases in which some victims might be armed while some of the offenders were armed. Moreover,

TABLE 44. *Sex Disparity and Degree of Harm*

DEGREE OF HARM	NO SEX DISPARITY (V/0)						SEX DISPARITY (V/0)						TOTAL	
	Male/Male (A)		Female/Female (B)		Total (C)		Male/Female (D)		Female/Male (E)		Total (F)			
	N	%	N	%	N	%	N	%	N	%	N	%	N	%
No or Minor Harm Number	77	65	9	75	86	66	2	50	25	68	27	66	113	66
(%)	(68)		(8)		(76)		(2)		(22)		(24)		(100.0)	
Serious Harm Number	41	35	3	25	44	34	2	50	12	32	14	34	58	34
(%)	(71)		(5)		(76)		(3)		(21)		(24)		(100.0)	
Total	118	100.0	12	100.0	130	100.0	4	100.0	37	100.0	41	100.0	171	100.0

Columns C × F: χ^2 = .02; d.f. = 1; $P < .90$.
Columns A × D: χ^2 = .01; d.f. = 1; $P < .95$.
Columns B × E: χ^2 = .02; d.f. = 1; $P < .90$.

TABLE 45. *Number Disparity and Degree of Harm*

NUMBER DISPARITY

DEGREE OF HARM	Victims Outnumber Offenders $V > 0$ (A)		Victims Equal to Offenders $V = 0$ (B)		Offenders Outnumber Victims $0 > V$ (C)	
	N	$\%$	N	$\%$	N	$\%$
No or minor harm	11	85	70	70	36	44
Serious harm	2	15	32	30	26	56
Total	13	100.0	102	100.0	62	100.0

Columns A, B, C: $\chi^2 = 4.07$; d.f. $= 2$; $P < .25$.
Columns A + B, C: $\chi^2 = 2.2$; d.f. $= 1$; $P < .25$.

"no weapon disparity" in this study means that neither the victim nor the offender was armed, although our definition of disparity is such that if a case were to arise in which both were armed, we would classify it as "no disparity."

The original hypothesis is confirmed, for presence of a weapon is significantly related to seriousness of harm, as can be noted in Table 46. If any kind of weapon is present during vis-à-vis offense, serious harm occurs in 72 per cent of the cases; but if no weapon is present, serious harm occurs in only 20 per cent of the cases.

TABLE 46. *Weapon Disparity and Degree of Harm*

WEAPON DISPARITY

DEGREE OF HARM	None		Present		TOTAL	
	N	$\%$	N	$\%$	N	$\%$
No or minor harm	104	80	13	28	117	66
Serious harm	26	20	34	72	60	34
Total	130	100.0	47	100.0	177	100.0

$\chi^2 = 39.90$; d.f. $= 1$; $P < .001$.

The age and sex of victims and offenders and the number of persons involved are normally recorded by the police in writing up their cases. But it could be argued that an offender's possession of a weapon is not regularly noticed; and that, therefore, it is not that weapons are likely to lead to serious harm but that weapons are only noticed and recorded as being present when they are used. This suggests that the presence of weapons means that they are most likely to be used, and if used the probability of severe injury is high. The following facts lead us to conclude that weapons do in fact lead to serious harm.

(1) The police examine all persons in the type of vis-à-vis offenses we have been discussing to determine whether anyone is in possession of a weapon. The carrying of a gun or a knife is itself an offense.

(2) In no case in our sample did the police discover an unused weapon. These two facts in combination imply that weapons are used if they are present.

(3) Certain types of weapons are more easily hidden than others. Knives and guns, for example, are more easily kept from view than are blunt instruments. When carrying a gun or a knife is an offense, these weapons are more likely to be concealed even if never used. But we have already indicated that the police investigate for concealed weapons. Blunt instruments are usually impromptu weapons picked up on the spot for immediate use and therefore would be easier to notice and detect at once even when they are not actually used to inflict harm. However, Table 47 shows that the difference in the frequency of serious harm when blunt instruments are used (74%) is

TABLE 47. Types of Weapon Disparity and Degree of Harm

	TYPE OF WEAPON					
DEGREE OF HARM	Blunt Weapon Only		Knife, Gun, or Multiple Weapons		TOTAL	
	N	%	N	%	N	%
No or minor harm	7	26	6	30	13	28
Serious harm	20	74	14	70	34	72
Total	27	100.0	20	100.0	47	100.0

not significantly different from the frequency of serious harm when a gun, knife, or multiple weapons are used (70%). If guns and knives were only noticed when used, the percentages should be different. These refined data strengthen the findings of an association between the presence of a weapon in the hands of the offender and severe injury for the victim.

Combined Disparities

Among the disparities, weapons and number of participants seem most important in the analysis of bodily injury. For this reason we were interested in how these two interrelate. None of the other disparities examined in combination yielded anything of significance, and in some tables cell size became too small to justify further testing. But most cases with serious harm involve either number or weapon disparities. Only 15 per cent of offenses with serious injury lack both these disparities. Most cases with no or minor harm involve neither disparity; as much as 62 per cent of such cases lack both.

Table 48 clearly shows that the presence of a weapon disparity is the most important factor leading to serious harm. The most illuminating observations to be made from this table are that (1) among offenses with serious harm, the highest proportion occur with a weapon disparity only (38%). (2) Among offenses with serious harm, there is the same frequency (18%) of cases with *both* number and weapon disparity as with *neither* number nor weapon disparity. (3) Of the four groups in the table, serious harm is lowest when neither weapon nor number disparity exists (21%), followed by number disparity only (33%), number and weapon disparity (69%), and finally weapon disparity only (75%).

Conclusion of the Disparity Analysis

Disparities of age and sex do not correlate importantly with the infliction of physical injury. Serious harm occurs somewhat more often when victims and offenders are of the same or similar age. A number disparity approaches but does not quite reach the level of significant association with serious injury. The significant relationship with serious harm vis-à-vis offenses is the existence of a weapon disparity.

Perhaps a major reason for these findings is that age and sex disparities are related to *who* the victim is whereas weapon and, to some extent, number disparities are related to *how* he is attacked. Thus, if the infliction of physical injury by juveniles is assumed to be a violent reaction of the juvenile offender to members of his peer

TABLE 48. *Number and Weapon Disparities and the Degree of Harm*

	DISPARITIES									
	Both Number and Weapon (A)		Number Only (B)		Weapon Only (C)		Neither Number nor Weapon (D)		Total	
DEGREE OF HARM	N	%	N	%	N	%	N	%	N	%
No or Minor Harm										
Number	5	31	31	67	8	26	73	79	117	66
(%)	(4)		(27)		(7)		(62)		(100.0)	
Serious Harm										
Number	11	69	15	33	23	74	11	21	60	34
(%)	(18)		(25)		(39)		(18)		(100.0)	
Total	16	100.0	46	100.0	31	100.0	84	100.0	177	100.0

Columns A × C: $\chi^2 = 0.14$; $P < .70$.
Columns B × D: $\chi^2 = 5.90$; $P < .02$.
Columns C × D: $\chi^2 = 37.68$; $P < .001$.
Columns B × C: $\chi^2 = 11.19$; $P < .001$.

group, the victim will be like the offender in age and sex. Because most offenders are males in their teens, most victims will also most likely be males in their teens. Therefore, the disparities of sex and age should not occur frequently; when they do, there is apparently no significant relationship to the degree of harm.

Furthermore, even the armed juvenile offender whose weapon produces the disparity of greatest significance in relation to the harm inflicted on his victim does not usually cause injury in order to accomplish some other offense, i.e., violence in general is not used instrumentally. Such instrumental injury typically could occur in offenses like robbery or in certain sex offenses, for in these the offender injures in order to take property from, or sexual advantage of, the victim. But in only 14 out of the total 177 vis-à-vis offenses was any money or property stolen, and the total amount stolen was only 200 dollars. Damage to property occurred in only three other cases, and forcible sexual activity occurred in only six cases. Most of the cases were assaultive offenses in which the injury, if any, occurred by itself and was not incidental to some other offense.

Finally, the disparity study has revealed some possible leads for index construction, even though some of our original assumptions about these disparities have proved to be incorrect. A statistically significant association of the presence of a weapon in possession of the offender with severe bodily injury to a victim does confirm our assumption and suggests that this factor should be taken into account in rating the relative seriousness of offenses used in constructing an index of delinquency.

14
Property Theft and Damage

According to the classification scheme used in the present research, Categories B and C refer to offenses involving property theft and damage, respectively. It should be remembered that our categories as defined are mutually exclusive but that some specific items of occurrence may appear in other categories. Thus, for example, no events classified under B or C involve bodily injury although some cases with bodily injury also involved property theft and consequently will be found in Category A. These are robberies which will be separately examined later.

There are many different ways of analyzing property offenses, depending on the purpose of the analysis. Our purpose is part of an effort to establish a delinquency index. But because we are concerned with knowledge available to us about qualitative differences in property offenses, we shall examine more than the mere quantity of these acts. First, we shall look at the 359 property theft and damage cases combined that involve no offenses against the person and that are completed acts. Second, we shall analyze in some detail property offenses that include violation of a place, have a known amount of monetary theft or damage, involve a known legal or illegal presence of the offender, and a known use or absence of force at entry and violence after entry. From this universe of 298 offenses we have excluded thefts from the person, all attempts, automobile theft, or thefts with unknown amounts stolen or damaged or an unknown modus operandi. Third, 27 robberies, even those including physical harm, are analyzed; and fourth, 35 automobile thefts are separately examined because they represent a particular kind of theft in which recovery rates are exceedingly high.

Some question might be raised about the monetary value of property theft or damage recorded by the police on their offense reports. It might be argued that victims are prone to overstate the value, and that the police may also overstate it for some reason. It has been suggested also that the police, skeptical of the reports of complainants who may be seeking insurance payments, particularly when automobiles are involved, will sometimes downgrade the reported values when writing up reports. How much over- or underestimating is actually done is difficult to say, and whether the two counterbalance one another is not known. Whatever may be the case with delinquents, the amounts actually recorded are relatively small and there is no indication from a close reading of these reports that inaccurate amounts were used. When we had doubts about the values of some items, such as the cost of replacing windows of certain sizes, we checked on current local prices to determine whether the estimates given were substantially accurate. There seems to be a tendency to report values in rounded dollar and 5-dollar amounts. We have collapsed the amounts into groups for analytic purposes and assume that the influence of this rounding factor thereby is reduced.

The values in Categories B and C combined, as we suggested, are low. As indicated in Table 49, 14 per cent of these cases involved one dollar or less, 33 per cent 5 dollars or less, and nearly 50 per cent 15 dollars or less. These figures are based on those which include even the values of automobiles stolen or damaged.

The comparison of our Category B (theft) and Category C (damages) to the offense types listed in Part 1 and Part 2 of the Uniform Crime Reports is shown in Table 8. Of the 359 offenses of theft or damage of property, 294 fall within the UCR Part 1, but only 131 of them, or 44 per cent, would constitute UCR "index crimes." Because current procedure now defines robbery, burglary, automobile theft, and larceny of 50 dollars and over as the only property offenses among these "index crimes," it is especially interesting to note that an additional 26 property theft and damage offenses involving 50 dollars or more in value appear in our Categories B and C. They fall in the UCR Part 2 group. Moreover, these 26 offenses make up 40 per cent of the 65 offenses in Categories B and C that are Part 2 types in Uniform Crime Reports. In short, even if 50 dollars and more were accepted as a cutoff point for the inclusion of an offense in an index, it is obvious that the Uniform Crime Report index misses a considerable number of serious property violations among those

TABLE 49. *Size of Monetary Loss in Property Offenses (Categories B and C), by Uniform Crime Code Classification*

UNIFORM CRIME CODE	LOSS IN DOLLARS													TOTAL N	TOTAL %
	1	2	3	4	5	6–10	11–15	16–20	21–50	51–100	101–200	Over 200	Un-known	N	%
Robbery	4	1	…	…	1	…	1	1	…	2	…	…	…	10	2.8
Burglary	6	1	2	2	5	5	3	3	14	8	12	11	1	73	20.3
Larceny	34	11	9	12	8	20	20	16	34	8	3	…	1	176	49.0
Auto theft	…	…	…	…	…	…	…	…	…	2	3	29	1	35	9.7
Simple assaults	…	…	…	…	…	…	…	…	…	…	…	…	1	1	0.3
Forgery and counterfeiting	…	…	…	…	…	…	…	…	…	…	…	…	1	1	0.3
Embezzlement, fraud, and stolen property	…	1	…	…	…	…	…	…	1	…	…	…	…	2	0.6
Disorderly conduct	…	…	…	…	…	…	…	…	1	…	…	…	…	1	0.3
Operating vehicle without consent of owner	…	…	…	…	…	…	…	…	…	…	1	…	…	1	0.3
Violation of ordinances	…	…	…	…	1	…	…	…	…	…	1	…	…	2	0.6
Threats to do bodily harm	…	…	…	…	…	…	…	…	1	…	…	…	…	1	0.3
Damage to city property	…	…	…	…	1	…	…	…	…	…	…	…	…	1	0.3
Trespassing	…	…	…	…	…	1	…	…	…	1	…	…	…	2	0.6
Malicious mischief	5	3	1	…	9	5	…	2	12	7	5	1	1	51	14.2
Arson	…	…	…	…	…	…	…	…	1	1	…	…	…	2	0.6
Total															
N	49	17	12	14	25	31	24	22	64	29	25	41	6	359	
%	13.6	4.7	3.3	4.0	7.0	8.6	7.0	6.1	17.8	8.0	7.0	11.4	1.7		100.0

* Total per cent rounded to 100.0.

211

labeled as receiving stolen goods, disorderly conduct, operating a motor vehicle without consent, damage to city property, trespassing, malicious mischief (especially), and arson.

The rate per 10,000 juvenile population, 7 to 17 years of age, of all property theft and damage offenses is 104.9 and is two and a half times as high as offenses involving bodily injury. In the absence of some method of evaluating the importance of a bodily injury relative to a property injury, the two types of injuries are given even values, as in Uniform Crime Reports. Thus relatively small changes in the number of property offenses can offset relatively large changes in the number of offenses with bodily injury. For this reason, we believe that it is extremely important to develop some common base or single dimension for a more realistic weighing of the two sets of phenomena.

We have previously referred to how and when Category B and Category C offenses were discovered and noted that only 22.5 per cent

TABLE 50. *Property Offenses by Discovering Group and Amount of Theft or Damage*

| | DISCOVERING GROUP | | | | | |
| | Police | | Nonpolice | | TOTAL | |
AMOUNT IN DOLLARS	N	%	N	%	N	%
1	11	14.7	38	13.4	49	13.7
2	1	1.3	16	5.6	17	4.7
3	3	4.0	9	3.2	12	3.3
4	4	5.3	10	3.5	14	3.9
5	5	6.7	20	7.0	25	7.0
6– 10	4	5.3	27	9.5	31	8.6
11– 15	7	9.3	17	6.0	24	6.7
16– 20	6	8.0	16	5.6	22	6.1
21– 50	10	13.3	54	19.0	64	17.8
51–100	5	6.7	24	8.5	29	8.1
101–200	5	6.7	20	7.0	25	7.0
Over 200	13	17.3	28	9.9	41	11.4
Unknown	1	1.3	5	1.8	6	1.7
Total						
N	75	100.0	284	100.0	359	100.0
%		(20.9)		(79.1)		(100.0)

of the theft cases and 14 per cent of the damage cases were discovered by the police. Combined, 284 or 79 per cent of the 359 offenses were discovered by nonpolice groups, mostly by the victims (Table 50). No striking patterns emerge when the discovering group is related to amount of theft or damage; for both offenses with loss or damage valued at 20 dollars or less and at more than 20 dollars were discovered by nonpolice groups in 79 per cent of the cases. Expressed in terms of each discovering group, 41 or 55 per cent of the 74 offenses with known amounts discovered by the police were 20 dollars or under and 153 or 55 per cent of the 279 offenses with known amounts discovered by nonpolice groups were 20 dollars or under. Other reasonable and meaningful divisions of amounts also indicated no significant differences between amount and discovering group (Table 51).

There were 696 juveniles involved in these 359 offenses, an average of nearly two offenders (1.9) per offense compared to an average of 1.8 for Category A, Bodily Injury, and of 1.6 for all types of offenses. In general, the fewer the number of offenders participating in an offense, the lower was the value of property theft or damage. Table 52 clearly shows the direction of this relationship. When a juvenile commits one of these offenses alone, the monetary value is 20 dollars or under in 61 per cent of the cases; but if he is part of a group of five or more, the value is that amount in only 31 per cent of the cases. The differences between two-, three-, and four-offender events are not significant, but it is logical to dichotomize offender participants in single events into (a) those events with one offender and (b) those with two or more offenders. When this is done (Table 53) 93, or 61 per cent, of the 152 offenses with one offender involved theft or damage of 20 dollars or under, but among the 201 offenses, each

TABLE 51. *Property Offenses by Discovering Group and Amount of Theft or Damage*

| | DISCOVERING GROUP | | | | | |
| AMOUNT | Police | | Nonpolice | | TOTAL | |
	N	%	N	%	N	%
$20 and under	41	21.1	153	78.9	194	100.0
Over $20	33	20.8	126	79.2	159	100.0
Total	74	21.0	279	79.0	353	100.0

TABLE 52.   *Number and Per Cent of Property Offenses, According to Number of Offenders in Each Offense, by Amount*

NUMBER OF OFFENDERS IN EACH OFFENSE

AMOUNT IN DOLLARS	One N	One %	Two N	Two %	Three N	Three %	Four N	Four %	Five N	Five %	Total N	Total %
1	28	18.3	15	13.9	3	5.9	3	10.0	...	...	49	13.7
2	9	5.9	2	1.8	4	7.8	2	6.7	...	...	17	4.7
3	5	3.3	5	4.6	1	2.0	1	3.3	...	...	12	3.3
4	8	5.2	3	2.8	2	3.9	1	3.3	...	...	14	3.9
5	15	9.8	8	7.4	1	2.0	1	3.3	...	...	25	7.0
6- 10	12	7.8	8	7.4	7	13.7	3	10.0	1	5.9	31	8.6
11- 15	9	5.9	6	5.6	5	9.8	3	10.0	1	5.9	24	6.7
16- 20	7	4.6	9	8.3	2	3.9	1	3.3	3	17.6	22	6.1
21- 50	27	17.7	16	14.8	13	25.5	4	13.4	4	23.5	64	17.8
51-100	12	7.8	11	10.2	2	3.9	2	6.7	2	11.8	29	8.1
101-200	10	6.5	7	6.5	3	5.9	3	10.0	2	11.8	25	7.0
Over 200	10	6.5	14	13.0	8	15.7	6	20.0	3	17.6	41	11.4
Unknown	1	0.7	4	3.7	...	...	...	...	1	5.9	6	1.7
Total	153	100.0	108	100.0	51	100.0	30	100.0	17	100.0	359	100.0

committed by two or more offenders, 101, or 50 per cent, involved that amount. This is barely a significant difference ($\chi^2 = 3.74$; d.f. $= 1$; $P \cong 05$), and the direction retains our finding of an association between size of the offender group in a property offense and the monetary value of thefts or damages.

TABLE 53.   *Property Offenses (Categories B and C) Committed by Single Offenders or by Two or More Offenders, by Amount of Loss*

OFFENDERS

AMOUNT*	One Offender N	One Offender %	Two or More Offenders N	Two or More Offenders %	TOTAL N	TOTAL %
$20 or under	93	61.2	101	50.3	194	55.0
Over $20	59	38.8	100	49.7	159	45.0
Total	152	100.0	201	100.0	353	100.0

* Amount unknown in 6 cases.
$\chi^2 = 3.74$; d.f. $= 1$; $P \cong .05$.

TABLE 54. *Number and Per Cent of Property Offenses by Amount and Type of Victimization*

	TYPE OF VICTIMIZATION							
AMOUNT IN DOLLARS	Primary		Secondary		Tertiary		Total	
	N	%	N	%	N	%	N	%
1	26	53.1	21	42.8	2	4.1	49	100.0
2	7	41.2	10	58.8	...	...	17	100.0
3	4	33.3	7	58.4	1	8.3	12	100.0
4	4	28.6	6	42.8	4	28.6	14	100.0
5	15	60.0	5	20.0	5	20.0	25	100.0
6– 10	17	54.9	13	41.9	1	3.2	31	100.0
11– 15	15	62.5	8	33.3	1	4.2	24	100.0
16– 20	19	86.4	3	13.6	...	...	22	100.0
21– 50	45	70.3	16	25.0	3	4.7	64	100.0
51–100	22	75.9	7	24.1	...	...	29	100.0
101–200	17	68.0	6	24.0	2	8.0	25	100.0
Over 200	36	87.8	5	12.2	...	...	41	100.0
Unknown	3	50.0	1	16.7	2	33.3	6	100.0
Total	230	64.1	108	30.1	21	5.8	359	100.0

Another interesting fact about these offenses is that as the monetary value increases, the proportion of primary victimization increases whereas secondary and tertiary victimization decreases (Table 54). This association between type of victimization and amount stolen or damaged is statistically significant, as Table 55 indicates. More persons suffer property theft or damage as primary victims (64.3%) than do commercial establishments and the community combined (35.7%). But primary victimization increases from 48 per cent when the property offense is 5 dollars or under to 79 per cent when the offense is over 50 dollars; whereas secondary victimization drops from 42 per cent at 5 dollars and under to 19 per cent at any amount over 50 dollars; tertiary victimization drops from 10 per cent to 2 per cent. No matter at what point a division of money value is made, the relationship remains between type of victimization and amount. The table shows this association and significant differences when a meaningful nearly equal division is made at 20 dollars. The association between primary victimization and greater property injury is most evident when we note that the percentage of offenses over 20 dollars

TABLE 55. Relationship between Type of Victimization and Amount of Property Theft or Damage by Four Groups of Amount

TYPE OF VICTIMIZATION

AMOUNT	Primary		Secondary		Tertiary		TOTAL	
	N	%	N	%	N	%	N	%
$5 or under	56	47.9	49	41.9	12	10.2	117	100.0
$6–$20	51	66.2	24	31.2	2	2.6	77	100.0
$21–$50	45	70.3	16	25.0	3	4.7	64	100.0
$51 and over	75	78.9	18	19.0	2	2.1	95	100.0
Total	227	64.3	107	30.3	19	5.4	353	100.0

$\chi^2 = 26.55$; d.f. $= 6$; $P < .001$.

TABLE 56. Number and Per cent of Property Offenses by Police Disposition and Amount

POLICE DISPOSITION

AMOUNT IN DOLLARS	All Arrested		All Remedial		Mixed		TOTAL	
	N	%	N	%	N	%	N	%
1	14	28.6	35	71.4	...	...	49	100.0
2	6	35.3	11	64.7	...	...	17	100.0
3	6	50.0	6	50.0	...	...	12	100.0
4	6	42.9	8	57.1	...	...	14	100.0
5	6	24.0	19	76.0	...	...	25	100.0
6– 10	7	22.6	23	74.2	1	3.2	31	100.0
11– 15	13	54.2	11	45.8	...	...	24	100.0
16– 20	17	77.3	5	22.7	...	...	22	100.0
21– 50	33	51.5	30	46.9	1	1.6	64	100.0
51–100	17	58.6	12	41.4	...	...	29	100.0
101–200	19	76.0	6	24.0	...	...	25	100.0
Over 200	34	82.9	6	14.6	1	2.5	41	100.0
Unknown	4	66.7	2	33.3	...	...	6	100.0
Total	182	50.7	174	48.5	3	0.8	359	100.0

is 1.4 times *greater* than those 20 dollars and under, whereas for secondary victimization it is 1.8 times *less*, and for tertiary victimization 2.3 times *less*. The reason is partly due to the fact that nearly three-fourths (29/40) of all property offenses over 200 dollars are automobile thefts and, in the sample, involve only primary victims. In the next section we shall analyze this relationship between type of victimization and property values by excluding automobile thefts.

From the point of view of examining police statistics compared to juvenile court statistics for index purposes, it is useful to compare offenses and offenders by disposition and property values. Tables 56 and 57 show these distributions. Abbreviated versions, dividing property injury at 20 dollars, show more clearly the positive association between disposition and amount or, more specifically, between an arrest disposition and amounts over 20 dollars. The percentage distributions are similar for both offenses and offenders, and, as expected, arrest dispositions are significantly more likely to be made in the higher value offenses. But perhaps most important for considerations of an index is the fact that 172, or 49 per cent, of the 350 offenses and 331, or 49 per cent, of offenders never go beyond police records and are thus lost to juvenile court statistics. It is equally important that as many as 34 per cent of offenses and 38 per cent of offenders (Table 58) involving more than 20 dollars are so lost.

If 50 dollars instead of 20 dollars were used as a cutoff point, very little difference is seen, for as high as 29 per cent of offenses and 27 per cent of offenders involving theft or damage over 50 dollars are remedialed and hence do not become part of juvenile court data.

TABLE 57. Disposition of Offenses by Amount of Property Theft or Damage

| DISPOSITION | AMOUNT | | | | TOTAL | |
| | $20 and under | | Over $20 | | | |
	N	%	N	%	N	%
Arrest	75	38.9	103	65.6	178	50.9
Remedial	118	61.1	54	34.4	172	49.1
Total	193	100.0	157	100.0	350	100.0

$\chi^2 = 23.71$; d.f. $= 1$; $P < .001$.

TABLE 58.   Disposition of Juvenile Offenders by Amount of Property Theft
or Damage

	AMOUNT*					
	$20 and under		Over $20		TOTAL	
DISPOSITION						
	N	%	N	%	N	%
Arrest	147	41.8	203	61.8	350	51.4
Remedial	205	58.2	126	38.2	331	48.6
Total	352	100.0	329	100.0	681	100.0

* Amount unknown in the case of 11 arrested and 4 remedialed.
$\chi^2 = 26.27$; d.f. $= 1$; $P < .001$.

SELECTED PROPERTY OFFENSES

In order to examine property theft and damage with greater refinement, we shall examine only property offenses *other* than automobile theft, those against the person directly, those with incomplete acts (attempts), unknown amounts and unknown modus operandi. The residual group for analysis contains 298 cases.

Because we have abandoned legal categories, our interest focuses on the amount of theft or damage and certain other variables connected with these offenses. Damage to property without theft (except to motor vehicles) is considered in Uniform Crime Reports; yet we believe that to convert these offenses to costs and to consider them in an index is a more realistic and meaningful procedure. Moreover, information regularly collected by the police and considered important by the community in evaluating the seriousness of offenses shows whether property was stolen, damaged, or both stolen and damaged; whether the offense was committed by an offender whose presence at the scene of the crime was legal or illegal; whether, if illegal, force was used to gain entry; and whether violence was used after entry. These sets of data, providing alone 18 different combinations of events, appear in Table 59.

The 298 offenses resulted in a loss of 14,007 dollars, with a mean of 47 dollars and a median of 15 dollars. More property is stolen (67%) than is damaged (33%); and more is stolen only (52%) than is damaged only (25%) or stolen and damaged in the same event (23%). But the average dollar loss is, in reverse order of frequency, highest for the combined stolen-damaged property offense (mean,

$104.50; median, $42.50), next for damage alone ($50.08; $25.00), and finally for stolen alone ($37.14; $11.00).

Criminal law reflects the community's greater concern with the offender who enters a place illegally than legally in order to steal or damage property. Illegal presence means that the perpetrator either breaks into a building or otherwise enters without legal permission. In larceny from a parking meter or by shoplifting the offender had a legal right to be in the street or in the store at the time. But the victim of a house burglary is usually very disturbed by the fact that the offender had the effrontery to enter the house illegally, and the

TABLE 59. *Selected Types of Property Offenses by Amount of Loss**

Type of Property Offenset	N	Total Theft (in Dollars)	Total Damage (in Dollars)	Total Theft Plus Damage (in Dollars)	Mean	Median	Per Cent above Median
T V̄ L	115	2,033	...	2,033	$17.68	$17.68	0.35
T V̄ IN	55	3,330	...	3,330	60.55	20.00	0.62
T V IF	21	1,922	...	1,922	91.52	25.00	0.62
T V L	4	22	...	22	5.50	4.50	0.00
T V IN	...	...	...	...	...	...	...
T V IF	2	9	...	9	4.50	4.50	0.00
D V̄ L	4	...	250	250	62.50	22.50	0.75
D V̄ IN	2	...	105	105	52.50	52.50	0.00
D V̄ IF	7	...	95	95	13.71	20.00	0.57
D V L	49	...	2,126	2,126	43.39	25.00	0.55
D V IN	7	...	875	875	125.00	20.00	0.57
D V IF	2	...	105	105	52.50	52.50	0.50
TD V̄ L	...	...	...	...	...	...	...
TD V̄ IN	1	4	5	9	4.00	9.00	0.00
TD V̄ IF	14	1,518	285	1,803	128.78	22.00	0.77
TD V L	5	4	14	18	3.60	4.00	0.00
TD V IN	4	140	245	385	96.25	72.50	100.00
TD V IF	6	430	490	920	153.33	177.50	100.00
Total	298	9,412	4,595	14,007	47.00	15.00	

* Excludes auto theft, offenses with theft directly from the person, unknown amount of theft or damage, unknown modus operandi.

† D = Damage   V̄ = No Violence   L = Legal   F = Force
   T = Theft   V = Violence   I = Illegal   N = No Force

chain store is more outraged by theft from a warehouse, where the offender has no business, than from the store where his presence is legal during store hours. For these and similar reasons, breaking and entering as well as burglary carry more severe sanctions in the law. For the same reasons we have considered this variable in the scaling design.

If the presence of the offender is legal (Table 60) (mean, $25.14, median $10,000) the amount of property loss is proportionately only about one-third of the amount in those cases in which his presence is illegal ($78.99; $25.00). Moreover, illegal presence is a more significant factor in high property loss than in the nature of the loss—damage or theft. As we have noted, damage to property results in a greater average loss than does theft; but analysis of the legal or illegal presence of the offender during commission of property damage or theft reveals an interesting rank order of loss. This finding results from dividing cases into those below and those above the median value of 15 dollars for all of these property offenses in which the combined sets of information were available. The ranking is made on the basis of the proportion of cases in each set above the median value. Table 61 shows these data in detail. Ranking according to the proportion of cases above the median dollar loss yields the following order:

TYPE	PER CENT ABOVE MEDIAN	ACTUAL TOTAL DOLLAR LOSS
(1) Illegal, damage	73.8	$ 4297
(2) Illegal, theft	60.0	$ 5261
(3) Legal, damage	51.7	$ 2394
(4) Legal, theft	33.3	$ 2055
		$14,007

Thus the type of presence during which an offense occurs is an important variable, for in all these kinds of property offense a statistically significant proportion of cases are above the median dollar loss if they were performed with illegal presence. Whether the amount of property loss, illegal presence, or both are of equal importance in a rating of the seriousness of an offense is a matter to be further examined in our scale analysis.

There is an insufficient number of cases to analyze in similar detail the use or nonuse of force to gain illegal entry in order to commit a property offense. But as Table 62 reveals, there is no significant difference between offenses in which force was present or absent relative to value of loss. The median value for both is 15 dollars.

Violence, as defined in these property offenses, refers so some forcing action that occurs after legal or illegal entry. For example, an

TABLE 60. *Summary of Selected Types of Property Offenses by Amount of Loss*

Type of Property Offense*	N	Total Theft (in Dollars)	Total Damage (in Dollars)	Total Theft Plus Damage (in Dollars)	Mean	Median
T	197	7,316	...	7,316	$37.14	$11.00
D	71	...	3,556	3,556	50.08	25.00
T and D	30	2,096	1,039	3,135	104.50	42.50
L	177	2,059	2,390	4,449	25.14	10.00
IN	69	3,474	1,230	4,704	68.17	25.00
IF	52	3,879	975	4,854	93.35	25.00
I	121	7,353	2,205	9,558	78.99	25.00
V	79	605	3,855	4,460	56.46	25.00
$\overline{V}$	219	8,807	740	9,547	43.59	15.00
All offenses	298	9,412	4,595	14,007	47.00	15.00

* D = Damage $\overline{V}$ = No Violence   L = Legal   F = Force
  T = Theft   V = Violence   I = Illegal   N = No Force

offender may without force enter a building where his presence is illegal, but may employ some destructive physical effort to perform the acquisitive offense inside. An offender who illegally enters a house through an open door but has to force open a jewel box has

TABLE 61. *Selected Property Offenses by Type of Presence and Amount of Loss*

	TYPE OF PRESENCE					
Amount	Theft *a*	LEGAL Damage* *b*	Total *c*	Theft *d*	ILLEGAL Damage* *e*	Total *f*
	N %	N %	N %	N %	N %	N %
Below median	74 66.7	28 48.3	102 60.4	30 40.0	11 26.2	41 35.0
Above median	37 33.3	30 51.7	67 39.6	45 60.0	31 73.8	76 65.0
Total	111 100.0	58 100.0	169 100.0	75 100.0	42 100.0	117 100.0

* Damage in this table refers to damage alone and damage-theft combination.
Columns $a \times d$: χ^2 = 11.86; d.f. = 1; $P < .001$.
Columns $b \times e$: χ^2 = 4.10; d.f. = 1; $P < .05$.
Columns $c \times f$: χ^2 = 16.72; d.f. = 1; $P < .001$.
Columns $a \times b$: χ^2 = 4.64; d.f. = 1; $P < .05$.
Columns $d \times e$: χ^2 = 1.68; d.f. = 1; $P < .20$.

TABLE 62. *Selected Property Offenses with Illegal Presence and Use of Force at Entry, by Amount of Loss*

	FORCE		NO FORCE		TOTAL	
AMOUNT	N	%	N	%	N	%
Below median	17	33.0	24	37.5	41	35.0
Above median	34	67.0	42	62.5	76	65.0
Total	51	100.0	66	100.0	117	100.0

$\chi^2 = .02$; d.f. $= 1$; $P < .90$.

used violence. The jewel box may or may not be damaged, but violence most commonly is accompanied by damage to the property. Among all 186 offenses of theft alone, only 6 occurred with violence, all below the median value.

Table 63 indicates that no significant association exists between violence and amount of property loss although in general the median value with violence ($25) is higher than without violence ($15).

In general, analysis of offenses in this section reveals that the amount of money loss per event is relatively small. For all cases, the first quartile (Q_1) falls at 4 dollars, Q_2 at 15 dollars, Q_3 at 45 dollars. Figure 4 shows this distribution. However, differences may be observed when theft, damage, theft and damage offenses, legal versus illegal presence, and violence versus nonviolence are compared. As Figure 5 makes clear, in summary form, damage to property has a higher probability of resulting in property loss above the median value of all offenses, and when combined with theft has the highest

TABLE 63. *Selected Property Offenses and Use of Violence Other than Entry, by Amount of Loss*

	VIOLENCE		NO VIOLENCE		TOTAL	
AMOUNT	N	%	N	%	N	%
Below median	37	46.8	106	51.2	143	50.0
Above median	42	53.2	101	48.8	143	50.0
Total	79	100.0	207	100.0	286	100.0

$\chi^2 = .28$; d.f. $= 1$; $P < .70$.

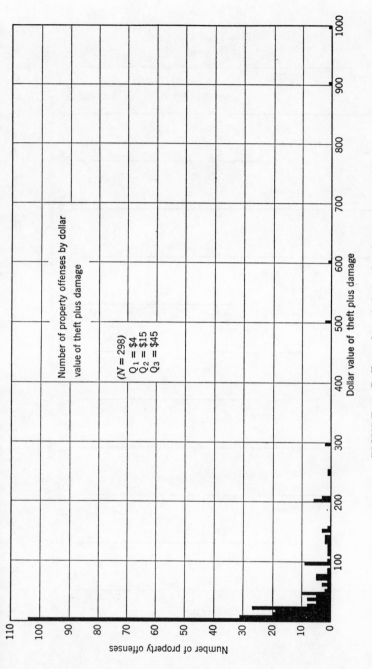

FIGURE 4. Dollar value of theft plus damage.

223

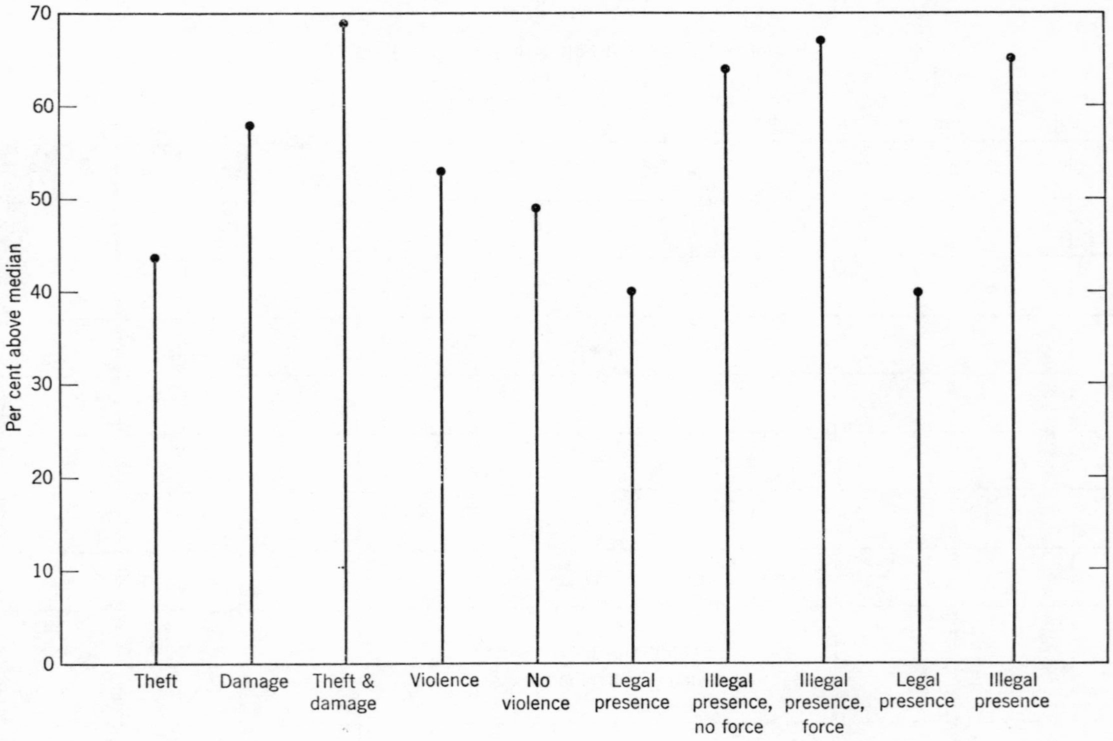

FIGURE 5. Property offenses by type, represented by percentage above median property loss (N = 286).

probability. These differences are statistically significant. Moreover, if the offense was performed in a place to which the offender did not have legal access the amount of loss is again significantly greater than when at least the offender's presence was legal. Whether force was used to make the illegal entry has no important relationship to the amount of property loss. Most cases of theft without damage are larcenies, including shoplifting, bicycle theft, and some burglaries. Most offenses with damage to but no theft of property are cases of malicious mischief, and most of those with both theft and damage in a single event are burglaries of commercial establishments, with illegal entry at night.

All other things being equal, we may probably assume that a theft of little amount is less likely to be reported than a theft of a great amount. But we are impressed by the high number of theft cases with relatively small amounts of money that are included in our sample. Yet malicious mischief costs the community much more than do thefts. Moreover, the community may be more outraged by a damage with small property loss than by a theft without violence or illegal entry. The middle class quasi-sacred respect for property may be more injured by destruction than by outright theft. If a building is simultaneously entered without authority, and force is used both upon entry and within, the affront to the value system is compounded certainly in terms of dollar loss, but perhaps equally in terms of rated seriousness. There are important and intricately related issues for determining the qualitative weights to be applied to these varied acts. The empirical data are revealing, for they tell us which known variables in the event are significantly associated with the greatest amount of property loss. These variables will be used in our scaling analysis, and the empirical confirmation of their importance adds reason for their use, no matter how the ratings of seriousness may relate to the variables.

ROBBERY

Robbery is of special concern to the community, and this concern is revealed in the usually more severe penalties assessed for it than for other types of theft in law and judicial sentencing.[1] In robbery the victim is aware of his having property, usually money, taken from his person. Some exception is recognized in the law when the

---

[1] Edward Green, *Judicial Attitudes toward Sentencing* (viii, 149 pp. London: Macmillan, 1961).

victim is a corpse or perhaps unconscious under some circumstances. Because robbery is at once an acquisitive offense and one involving personal confrontation, both the law and criminal statistics show confusion in classifying it. Some penal classifications, such as the one used in federal statutes, place robbery among property offenses; others, such as the Pennsylvania Penal Code, place it among offenses against the person. In statistics the percentage of offenses cleared by arrest and the percentage of offenders found guilty from among persons charged with robbery consistently fall midway between offenses against the person and offenses against property, thus reflecting the dual and overlapping character of robbery.

The legal label masks the variegated dimensions of robbery; the amount of property stolen, the kind of intimidation (verbal, restraint, with gun, knife, other weapon), and the presence or absence of physical injury to the victim. Of course, traditional criminal and delinquency statistics do not reflect these variations either, and they usually include attempts with completed acts. In the classification we have developed, robbery may appear in Category A because bodily injury was part of the event, in Category B, property theft, or in Category D, intimidation only.[2] We have argued that if there is threat to take property from the person but no theft occurs, the event is similar to an unfulfilled threat to do bodily harm. If a bodily injury occurs during a robbery, the assault and physical harm are omitted from, or are masked by, the statistical category of robbery. We have, instead, classified robbery with physical injury among other events involving like injury. Thus, the crime of robbery presents one of the major problems in describing the amount and quality of delinquency in a community—that of reducing a physical harm and property theft to a single dimension that can be weighted and used as a measurement to observe changes over time and space.

There are only 27 cases of robbery among our Class I offenses (Table 64), of which four are attempts, although each of these attempts involved bodily injury. This is a rate of *offenses* of only 7.9 per 10,000 juveniles. There are 55 juvenile offenders (and one adult), or a mean of 2 per offense and a rate of juvenile *offenders* of 16.1. In the 23 cases with any property stolen, the total property loss is but 354 dollars and the mean, median, and mode are only 5 dollars, or 10 dollars less than the median for all property offenses (excluding automobile theft). No damage to property occurred in any of these robberies. The range is from 5 cents to 66 dollars, and only four cases

---

[2] There were only two cases of robbery without harm or loss. They are not included in the present analysis, which comprises only Class I offenses.

TABLE 64. Robbery, Bodily Injury, and Theft of Property

	Any Bodily Injury		No Bodily Injury		Total	
	N	%	N	%	N	%
Theft	13	76.5	10	100.0	23	85.2
No theft	4	23.5	...	...	4	14.8
Total	17	100.0	10	100.0	27	100.0

$\chi^2 = 1.21$; d.f. $= 1$; $P < .30$.

produced a loss of over 20 dollars. All but one of the 27 offenses occurred on the street or in the open, to which the offenders had legal access. A gun was used in only one case, which involved secondary victimization of a commercial establishment; the remaining 26 cases were primary. Total recovery of stolen property is noted in 9 cases, partial recovery in 4, none in 11, and unknown in 3; thus there was at least some recovery in approximately half of these robberies.

There was one victim per robbery except in two cases, each of which had four victims, and with the exception of the five purse snatching robberies, all victims were males. In 14, or 52 per cent of the cases, the victims were juvenile, in 12 they were adult, and in one case with four victims, they were mixed juvenile and adult. Relative to the juvenile or adult status of the victim, the hypothesis seemed reasonable that proportionately more loss would occur when the victim was an adult instead of a juvenile. Excluding the one mixed case, the 13 juvenile victims suffered a median loss of less than 5 dollars, and the 10 adult victims a median loss of 18.50 dollars. The adult loss is significantly higher and could not have occurred by chance (rank-sum z score $= 1.77$; $P < .05$).[3]

Of special interest in robbery offenses is the method of intimidation, whether an offensive weapon was present, and whether physical harm resulted. Verbal threats only were employed in one case, a knife in 4, a blunt instrument or physical force in 23, and a gun in only one.

[3] Virginia L. Senders, Measurement and Statistics (xvi, 594 pp. New York: Oxford University Press, 1958), p. 439. The formula for the rank-sums test is:

$$z = \frac{2Ti - Ni(N + 1)}{\dfrac{\sqrt{N1 \cdot N2 \cdot (N + 1)}}{3}}$$

The advantage of this test is that it is not dependent upon normal distribution.

Bodily injury resulted in 63 per cent of the cases (17/27) and we hypothesized that a significant association should exist between completed thefts and bodily injuries. Table 64, however, shows that there is a negative nonsignificant relation between harm and theft. The 17 cases of harm were less serious than the total of all Category A offenses involving physical injury: Robbery had 76.5 per cent with minor harm, compared to 55.9 for all assaults; 23.5 per cent of the robberies (4/27) had serious harm compared to 42.8 per cent of all assaults. None of the robberies resulted in hospitalization, but among simple assaults, 21 per cent of the victims required medical treatment and another 7 per cent were hospitalized, making the proportion of serious harm—28 per cent—higher than in robbery.

The amount of money or other property stolen in robbery was, in the average case, only one-third of that in all other types of theft, excluding larceny of automobiles. Moreover, only 354 dollars was stolen in the robberies compared to 14,000 in other thefts. On the basis, then, of injury or property loss caused by juveniles, robbery is an offense that empirically is less serious than simple assaults and petty larcenies. As we shall see, the presence or absence of bodily injury in robbery is the fact of importance to the community. If theft and injury are combined in a single event we assume that the harm is of sole importance in rating the seriousness of that event. Our data indicate that the amount of the theft, as well as its completion, is unrelated to the condition of physical injury. When bodily harm occurs, therefore, it is the factor of prime importance in the event.

AUTOMOBILE THEFT

Automobile theft in the United States is committed mostly by juveniles. For many years national statistics have consistently shown that nearly two-thirds of all automobile thefts resulting in arrest were by persons under 18 years of age, which is a higher proportion than for any other Part 1 offense. Several special studies have examined this phenomenon descriptively and have interpreted it in psychological and sociological terms.[4] Our task is not to explain juvenile automobile theft but to relate it to an index of delinquency. In the second section of this chapter we excluded automobiles from

---

[4] William W. Wattenberg and James Balistrieri, "Automobile theft: a 'favored-group' delinquency," *Amer. J. Sociol.* 57:575–579 (May 1952).

T. C. N. Gibbens, "Car thieves," *British J. Delinq.* 8:257–265 (April 1958).

Leonard D. Savitz, "Automobile thefts," *J. Crim. Law, Criminol. and Police Sci.* 50:132–143 (August 1959).

our analysis of property theft because: (1) The dollar value of a motor vehicle is extremely high compared to property in the other common types of theft, where the median value is only 15 dollars. (2) Most automobiles taken are recovered, so that the actual loss to the victims is minimal and is reduced to damage, if any, of the vehicle during its absence or to inconvenience to the owner. (3) Most automobiles are recovered within a short period of time (usually 48 hours), having been abandoned by the offenders, thus suggesting that only temporary use was intended. As we have several times said, an index cannot measure intent, but the reality of "joyriding" is widely acknowledged and is supported by the empiric fact of quick recovery of stolen automobiles. If this kind of larceny is mainly for temporary use only, then obviously it differs from the acquisitive property offenses. For these reasons, including automobile thefts in a general analysis of property thefts without special examination of the automobile thefts distorts the property thefts in terms of the value of property loss and consequently the seriousness of property offenses in general.

But stealing an automobile is still a violation of the law and of the value system that places high priority on respect for another's property. Nor can we overlook the fact that automobiles taken for temporary use are sometimes damaged. For measurement purposes, the injury and its monetary value are, then, no different from the loss of property due to conduct labeled malicious mischief or disorderly. For these reasons, qualitative differences in the character and results of automobile theft should be considered in a rating of the seriousness of the act. Moreover, the theft of an automobile is highly reportable and otherwise satisfies logical requirements for inclusion in an index.

Descriptively there are a few items of interest. The police discovered 11 or 31 per cent of the 35 automobile thefts, which is a relatively high proportion among Class I offenses whose discovery by the police is only 16 per cent. This means than in nearly a third of the cases of automobile theft in which the juvenile offender became known through being taken into custody, the police discovered the thefts before the victim reported his car stolen. The police use of "safety checks" most likely accounts for this high proportion. That the victim would shortly have reported the loss of his car anyway is almost undeniable; that the offender would have been apprehended anyway is doubtful. We are not suggesting that "aggressive police action" through these safety checks of "suspicious" cars or drivers is defensible, for we have no way of knowing what proportion of these checks result in a successful operation or what kinds of civil rights may be jeopardized.   But that nearly one-third of these automobile thefts are discovered by the police is some reflection of police activity, although sufficiently low not to eliminate the offense from an index necessarily.

There was no bodily injury resulting from these automobile thefts, but 16 or 46 per cent had some damage to property, mostly to the stolen cars.   The amount of damage is known for 15 cases and totals 7700 dollars, with a mean of 513 and a median of 200.   For the 19 cars stolen and undamaged, the total theft value was 13,550 dollars; a mean of 713 and a median of 500.   For the cars stolen and damaged the total property value was 20,730 dollars; a mean of 1382 and a median of 700.   Thus, the total amount of the stolen value of the cars plus the property loss through damage was 34,280 dollars, with a mean of 1008 and a median of 525.

In this context it is important to note that the recovery of these automobiles was total.   The net loss must rest on the damage to property caused by or to the automobile, which amount is the 7700 dollars.   Police reports perhaps should record whether there was theft insurance on the automobile (as they should record this for all property thefts) if the net loss were to be considered in the measurement of the offense.   But again we must be cognizant of the fact that recovery of these cars is practically built into the definition of this delinquency, which means that the offenders necessarily had to be taken into custody to be designated juveniles and that the character of the offense suggests that if apprehension occurs at all it will be accomplished by recovery of the stolen object.   Unlike perishable items or goods easily disposed of through use or hidden transference (jewels to a receiver of stolen goods), an automobile stolen by juveniles is most likely abandoned and recovered without apprehension of the offenders, or is recovered before abandonment takes place.   If the latter, then the juveniles are usually found in the cars or readily traced to them.

RECOVERY OF PROPERTY

Although an index of delinquency must be based on the number of certain types of offenses committed, including property offenses, the net loss to the community is an interesting piece of information. Were it not for the complexity of variables of which net loss is a function, such loss might conceivably be used to measure the injurious effects of property offenses committed by juveniles.

Data from our sample of property thefts can be analyzed in terms of amount stolen and amount recovered. Offenses which involve damage to property cannot be examined in this way unless knowledge of restitution by the offenders or their families is available. Moreover, we do not know in all cases of either theft or damage whether victims had insurance to cover their losses. We suspect that there may be some relationship between having insurance and willingness to report a theft or damage to the police because insurance companies generally require that theft or malicious damage be reported if payment is to be made to the policy holder.

Table 65 presents data on the number of theft cases, the value of property stolen and recovered by specific types of offenses. As we have elsewhere indicated, the police generally record the reported value of both the stolen and the recovered property. If they have occasionally failed to indicate the amount in dollars, specific descriptions of the stolen items have made possible our estimating the loss. For only 9 of the 302 cases of theft was the description of the property so inadequate that we could not make a good estimate in dollar values.

Most of the 293 cases involving known amounts of theft and recovery are contained in our Category B, but a few were accompanied by physical harm—Category A—or damage as well. The summary reviews these overlappings of categories. In these 293

TABLE 65. Number and Value of Property Stolen and Recovered by Uniform Crime Code*

| Uniform Crime Code | Number of Thefts | Value of Property | | | Per Cent of Value Recovered |
		Stolen	Recovered	Not Recovered	
Robbery	20	$ 266	$ 204	$ 62	77
Burglary	62	6,394	4,303	2,091	67
Larceny	174	3,061	2,625	436	86
Auto theft	35	27,080	27,080	. . .	100
Fraud	1	2	2	. . .	100
Receiving stolen property	1	25	25	. . .	100
Total	293	36,828	34,239	2,589	93
Total excluding auto theft	258	9,748	7,159	2,589	73

* Excludes nine cases with unknown amount either stolen or returned.

cases the value of property stolen was 36,828 dollars and the value of property recovered was 34,239, leaving a net or residual loss of only 2589. These figures are swollen by their containing 35 automobile thefts, for, as noted, this form of theft amounts to 27,080 dollars. Excluding automobiles, the number of cases is 258, the total amount stolen is 9748 dollars, recovery amounts to 7159 dollars, and the net loss remains at 2589 dollars because the automobiles were totally recovered. Proportionately, the dollar value returned to owners victimized by property theft is as high as 93 per cent, if automobiles are included, and 73 per cent if automobiles are excluded. The rank order of proportionate return of property by the legal labels of offenses is automobile theft (100%), larceny (86%), robbery (77%), and burglary (67%). (The one case of fraud and the other of receiving stolen property both resulted in total recovery but, of course, cannot be used to generalize.)

The recovery value of property theft is high. For a city of approximately two million persons and 342,000 juveniles the net loss of about 26,000 dollars seems surprisingly low. Relative to the number of known juveniles committing these offenses, the net loss may be viewed as no more than 4 dollars per offender; and relative to the number of juveniles in the city, it is about 75 cents per juvenile.

But there are several interpretative factors to keep in mind. The universe of *all* offenses committed by juveniles is still unknown, i.e., offenses committed by juveniles whether apprehended or not by the police. Our data cannot indicate what proportion of offenses not cleared by arrest but resulting in property recovery are juvenile offenses. It is necessary, as we earlier asserted, to define delinquency for measuring purposes in terms of persons apprehended if we are to be certain of the age of the person committing the offense. There is no systematically derived evidence, but there is wide acceptance for the argument that juveniles are more easily and speedily apprehended than are adults. And the speed of apprehension is probably directly related to the proportion of offenses cleared by arrest as well as to the amount of stolen property recovered. Most persons who steal property are not caught, but among those who are the probability of being caught in possession of the property they stole seems relatively high, as indicated by the percentage recovered of the dollar value taken.

THE RELATIONSHIPS AMONG CLASS I OFFENSES

In our classification system we have selected events assumed to be useful for construction of an index and have referred to them as

Category A, Bodily Injury, Category B, Property Theft, and Category C, Property Damage. These three categories comprise our Class I offenses. The single item used for sequential ordering of these categories has been, first, the presence of physical injury; then the fact of some property stolen, and, finally, the fact of some property damage. This item order was chosen for two major reasons. (1) We assumed, with supportive reasons to be empirically confirmed later, that the item of major concern to the community was whether a victim was physically injured in any way. (2) There was no necessity to make assumptions about the relative importance of property thefts and damages because both types of legal norm violation could and should be analyzed together, for both are readily reducible to a single dimension of value in terms of monetary costs. As a matter of fact, both types of property offenses could have been combined into one category, but because society traditionally provides much more severe sanctions for theft than for criminal damage of property and because we wanted to retain the differences in a scale analysis of attitudes of certain groups toward these offenses we separated them in our categories. Primarily because of more severe penalties for theft than for damage but partly because of their greater number, property theft preceded property damage in the classificatory ordering.

But any ordering would theoretically embrace and, in the real world, experience some combinations of harm, theft, and damage. In order to equate a physical injury with a property theft or a property damage it is ultimately necessary to express all in terms of some single dimension. And if both theft and harm occur in the same event questions arise about the relationship between the two. Are these additive items, or does one item so completely dominate the other in the weighing of them that only the one need be considered for measurement? These questions we shall seek to answer in the final chapters.

For the present we are interested in the descriptive analysis of the relationships among injury, theft, and damage. The evidence accumulated thus far generated two hypotheses, the one being a corollary of the other: (1) Events involving physical injury are significantly isolated from property theft or damage. (2) Events involving property theft or property damage are in significant proportions interrelated. In short, cases of physical harm stand more or less by themselves; and cases of theft and damage often occur together in the same delinquent event.

The Venn diagram (Figure 6) on the following page clearly shows these relationships. The number of offenses in Categories A, B, and

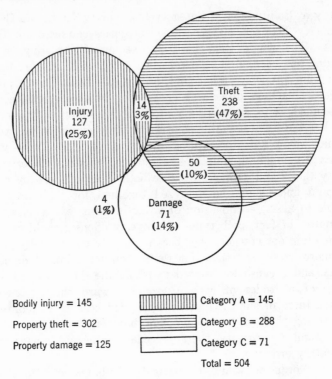

Bodily injury = 145   ▓▓▓▓▓ Category A = 145

Property theft = 302   ▓▓▓▓▓ Category B = 288

Property damage = 125   ☐ Category C = 71

Total = 504

FIGURE 6. Absolute number and percentage distribution of Class I offenses.

C respectively is 145, 288, 71. Because our ordering of categories begins with bodily injury, the number of these cases is the same, 145. But there were 302 cases of property theft, 14 of which are contained in Category A because theft accompanied the injuries, and there were 125 cases of property damage, four of which are contained in Category A because damage accompanied the injuries, and 50 of which are contained in Category B because damage accompanied the thefts. The total number of single events is 504; the total of additive violations is 572. There was no event in which harm, theft, and damage occurred simultaneously. In the diagram showing these relationships as a percentage of the 504 events, the order of frequency is revealed as (1) theft only (47%), bodily injury only (25%), damage only (14%), theft and damage together (10%), injury and theft together (3%), and injury and damage together (1%).

The hypotheses are confirmed by a statistical test of the probability that the observed distribution of events differs significantly from an expected distribution. In the analysis we have moved from first to third order levels of association, or from harm, theft, and damage, irrespective of combinations to three-dimensional combinations. Thus, if the probability of any harm equals the number of cases involving harm (145) divided by all offenses (1313), the probability of any damage (125) divided by all offenses, then we may compute the theoretical or expected number of combinations in the following manner, where p = probability; H = harm; T = theft; D = damage. The crossbars over letters refer to the absence of the item.

		EXPECTED	OBSERVED
$p(HTD) = p(H) \cdot p(T) \cdot p(D) \cdot N$	=	3.2	0
$p(HT\bar{D}) = p(H) \cdot p(T) \cdot 1 - p(D) \cdot N$	=	30.2	14
$p(\bar{H}TD) = 1 - p(H) \cdot p(T) \cdot p(D) \cdot N$	=	25.6	50*
$p(\bar{H}T\bar{D}) = 1 - p(H) \cdot p(T) \cdot 1 - p(D) \cdot N$	=	243.1	238
$p(H\bar{T}D) = 1 - p(T) \cdot p(H) \cdot p(D) \cdot N$	=	10.6	4
$p(H\bar{T}\bar{D}) = p(H) \cdot 1 - p(T) \cdot 1 - p(D) \cdot N$	=	101.0	127*
$p(\bar{H}\bar{T}D) = 1 - p(H) \cdot 1 - p(T) \cdot p(D) \cdot N$	=	85.6	71
$p(\bar{H}\bar{T}\bar{D}) = 1 - p(H) \cdot 1 - p(T) \cdot 1 - p(D) \cdot N =$		813.7	809

$$\chi^2 = 24.39; \text{d.f.} = 7; P < .001$$

Comparison of these two distributions reveals that there is a statistically significant difference, thus indicating that in the observed data certain types of combinations do not occur by chance. The two starred figures in the observed distribution are the only combinations that exceed the expected number. These are theft and damage without harm in the same event, and harm without theft and damage. Therefore, our hypotheses remain, i.e., cases involving harm are likely to appear with harm alone, whereas cases involving theft or damage often appear in combination.

These findings suggest that if no unidimensional basis were possible for measuring all offenses considered useful in an index, two indexes could be employed, one for bodily injury and one for property offenses that contained no bodily injury. Moreover, if we can employ a single dimension for all offenses, with an event containing both injury and a property offense, we could use injury alone for positioning the event on a scale. In either approach, only an insignificant set of combined items in the universe of all sets would be lost. Our next stage of analysis will determine how these problems can most efficiently and validly be resolved.

15

Theory, Design, and Procedure
for the Scaling of Offenses

We have said earlier that in order to measure delinquency qualitative
elements must be taken into account and that this accounting requires
the application of some kind of weighting system. We have also
asserted that the act of causing social harm—whether bodily injury,
property loss or damage—is an important and mensurable variable.
There still remains the problem of determining weights for other
associated variables if we are to arrive at an administratively and
sociologically meaningful and functionally efficient index of delinquency. In this chapter, we shall briefly discuss the theoretical
framework for the scaling of offenses and describe the design and
procedures used to obtain responses from selected subjects.

THEORETICAL FRAMEWORK

The underlying theory we are using for the scaling of delinquency
events is based upon work in psychophysics. Discussion of that work
here must necessarily be brief but should be sufficient to enable
readers unacquainted with that literature to appreciate its importance
and relevance to our problem.[1]

Our major purposes for scaling offenses were:

1. to select from multidimensional features of delinquency a single
   dimension, taking into account the relative gravity or seriousness
   of delinquent acts;
2. to produce an empirical, objectively ascertained set of components

[1] Research references in this and subsequent chapters provide a useful list for

236

of delinquency that would be examined by socially significant groups whose evaluations could be used as a basis for scoring;

3. to arrive at a system of weights for delinquency events for use in the construction of an index.

But if an event is to be weighted, should the relative importance of its individual components be determined arbitrarily or in some objective way? The criteria for determining degrees of seriousness of crimes must ultimately be determined by someone's or some group's subjective interpretation. If weights were assigned by a few criminologists engaged in the task of constructing a mathematical model, we should regard this as an arbitrary determination. But if judgments were elicited from theoretically meaningful and large social groups, consensus might produce a series of weighted values that would have validity. Therefore, we sought to obtain such judgments from purposively selected groups. Although no external objective criteria, beyond people's judgments, exists for producing a continuum of seriousness of delinquent acts, there are objective methods of measurement which have been developed into psychological "laws" relating two different kinds of psychological scales. These methods can be applied to such nonphysical dimensions as the graded seriousness of deviant behavior.

The conversion of qualitative intuitions of magnitude into quantitative variables is more or less straightforward in the physical sciences. Measurement of two of the three fundamental variables of physics was well understood by the Egyptians, even though fairly precise measures of the third, temporal, duration generally languished until the fifteenth century. Although empirical physical methods of measurement were well developed by the end of the nineteenth century, the theory of measurement was just beginning. The publication of Campbell's *Physics, the Elements*, in 1912 was one of the first attempts to show the underlying mathematical ideas in measurement.

In the mental and behavioral sciences, ideas of measurement, although commonplace since Bernouilli, were difficult to implement. The first serious attack on the problem was directed toward a specific issue—the relation of mind and body—and it was the partial solution of this problem that made one important point clear. Mental measurement requires some measurement theory before practical techniques can be invented. The observable relations among physical measures that serve to justify them are not easy to come by in mental

---

further study of these theories. Comments on scaling efforts using Guttman and other approaches appear in Chapter 20.

measurement. In fact, from the beginning it was clear that justification of mental measures would have to be based on some indirect theoretical arguments that connected one measurement with another. From the viewpoint of G. T. Fechner,[2] who first achieved important results in mental measurement, the mind-body problem concerned the nature of the rule that connected physical measures of energy, to which people were sensible, to their mental effect. Thus a "heavy" weight weighed more than a "light" weight. But how many more grams were added to a weight of ten grams to make it twice as "heavy"? Obviously not ten grams, if "heavy" and "light" refer to the psychological effect of the weights. To find this psychophysical rule, Fechner had to have a measure of "heaviness," and this he did not have. However, he conjectured a theory of psychological measure and used this theory along with some facts to establish the psychological scale. He then derived the psychophysical rule about the relation between mental and physical measures.

In foreshortened form, Fechner's conjecture is simplicity itself. If physical energies A and B are as confusible with each other as are physical energies C and D, then the psychological difference between the psychological effects of A and B $[\psi(A) - \psi(B)]$ are equal to the difference between the psychological effects of C and D $[\psi(C) - \psi(D)]$. Thus equal confusibility means equal psychological differences. This principle, coupled with the fact that the confusibility of the neighborhood of any particular physical event is proportional to the physical magnitude of the event (Weber's law), leads to Fechner's law: *The psychological measure of a physical event is equal to the logarithm of the physical measure (multiplied by a constant of proportionality).* Therefore, for intensive physical variables the psychological measure is simply the logarithm of the physical variable.

The ramifications of Fechner's ideas led to a variety of researches in psychophysics, all seeking firmly to establish or generalize Fechner's results. But these psychophysical relations gave no leverage to the general mental measurement problem. If we did not have a physical variable to measure, we could not assign psychological values to your presumed psychological variable. But Fechner's idea—that equal confusion between events could be interpreted as equal psychological units—suggested to L. L. Thurstone[3] that if one knew how confusions arose, then even without Weber's law (and its dependence on physical measures) confusions could be used as a psychological unit in their

[2] G. T. Fechner, *Elemente der Psychophysik* (Leipzig: Breitkopf and Hartel, 1860).

[3] L. L. Thurstone, "A law of comparative judgment," *Psychol. Rev.* 34:273–286 (1927).

own right. Thus, psychological events with no intrinsic physical counterpart could be given quantitative values. Only the interpretation of the confusion measures was arbitrary. Thurstone's scaling techniques were widely adopted and psychological measures became the common currency of much of social psychology. The applications of Thurstone's technique quickly gave rise to the search for laws governing relationships between psychological measures. Much of social science occupied itself with questions of how attitudes (psychologically measured) were related to interests (psychologically measured) or other such questions.

But the nub of the problem of "pure" psychological measurement remained. It involved the adequacy of Fechner's and Thurstone's intuition. If they were wrong the propositions were wrong. The question remained of how to decide if they were right. Some form of internal consistency usually appeared as a justification. The problem was that the internal consistency often existed by the very nature of the techniques. The techniques were too weak to place stringent demands on the data. What was needed was some internal "inconsistency," some differences in measurement of the same mental events with sufficient generality over events to let one know that measures of one kind of event conform to measurements of another.

In the middle and late 1930's, while studying psychophysical relations and measurement problems, S. S. Stevens developed a number of techniques for the assessment of psychological magnitudes of physically measurable events. One of the methods, ratio estimation and production, yielded results that were at variance with those of Fechner. In the measurement of "loudness," the psychological attribute of acoustic energy, he found that the relation between the physical measure and the psychological one was not Fechner's logarithm but appeared to be closer to the one-third power of energy. With these results, he challenged Fechner's law in psychophysics and the Fechner and Thurstone methods of measurement. The culmination of his position is set forth in a paper on the psychophysical law.[4]

The important issue for us is the disparity between Stevens and Fechner, and not the psychophysical question at all. What seems to be implied is that two different measurement methods give rise to two different results. The simple character of this statement conceals its real importance. In an extensive series of experiments, Stevens and Galanter[5] showed that, for a variety of physical continua, the two methods of measurement gave scales of psychological magnitude

[4] S. S. Stevens, "On the psychophysical law," *Psychol. Rev.* **64**:153–181 (1957).
[5] S. S. Stevens, and E. Galanter, "Ratio scales and category scales for a dozen perceptual continua," *J. exp. Psychol.* **54**:377–411 (1957).

that were indeed different, but were similarly (if not identically) related for each of the continua. One measure when plotted against another showed the same relation independent of the physical variable that happened to be involved. Thus they demonstrated a psychological law relating two different kinds of psychological scales. Stevens and his collaborators have extended this result to many other continua; Galanter and Messick[6] have shown the precise form of the psychological principle; and Galanter[7] has shown that the method can be applied to nonphysical dimensions.

To summarize what we know at this point: We see that Thurstone had provided a way to make psychological measurements based on Fechner's principle; that Stevens had shown that these measures are not unique; that Stevens and Galanter have later shown that they are uniquely related, independent of the objects of the measurement; and that Galanter has shown that Stevens' methods work for nonphysical continua. What remains to be seen is whether the psychological law demonstrated by Stevens and Galanter extends to many nonphysical continua. In the present study we are, of course, interested in knowing whether the formulation applies to the nonphysical continuum that represents the relative gravity of delinquent acts. If we were to find interrelations revealed by this psychological law, we would be in a position to assign values from the one or the other scale to the delinquency events in which we were interested and show how other values, concordant with these psychological values, could be obtained for other delinquent events on the same continuum.[8]

[6] E. Galanter and S. Messick, "The relation between category and magnitude scales of loudness," *Psychol. Rev.* **38**:363–372 (1961).

[7] E. Galanter, "The direct measurement of utility and subjective probability," *Amer. J. Psychol.* **75**:208–220 (1962).

[8] Application to many such continua permits a study of the parameters of this psychological relation to learn something about the people who gave rise to the actual measurements themselves. Even though the form of this psychological law may be the same for all people, the absolute values of the constants of the law may depend on social or cultural variables.

For some additional discussions of the theoretical formulation underlying our scaling design and for substantive findings of related interest, see the following:

E. Adams and S. Messick, "An axiomatic formulation and generalization of successive intervals scaling," *Psychometrika* **23**:355–368 (1958).

G. Diederich, S. Messick, and L. Tucker, "A general least squares solution for successive intervals," *Psychometrika* **22**:159–173 (1957).

H. Gulliksen, "A least squares solution for successive intervals assuming unequal standard deviations," *Psychometrika* **19**:117–139 (1954).

H. Gulliksen and S. Messick, *Psychological Scaling: Theory and Applica-*

DESIGN AND PROCEDURES

Offense Variables

The number of combinations of conceivable variables included in delinquency events is enormous. It was obviously impossible, within our time limits, to obtain any group's attitude toward them all; nor was it necessary, because we safely assumed, as subsequent analysis indicated, that some offenses are judged by one major component variable, most of the other components being considered inconsequential. In murder, for example, the offender's legal or illegal presence at the scene is irrelevant. Furthermore, all variables that conceivably could occur in any delinquent event were not available for research. The restrictions on known data considered useful for our general purposes were few but still limited to the information in the police officer's offense and investigation report. From this information and with the set of variables we considered important for index construction, we re-examined each of the items in the list of offenses in the Philadelphia Crime Code in order to select a subuniverse for scaling analysis. We purposely did not exclude items which would have no logical place in an index list. This was done in order to obtain, empirically and from different groups, an evaluation that could be compared with our own perspective. Running away, being truant or incorrigible, among others, were thus included for testing. However, because all our preceding logical and statistical analyses had suggested that bodily injury and property theft and damage were the most important, objectively verifiable, and valid categories to be con-

---

tion. (xvi, 211 pp. New York: Wiley, 1960).

R. D. Luce, "On the possible psychophysical laws," *Psychol. Rev.* **66**:81–95 (1959).

W. A. McGill, "The slope of the loudness function: A puzzle," H. Gullicksen and S. Messick (Eds.), *Psychological Scaling: Theory and Applications*, (211 pp., New York: Wiley, 1960).

S. Messick and R. P. Abelson, "Scaling and measurement theory," *Rev. Educ. Res.* **27**:487–497 (1957).

G. A. Miller, "Sensitivity to changes in the intensity of white noise and its relation to masking and loudness," *J. acoust. Soc. Amer.* **19**:609–619 (1947).

B. Scharf and J. C. Stevens, "The form of the loudness function near threshold," *Proc. 3rd International Congress on Acoustics* (1960).

S. S. Stevens, "The direct estimation of sensory magnitudes: Loudness," *Amer. J. Psychol.* **69**:1–25 (1956).

S. S. Stevens, "Tactile vibration: Dynamics of sensory intensity," *J. exp. Psychol.* **59**:210–218 (1959).

W. S. Torgerson, *Theory and Methods of Scaling* (460 pp. New York: Wiley, 1958).

sidered for index purposes, we decided to use the greatest number of versions among these categories. This spread was produced by various combinations of presence or absence of bodily injury, type of bodily injury, method used to inflict injury, whether property was stolen or damaged, whether intimidation was present and by what means; whether much or little property was stolen or damaged; whether violence had been involved in the property offense, or the presence of the offender was legal or illegal; whether, in automobile offenses, the cars were locked, unlocked, abandoned, returned, or damaged; and finally the type of victimization. Thus, for example, under robbery (310 and 311) there are twenty combinations, each of which includes the presence or absence of (a) the amount stolen (much or little), (b) the method of intimidation (by gun, blunt instrument, physical, verbal), (c) the method of inflicting harm (by gun, blunt instrument, physical), and (d) the degree of harm (hospitalization, minor). All told, 141 different specified events emerged from these various combinations. It was not theoretically necessary to expand some of the legal or traditional statistical categories, because a brief description of the legal offense included all elements needed for rating.

A list of the Philadelphia Crime Code offenses used in the analysis, along with their variations, follows.

ITEM NO.	PHILA-DELPHIA CRIME CODE	DESCRIPTIVE TITLE OF OFFENSE	VARIABLES 1 2 3 4	
1	111	Wilful killing		
2	111	Felony murder (+ robbery)		
3	111	Felony murder (+ rape)		
4	121	Manslaughter by auto		
5	211	Forcible rape (+ Agg. A & B)		
6	211	Forcible rape		
7	233	Ravish, attempt rape		*Key for Items 8–27*
8	311	Robbery	+ G G H	*Col. 1, Amount stolen:*
9	311		+ G G M	+ = Much
10	311		+ G O O	− = Little
11	310		+ B B H	*Col. 2, Means of*
12	310		+ B B M	*intimidation:*
13	310		+ B O O	G = Gun
14	310		+ P P H	B = Blunt instrument
15	310		+ P P M	P = Physical
16	310		+ P O O	V = Verbal

ITEM NO.	PHILA-DELPHIA CRIME CODE	DESCRIPTIVE TITLE OF OFFENSE	VARIABLES 1 2 3 4	
17	310		+ V O O	Col. 3, Method of inflict-
18	311		− G G H	ing harm:
19	311		− G G M	G = Gun
20	311		− G O −	B = Blunt instrument
21	310		− B B H	P = Physical
22	310		− B B M	O = None
23	310		− B O O	Col. 4, Type of harm:
24	310		− P P H	H = Hospitalization
25	310		− P P M	M = Minor
26	310		− P O O	O = None
27	310		− V O O	
28	404	Aggravated assault	G M	Key for Items 28–37
29	404		G T & D	Col. 1, Method of inflict-
30	404		G H	ing harm:
31	404		K M	G = Gun
32	404		K T & D	K = Knife
33	404		K H	B = Blunt instrument
34	404		B M	P = Physical
35	404		B T & D	Col. 2, Type of harm:
36	404		B H	H = Hospital
37	404		P H	T & D = Treated & dis-
				charged
				M = Minor
38	538	Burglary	+ P V	Key for Items 38–49
	548			Col. 1, Amount stolen:
39	538		− P V	+ = Much
	548			− = Little
40	538		+ P O	Col. 2, Type of
	548			victimization:
41	538		− P O	P = Primary
	548			S = Secondary
42	534		+ S V	T = Tertiary
	544			Col. 3, Presence of
43	534		− S V	violence:
	544			V = Violence
44	534		+ S O	O = No violence
	544			
45	534		− S O	
	544			
46	510		+ T V	
	520			

ITEM NO.	PHILA-DELPHIA CRIME CODE	DESCRIPTIVE TITLE OF OFFENSE	VARIABLES 1 2 3 4
47	510 520		− T V
48	510 520		+ T O
49	510 520		− T O
50	617	Larceny	+ P V L
51	614		+ P V I
52	632		− P V L
53	624		− P V I
54	617		+ P O L
55	614		+ P O I
56	616 626 636		− P O L
57	616 626 636		− P O I
58	617		+ S V L
59	617		+ S V I
60	627		− S V L
61	627		− S V I
62	613		+ S O L
63	617		+ S O I
64	623		− S O L
65	627		− S O I
66	617		+ T V L
67	618		+ T V I
68	647		− T V L
69	627		− T V I
70	617		+ T O L
71	617		+ T O I
72	627		− T O L
73	627		− T O I
74	611	Pocket picking	+ P O L
75	621		− P O L

Key for Items 50–75
Col. 1, Amount stolen:
  + = Much
  − = Little
Col. 2, Type of victimization:
  P = Primary
  S = Secondary
  T = Tertiary
Col. 3, Presence of violence:
  V = Violence
  O = No violence
Col. 4, Presence of offender:
  L = Legal
  I = Illegal

ITEM NO.	PHILA-DELPHIA CRIME CODE	DESCRIPTIVE TITLE OF OFFENSE			

					Key for Items 76–81
					Col. 1, Locked or
					unlocked:
					L = Locked
					U = Unlocked
					Col. 2, Disposition of
76	700's	Automobile theft	L	A D	*auto:*
77	700's		L	A O	A = Abandoned
78	700's		L	R O	R = Returned
79	700's		U	A D	*Col. 3, Condition of auto:*
80	700's		U	A O	D = Damaged
81	700's		U	R O	O = Not damaged

82	801	Assault & battery, primary minor
83	801	Assault & battery, primary T & D
84	902	Forgery
85	1001	Embezzlement $1000
86	1001	Embezzlement $5
87	1005	Passing worthless checks
88	1101	Receiving stolen goods
89	1201	Weapons (found when searched)
90	1201	Weapons (firing rifle)
91	1203	Other weapons
92	1301	Pandering
93	1302	Bawdy house proprietor
94	1303	Bawdy house inmate
95	1305	Prostitution (performs act)
96	1305	Prostitution (solicits)
97	1401	Incest (stepfather-stepdaughter)
98	1401	Incest (brother-sister)
99	1402	Indecent assault
100	1403	Corrupting
101	1405	Sodomy (no force)
102	1405	Sodomy (force)

ITEM NO.	PHILA-DELPHIA CRIME CODE	DESCRIPTIVE TITLE OF OFFENSE
103	1405	Sodomy (solicitation)
104	1406	Adultery
105	1407	Fornication
106	1408	Public indecency
107	1409	Enticing
108	1410	Statutory rape
109	1601	Drug selling—heroin
110	1601	Drug selling—marijuana
111	1602	Drug possession—heroin
112	1602	Drug possession—marijuana
113	1603	Drug using—heroin
114	1603	Drug using—marijuana
115	1703	Illegal possession of intoxicants
116	1710	Maintaining unlawful drinking place
117	1802	Intoxication
118	1804	Intoxication, minors
119	1901	Bawdy house frequenter
120	1903	Corner lounging
121	1904	Disorderly conduct
122	1909	Frequenter of unlawful drinking place
123	2001	Loitering
124	2002	Vagrancy
125	2103	Gambling on highway
126	2104	Gambling house, proprietor
127	2105	Gambling house, frequenter
128	2109	Lottery, numbers
129	2601	Abortion
130	2615	Threatening letters
131	2619	Truancy
132	2621	False alarm
133	2622	Trespassing
134	2623	Incorrigible
135	2624	Runaway
136	2626	Malicious mischief $1000
137	2626	Malicious mischief $5+
138	2628	Arson
139	2641	Kidnapping
140	2646	Perjury
141	2653	Obscene phone calls

Offense Descriptions

Variations were introduced where they were useful. Some offense types have some characteristics inherent in their legal definition, for example, criminal homicides, rapes, most robberies and assaults, all of which involve primary victimization; hence, no other kind of victimization variation can be tested. Furthermore, many of the offenses from items 84 through 141 are "mutual," "tertiary," or "no victimization" by our previous definitions. We have, as mentioned, concentrated variables in the offenses most commonly involving some degree of physical harm, loss of, or damage to, property.

After these items had been carefully selected, a brief description of each was typed on 3 x 5 cards for presentation to a group for trial testing. Phrasing the descriptions in order to eliminate an unconscious and unaccounted-for bias by the writer or by the subjects (judges) was an important process. Descriptions had to be brief to retain attention yet clear and unambiguous, and had to avoid extraneous adjectives. We tried to eliminate any reference to offender or victim variables except where obviously necessary (as in rape). The focus was on the act. Few assumptions were made about the judges' understanding of quasi-legal terminology. Robbery, burglary, or larceny, for example, were terms not used alone, for many persons are unaware of differences in their meanings. However, being truant from school, committing an illegal abortion, embezzling funds from an employer, and the like were offenses requiring little additional description to communicate the character of the offenses. Descriptions of the 141 offense items finally used in the scaling analysis are found in Appendix D.

Trial Run, Category, and Magnitude Scales

Seventeen subjects, most of whom were university students of both sexes, were used in the trial run for scoring all 141 offenses on an equal-interval scale of seriousness ranging from 1 to 7, where 1 represented "least serious" and 7 "most serious." The test was made to determine the adequacy of the description of each event and the modality of response. The descriptions appeared to be quite adequate and caused no misunderstanding. From the 2397 judgments (n items times s subjects) on the seven-point scale, median scores for particular offense items were determined. For each of the seven-scale divisions three offense items, whose medians represented the midpoint of the category and whose variability was at a minimum, were selected for testing with larger groups of subjects. This process was necessary in order to keep the total judgments within manageable proportions. Moreover, these offense items provided critical points on a continuum with which the remaining 120 items could subsequently be tested for positioning.

The next step involved a determination of types of scales to be used in the final testing experience. The previously mentioned studies in contemporary psychophysics, particularly those by Stevens and Galanter and Galanter and Messick, suggested the use of two types of scales: an eleven-point category scale and a magnitude estimation or ratio scale, the one scale to be plotted against the other to determine their relationship.[9]

The category scale used in the present study is common to much sociological research. It has lower and upper limits, in this case ranging from 1 and 11, with each division representing an equal distance between them. Consequently, judgments are to some extent "forced" within the arbitrary range with obvious restrictions on sensitivity because of limited discriminatory points. Theoretically the magnitude estimation scale has, by contrast, no established or assigned upper limit, and any number greater than zero could be used as the lower limit. An infinite number of discriminatory points are available for use in judging any phenomenon, each judgment being a ratio of a standard item positioned at the outset of the rating process. The assigned position of the standard item may be any number, since it is used merely as a base. The results of plotting the one scale against the other and the mathematical procedures for analyzing them are discussed in Chapter 16.

Choice of Judges

One group of the major issues in the scale analysis was the choice of groups to judge the relative seriousness of the twenty-one offenses and the total 141 offenses. The phenomena under investigation— delinquent acts—and the purpose of scaling these phenomena by their evaluated seriousness to the community were the principal guides for determining which groups should ultimately be selected. The ease or difficulty of obtaining some groups compared to others was considered partly in relation to time and resources available but did not constitute a major or serious limitation on the theoretical require-

---

[9] See especially, Galanter and Messick, *op. cit.* In this study the authors used loudness judgments of 20 stimuli obtained from 71 subjects on both magnitude estimation procedures and category judgments with eleven categories.

ments of the research design. We considered several groups among which the most suitable for our purposes seemed to be a sample of:

1. University students.
2. Police line officers.
3. Police assigned to the Juvenile Aid Division.
4. Juvenile court judges.
5. Criminal court judges.
6. The general population of the entire community, or some sub-sections of the community, including victims of delinquent or criminal acts.
7. The list of persons originally selected for jury duty.

If the purpose of assigning weights of seriousness of delinquency were to reflect an entire community's sentiment, a kind of Durk-heimian "collective conscience," then clearly a representative random (or perhaps stratified) sample of the population of the entire community should be chosen—with all socioeconomic classes, with offenders and victims, all races, both sexes, and perhaps all ages above the common-law age of criminal responsibility. In our deliberations, we came close to adopting group (6) or (7) above. Group (7) would have been more restricted but still an important, large, and representative segment of the general community population, for it comprises not only those registered voters who served as jurors but also those who were selected for jury duty by a random process, many of whom never did serve for various reasons. Essentially, groups (6) and (7) both fell within the "community sentiment" concept.

Several theoretical and practical reasons caused us to use groups (1) university student, (2) police line officers, (3) Juvenile Aid Division officers, and (4) juvenile court judges. There was the practical problem of accessibility of subjects. University students were present and traditionally captive for such experimental research. The administration of the police department was continually coopera-tive and willing, as we shall see, to set up the elaborate machinery for having a large body of police officers available for the ratings. This cooperation included both regular line officers and juvenile aid officers.

But beyond the practical reasons were important theoretical ones. The philosophy and the sociology of the criminal law suggest that principal culture themes of legal prescriptions and sanctions come from the middle-class value system. Representatives of this value system legislate and adjudicate. Thus the definition of crime and the administration of criminal justice are institutionalized expressions of the normative structure of the dominant middle class in American society. If this argument is correct, it may be asked why we did not ask a sample of the middle class in our urban setting to rate the seriousness of specific delinquent acts. This would have been an enormous task consuming resources beyond the limits of the study, but more than this, we were not convinced of its necessity. Despite their occasional revolt against authority while part of the teen-age culture, university students like their parents, generally hold the middle-class values embodied in the common law. Avoidance of physical aggression in the form of assaultive behavior, a quasi-sacred respect for property, the importance of using leisure time wholesomely and productively, emphasis upon ambition, etc., are components of the middle-class ethic and are values commonly shared by most university students. Although there is undoubtedly considerable diversity among some value orientations within any large student body, it seems safe to assume much homogeneity regarding attitudes toward crime and especially toward the offenses that logical inference and empirical reference point to as index offenses. We therefore considered a group of students to have typical middle-class values toward the 141 offenses or any selection of them.

Except for some higher administrative positions, police officers by education, occupation, and income generally belong in a lower stratum of the class structure. But they are also guardians and executors of the law, which, as we have contended, reflects middle-class values. Whether police officers in the field function as carriers of middle-class values, at least with respect to law violation, is not fully known. The social organization and value system of this group have not yet been adequately analyzed by sociologists. That there are role conflicts and concomitant value conflicts among the police is suggested in some of the literature,[10] but whether the police execute their

---

[10] Jacob Chwast, "Value Conflicts in Law Enforcement," Paper presented to the annual conference of the American Society of Criminology, Denver, Colorado (December 30, 1961).

T. C. Esselstyn, "The social role of a county sheriff," *J. Crim. Law, Criminol. and Police Sci.* 44:177–184 (July-August 1953).

Caleb Foote, "Vagrancy-type law and its administration," *University of Pennsylvania Law Rev.* 104:603–650 (March, 1956).

Nathan Goldman, "The Differential Selection by Police of Juvenile Offenders for Court Appearance," Ph.D. dissertation, University of Chicago (1950).

G. Douglas Gourley, "Recognition and status for rank and file policemen,"

roles with a middle- or lower-class value orientation is difficult to determine at this time. A comparison of their scale scores of offenses with those of university students provides some clues to this issue and is discussed below.

There is a more cogent reason for using the police in the scale analysis. Except for the citizen complainant or victim (and the two are not always synonymous) who witnesses a crime, the police are the first to come into contact with the offender. In many cases the police are the complainants, representing the community. In other than vis-à-vis offenses, the victim does not encounter the offender personally. The police are society's reconnaissance troops, literally the front-line patrols from legislative and judicial headquarters. It is usually their action that sets the whole machinery of justice into operation in particular cases and that determines, through their decision to make or not to make an arrest, whether the full apparatus will be used to deal with an offender. Particularly with juveniles, the police have wide choices in their initial handling of cases. Only if the police decide to arrest does the court also receive the case.[11]

The attitude of the police, therefore, plays an extremely important part in the collection of delinquency statistics. How serious the police think an offense to be affects their discretion and their decisions. Their judgments are critical and their weighing of the gravity of offenses, albeit without purposive precision, is fundamental to our problem of constructing a quantitative index that takes into account qualitative variations.

J. Crim. Law, Criminol. and Police Sci. **40**:75–84 (May-June 1949).

William M. Kephart, *Racial Factors and Urban Law Enforcement* (209 pp. Philadelphia: University of Pennsylvania Press, 1957).

Robert S. Lynd and Helen M. Lynd, *Middletown* (xii, 550 pp. New York: Harcourt, Brace, 1929).

Robert S. Lynd and Helen M. Lynd, *Middletown in Transition* (xviii, 604 pp. New York: Harcourt, Brace, 1937).

Bruce Smith, *Police Systems in the United States* (xx, 384 pp. New York: Harper, 1940).

William A. Westley, "Violence and the police," *Amer. J. Sociol.* **49**:34–41 (August, 1953).

William Foote Whyte, *Street Corner Society* (xxii, 366 pp. Chicago: The University of Chicago Press, 1955).

O. W. Wilson, *Police Administration* (x, 540 pp. New York: McGraw-Hill, 1950).

[11] John I. Kitsuse and Aaron V. Cicourel, "A note on the uses of official statistics," *Social Problems* **11**:131–139 (Fall 1963), emphasize this same point: "The theoretical conception which guides us is that the rates of deviant behavior are produced by the actions taken by persons in the social system which define, classify and record certain behaviors as deviant" (p. 135).

The juvenile court judge may also have value conflicts in his role, especially if he is not on full time in juvenile court and presides now and then in adult criminal proceedings. His disposition of a case is a function of many more variables than those associated with the offense, for principal focus in the juvenile court is on the offender, his age, previous record, attitude, and so forth. Still, the juvenile court judge, who probably, and more than the police, reflects middle-class values, is acutely aware of delinquent acts and is a knowledgeable observer whose opinions on the subject command respect in the community. The degree to which his ratings of offenses are concordant or discordant with those of university students and of the police was considered useful to our problem of weighting offenses.

The Offender Variable

We were concerned with offender variables in the rating of seriousness, but we could not ignore the fact that any addition of offender information would require a proportionately greater number of subjects judging the offenses. Moreover, we could not lose sight of the basic issue of constructing an index, else all kinds of interesting associational factors could be queried in the ratings, such as the sex and race of the offender, victim-offender relationships, group versus individual offenders, and so forth. It was necessary to remain within the frame of our problem for obvious reasons, but because we were dealing with juveniles it seemed equally important to try to obtain responses that might differentiate acts committed by juveniles from acts committed by adults when a rating of seriousness of the same act is being judged. To do so, we introduced offender age variables while keeping the descriptions of offenses constant. Because the vast majority of delinquents are males, the sex of the offender was always given as male except in a few offenses peculiar to females (items 94–96). The description of the offender was either

(a) the offender is a male,
(b) the offender is a male 27 years of age,
(c) the offender is a male 17 years of age, or
(d) the offender is a male 13 years of age.

The male of unidentified age was used primarily because we intended to concentrate attention on the act committed, on the physical injury done, or on the theft or damage produced. The rater was expected to respond primarily to the degree of gravity of an offense and secondarily, if at all, to the characteristics of the offender. We have suggested elsewhere that the victim of a theft probably is more concerned with the amount stolen than with who stole it or how many persons participated. The choice of age 27 was purposefully made to have an offender of typical adult criminal age sufficiently far removed from a "youth" status. Age 17 was used because this is the upper limit of the juvenile court age in many states (including Pennsylvania) and constitutes an age which may be presumed by many subjects to possess the greatest degree of responsibility, among all juveniles, for "rational" and "volitional" conduct. We also were seeking to determine whether a delinquent act is regarded as more serious when committed by an older rather than by a younger juvenile. Finally, we wanted an offender having an age that would be still younger yet not so young as to preclude his committing most of the offenses on our list. Age 13, therefore, represented the offender sufficiently distant from one aged 17 while still possessing the image of a potentially destructive juvenile needing social intervention when he committed violations of the law.

Randomization

The mechanical procedure for preparing the scale requires a brief description because the ordering in which the offenses to be rated would be placed might have an effect on the raters. A larceny following a disorderly conduct might be judged more serious than a larceny following a murder; a charge of intoxication might be judged more serious if it followed a runaway offense than if it were preceded by a larceny; and so forth. We could not be sure of the specific effect of any particular order, and consequently balanced the unknown effect of any sequence by randomizing the order. Randomizing was achieved by writing down on cards a number assigned to each offense, shuffling the cards, and sequencing the offenses in the shuffled order. Instead of merely randomizing once and in the same way for all raters, we randomized each set of offenses for each rater. No two raters received an identical ordering of offenses. The influence of offense order was therefore reduced entirely to chance variations.

Instructions and Testing

Each rater was told that his name would remain anonymous on the test and was given a small booklet (8½ x 5½) which contained on separate pages the university address of the project, the instructions for filling out the booklet, two examples of the category scale or one example of the magnitude scale, and the offenses to be judged. Each offense description appeared on a separate page, at the top of which the specific offender description was given which remained the same throughout each booklet. At the bottom of each page for the category rating was the following:

										Most
Least										Serious
Serious										
1	2	3	4	5	6	7	8	9	10	11

The instructions for the *Category Scale* were carefully phrased:

This booklet describes a series of violations of the law; each violation is different. Your task is to show how serious *you* think each violation is, *not* what the law says or how the courts might act.

You do this by circling a number from 1 to 11 on each page which shows how serious each violation seems to you. The first two violations have been done as examples. The first one describes a violation in the most serious category and 11 was circled; the second crime is in the least serious category and 1 was circled. You should read each of the following violations and circle the number you think best fits it. If you think it is in the least serious category circle 1. If you think it is of middle seriousness circle 6. If you think it is the most serious category circle 11. You may circle any number 1, 2, 3, 4, 5, 6, 7, 8, 9, 10 or 11 just so long as it shows how serious you think the violation is. Each of the eleven categories is an equal step on the scale of seriousness so that 6 is one step more serious than 5 and 10 is one step more serious than 9, and so forth.

Take your time. Every page should have one circle on it. Do not turn back once you have finished a page. Remember, this is not a test. The important thing is how *you* feel about each violation. Do not write your name on any of the sheets for you will not be identified.

If the booklet was designed for the *Magnitude Estimation Scale*, a large empty score box was placed at the bottom of the page on which each offense was described. The instructions for the *Magnitude Scale* were as follows:

This booklet describes a series of violations of the law; each violation is different. Your task is to show how serious *you* think each violation is, *not* what the law says or how the courts might act.

You do this by writing down in a score box on each page a number which shows how serious each violation seems to you. The first violation has been done as an example. It shows a violation which is given a seriousness score of 10. Use this violation as a standard. Every other violation should be scored in relation to this standard violation. For example, if any violation seems ten times as serious as the standard violation, write in a score of 100. If a violation seems half as serious as the standard, write in a score of 5. If a violation seems only a twentieth as serious as the standard, write in a score of ½ or .50. You may use *any* whole or fractional numbers that are greater than zero, no matter how small or large they are just so long as they represent how serious the violation is compared to the standard violation. Take your time. Every page should have a number in the score box. Do not turn back once you have finished a page. Remember, this is not a test. The important thing is how *you* feel about each violation. Do not write your name on any of the sheets for you will not be identified.

Experimental psychological testing of university students is a common episode on many campuses and the procedures used in the present study were not unlike those employed in other testings and attitude studies. Our total number of university subjects was 251; some took the category scale, others took the magnitude scale. Because major focus was placed on the offense and the seriousness of the injury inflicted on the community, a larger portion of the raters were asked to rate offenses committed by a male of unidentified age. Besides the 21 offenses with highest modal heaping discovered on the trial run, the remaining 120 offenses were randomly grouped into four sets of 30 and each set, like the original set of 21, was randomly ordered for each rater. Some, then, were asked to rate not only the 21 offenses rated by everybody, but an additional 30 that were placed at the end of the set of 21. Although no raters in the trial run objected to the large number of offenses (141) to be judged, apparently because the task was more simple to rate on a seven-point scale, we felt that to ask any single individual to rate more than 51 offenses on a magnitude scale might produce fatigue which would reduce the validity of the testing device.

Male students enrolled in courses of introductory sociology in two local universities (Temple and Penn State Ogontz Center) were used. There was no need to take a random sample of students. Most students enroll for the course in introductory sociology without any special factor of student enrollment that might cause them to cluster in a particular way.

Rating done on a given campus was completed in a single day under circumstances allowing no communication about the test among raters before or during the rating. Table 66 shows the distribution of 251 students according to type of scale, number of offenses being evaluated, and offender variables.

With cooperation from the police department, 310 police officers were selected and asked to appear at five separate centers throughout the city on the same day and at the same hour to rate the seriousness of offenses. It was important that we had sufficient numbers of police raters by scale type and offender variables to make comparisons between the police and the university students. Consequently, a larger

TABLE 66. *Number of Raters in Various Groups Who Scaled 21 Offenses, by Scale Type and Offender Style*

AGE OF MALE OFFENDER	CATEGORY				MAGNITUDE				
	UNIVERSITY STUDENTS		POLICE OFFICERS	JUVENILE COURT JUDGES	UNIVERSITY STUDENTS		POLICE OFFICERS	JUVENILE COURT JUDGES	TOTAL
	Temple	Ogontz			Temple	Ogontz			
Unidentified	21	45	55	...	20	37	47	...	225
13 years	22	...	33	20	18	...	29	18	140
17 years	21	...	29	...	19	...	34	...	103
27 years	21	...	27	...	21	...	32	...	101
Total	85	45	144	20	78	37	142	18	569

number of police were asked to rate offenses with male offenders of unidentified age. The absence of communication prior to and during the rating was especially important in the case of police officers, for we knew them to be very sensitive to any testing procedures, feeling either that their status might be threatened or that they themselves were being judged for promotion or for some similar reason associated with their work. Despite the difficulties of having many police officers available and off patrol duty, simultaneity was achieved. After a meeting of district inspectors, including the inspector of the Juvenile Aid Division, who were briefed on the purpose of the rating, each inspector was asked to select a reasonably representative group of line officers from his district to participate in the scaling. The requirements for selection did not have to be rigid. Because of the size of the group, we had no reason to believe that any rating differences would escape us. We asked that there be a general selection of these men by different lengths of service, age, and diversity of experience. The number selected from each district was roughly proportional to the size of the force in the district.

Table 67 shows the distribution of the 286 police officers who turned

TABLE 67. Number of Police and Ogontz Raters Judging One of Four Sets of the 120 Offenses with Male Offender of Unidentified Age, by Scale Type

	TYPE OF SCALE						
	CATEGORY			MAGNITUDE			
OFFENSE GROUPS[a]	Police	Ogontz	Total	Police	Ogontz	Total	Grand Total
A	11	12	23	12	10	22	45
B	11	11	22	12	11	23	45
C	11	11	22	12	11	23	45
D	11	11	22	11	11	22	44
Total[b]	44	45	89	47	43	90	179

[a] Each group (A, B, C, D) of offenses included 30 offenses to be rated. By rough approximation, each group of 30 contained similar types of offenses, but the four groups combined comprised the 120 different offenses.

[b] Because the A, B, C, D partial sets of offenses made up the complete set of 120 offenses, the number of times the complete set was rated equals the minimum number in that column.

in usable booklets according to the type of scale, number of offenses being evaluated, and offender variables.

When the groups were assembled, a member of the research staff briefly described the purpose of the ratings as being solely one of obtaining their opinions of the seriousness of law violations. Again, because we focused on the act, we did not mention the title of our research project (which contains the word "delinquency"), especially because some raters were evaluating offenses committed by a male offender of unknown age or by a male 27 years of age. The raters were told that this was an experiment to find out how they judged seriousness of offenses and that they were to make their judgments as they felt, not as the law says or as the courts might act. They were told that their names were not to be recorded on the booklets. Students are accustomed to such instructions, and from our discussions with them *after* the scaling operation, we were sure that the students took the experiment seriously. The police officers, less used to such testing, knew that their names were recorded on the police district roll by the district inspectors or other administrative heads and as a group they were impressed with the importance of taking the experiment seriously. Essentially, the same instructions that appeared in written form in the booklet were orally given before each group and no additions were made.[12]

Finally, of the 64 juvenile court judges in Pennsylvania who received test booklets, 38 returned them. This was the only group instructed by mail. There appeared to be no regional factor among those who returned them which would distinguish them from the rest and therefore bias the returns.

In the chapters that follow, references are made to the various groups of raters. "Judges" will refer to the juvenile court judges; "Temple" means students from Temple University; "Ogontz" means students at the Ogontz Penn State Center in Philadelphia; "police" refers to the police officers who participated in the rating; and in Chapter 17 reference will be made to a final group of raters, "U of P," referring to the testing of and ratings by students from the University of Pennsylvania.

---

[12] Those doing the magnitude scale were given more detail, for the experimenter checked on their understanding by giving them problems: for example, "If the second offense seems twice as serious as the standard violation, Sgt. Brown, what number would you give it?" "If the second offense seems half as serious as the standard violation, Sgt. Smith, what number would you give it?" After an average time of 30 minutes, the booklets were collected.

16

The Category and Magnitude Scales: results of the testing

THE RELATION BETWEEN THE TWO SCALES

One preliminary question must be answered at the outset. Specifically, are the category scale and magnitude scale for the social variable of the seriousness of delinquency related to each other in a fashion analogous to what would have been observed if a physical variable had been scaled in this way? What has now become the classical result[1] is that the mean category values plotted as a function of the means of magnitude estimation in arithmetical coordinates yield a function that is concave downward. Figure 7 shows part of the results for the 21 offenses judged by the juvenile court judges for 13-year-old offenders. It is obvious that one could form a concave downward curve through these points. That the two scales are not related by the logarithm can be shown by taking the logarithm of the means of the magnitude estimations and plotting the points as in Figure 8. If this logarithmic transformation linearized the data points, we should be surprised insofar as Stevens and Galanter have shown that for physical variables the data are consistently not logarithmically related. On the other hand, Galanter and Messick[2] and Luce and Galanter[3] argue that the mean category values do not com-

[1] S. S. Stevens and E. Galanter, "Ratio scales and category scales for a dozen perceptual continua," *J. exp. Psychol.* **54**:377–411 (1957).

[2] E. Galanter and S. Messick, "The relation between category and magnitude scales of loudness," *Psychol. Rev.* **38**:363–372 (1961).

[3] R. D. Luce and E. Galanter, "Psychophysical scaling," Chapter 5 in R. D. Luce, R. Bush, and E. Galanter, Eds., *Handbook of Mathematical Psychology*, Volume I (xiii, 491 pp. New York: Wiley, 1963).

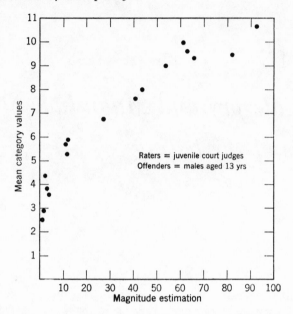

FIGURE 7. Magnitude and category scale scores, linear coordinates. Not all values are shown.

prise a reasonable scale at all. The numbers given by the raters are marked off on the graph with equal spacing between the intervals. But the particular numbers that the raters used are quite arbitrary. Any set of numbers, or even letters or adjectives of quantity could have been used (Stevens and Galanter, 1956). What justification is there, then, to assume equal spacing between the categories? Obviously, none at all. The fact that these numbers are plotted in an equally spaced fashion on a piece of paper, when the experimenter could have chosen any set of numbers or even names to indicate the categories, suggests that this scale, although it is probably a good approximation, is not the category scale that we should use. Rather, we suspect that we should transform the category values assigned by the rater into scale values by techniques similar to those developed by Thurstone and Fechner. That is to say, we should take into account the confusibility of the various category assignments.

To accomplish this, we make use of Thurstone's theory and the method of successive intervals developed originally in 1939 by Saffir.[4]

[4] M. Saffir, "A comparative study of scales constructed by three psychophysical methods," *Psychometrika* **2**:179–198 (1937).

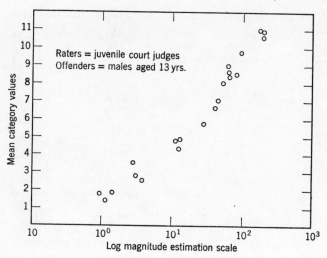

FIGURE 8. Magnitude and category scale scores plotted on a logarithmic scale.

Actually, the method of Saffir was generalized in 1959 by Helm, Messick, and Tucker[5] to eliminate the rather untenable assumption that the confusibility of the items is uniform over the entire scale. Because the Helm et al. method requires the use of high speed computing machines to calculate the scale values, all the category scale values of our various groups of subjects were converted into "processed" category scales.[6] This procedure involves conversion to homoscedasticity of the variance at different scale points. Figure 9 shows the relation between the magnitude scale and the "processed" category scale for the same data as shown in Figures 7 and 8. The slight curvilinearity has been eliminated by this processing procedure, and the relation between the scales is thus shown empirically to be logarithmic.[7]

We are satisfied that the *relation* between processed category judg-

[5] C. Helm, S. Messick, and L. Tucker, *Psychophysical Law and Scaling Models* (Princeton, N.J.: Educational Testing Service Research Bulletin, No. 59-1, 1959). See also Goesta Ekman, "Measurement of moral judgment: A comparison of scaling methods," *Perceptual and Motor Skills* 15:3–9 (1962).

[6] We should like to express our gratitude to Samuel Messick and Henrietta Gallagher of the Educational Testing Service of Princeton, N.J., for assistance and cooperation in this procedure.

[7] The processing procedure of Helm et al. requires the existence of variability in the raters' use of the categories. For some groups of raters, insufficient var-

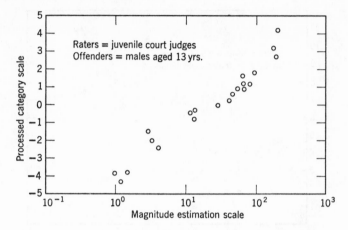

FIGURE 9. Magnitude and processed category scale scores.

ments and magnitude judgments for these offenses behaves in a way analogous to judgments of physical variables. We are now in a position to ask questions about whether the psychological "law" or parameters of the psychological law that relate these two kinds of judgments depend upon other variations in our experimental treatments.

Two major aspects of variation were employed in the current study. On the one hand, as previously indicated, we varied the content of the items that we presented to our groups of raters by varying the nominal age of the hypothetical offender. That is to say, some groups of raters made judgments about the offenses relative to a 13-year-old offender, other groups made judgments about a 17-year-old offender, others, an offender 27 years old, and still others made judgments about an offender who was identified only as being a male.

We now can ask whether the age of the ostensible offender alters either the form or the parameters of the psychological relation between these two scale values for the people who are making the judgment.

On the other side of the experimental coin, we also varied the sociocultural category of the groups who were making the judgments.

iability was present in a few of the end categories to make these values reliable. When this happened, the data points were deleted from the subsequent analysis. This condition is indicated in Table 68 by an asterisk (*). The number of deleted points can be determined from the figures. In no case does it exceed 3 of the original 21 offenses.

We had as groups of raters police officers, college students, and juvenile court judges. We could reasonably expect that these different sociocultural groups would reveal differences in the form or parametric values of the relation between the two psychological scales of the seriousness of offenses.

Finally, we can ask whether there is any interaction or interdependence between the people who are doing the judging and the nominal age of the offender. Thus, for example, police officers might alter their judgments relative to adult males and 13-year-olds whereas college students might not.

NO SIGNIFICANT DIFFERENCES BY AGE OF OFFENDER OR GROUPS OF RATING SUBJECTS

Before we begin to make comparisons of various experimental treatments, we must find some way to characterize the relations that we observe. That is, we must find a way to assign to each set of data numbers that represent one or more features of these data. These numbers can then be compared in order to find out whether any meaningful results have emerged.

If all the data of the study give rise to relations similar to that in Figure 9, namely that all the relations between the magnitude and category scales for all the offenders and all the various raters yield straight lines when plotted in this semilogarithmic coordinate system, we can assume that the principle operating in every case is the same, and that the only variation that could possibly occur is variation in the slope and intercept of the line representing this principle. This supposition is well founded. Each of the rater groups who made judgments about each of the offender/offense examples produced data which when plotted as in Figure 9 yield straight line relationships. Of course, this assertion must be qualified by the fact that the data consist of points scattered over each graph. But the general feature of the scatter of points is that to a first approximation they can be represented by a straight line. Figure 10, *a–j*, shows the various empirical functions for the ten conditions. The essentially linear form of each condition is readily apparent by inspection.

Now observe that when the raters make judgments under category instructions, they are told to use the first category for the least serious offense and the last category for the most serious. In addition, they are given examples of these offenses so that they will understand the use of these end categories. The raters are therefore limited in the range of values that they can assign. The only way that they can

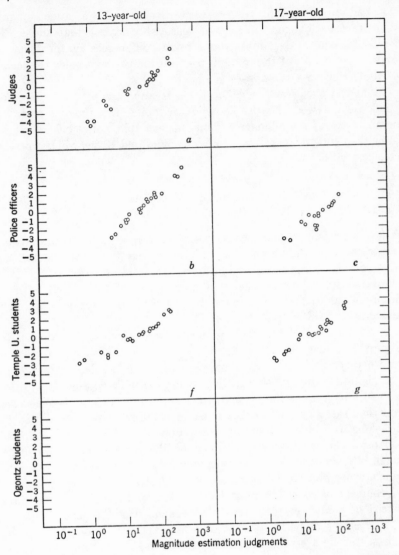

FIGURE 10. *Processed*

vary their assignment of category values to the offenses is by varying the relative spacing of the categories they use.

When the raters are making judgments under magnitude estimation instructions, however, they are given only a single offense and asked to consider it the modulus. From that point forward, they are free

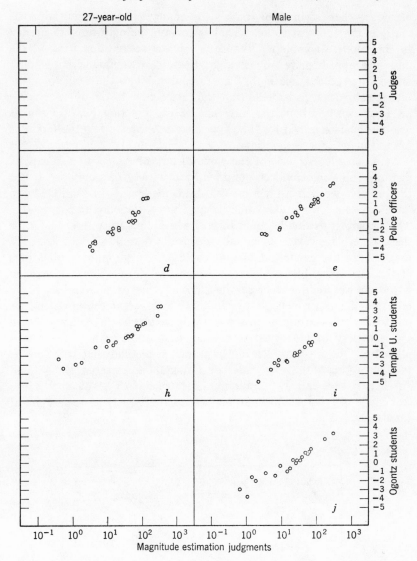

category scales.

to use any positive numbers that they choose, therefore, the relative
seriousness of the offenses can range over an indefinite domain of
numbers. Hence, if the form of the relation between the two scales
remains constant (i.e., logarithmic) and the range of category assignments is fixed by the instructions, then the only changes that can

occur are changes in slope induced by changes in the magnitude estimations the subjects make. That is to say, the only number needed to characterize completely the data (on the assumption that all the data are approximated by straight lines in a semilogarithmic plot) is the slope of the relation. This is equivalent to the range of magnitude estimation judgments that the raters gave to the offenses. We need not worry about the intercept of the function because this is arbitrarily determined by the experimenter when he sets the modulus for the magnitude estimations.

A reasonable estimate of the slope of any of the particular experimental conditions could be obtained by a variety of techniques. For the present, we will use simple graphical methods. In Figure 11, we have drawn a least squares line through the data points in Figure 10a. The slope of this line is equal to 0.29 which constitutes a statistic for these data. However, as in all empirical work, these data are only a sample of the possible data that could arise from many replications of the same experiment. That is to say, we do not know how much variation we could expect in the slope of this particular line if we repeated the experiment many times. To represent this problem, we must take into consideration the intrinsic scatter of the points. There are a variety of numerical techniques that could be used to accomplish this, but we have selected a graphical method that will give us two slopes, one that we call the "maximum expected slope" and another that we call the "minimum expected slope." We can then use this range of possible slopes in making comparisons with experimental conditions.

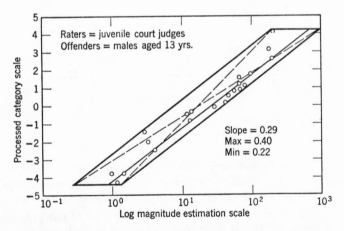

FIGURE 11. *Maximum and minimum slope of seriousness.*

These numbers are constructed in the following way. We draw a parallelogram whose sides are parallel to the line that represents the data, and whose width and length are just large enough to encompass all the data points on the graph. This "envelope" is shown by the heavy lines in Figure 11. The long and the short diagonals shown by dotted lines constitute the maximum and the minimum expected slope for these data. The particular statistics have an arbitrary character but they are simple to reproduce and are transparent in their intended representation.

We are now in a position to make our analysis of the effects of our experimental variations on the judgments made by our various groups of raters. Table 68 constitutes a summary of all of the data. The columns in the table represent the nominal age of the offenders about whom the judgments were made. The rows in the table refer to the various groups of people who served as raters. The entries in each cell show the slope of the psychological principle and the maximum and minimum expected slopes as determined by the graphical technique used in Figure 11.

The overwhelming impression conveyed by Table 68 is the extreme similarity in the slopes of the functions relating the magnitude to the category judgments. The similarity is perhaps strongest within a particular treatment group, but when we examine the range of possible slopes by comparing the difference between the maximum and

TABLE 68. *Raters and Offenders; Range of Slope of Seriousness*

Raters	MALE OFFENDER, BY AGE							
	13 Years		17 Years		27 Years		Unidentified Age	
Juvenile court judges	0.29							
	Max. 0.40	Min. 0.22						
Police officers	0.31		0.30 *		0.27		0.26	
	Max. 0.40	Min. 0.29	Max. 0.57	Min. 0.25	Max. 0.42	Min. 0.24	Max. 0.34	Min. 0.23
Temple University students	0.24		0.27		0.22		0.28 *	
	Max. 0.35	Min. 0.19	Max. 0.37	Min. 0.23	Max. 0.26	Min. 0.16	Max. 0.33	Min. 0.24
Penn State University, Ogontz Center, students							0.26 *	
							Max. 0.34	Min. 0.22

the minimum slope in each of the cells, we see that the slope value of any one cell could very well have arisen in any other cell.

Considering the police officers and the Temple University students on whom most of the data were collected, we might possibly conjecture that the police officers show slightly steeper slopes than the Temple students. This is reflected by the fact that the range of magnitude estimation judgments used by the police officers fall within a narrower range than that used by the Temple University students. Although these differences might, under repeated measurements, turn out to be significant, the differences are small, and the impressive quality of the data is their over-all similarity. Subtle differences could be selected and elaborated upon, for example, the greatest similarity in functions appears to obtain over the various raters for items in which the age of the offender was not identified. But even here some care must be exercised insofar as two of the three sets of data are truncated because of insufficient variability in the construction of the processed category scale.

The most strongly supported conclusion on the basis of the data at hand is that all the raters, although unconstrained in their use of the magnitude scale assignments, tended to so assign the magnitude estimations that the seriousness of the crimes is evaluated in a similar way, without significant differences, by all the groups. The age of the offender does not particularly color a person's judgment about the seriousness of the offense. A pervasive social agreement about what is serious and what is not appears to emerge, and this agreement transcends simple qualititative concordance; it extends to the estimated numerical degree of seriousness of these offenses.

Because of the inherent ratio quality of the magnitude judgments, the particular numbers used by the raters are not especially relevant; rather, it is the ratios of offense seriousness that are preserved intact. Thus a particular offense may be judged to have seriousness 20 by a police officer and seriousness 2 by a university student. What this means is that if the police officers judge another offense as twice as serious and therefore call it 40, then the university students when judging the same offense will call it 4. It is the ratios of the offense that remain constant from one class of raters to another.

STABILITY OF RATINGS

We might reasonably ask at this point how stable these judgments are, i.e., are the particular numerical assignments, and therefore the particular ratios of differential offensiveness, contingent upon the

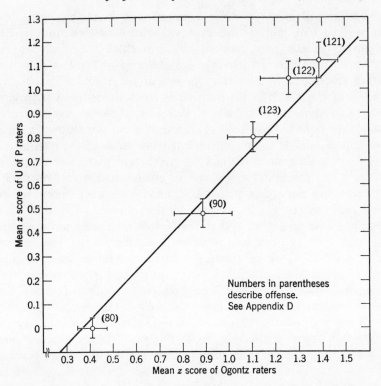

FIGURE 12. Mean standard scores (z) ± standard error of the mean (δ∓) on the magnitude scale of seriousness for five offenses judged in two contexts. (Line describes perfect relation.)

particular set of offenses that were scaled? We can partially examine this question by comparing the scale values of some of these 21 offenses judged in their own context, with scale values assigned to them when they occur in the context of other offenses. To accomplish this, five of the original 21 offenses were extracted from 20 offenses adapted from our pool of 141. These five items are from a narrow range of scale values and consequently make this test as powerful as possible. This new task was given to 195 University of Pennsylvania undergraduates who were asked to make magnitude estimations of these items.[8]

In Figure 12 we show the magnitude scale values of the five offenses taken from the judgments made by the Ogontz students plotted

[8] See *infra*, pp. 281–284 for more details on this later test.

against the judgments of these same offenses in their new context. The vertical bars indicate one standard error estimated from the 105 judgments in the new context; the horizontal bars indicate one standard error estimated from the Ogontz raters. The line represents perfect agreement between the two sets of judgments. The relative position of the five offenses remains fairly constant even with large changes in context. We believe, therefore, that the assignment of numerical values to the offenses is independent of the context in which they appear, and is associated with the substance of the offense.

The result suggests a method by which any particular offense or statement not previously scaled can be given a numerical value. We may take any particular offense that has been scaled before, for example, any one of the 21 offenses that we have used in our initial experiment; we then present that offense to a rater, assign it a number (the modulus), and ask him to assign a number to the new and unscaled offense. If we do this for a number of raters, i.e., ask them to make only a single numerical judgment about the new offense, then the mean score of that new offense, relative to a normalized modulus (multiplying or dividing the new offense by a factor that will make the modulus equal for all of the raters), gives us immediately the value of the new offense relative to this scale. Even if a different offense is used for each judgment and assigned an arbitrary value, the score for the new offense should not systematically depend on the choice of the offense that is the basis of the judgment. This invariance of judgment makes it possible to use an easy method for ascertaining the seriousness of previously unscaled offenses, simply by asking a question of a variety of raters.

The technique just described also permits an investigation of sets of hypotheses about cultural, subcultural, or social differences among raters. Differences among the various populations will be revealed by differences in the ratios of the old to the new offense. Insofar as those ratios do not differ among populations, we may conclude that their judgments conform, at least as a first approximation, to the judgments that we have observed in this study. Further examination of testing new offense variations among new raters appears in Chapter 17.

These various analyses can contribute to our understanding of the nature of the psychological proposition discussed earlier, its dependence upon the form of the questions we have asked, and the sociocultural aspects of the respondents. Once we have extracted this information, we will turn to another class of questions that relates to the practical problem of indexing offenses in such a way that we can measure "offensiveness," taking into account not only the number of particular delinquencies committed but also their relative seriousness. We have consistently argued that by using such a procedure we can better measure the "amount of delinquency." It may well be that preventive social activity can reduce the total "offensiveness" of criminal acts even though their actual number is not altered. Given scale values for these offenses, we should be able to construct indices of crime without having to rely on the equating of all criminal offenses or on some arbitrary and often highly personal weighing scheme.

THE CHOICE OF THE MAGNITUDE SCALE FOR EVALUATING SERIOUSNESS

It should be clear to the reader by now that we have only been discussing the relation of two highly reliable and reproducible scale functions on offenses. It has been demonstrated that these two scales relate to each other in a consistent and reproducible fashion independent of the effects of social variables that could reasonably be construed as having a marked influence upon them. The fact that the scales reveal this highly desirable consistency appears to present a choice to the researcher as to which scale he will select for use in an index of the seriousness of an offense. We have already pointed out the ease and simplicity with which new offenses can be scaled using the method of magnitude estimation, but perhaps this prejudges the question of whether magnitude estimation or category scaling is the more appropriate technique. It is certainly the case that category scales are the most commonly used in social research, and to suggest to the researcher that these scales should be supplanted by magnitude estimation scales requires justification.

The justification for the use of magnitude scales as an appropriate method for a delinquency index or for generating indices of other social events, attitudes, or opinions is based upon a number of quite independent factors. We move from the most abstract to the most concrete of these. First, the relation between the magnitude and category scales shown in this study precisely duplicates the form of relation that has emerged in a variety of psychophysical studies where the physical scale was well known.[9] In the area of psychophysics, a

---

[9] It should, however, be made explicit that the truth claims made for the scales in psychophysical studies and for the scale in the present study are not necessarily identical. There are similarities and no contradictions; but there are some issues not examined by both sets of studies.

strong case has been made for the use of magnitude scales as appropriate characterizations of the mental effect of the stimulus. This case has been made on the grounds of scientific parsimony, high reproducibility, and the effectiveness of predictions in new situations from a knowledge of scale values based on prior experimentation. A description of this form of justification can be found in an essay on psychophysical scaling by Luce and Galanter.[10] These authors justify a preference by many psychophysicists for the magnitude scale relative to the category scale on the basis of the meaning that can be assigned to the average scale values of either of them. They ask ". . . what meaning can we attach to an average of the numerical responses that a subject emits to a stimulus? Is it defensible or not to treat this as a measure of subjective sensation?"[11]

We criticized an . . . averaging procedure in category scaling, and we might be expected to apply the same objections here with only a slight rewording. We shall not, however, for this reason. The trouble [with averaging category responses] was that the category numbers were assigned by the experimenter in a way that is arbitrary except for their ordering. Assuming that the subject's responses are independent of the labeling used, the experimenter can generate any monotonic function he wishes by his choice of numbers to relate the mean category judgments to the physical scale. Magnitude estimation differs in that the subject, not the experimenter, chooses the numbers, and so they can not be considered arbitrary in the same sense; it requires empirical evidence to know just how arbitrary they are.[12]

The heart of this point is that the magnitude estimation scale values are a product of the rater rather than the experimenter, and as such have an inherent validity that cannot be claimed for the imposition of a fixed range of category values by the experimenter on the rater's judgment.

Another reason for choosing the magnitude scale values as the appropriate estimation of the seriousness of offenses is the inherently greater nuance that can be exhibited by the rater in his selection of responses. Whether or not he really has all the numbers of the real number continuum available to him is not relevant here. The fact is that in making these judgments the rater uses a range of numbers that extends over two to three logarithmic units, i.e., spans a range from the least to the most serious offense of between 100 and 1000 to 1. The category scale on the other hand, even with a large number

[10] Luce, Bush, and Galanter, Eds., *loc. cit.*
[11] *Ibid.*, p. 278.
[12] *Ibid.*

of categories, rarely exceeds a single logarithmic unit. More often than not, the range of average category values with an eleven-point category scale is from two to ten, a factor of five to one in the relative magnitudes of the seriousness of the offenses. The freedom in the range of possible responses available by the magnitude estimation technique provides intrinsically more information about the raters' judgments than the severely limited categories.

17

Deriving Scores

THE MAGNITUDE SCORES AND THE PRIMARY INDEX SCALE

We have seen that the scaling data suggest an impressive invariance across subjects and offenders, and are uninfluenced by the context in which offenses appear. Each of the rating groups showed remarkable consistency when the category scale was plotted against the magnitude scale for an original set of twenty-one offenses and when these plots were compared between groups. The age of the offender did not significantly alter the judgment of seriousness among any of the rating groups, and when some offenses were placed in a different context, they retained their same relative positions. Moreover, we have tried to justify our choice of the magnitude estimation scale over the category scale as the basis for establishing weights of seriousness and were therefore led to pursue further the analysis of the magnitude scores. For the sake of comprehensiveness, all the mean raw scores for the offender groups by rating groups are presented in Appendices E-1-4. The raw score of each offense judged by a particular group is an arithmetic mean in the category scale and a geometric mean in the magnitude estimation scale.

The original set of 21 offenses, which covered a wide range of seriousness, was evaluated by all subjects mentioned thus far ($N = 569$). Altogether, 275 subjects rated these offenses on the magnitude scale, thereby providing a large number of raters to which we shall refer as our "population." By combining the ratings for each offender group and each rating group we obtain for each offense a mean of the geometric means on the magnitude estimation scale. Appendix

E-2 shows the mean scores for the 21 basic offenses that form an important part of our subsequent analysis. We refer to them as our Primary Index Scale. They do not constitute our final weights but they do provide the basis for producing them. Without these scores the weights that were finally developed could not have the reliability, validity, refinement, nor elegance of derivation that they should possess.

SELECTING RATINGS FOR OFFENDERS WITH UNIDENTIFIED AGE

It should be recalled that all rating groups plotted similarly and had slopes without significant differences. This invariance on the original set of 21 offenses was repeated when the total set of offenses was plotted. Further, although absolute numerical scores varied among rating groups, with the police scores generally higher, the inherent ratio quality of the magnitude judgments means that the numbers used by the raters are not particularly relevant and that the only fact of real importance is the ratios of offense seriousness which are preserved intact. Therefore, on this basis alone, it is of little concern whether a particular rating group or all rating groups combined is used for further analysis. Because the largest number of raters judged offenses committed by males of unidentified age, because the age of the offender was a variable without significant influence on the ratings of seriousness, because our theoretical focus has been upon the type of social injury inflicted on members of the community rather than on the perpetrator, and because of potentially wider applicability beyond juvenile offenses, we have used for further refined analyses the ratings for offenses committed by males not identified by age. Our subsequent discussion of specific statistics is based principally on this group of ratings.

SELECTING THE RATING GROUP

Although analysis indicated that we could have used scores from any of the rating groups, we selected those from the Ogontz Penn State Center. Our choice was not merely arbitrary. Ratings for the 92 descriptions of Class I offenses among the total of 141 were arranged in tabular form (see Appendix E-4) for the two rating groups with the largest number of raters (Police and Ogontz) and examined for internal consistency. The group with fewer inconsistencies was selected as the more functionally useful and efficient. Consistency was considered only when objectively derivable. For example, except for murder, assaults against the person were described with three possible injury outcomes—hospitalization, treated and discharged, minor—and with four modes of attack—gun, knife, blunt instrument, fists. We were unwilling to make assumptions about the rank order of the weapons used in assaults, but we did consider the description of the result of the injury as being ordered objectively. By examining the means of the geometric mean scores in a 3 x 4 table, we could readily observe consistency; i.e., if the mean score for minor harm was higher than the mean score for treated and discharged, we counted this as an inconsistency or a paradox. If in the many versions of robbery, burglary, and larceny in which all other facts presented were the same save the amount of money stolen, we considered as an inconsistency a rating which was higher for the lesser amount of money. Of the nearly 100 interrelationships for which consistency was examined, the Police had 28 and the Ogontz students 10 inconsistencies. In most of these situations the rating differentials were indeed slight but we counted only the presence or absence of a paradox. Combining the Police and Ogontz did not reduce the Police number substantially. On the basis of the large number of raters and of fewest inconsistencies the Ogontz group was selected for additional analysis.

REDUCING INDIVIDUAL SUBJECT VARIANCE: STANDARD SCORES (z)

It is not surprising that some paradoxes existed. It might even be said that the small number found was surprising, even for the versions of the 92 Class I offenses. For no single person rated all 141 or even all of the 92 offenses; hence, any one rater's "field," or range, was randomly produced and delimited rather than the whole spectrum. In effect, we created for each subject a somewhat different field situation through randomization. For example, some subjects had only "death" and "minor harm" in their field of assault outcomes while others had "treated and discharged" as the upper limit to compare with "minor harm." Further, the instruction requiring the raters not to turn back in a booklet, combined with these partial sets of offenses, was confounding. The reasons for this instruction are the obvious and traditional ones in psychological testing.[1]

---

[1] While raters were requested not to turn back to their ratings of offenses which appeared earlier in the booklet, some limited cross-referencing was obviously done, especially among those raters who rated a maximum of 21 offenses. Differential degrees of retention must have occurred, but they appear not to

It will be recalled that all the offenses in the original set of 21 were judged by all raters, and it was therefore possible to standardize the scores using the means for the sets and raters. However, as just noted, in the present case, in which the additional 120 offenses were used, not all raters judged all offenses. It was not considered desirable to request persons to rate 141 offenses because fatigue might have been reflected in the results obtained. Accordingly, as we indicated in the previous chapter, each rater was provided with a random set of no more than 51 offenses which included the original 21.

When the magnitude scales used by the raters were examined it was noted that some persons had used scales with very large ranges and variance, whereas others had used scales with limited ranges and variance. But as has been reasoned and demonstrated earlier, the choice of scale is arbitrary. In view of the results of comparisons between scales and ratings and other results, it was decided to standardize each rater about his own mean, thus reducing the variance between raters due to choice of range, and providing a more powerful discrimination between the ratings for different offenses. Since it is our purpose to compare offenses, differences among raters was not relevant. It is, however, known that different classes of raters are equally likely to select varying scale ranges (i.e., Police, Judges, Students). The probability of a person's having a propensity to select a wide range being included in the group of raters who rated a particular set of offenses was relatively small, being distributed approximately in Poisson series. Thus, all offenses in a set rated by a group which, by chance, included two or three wide-range selectors, would show heavier weights due to the inclusion of these unusual raters; similarly, a set of offenses rated by a group which did not include any of the unusual raters or, only one, would be down-weighted even after logarithmic transformation.

To reduce rater variance, the following procedure for obtaining standard scores, or z scores, was adopted for the 141 offenses rated by the Ogontz students:

(a) Each individual rater's score for each offense was transformed to its logarithm.

(b) The transformed score for each rater was standardized.

(c) The standard measure scores were substituted based on each

---

have affected the mean judgments because no differences are noted for raters with 51 offenses to judge. In our analysis, of course, we used limited cross-referencing in order to obtain comparative mean judgments for the complete set of offenses.

rater's mean and variance for each offense rating; thus, all raters had a similar mean and variance in their ratings.

(d) In order to ensure comparability with the original set of 21 offenses used in the earlier analyses, the standard scores were transformed to the same scale (with mean and σ) as that used in Appendix E-2, referred to as the Primary Index Scale.

This procedure removed the correlation between the mean and the variance of each rater's scores over offenses rated. Apart from the logarithmic transformation, this procedure will be recognized as similar to that which is usual in the standardization of intelligence test measurements when raw scores on tests are transformed to standard measure according to the age of the testees.[2]

It should be emphasized that this procedure rests upon the results noted earlier, namely, that individual differences between raters in respect of their choice of scale are irrelevant to comparisons between offenses. It seems reasonably certain that the phenomenon of scale choice under conditions of fixed origin (where the standard violation was assigned a score of 10) is a function of personality variability or other individual differences and is not in any way a function of the subject under consideration. It is agreed that the former function is an interesting fact but it is not one which the present study was directly concerned to examine.[3]

TRANSFORMING THE z SCORES

To maintain comparability with the original set of 21 offenses and to retain the results of these earlier analyses, the z scores of the Ogontz raters were transformed to the numerical equivalents of the Primary Index Scale. That is, by having standardized the scores on the original set of 21 offenses rated by the Ogontz group, we then compared these z scores with the scale scores of the population, or the set of offenses rated by all subjects. This process links the subsample sets to the total sample of raters used in the analysis in Chapter 16. As expected from previous analysis, the correlation is very high ($r = .99$). Figure 13 shows this comparison with its regression line using the general regression equation ($\log Y = \log A + b \log X$, where $a = 1.43451$, $b = 0.72671$) from which the standard scores were trans-

---

[2] The standard or z score is simply a number which indicates how many standard deviation units a score is from the mean and is defined by the formula $Z = (X - \overline{X})/\sigma$.

[3] See *infra*, p. 321, n. 3.

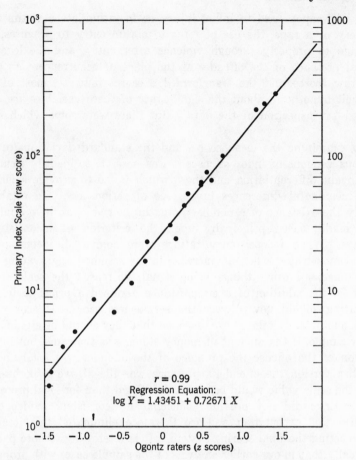

FIGURE 13. z scores for 21 offenses from the magnitude scale, Ogontz raters, and all raters on the primary index scale.

formed to the magnitude scale scores. Appendix E-5 gives the *z* scores for the 141 offenses; the transformed scale scores for the index offense versions were calculated from the regression line.

ELIMINATING SOME OFFENSE VARIABLES

There were many offense versions involving bodily injury, property theft, and property damage because these delinquent acts constitute our index events. We had assumed that subsidiary important variables included such things as the type of resulting physical harm, the kind of weapon used to inflict injury or to intimidate a victim of a robbery or a rape, the use of force to obtain entry to premises, the damage to property through violence after entry, and the legal or illegal presence of the offender at the place of occurrence. As both the raw scores and the transformed z scores indicate, most of the implicit hypotheses about the significance of these variables are confirmed by inspection of the data. But there were some which were not.

By examining the mean scores and the standard deviations of the various versions of index offenses it was possible to identify items of significant differentiation and those which failed to provide sufficient and meaningful differences in degrees of seriousness. To establish firmly the existence of a nondiscriminating variable, an item analysis was made, based principally upon the criterion of inconsistency ratings. When inconsistency ratings were compared, inconsistency was demonstrated when an increase in an assumed aggravating circumstance, all other things being equal, decreased the scale score. That is, the addition of a circumstance assumed a priori to be aggravating should never lower the seriousness score. If scores are not monotonically related, we reasoned that they should be eliminated. For example, if the amount of money stolen was the same, but in one version of the offense the presence of the offender was legal and in another version the offender's presence was illegal, we hypothesized that the scale value would be higher for illegal than for legal presence. The ratings did not provide sufficient and consistent evidence to confirm this expectation and we therefore eliminated this item in constructing the final scoring system. It is interesting to note parenthetically that in our earlier analysis of the sample cases with property offenses, by amount of loss, theft with no violence and legal presence of the offender had a median dollar loss no different from theft with no violence and illegal presence. In the various combinations of theft, damage, forcible or nonforcible entry, violence versus nonviolence to property after entry, and legal or illegal presence, there were significant differences in the observed mean or median dollar loss. But these differences could be accounted for through score values assigned to the amount of property loss alone rather than through some other or additional factor. In short, other than the amount of money lost through theft or damage and except for forcible entry, our item analysis indicated that none of the other items tested in the scaling was considered sufficiently aggravating to be significantly discriminating. The items eliminated from further study were the following: (a) presence of the offender in property offenses (legal, illegal); (*b*) use of violence after entry in property offenses (violence, no violence); (*c*) type of victimization in property offenses (primary, secondary, tertiary); (*d*) specific type of weapon in assaults (gun, knife, blunt instrument, physical); (*e*) certain items in motor vehicle theft (locked, unlocked; abandoned, returned). There remained a residual core of offenses and their concomitant variables which are theoretically and empirically significant and which also have seriousness scores of sufficient discrimination to warrant their use.

REFINING DISCRIMINATION

Item analysis of the Ogontz *z* scores revealed that some versions of offenses to be used in an index had not been sufficiently refined to obtain scores with adequate specificity in some circumstances. Although the paradoxes discussed earlier had been reduced 50 per cent (to only five in number) by obtaining the standard scores, we considered it necessary to run a retest of these items in order to increase the size of the sample and to procure refinements in other items. For example, we originally had only two points of reference for money values, 5 dollars and 1000 dollars; left with these we would have been forced to assume a linear function for seriousness ratings of money loss, interpolating too extensively to be satisfactory.[4]

The final stage of our scaling test procedures was set up using 195 students from the University of Pennsylvania (U of P). Twenty offense versions were presented in booklet form, with the same instructions previously used with the magnitude estimation scale. As an interesting methodological refinement, 105 students received the completely randomized set of offenses while 90 students received a set randomized for all offenses *except* physical assaults by injury outcome and larceny by amounts of money stolen. In short, the 105 students were presented with a random "sequential" set of offenses and 90 students with a partially random, partially "simultaneous" set of offenses. The reference points for money values were increased to five: 5, 20, 50, 1000, and 5000 dollars. In the sequential ordering, the larceny offenses describing these money losses were separated and randomly distributed among the other offenses. In the simultaneous ordering the money values were presented on a single page and ordered from the least to the most. The same was done with the personal assaults so that on a single page in the simultaneous set

---

[4] As discussed below, to have assumed a linear function would have been incorrect.

injury outcomes were listed (in reverse order from the money values) from death to minor harm. Full descriptions of the offenses used in this final scale test and the z scores for both the sequential and the simultaneous presentations, appear in Appendix E-7.

The first task in analyzing the results was to compare the sequential and simultaneous tests. Although the correlation of the z scores was high, $(r = .92)$, within our context of rating comparisons it was the lowest observed (see Figure 14), principally because the items of bodily injury displayed the widest scatter. Death was directly positioned on the slope but lesser injury outcomes spread. The reason became obvious, death was the gravest injury; as the first to be rated on the simultaneous presentation it thereby set the anchor point for evaluating the lesser injury outcomes at the same time. But in the sequential presentation the first type of injury outcome rated appeared

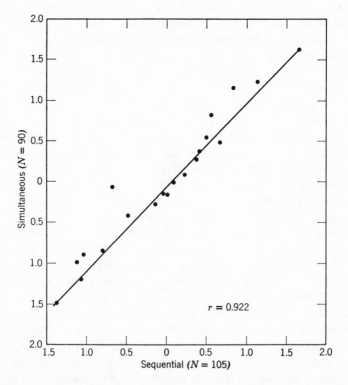

FIGURE 14. *Sequential and simultaneous standard scores, University of Pennsylvania raters.*

by random distribution and could have been any one of the four outcomes.[5]

The simultaneous test provided, then, nothing which we could not have from the sequential test; indeed, the former possesses the disadvantages noted which led us to reject its use. The underlying theory for randomly distributing these items and the absence of any paradoxes in either test supported continued use of results from the sequential test.

Before these results could be used further, it was necessary to determine the degree to which they were correlated with previous test scores. Eight of the twenty offenses in the U of P test were identical in description to ones used in the Ogontz test; the z scores for both groups were compared and produced a correlation near unity ($r = .986$). Eight additional offense versions with slight variations in phrasing were used in the U of P test. For example, in the previous tests, the specific type of weapon (gun, knife, etc.) was mentioned when describing an assault. But having discovered that the particular weapon was not of sufficient discriminatory power, the U of P test presented a description of an assaultive or intimidating offense which simply mentioned the presence or absence of a weapon. To make comparisons between the U of P test scores on these items with the Ogontz scores we used the mean score for all weapons described in the same offenses in the Ogontz test. There were no comparisons possible for the four new money values in the U of P test, but of course one of the reasons for the U of P test was to obtain new reference points for these items. Using, then, the sixteen offenses for comparative purposes and for linking this final testing stage to the previous analyses, the correlation of the U of P standard scores to the Ogontz standard scores was computed and found to be .987. (See Figure 15.) This extremely high correlation near unity gave us confidence both in the reliability of the scale and in the theoretical and empirical connection to the previous analyses of invariance across raters and offender variables. It remained only to examine money values, to transform once more from z scores to scale scores and to convert results to the most efficient form of weights for application.

---

[5] If response is a positive monotonic function of stimulus, then the order of presentation should be from least to most in order to minimize the bias of previous response upon present response. Thus, money was presented in this fashion from least to most but physical injury was not.

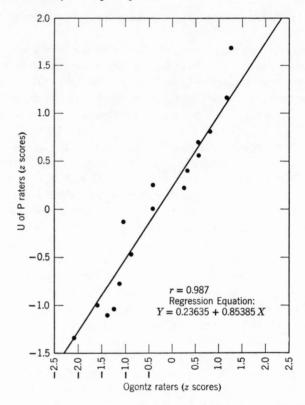

FIGURE 15. z scores for 16 similar offenses from the magnitude scale, University of Pennsylvania raters, and Ogontz raters.

THE POWER FUNCTION OF MONEY

It will be recalled that in the final testing stage the money values of simple larcenies judged by 195 raters was increased from the earlier two to five. From the sequential set randomly distributed among all offenses presented, the raters judged the following offense version with varied amounts of money: "Without breaking into or entering a building and with no one else present, an offender takes property worth ($5), ($20), ($50), ($1000), ($5000)." The mean magnitude scale score was computed for each larceny by using the regression equation for money values ($\log Y = 1.22877 + .16515 \log X$) with the following results: \$5:22.09; \$20:27.77; \$50:32.31; \$1000: 52.99; \$5000:69.13. These values were plotted on arithmetic co-ordinate and then on log-log paper as shown in Figures 16 and 17.

It became quite clear that the computed relation between the scores and the selected reference points of money value is a power function of the form $X = 16.93Y^{0.165}$. When two variables are related by a power function, a geometric change in the one variable is associated with a geometric change in the other variable.

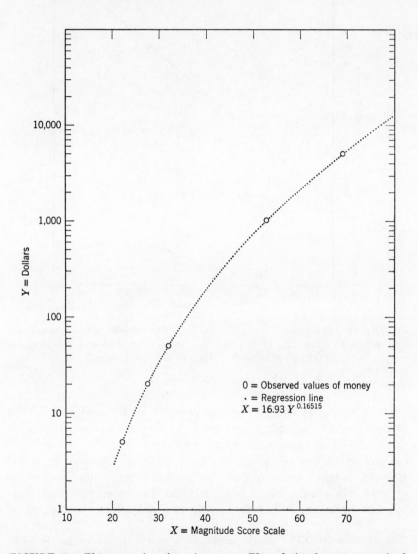

FIGURE 16. *The power function of money. The relation between magnitude scale scores of University of Pennsylvania raters ($N = 105$) and points of the value of money thefts.*

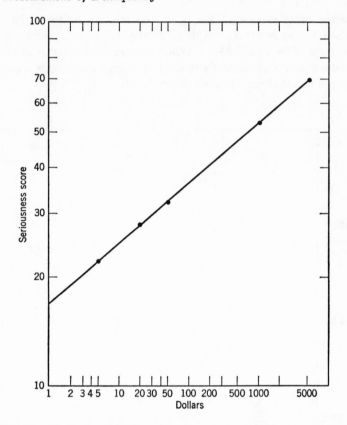

FIGURE 17.   *The power function of money. The relation between magnitude scale scores of University of Pennsylvania raters (N = 105) and points of the value of money thefts (log-log plot).*

These results fit closely previous research on the subjective utility of money.[6] Although this is not surprising, they are an important addition to this literature because the present study is the first to show the power function of money in an experimental situation for which different assigned amounts described as stolen constitute loss instead of gain. It should be emphasized that the raters did not scale amounts of money but, rather, their own subjective reaction, along

---

[6] Eugene Galanter, "The direct measurement of utility and subjective probability," *Amer. J. Psychol.* **75**:208–220 (June 1962). Galanter here suggests the general Form $U = kM^n$ to express the relation of utility to money as a power function.

an implicit continuum of seriousness, to the loss of different amounts of money. The data show that the form of the function relating the seriousness of the offense to the amount of money stolen is similar to ratio scales for many other analogous perceptual continua.[7]

CONVERTING TO SCORES (WEIGHTS) WITH ADDITIVITY

Although the theory, design, and procedures for arriving at the present stage of our analysis have been complex and technically somewhat complicated, with the knowledge at hand it now becomes possible, through the usual process of transforming the U of P standard scores to scale scores, to obtain the simplicity needed for application.

From the beginning we had made several theoretical assumptions, partially based on the historical review of efforts to measure crime and delinquency, about the desiderata in constructing an index of delinquency. Certain delinquency events were excluded from consideration because they failed to satisfy the logical inferences made about index offenses that become known to public authorities. The residual events involving harm, loss or damage, either of singular or plural character, constituted the group which we provisionally classified as index events. Statistical analysis of our sample of events supported the major assumptions and operationalized hypotheses. Certain implicit assumptions were built into the scaling design about aggravating factors that were expected to reveal significantly differential degrees of seriousness. Some of these factors were dropped when they failed to provide consistent patterns of ratings. After examination of the Ogontz magnitude standard scores, there remained a core set of offenses with accompanying aggravating factors that were extractable and presented in a final retesting situation. From this last analysis score values were provided for specific types of events with the extracted factors.

It became evident early in the scaling analysis that certain items

---

[7] See S. S. Stevens, "On the psychological law," *Psychol. Rev.* **64**:153–181 (1957); S. S. Stevens and E. H. Galanter, "Ratio scales and category scales for a dozen perceptual continua," *J. exper. Psychol.* **54**:377–411 (1957).

Stevens has strongly asserted elsewhere that "If utility is a prothetic continuum, and if it behaves like the dozen or more other prothetic continua that have been explored, then the expectation is that utility is a power function of dollars. Furthermore, if it is true that marginal utility is a diminishing function of dollars, the exponent of the power function must be less than 1.0." S. S. Stevens, "Measurement, psychophysics, and utility," Chapter 2 in C. W. Churchman and Philburn Ratoosh (Eds.) *Measurement: Definitions and Theories* (247 pp. New York: Wiley, 1959), p. 53.

could be isolated for special rating because of the assumption of additivity. Of course, the design of a scale which seeks to convert a generally assumed qualitative factor (seriousness) to a unidimensional quantitative measurement contains elements suggesting additivity. For example, to a 5 dollar theft a given increment of seriousness is added as the theft changes from a simple larceny to one following upon a forcible entry into a building, or to a robbery involving immediate threat to a victim. The score value of a forcible entry or of intimidation (if followed by harm, property loss, or damage) is thus an extractable and additive feature of the event.

In Table 69 are listed these offense items taken from the U of P testing with the scale scores derived from (a) the Ogontz scores because of their virtual identity (Figure 15) which were in turn derived from (b) the near identity to and the general regression equation (log $Y = 1.43451 + .72671X$) with the population (Figure 13), and (c) the analysis of money values (Figures 16). The column to the far right gives these score values as weights after dividing each scale value by the lowest score among these items, namely, by using the estimated scale score for a theft of one dollar (16.93) as the divisor. In this way the ratios between offenses are obviously preserved.[8] Decimals are eliminated because they provide at this stage only misleading or at best unwarranted precision and reduce functional simplicity. The analysis of money values as described above yields the following offense scores or weights for theft or damage of property based upon the power function of these money values, with division by the lowest scale value and adjustment by rounding.

DOLLAR LOSS	SCORE
Under $10	1
10– 250	2
251– 2000	3
2001– 9000	4
9001–30,000	5
30,001–80,000	6
Over 80,000	7

We have used a score of 7 for the amount of property theft or damage involving anything over 80,000 dollars. The lower limit to the open end for this amount is more than large enough for juvenile delinquents and is a sensible point to drop higher score values. Were all crimes and adult criminality to be scored, extensions of money

---

[8] See *infra*, pp. 342 ff., regarding the assignment of numbers to represent positions on the scale and the relations between these positions.

TABLE 69. *Offense Scores Derived from Magnitude Scale Values in Last Stage of Testing*

OFFENSE ITEM	MEAN MAGNITUDE SCALE VALUES	SCORES (SCALE VALUES/16.93, ADJUSTED)
ᵃLarceny $1	16.93	1
Larceny $5	22.09	1
Larceny $20	27.77	2
Larceny $50	32.31	2
Larceny $1000	52.99	3
Larceny $5000	69.13	4
ᵇBurglary $5	40.62	2
ᶜRobbery $5 (no weapon)	52.25	3
ᵈRobbery $5 (weapon)	86.33	5
Assault (death)	449.20	26
Assault (hospitalized)	115.60	7
Assault (treated & discharged)	69.32	4
Assault (minor)	22.50	1
ᵉRape (forcible)	186.30	11
Auto Theft (no damage)	27.19	2
ᶠForcible Entry	18.53	1
ᵍIntimidation (verbal)	30.15	2
ʰIntimidation (weapon)	64.24	4

ᵃ Derived from analysis of money values.

ᵇ Burglary $5 has a score of 2, which includes a score of 1 for the money value and a score of 1 for the forcible entry.

ᶜ Robbery $5 (no weapon) has a score of 3, which includes a score of 1 for the money value and a score of 2 for verbal intimidation.

ᵈ Robbery $5 (weapon) has a score of 5, which includes a score of 1 for the money value and a score of 4 for intimidation with a weapon.

ᵉ Rape (forcible) has a minimal score of 11, which includes a basic score of 8 for the forced sex act, a score of 2 for the minimal intimidation (verbal), and a score of 1 for the minimal physical injury (minor).

ᶠ The score for Forcible Entry (18.53) may be seen as the result of Larceny $5 (22.09) subtracted from Burglary $5 (40.62), divided by 16.93.

ᵍ The score for Intimidation (verbal) (30.15) may be seen as the result of Larceny $5 (22.09) subtracted from Robbery $5 (no weapon) (52.25), divided by 16.93.

ʰ The score for Intimidation (weapon) (86.33) may be seen as the result of Larceny $5 (22.09) subtracted from Robbery $5 (weapon) (86.33), divided by 16.93.

values and weights could readily be computed from the equation used in the money analysis.[9]

Most of the terms used in this final set of items have been fully described elsewhere, but a few points require clarification. In plotting the regression line from the z scores of the U of P and Ogontz subjects, the offense describing minor harm appeared as the most anomalous. It had the greatest standard deviation of any offense used (.89). Inspection of the phrasing shows the minimization of harm presented to the U of P subjects ["An offender shoves (or pushes) a victim. The victim does not require any medical treatment."] compared to the presentation to the Ogontz subjects ("The offender beats a person with his fists. The victim is hurt but requires no medical treatment."). To derive a more workable solution, we used the Ogontz z score ($+$.178) as the upper limit of minor harm and the U of P z score ($-$.667) as the lower limit, transformed to normalized scale scores (36 and 9, respectively) and obtained a mean scale score (22.5) as our working score for minor harm. Converting to an offense score and rounding produced a weight of 1.

"Rape (forcible)" refers to sexual intercourse with force and may include sodomy performed under compulsion. Almost every forcible sex act includes intimidation (unless the victim is rendered unconscious first and without knowing why) and at least minor physical harm. Thus, as our more detailed discussion of scoring methods will show in Chapter 18, the minimum score for a forcible rape is 11. "Intimidation" in the scale values applies only to sexual intercourse with force and to theft from the person in a vis-à-vis relationship (like robbery). "Forcible entry," as previously defined, refers to entrance into a building or other property. It should be understood, however, that intimidation alone, not followed by a theft or a forcible sex act, does not constitute an index offense. From our discussion of money values the scale values given for different amounts of money

---

[9] The upper dollar limit for each of the score values was as follows:

UPPER DOLLAR LIMIT	SCORE
11.64	1
256.20	2
1,948.00	3
9,004.00	4
30,370.00	5
83,270.00	6
198,800.00	7

The lower and upper limits used in the scoring system are the adjustments from rounding.

should be clear. Only the methods of counting multiple thefts in a single event require fuller discussion. Motor vehicle theft is given a weight of 2 when the vehicle is stolen, undamaged, and either returned or abandoned; any property loss through unrecovered theft or because of damage is an addition to this basic score.

These scores represent the weight of seriousness to be applied to elements in various types of delinquent events. Any score represents the gravity involved in passing from lawful conduct to conduct which is unacceptable by legal norms and registers an estimated quantitative degree of seriousness of deviation. In accord with the best work in psychophysics, we are asserting that empirically these scores constitute a ratio scale and that the numbers represent the degrees of seriousness attributed to certain properties of delinquent events.[10]

These weights, then, constitute the final result of our search for a means to escape the traditional scheme of treating all delinquent acts as if they were equal and for providing a sociologically and mathematically more meaningful way of measuring the amount of delinquency.

---

[10] For a fuller discussion of this assertion see *infra,* pp. 341 ff.

18
Indexing Delinquency

In previous chapters we have sketched the history of ideas concerning the measurement of criminality and delinquency. We have discussed the limitations of a legal definition of delinquency for index purposes. We have described our study of a sample of one year's events of delinquency known to the police of Philadelphia—the character of the record system maintained by the police, the method of sampling we used; the assumptions underlying the transcription of data from the offense reports; the classification we devised for the analysis of the events; this analysis itself in the light of our assumptions. We have finally described our experiment of securing a scale that would allow us to evaluate the degree of seriousness of an event, isolate its components, and give them differentiated numerical weights, which when added together would give the event a score that would represent its delinquent "value." One matter that remains is to suggest how such data may be used for the construction of an index of delinquency.

THE UCR METHOD

Conventional criminal statistics are designed to show both the frequency and the degree of seriousness of violations of the criminal law. The frequency is shown by counting the offenses committed; the seriousness, by grouping the offenses counted in categories according to legal definitions and arranging these categories in an order with the one containing the most serious offenses at the top and listing the rest in a decreasing order of seriousness. This, at least, is the system adopted by Uniform Crime Reporting system now in common use in the United States and briefly described in Chapter 6. Other systems of classification exist, of course. The most popular ones either group appropriate subclasses of offenses into main classes entitled "offenses against the person," "offenses against property with violence," "offenses against property without violence," "malicious injuries to property," "forgery and offenses against the currency," "other indictable offenses," and "nonindictable offenses"—the British system—or group by chapter, section, and subsection of the penal code, as in Italy and Sweden, for instance. In all systems, the main classes contain offenses varying in degree of seriousness.

One of the aims of the system of reporting and classifying offenses known to the police in the United States and described in the *Uniform Crime Reporting Handbook* issued by the Federal Bureau of Investigation is to provide data for an index of criminality. Of the 26 classes, only seven are said to contain data that would serve this purpose. They contain the "index crimes": non-negligent criminal homicide, forcible rape, robbery, aggravated assault, burglary, theft of values of 50 dollars or more, and automobile theft.

The method of counting these "index crimes" by the UCR method is governed by certain arbitrary rules.

1. The number of non-negligent homicides, forcible rapes, and aggravated assaults is equivalent to the number of victims.

2. The number of other index crimes is determined in the following manner:

Robbery. Each distinct robbery is counted, regardless of the number of victims.

Burglary. Each unlawful entry, with or without force or "breaking," is counted. However, if several rooms in a hotel, motel, or lodging house are entered on the same occasion, only one entry is counted.

Larceny (except automobile theft). Each "distinct operation" of wrongful taking or carrying away of property from the possession or constructive possession of another, not connected with burglary or robbery, is counted. It should be recalled, however, that embezzlement, or money obtained through fraud, forgery, or writing worthless checks, is not included under "larceny-theft" or anywhere else among the UCR "index crimes." A theft of personal articles from automobiles, even when the car is broken into, is counted as a larceny and so is purse snatching where no more force is used than to grab the purse. The forcing of a coin-operated device for purpose of theft is a larceny. Each parking meter so forced is a "distinct operation," as is each theft from automobiles parked in the same block at about the same time, but thefts on the same occasion from several cars parked in a used car lot, private parking lot, or public parking garage are counted as a single larceny.

Automobile Theft. Each theft of a motor vehicle, i.e., any self-propelled vehicle that runs on the surface, not on rails, is counted, if it is committed by a person who does not have lawful access to the vehicle.

3. An attempt to commit one of the *index crimes* is counted as though it were a completed offense, except that an unsuccessful attempt to kill someone is counted as an aggravated assault and an attempt to commit a larceny other than a motor vehicle is not counted as an index crime.

4. Each index crime is counted as one unit even if this unit involves several different offenses committed at the same time or occasion by one person or by several persons acting in concert. Thus, if in one "distinct operation" a rape-murder is committed, preceded by a burglary and a robbery, only one of these offenses will be counted. The selection of that offense is governed by the order in which these offenses are listed in the Uniform Classification. Because non-negligent homicide heads the list, only the murder will be counted. Similarly, only the burglary will be counted when theft of property of any kind, including motor vehicles, conjoins it; if it is associated with an aggravated assault, only the assault will become a statistic; and if, in addition the victim is raped, the rape alone will be counted.

The method of counting and classifying offenses for index purposes just described has two inherent deficiencies. By counting only one offense, when several are conjoined, it provides only a partial enumeration of the specific criminal offenses known to the police, and by equating all offenses which carry the same legal label, differences in the degree of seriousness of offenses within any given category are concealed. *In other words, the UCR method provides no solution for the problem of how to deal statistically with a complex of offenses or with simple offenses that vary in seriousness but carry the same legal title.* This suggests that the problem of measuring criminality or delinquency should be approached in some different manner, but it does not imply that some other source than police data be used. We firmly believe that the information possessed by the police about violations of the criminal law remains the best source of data for index purposes.

A NEW APPROACH

On one point we are in full agreement with those who developed the Uniform Classification and set aside "index crimes," namely, that an index must be based only on *certain kinds* of offensive conduct known to the police. However, instead of selecting these kinds of conduct according to the title given them by the criminal code, we believe that the nature of the harm inflicted should govern the selection. *We have arrived at the conclusion that an index should be constructed from information about certain events involving violations of the criminal law that inflict some bodily harm on a victim and/or causes property loss by theft, damage, or destruction and that these effects are more important in this connection than the specific legal labels attached to the events.*

The above criterion of selection differs in two respects from the one used in Uniform Crime Reports. It does not permit the inclusion of attempted offenses that lead to none of the consequences mentioned, and it includes many offenses not counted among the "index crimes" in those Reports. The omitted violations either possess characteristics which cause them to be mostly unreported to the police or are of kinds that fluctuate statistically depending on increases or decreases in the activity of police patrols. In any case, the information available to the police is too scanty or too conditioned by administrative policy and practices to provide an adequate basis for an index. It was similar considerations that led the framers of the Uniform Classification system to adopt the concept of "index crimes," but we believe that the approach we have chosen will lead to more valid measurement.

We furthermore propose that the class of violations, which we have broadly indicated above, be subdivided into three categories: (a) events that produce bodily harm to a victim or to victims, even though some property theft, damage, or destruction may also be involved; (b) events that involve theft, even when accompanied by property damage or destruction; and (c) events that involve only property damage or destruction. *Although such a subclassification is not essential to the construction of a delinquency index, its use will permit the formation of subindices and allow comparisons between and among the three categories in various ways.*

The proposed classification includes only delinquency events which are presumed to provide data for the construction of an index or indices. It is not designed to replace conventional classifications based on other conceptual frameworks, legal or otherwise. The police and other agencies of law enforcement, adjudication, and corrections will, for purposes of their own, continue to provide statistics on offenses and offenders and use appropriate traditional systems of classification. Rather, our classification should be regarded as a supplementary one having but one purpose, namely, facilitating the construction of a more nearly valid index of criminality or delinquency. As a matter of fact, because of the manner in which we propose to deal with the class of violations in which we are interested, strict comparability of any kind between our results and those achieved by the Uniform Crime Reporting system is virtually impossible.

Parenthetically speaking, the above classification is maintained primarily because we have found it useful in categorizing the data of our research and have made it the basis of our analysis of these data. In Table 6 of Chapter 10, however, the possibility of a more flexible system is indicated, and in the manual of instructions that we have prepared for the possible use of police departments and others concerned[1] we have proposed that instead of labeling an event as falling into Class A, B, or C, the label should indicate the presence in the event of one or more of the traits of bodily injury (I), theft (T), and property damage (D). This would, then, permit the grouping of events into those that contain only I; I and T; I and D; and I, T, and D (the Class A events above)—those that contain only T; and T and D (the Class B events)—and those that contain only D (the Class C events). The information would also permit the segregation of all events in which theft or damage occurred.

A second feature of this approach to the construction of an index is that it is not concerned with the counting of offenses, as presently practiced, but with the evaluation of the degree of seriousness of offensive *events*, thereby providing a solution to the problem of dealing statistically with complex events.

The concept of a criminal or delinquent event is quite familiar to the police, who sometimes call it a case, complaint, or incident, no matter how they may later dissect it for statistical reporting. An event is, in short, a happening (a) which causes someone to call it to the attention of the police and which upon investigation is found to involve one or more violations of the criminal law; or (b) which the police themselves discover, directly or indirectly, during routine patrol and is found to exhibit one or more such violations.

Most events are of a simple nature. This does not mean that they are necessarily insignificant but that they are uncomplicated, such as a simple theft or a simple assault. Other events are more or less

---

[1] *Constructing an Index of Delinquency—A Manual* (16 pp. Philadelphia: Center for Criminological Research, University of Pennsylvania, 1963).

complex because they are of a continuous character, like embezzlement, or because they involve more than one distinct violation of the criminal law. For instance, more than one victim may be injured during the event or both physical harm and property theft may occur. *Each violation of the law occurring during an event is a component thereof, and in the evaluation of an event account must be taken of all its components and not merely of the most serious one.* The system here proposed is focused on the total event. It is not concerned with 'index crimes" but with "index events" that fall within the tripartite classification already mentioned. We shall reserve for the moment the question of how to define an index event in more specific terms.

The evaluation of an event requires the existence of a scale by which it is possible to assign different weights to its components. Such a scale has been described in previous chapters. In assaultive events the scale takes into account the degree of objectively ascertained injury to a victim, and in connection with the theft, damage, or destruction of property it takes into consideration the amount of loss in dollar value.

An event should not be evaluated solely in terms of such injuries or losses. Account must also be taken of certain factors of the event that aggravate it. A theft from a person, regardless of the amount taken, is aggravated if the victim is intimidated, especially if a dangerous weapon is used for that purpose, and the use of such a weapon to accomplish a rape also aggravates that event. Furthermore, theft or damage to property in a building or an assaultive event inside a building is aggravated if force was used to enter the premises. *The scale in question takes account of both the components and the aggravating factors of an event.*

It should be noted, of course, that our scale is based on the evaluation by Philadelphians of offensive conduct. Whether or not the same scale would be applicable elsewhere could only be answered by replicating our scaling procedure in other communities. We suspect, however, that so far as the elements (components and aggravating factors) are concerned that enter into our scoring of the events in the tripartite classification, considerable uniformity of judgment would be found to exist in the United States.[2]

In order to facilitate the reading of the following pages, we restate here the score values arrived at for the elements of the events in our classification.

[2] See Chapter 19 on reliability and validity.

ELEMENT	SCORE VALUE
Minor injury to victim	1
Victim treated and discharged	4
Victim hospitalized	7
Victim killed	26
Victim of forcible sex intercourse	10
Intimidated by weapon, add	2
Intimidation of persons in connection with theft, etc. (other than in connection with forcible sex acts):	
Physical or verbal only	2
By weapon	4
Forcible entry of premises	1
Value of property stolen and/or damaged:	
Under 10 dollars	1
10–250	2
251–2000	3
2001–9000	4
9001–30000	5
30001–80000	6
Over 80000	7
Theft of motor vehicle (recovered, undamaged)	2

SCORING THE EVENT

Evaluation involves an analysis of the event described by the investigating authorities in order to determine the presence of elements that can be given the score values listed above. This analysis will first of all reveal the category to which the event belongs. If a victim received bodily harm, it belongs to Category A; if no such harm occurred but a theft took place, it belongs to Category B; and if only damage or destruction to property was involved, it belongs to Category C.

The total score value of an event depends on the number of elements it contains and their relative values. The largest number of scoreable elements will be found in some events belonging to the A category and the smallest number in the C category, with the B category in an intermediate position; but all three categories will be found to contain some events that will have a total score of only 1.

Category A Events

An event in this category may involve more than one victim as well as some of the other elements in our list. Taking an extreme case, the following elements may have to be scored: (*a*) degree of injury to each victim separately; (*b*) forcible sex intercourse—each victim separately; (*c*) intimidation by weapon to achieve that intercourse, scored for the victim on whom such intimidation is used; (*d*) forcible entry of premises if it preceded the rape; (*e*) motor vehicle theft if conjoining the episode; and (*f*) value of property stolen and/or of the extent of property damage, including damage to recovered motor vehicle and/or value of property taken from it.

Illustration I. (The appropriate score values are given in the parentheses) Two girls are raped by a man (20); one requires hospitalization (7), the other is given medical treatment and discharged (4); one of them had been threatened with a knife (2); the rape occurred in a house to which the offender had secured entry by force (1) and upon leaving he took the pocketbooks of the girls, valued together with their contents at 25 dollars (2). Total score for event: 36.

Illustration II. A boy is assaulted by two companions and sustains a minor injury. Total score for event: 1.

Category B Events

In these events no victim suffers bodily harm. An extreme case would call for the scoring of the following elements: (*a*) intimidation by weapon regardless of the number of victims; (*b*) total value of property taken from the victim(s); (*c*) forcible entry of premises, if part of the event; (*d*) motor vehicle theft if part of the event; (*e*) value of property stolen and/or of extent of property damage, including damage to recovered motor vehicle and/or property taken from it.

Illustration III. A man breaks into a house (1), intimidates its occupants with a dangerous weapon (4), takes property from them and escapes in a car belonging to one of the victims (2). The car is recovered undamaged, but personal articles taken from it, together with the property taken during the holdup, are valued at 300 dollars (3). Total score for the event: 10.

Illustration IV. A boy steals a milk bottle from the stoop of a house. Total value of property stolen, 30 cents. Total score for event: 1.

Category C Events

In these events no bodily harm is inflicted on a victim and no property is stolen. Damage to property occurs, however. In an extreme case, the following elements would be scored: (*a*) intimidation by weapon; (*b*) forcible entry of premises, if part of the event; (*c*) extent of property damage, in dollars.

Illustration V. A man breaks into a building (1), intimidates its occupants with a dangerous weapon (4), forces them to stand by while he sets fire to the premises causing damage to the extent of 3000 dollars (4). Total score for event: 9.

Illustration VI. A boy smashes a number of light bulbs in the waiting room of a railroad station. Total value, 6 dollars. Total score for event: 1.

If we compare the conventional counting of index crimes in the six events in the above six illustrations with the scoring system proposed here, we arrive at the following results.

ILLUSTRATION	UCR COUNT	SCORES BASED ON PROPOSED SYSTEM
I	Two rapes	36
II	Not an index crime	1
III	One robbery	10
IV	Not an index crime	1
V	One burglary	9
VI	Not an index crime	1
Totals	Four index crimes	58

The lowest possible score values of events of the types described in Illustrations I, III, and V would have been: for I a score of 22, if the two victims had not been intimidated by a weapon and had received only minor injuries; for III, a score of 1, if the burglary was followed by no offense of any kind inside; and for V, a score of 1, if no intimidation of persons or damage to property occurred. The total score values of the six events, even so, would have been 27, whereas the UCR could count only 4 index crimes.

THE DELINQUENCY INDEX

The original purpose of the research described in this book was to examine the possibility of arriving at an index of delinquency that would be usable in testing the effectiveness of social action aiming at the reduction or prevention of delinquency, in other words *an index that would, as accurately as possible, measure the real or actual incidence of delinquency during a given period or in a given area.* We have observed that the source of data necessary for such purpose is available or can be made available by the police; that only certain kinds of delinquency events will yield the data that can be used in the construction of an index; that an analysis of these events in terms of these elements is necessary; and that different values are attached to these elements and must be recorded in accord with a scale which reflects community judgments of their relative importance or weight.

The sum of the scores of all the events analyzed and pertaining to a given community and period of time represents the sum total of what might be called the social injury inflicted on the community and its people during that period of time.

Would an index based on the scores of *all* these events be one of real delinquency or merely one of known events of the kinds we have dealt with? Throughout the discussions of measurement during the history of criminal statistics and especially in late decades doubt has been expressed about the utility for index purposes of data on certain petty offenses known to the police.

The framers of the UCR system excluded petty thefts and simple assaults from their "index crimes," because of the weight of these arguments. In previous chapters we have referred time and again to the fact that although we selected certain kinds of delinquency events for study, the possibility existed that all of them might not be useful in the construction of an index. Past experience, buttressed by some cogent findings in the analysis of our sample of events, have led us to the conclusion that a more reliable index of *real* delinquency *of the kind covered by our tripartite classification* will be found, if simple assaults that result in such minor injuries that no medical treatment is sought for them and petty thefts are excluded. The effect of this decision is to eliminate all events in our tripartite classification that would, if scored, have a total score of 1, i.e., assaults resulting in only a minor injury to a *single* victim and simple theft or damage cases in which the total value lost was less than ten dollars. It would not eliminate "forcible entry of premises," which by itself has a score value of one, for such entry is usually associated with some other scored element of the event, such as damage or theft of property. Nor would it eliminate simple assaults in which minor injuries were sustained by two or more victims or in which a minor injury to a single victim was associated with a theft of less than ten dollars. All events with *total* scores of 2 or higher would, thus, enter into the index. This emphasis on the total score also explains the reason for giving a score value at all to minor injury or petty theft in scored events; they are needed for the computation of the total scores of composite events. Parenthetically, it may be noted that in our proposed system of scoring, the uncomplicated incidents of minor injury or of petty theft are the only ones that receive the same score which is given by the UCR system to every "index crime," namely the score of 1.

In our 10 per cent sample of delinquency events in Class I, one third had total scores of 1 each (170 of the 504), but in the weighted rate based on the sum of the scores of all events they represented only 13 per cent (46.9 out of 367.7). It is, of course, conceivable that over the years, the number of events of assaults with minor injury and of petty theft may be found to maintain a constant ratio to the events included in the index.

If we consider the number of provoked "fights" occurring daily in schoolyards, playgrounds, streets, and alleys, and resulting in minor injuries, it is hazardous to assume that the proportion of such assaults that come to the attention of the police would remain constant. The same probably holds true for episodes of pilfering where the amount of monetary loss is small or the damage done to property slight.

The problem is to determine where to draw the line in separating thefts with low reportability from those with reportability high enough to permit the assumption of constancy in the proportion recorded by the police. That line cannot presently be fixed with a great degree of accuracy. The analysis of our scaling results only showed money loss as a power function, indicating that if the loss amounted to 10 to 250 dollars, the theft was considered twice as serious as one which caused the loss of less than 10 dollars in value. But this fact does not assure us that constant reportability begins with events resulting in losses valued at 10 or more dollars. Our decision to place the dividing line at 10 rather than at 50 dollars, therefore, is partly an arbitrary one[3] but is also based on the fact that the rating of seriousness reaches a point approximately twice as great at 10 dollars as at one, that the score of 2 is the first to span a wide range, as it does from 10 to 250 dollars, that a score of 2 is also assigned to an automobile theft and to minimal intimidation.

While a rating of seriousness does not directly yield information on reportability, there is some connection. Narcotics violations were rated highly serious, but we excluded them from the index on other grounds, it will be recalled. A property theft or damage does not involve the conspiracy of silence between victim and offender, nor is its being reported primarily dependent on discovery by the police. Its reportability is a function of the seriousness of the loss, the probability of recovery of the property, and apprehension of the offender

---

[3] A higher cut-off point could, of course, be used. If, for instance, any agency adopting our scale of weights would wish to score only larcenies involving 50 or more dollars this could be done by giving thefts of values between 50 and 250 dollars a score of 2 and giving thefts of larger amounts the appropriate scores from the scale in our table of weights. So far as simple thefts by juveniles are concerned, this would mean that almost all of them would be ignored for index purposes, as they now are in the UCR system.

as perceived by the victim. Moreover, larcenies reported to the police and later determined as unfounded are usually those involving small amounts of money, especially under 10 dollars. This leads to the conjecture that the individual who misses such small amounts of property is often uncertain that the money was lost, used, or stolen. The interrelation of all these factors as they affect the probability, the reliability, and the validity of reporting requires special and further research. For the present we must rely on the best available data and theory which suggest a score value of 2 as being the minimal level of use. After the elimination of simple events of minor personal injury or petty thefts with scores of 1, the index will then be constructed from the events with scores of 2 or more. To arrive at this index the sum total of the scores must be reduced to a rate, and for that purpose it is necessary to know the size of the juvenile population at risk in the community. This information makes it possible to establish an index figure per thousand or ten thousand of that population. Our view is that such a rate will more accurately than is done by present conventional methods indicate the degree of seriousness and, over a period of years, the trend of *real* juvenile misconduct which violates the criminal law and inflicts personal injuries and/or property loss.

Subindices for three categories of index events, similarly constructed, will provide measures of delinquency that involve bodily harm to persons compared with those leading to theft, damage, or destruction of property, and, if considered desirable, indices could be computed on the basis of several combinations of features of events: those involving (a) only personal injury; (b) personal injury and theft; (c) personal injury and property damage; (d) personal injury, property theft, and damage; (e) theft only; (f) theft and damage; and (g) damage only.

The proposed system could also be used for the development of an index of criminality in general, as known to the police, so long as it falls within the classification we have indicated. Rates for the community as a whole, based on the population at risk, could be computed. The total score values of all index events and of the three categories, as well as mean score values based on the number of events, could be shown for different police districts or other geographically delimited areas—since events are nearly always assignable to a specific place or locality—or distributed seasonally, monthly, weekly, by day and hour, as is now done with specific offenses. It might be inadvisable in some situations to compute interarea rates on the basis of the populations of the areas in which the events occur.

This is equally true of juvenile events. The reason is that in some areas most events are attributable to outsiders.

One problem remains, namely, the definition of an event, for if the event, rather than one or more of its constituent parts, is to be made the focus of scoring, the definition of its scope becomes important for two reasons. First, the frequency of delinquency events needs to be known. Regardless of the score values of events, it is desirable to know whether or not events increase or decrease in number. An increase may not lead to a rise of the sum of their scores, and a decrease may occur although the sum of the scores of the fewer events may grow larger. If it is desirable to know the mean score value of a delinquency event—and we believe that this is useful—the number of events must be established. Second, if intercommunity comparisons are to be made, uniformity in the definition of an event becomes important if valid comparisons are to be made.

The problem may best be illuminated by an illustration.

Suppose that a gas station is held up by a man armed with a gun and that an attendant and a customer are surprised by the robber. The attendant is killed and 400 dollars stolen from the cash register. The customer loses 300 dollars, is knocked down by the robber, and sustains an injury that requires his hospitalization.

The event described would result in a report of one homicide for inclusion in Uniform Crime Reports. Under the proposed system, the scoring of this incident would depend on whether it was counted as one event or, because of the two victims, as two events. In the former case the score would be intimidation by weapon (4); homicide (26); hospitalization (7); theft of 700 dollars (3), or a total score of 40. If the episode were broken down into two events, the scores would be: (a) intimidation (4); homicide (26); theft (3), or a total of 33; (b) intimidation (4); hospitalization (7); theft (3), or a total of 14. Grand total, 47. The mean score value of the episode seen as one event would be 40; as two events, 23.5. It is obvious that from our point of view *only one event* occurred and that during it the robber intimidated the victims with a gun, killed one, injured the other, and stole a total of 700 dollars and that these acts represent the elements that should be scored. If the second method is followed in scoring this type of episode as well as many others, it is equally obvious that the total number of events will be larger and the mean score value of an event therefore smaller.

We wish to emphasize that no matter how the police of a community define an event, the method of scoring in the proposed system can be used so long as the definition remains substantially unchanged over a period of time. The results will still be applicable to that community but would permit doubtful comparisons with the results arrived at in another community, which employs a different definition. In either case, the index produced would provide a measure of the delinquency of the community concerned, and the ratio of change in one community could be compared with the ratio of change in another community. However, we would strongly urge that the same definition of an event be used wherever the new approach is adopted.

It may be impossible to develop a theoretically valid as well as practically useful definition of an event. In our detailed instructions for scoring events (see Appendix F) we have attempted to provide specifications that should create sufficient uniformity to permit both inter- and intracommunity comparisons without imposing impossible administrative burdens on the police. If Philadelphia practice is any guide, an event is, in nearly all cases, likely to be synonymous with the happening that is described in the report of the "offense," given an individual identification or complaint number and investigated by the police. In some instances two or more such reports may cover different components of an event as we have defined it, and in such instances a consolidation or comparative analysis of these reports would be necessary before scoring. For instance, in Illustration I given on an earlier page of the chapter the police would probably prepare separate offense reports, each with its own complaint number, for each of the two victims raped. However, in the description of the event in each of the reports, the same facts would be given, including data concerning the second victim. If each report were to be regarded as the report of a separate event, it might occur that both these "events" would be scored as having two victims with the result that the total event would be scored twice. Some device would, therefore, have to be found that would enable the scorer to take both reports into consideration for scoring as one event with two victims.

So far, we have been dealing with events and not their perpetrators. In many events only one actor is found, but in others a considerable number may participate as offenders. Since, in juvenile delinquency, we can concern ourselves only with events that are cleared by the apprehension of someone whose age places him in the juvenile category, it is possible to give to a participant offender in an event a score that registers the degree seriousness of his delinquency. *The score applied to a delinquent is the score pertaining to the event in which he was the sole or a participant actor.* It may be true that if several offenders participate the involvement is not the same for every one of them. One could be the real perpetrator, others might lend him passive support, and one might be an unwilling participant, for instance. To attempt, however, to gauge such variations, which a court might well take into consideration in determining relative guilt or which even the police might take into account when deciding whether or not to prosecute all the offenders, would be a nearly impossible task. Therefore, we suggest the procedure already mentioned, even though we are aware of its limitations.

Events in which both adults and juveniles participate as offenders are here called mixed events. An arbitrary decision has to be made on whether or not such an event should be scored for use in constructing the delinquency index. It should be so scored *only* when the number of juvenile participants (offenders) exceeds the number of adults. When there is an equal number of juveniles and adults, the event should be omitted as being an adult one. Note, however, that the *juveniles* involved in such events should be included, when instead of a *delinquency index* an *index of delinquents* is constructed, each such juvenile given the score value attached to the event in which he participated. In our sample of "index events," there were 34 mixed events, of which 8 were, in accord with the classification here suggested, delinquency events.

The sum of the scores for the delinquents, transformed into a rate per thousand or ten thousand of the juvenile population at risk, will provide an index of the degree of juvenile participation in delinquent events of varying degrees of seriousness. Subindices for the three categories can be developed; specific age, sex, race, and area rates can be computed. Since both the number of offenders, as well as their scores, are known, an examination of the effect of social action programs in given areas of juvenile residence is made possible.

FORMULAS FOR COMPUTING INDEX STATISTICS

Table 70 presents the formulas for the various computations suggested by our earlier discussions. Along with the symbolization are the explanation of the symbols, the substitution of numbers from our observed data, the interpretation, and a short title of each statistic. It should be clear that we are using delinquency index events, i.e., omitting events involving an equal or greater number of adults (for these are defined as adult events), using only events with a total score value of 2 or higher. Each of the computed statistics provides a specific and different piece of information. Formula I provides the chief comparative statistic for a weighted index of delinquency based upon the juvenile population 7 through 17 years of age. The result-

TABLE 70. *Formulas for Computing Delinquency Index Statistics*

FORMULA	EXPLANATION	PHILADELPHIA 1960 ESTIMATE	INTERPRETATION	SHORT TITLE
I. $\dfrac{\Sigma fs}{j} k$	$\dfrac{\text{(Seriousness Summed Over Events)}}{\text{(Juvenile Population)}}$ (10,000)	$(10)*\dfrac{998}{342,252}\,10,000 = 291.6$	Average number of seriousness units, or weighted rate per 10,000 juveniles at risk.	Juvenile harm
II. $\dfrac{\Sigma fs}{p} k$	$\dfrac{\text{(Seriousness Summed Over Events)}}{\text{(Total Population)}}$ (10,000)	$(10)*\dfrac{998}{2,002,252}\,10,000 = 49.8$	Average number of seriousness units inflicted, or weighted rate per 10,000 population.	Community harm
III. $\dfrac{\Sigma fs}{f}$	$\dfrac{\text{(Seriousness Summed Over Events)}}{\text{(Events)}}$	$= \dfrac{998}{306} = 3.26$	Average number of seriousness units per event.	Seriousness per event
IV. $\dfrac{\Sigma fs}{\Sigma fn}$	$\dfrac{\text{(Seriousness Summed Over Events)}}{\text{(Offenders)}}$	$= \dfrac{998}{643} = 1.55$	Average number of seriousness units per offender.	Seriousness per offender
V. $\dfrac{\Sigma fns}{\Sigma fn}$	$\dfrac{\text{(Seriousness Summed Over Offenders)}}{\text{(Offenders)}}$	$= \dfrac{2141}{643} = 3.33$	Number of seriousness units in event involving average offender.	Average offender seriousness
VI. $\dfrac{\Sigma fns}{j}$	$\dfrac{\text{(Seriousness Summed Over Offenders)}}{\text{(Juvenile Population)}}$	$(10)*\dfrac{2141}{342,252} = 0.06$	Number of seriousness units in event involving average juvenile at risk.	Average juvenile seriousness
VII. $\dfrac{\Sigma fn}{\Sigma f}$	$\dfrac{\text{(Offenders)}}{\text{(Events)}}$	$= \dfrac{643}{306} = 2.10$	Average number of offenders per event.	Offenders per event
VIII. $\dfrac{\Sigma fn^2}{\Sigma fn}$	$\dfrac{\text{(Offenders Summed Over Offenders)}}{\text{(Offenders)}}$	$= \dfrac{2069}{643} = 3.22$	Number of offenders in event involving the average offender.	Offenders in average offender's event

* When using the Philadelphia data it was necessary to multiply by (10) to account for the fact that the data are from a 10 per cent sample.

TABLE 71. Sample Worksheet for Computing Delinquency Index Statistics
(Cell entries are events with indicated number of offenders and degree of seriousness)

OFFENDERS PER EVENT

Seriousness score	1	2	3	4	5	6	7	8	9	10	11	...		
1					(Omit)									
2	72	46	25	16	8	5								
3	15	19	5	2						1				
4	30	14	3	2	1			1						
5	8	2	3											
6	2	2								1				
7	9	2	1	2			1							
8											1			
9						1								
10														
11	1													
12														
13														
14	1	1												
15														
16	1													
.														
.														
.														
26	1				1									
.														
.														
.														
Σf	140	86	37	22	10	6	1	1	0	2	1		306	Events
Σfn	140	172	111	88	50	36	7	8	0	20	11		643	Offenders
Σfn^2	140	344	333	352	250	216	49	64	0	200	121		2069	Offenders summed over offenders
Σfs	491	255	99	60	46	19	7	4	0	9	8		998	Seriousness of events
Σfns	491	510	297	240	230	114	49	32	0	90	88		2141	Seriousness summed over offenders

TABLE 71.   Sample Worksheet for Computing Delinquency Index Statistics.
(Continued)

Example: to find for Column 6*

Σf $= 5 + 1 = 6$ = Sum of cell entries in column
Σfn $= 6 \times 6 = 36$ = Σf times column number
$\Sigma fn^2 = 36 \times 6 = 216$ = Σfn times column number
Σfs $= (5 \times 2) + (1 \times 9) = 19$ = Each cell entry in column times
                                                  row number summed
$\Sigma fns = 19 \times 6 = 114$ = Σfs times column number

---

* More specific formalization of the summations may be described as follows:

X_{ij} = number of events with ⁻(i) seriousness and (j) offenders.

$$\sum_{i=2}^{n} X_{ij} = \text{events}$$

$$\sum_{i=2}^{n} jX_{ij} = \text{offenders}$$

$$\sum_{i=2}^{n} j^2 X_{ij} = \text{offenders summed over offenders}$$

$$\sum_{i=2}^{n} iX_{ij} = \text{seriousness of events}$$

$$j \sum_{i=2}^{n} iX_{ij} = \text{seriousness summed over offenders}$$

---

ing statistic from Formula I answers the crucial question: Among a group of ten thousand juveniles in the community, what is the amount of seriousness of delinquency harm which they inflict? Formula II provides an index of the "community harm" or "social injury" burdening the whole community, and does this by distributing the total seriousness scores throughout the entire population. The result of Formula II answers the question: Among a group of ten thousand persons in the community, what is the amount of seriousness of delinquency harm inflicted upon them? Formula III provides information on the average seriousness score per delinquency event.

Formulas IV, V, and VI describe, respectively, the average seriousness per offender; the seriousness score in the event involving the average offender; the average juvenile's seriousness among the entire juvenile population. Formulas VII and VIII do not involve use of weights for events, and express simply the average number of offenders per event and the number of offenders in the event involving the average offender.

As a regular practice for maintaining an index of delinquency in a community, the statistics derived from Formulas I, II, III, and VI are recommended as the minimum for comparative purposes.

Table 71 shows in succinct form a simple yet comprehensive system for recording the three-dimensional phenomena of seriousness score, number of offenders, and number of events. The sums at the bottom of the table provide all the data needed to compute the statistics described in the frequency table. Although Table 71 is based on the combination of Categories A (bodily injury), B (theft), and C (damage), it should be obvious that three separate tables for each category, or seven separate tables for I (injury), T (theft), D (damage), and combinations of these (I-T, I-D, T-D, I-T-D), could, and perhaps should, be constructed by police departments using this model to produce subindices.

SCORES AND WEIGHTED RATES
FOR THE PHILADELPHIA SAMPLE

Before this chapter is concluded, it may be of interest to examine the weighted rates and the mean score values of the index events of our tripartite classification found in the sample of delinquency events which we have been studying. Although we have also included for comparison the count of the events according to the UCR method of counting "index crimes," we must reiterate that no complete comparison is possible because where we have scored all components of an event, the UCR counts only the most serious one according to the legal label it carries. Furthermore, where in assaultive events, the UCR counts each victim of an aggravated assault, a rape or a nonnegligent homicide, our event resulting in bodily harm may have more than one victim, even though each is separately scored. Finally, our events include many assaultive events or ones involving property theft or damage, which have been excluded by UCR from the categories of index crimes. Nevertheless, the juxtaposition of the two sets of data may have some interest. It should be kept in mind that all events whose total score was 1 and all "mixed" events with an equal or greater number of adults than of juveniles have been omitted from the following analysis that applies our model to the sample data from Philadelphia. Thus, the number of index events (306) is smaller than the number of all Class I events (504) which have been previously examined.

TABLE 72. *Number, Total Scores, and Unweighted Rates of Delinquency Index Events by Uniform Crime Reports Classification*

	CATEGORY OF EVENTS								Unweighted Rate per 10,000 Juveniles 7-17 Years
	A (Injury)		B (Theft)		C (Damage)		TOTAL		
UNIFORM CRIME REPORTS CLASSIFICATION	Number of Events	Score	Number of Events	Score	Number of Events	Score	Number of Events	Score	
UCR Index Offenses									
Criminal homicide	2	52	...	...	...	...	2	52	0.58
Rape, forcible	3	44	...	...	...	...	3	44	0.88
Robbery	17	85	10	38	...	...	27	123	7.89
Aggravated assault	28	140	...	...	...	...	28	140	8.18
Burglary	...	...	54	132	5	12	59	144	17.24
Larceny ($50+)	...	...	16	34	...	...	16	34	4.67
Auto theft	...	...	31	95	...	...	31	95	9.06
Total UCR Index	50	321	111	299	5	12	166	632	48.50
Unweighted Rate	14.61		32.43		1.46		48.50		
UCR Nonindex Offenses									
Larceny (under $50)	1	2	68	141	2	6	71	149	20.75
Other assaults	27	117	...	...	...	...	27	117	7.89
Sex offenses	2	8	...	...	...	...	2	8	0.58
Disorderly conduct	...	...	...	...	1	2	1	2	0.29
Traffic violations	...	...	...	...	1	2	1	2	0.29
Trespassing	...	...	...	...	2	4	2	4	0.58
Malicious mischief	...	...	...	...	30	61	30	61	8.77
Other	2	15	...	...	4	8	6	23	1.75
Total UCR Nonindex	32	142	68	141	40	83	140	366	40.90
Unweighted Rates	9.35		19.87		11.69		40.90		
Total	82	463	179	440	45	95	306	998	89.40
Unweighted Rates	23.96		52.30		13.15		89.40		

TABLE 73. *Average Seriousness Score per Delinquency Index Event by Uniform Crime Reports Classification*

UNIFORM CRIME REPORTS CLASSIFICATION	CATEGORY OF INDEX EVENTS			
	A (Injury)	B (Theft)	C (Damage)	TOTAL
UCR Index Offenses				
Criminal homicide	26.0	...		26.0
Rape, forcible	14.7	...	...	14.7
Robbery	5.0	3.8	...	4.6
Aggravated assault	5.0	...	...	5.0
Burglary	...	2.4	2.4	2.4
Larceny ($50+)	...	2.1	...	2.1
Auto theft	...	3.1	...	3.1
Total UCR Index	6.4	2.7	2.4	3.8
UCR Nonindex Offenses				
Larceny (under $50)	2.0	2.1	3.0	2.1
Other assaults	4.3	...	...	4.3
Sex offenses	4.0	...	...	4.0
Disorderly conduct	...	...	2.0	2.0
Traffic violations	...	...	2.0	2.0
Trespassing	...	...	2.0	2.0
Malicious mischief	...	...	2.0	2.0
Other	7.5	...	2.0	3.8
Total UCR Nonindex	4.4	2.1	2.1	2.6
Total	5.6	2.5	2.1	3.3

Table 72 shows the number of delinquent events and the sum of the scores, and Table 73 gives the mean seriousness scores for these index events. Table 74 presents the weighted rates per 10,000 juveniles aged 7 to 17 in Philadelphia in 1960, and Table 75 shows the weighted rates per 10,000 total population. As mentioned, the index events from our A, B, C categories cannot be completely compared to the Uniform Crime Reports classification, but there are some functions of each system, using the weighted rates, that might be shown. In effect, by using these categories, the score values as a ratio scale, our definition of events, and the scoring system, the tables show how the statistics would appear if distributed by the Uniform Crime Reports (UCR) classification. It should also be noted that because the data are from a 10 per cent sample, the computed statistics should be con-

TABLE 74. Weighted Rate of Delinquency Index Events by Uniform Crime Reports Classification, per 10,000 Juvenile Population (7–17 Years)

UNIFORM CRIME REPORTS CLASSIFICATION	CATEGORY OF INDEX EVENTS			
	A (Injury)	B (Theft)	C (Damage)	TOTAL
UCR Index Offenses				
Criminal homicide	15.19	...	...	15.19
Rape, forcible	12.86	...	...	12.86
Robbery	24.84	11.10	...	35.94
Aggravated assault	40.90	...	...	40.90
Burglary	...	38.56	3.51	42.07
Larceny ($50+)	...	9.93	...	9.93
Auto theft	...	27.76	...	27.76
Total UCR Index	93.79	87.35	3.51	184.65
UCR Nonindex Offenses				
Larceny (under $50)	0.58	41.20	1.75	43.53
Other assaults	34.19	...	...	34.19
Sex offenses	2.34	...	...	2.34
Disorderly conduct	...	...	0.58	0.58
Traffic violations	...	...	0.58	0.58
Trespassing	...	...	1.17	1.17
Malicious mischief	...	...	17.82	17.82
Other	4.38	...	2.34	6.72
Total UCR Nonindex	41.49	41.20	24.24	106.93
Total	135.28	128.55	27.75	291.58

sidered as the best estimates of rates and averages. As a summary account we note the following:

(1) Of the 306 events in our index, only 54 per cent would fall within the UCR crime index. The number excluded (140) is nearly the same as the number included (166). About half of these exclusions (71) are UCR larcenies, each of which in our scoring system has a score of 2 or an amount of theft over 10 and under 50 dollars. But 3 out of each 8 bodily harm events (32 of the 82 Category A) would be excluded from the UCR index, despite the fact that these 32 events resulted in relatively serious injuries requiring medical treatment, some with and some without hospitalization. One of the major differences between our model and the UCR system is again obvious,

TABLE 75.   *Weighted Rate of Delinquency Index Events by Uniform Crime Reports Classification, per 10,000 Total Philadelphia Population*

UNIFORM CRIME REPORTS CLASSIFICATION	CATEGORY OF INDEX EVENTS			
	A (Injury)	B (Theft)	C (Damage)	TOTAL
UCR Index Offenses				
Criminal homicide	2.60	...	...	2.60
Rape, forcible	2.20	...	...	2.20
Robbery	4.24	1.90	...	6.14
Aggravated assault	6.99	...	...	6.99
Burglary	...	6.59	0.60	7.19
Larceny ($50+)	...	1.70	...	1.70
Auto theft	...	4.74	...	4.74
Total UCR Index	16.03	14.93	0.60	31.56
UCR Nonindex Offenses				
Larceny (under $50)	0.10	7.04	0.30	7.44
Other assaults	5.84	...	...	5.84
Sex offenses	0.40	...	...	0.40
Disorderly conduct	...	...	0.10	0.10
Traffic violations	...	...	0.10	0.10
Trespassing	...	...	0.20	0.20
Malicious mischief	...	...	3.05	3.05
Other	0.75	...	0.40	1.15
Total UCR Nonindex	7.09	7.04	4.15	18.28
Total	23.12	21.97	4.75	49.84

namely, that the UCR makes assumptions about consistency of reporting based on the penal code titles of offenses while our model makes these assumptions (partially verified) based on the objective characteristics of events in terms of certain levels of harm, theft, and damage, ignoring the legal labels.

(2) The bodily harm events excluded from the UCR index are nearly as serious as the harm events which are included. For example, the average weighted seriousness score of the 50 Category A events that fall within the UCR index, including homicide, is 6.4 and of the UCR's aggravated assaults is 5.0. The average weighted seriousness score of the 32 Category A events excluded from the UCR index is 4.4. Moreover, the average seriousness score for UCR index events is 3.8 while the same computation for our model index is 3.3,

which indicates in another way that the UCR system is excluding reportable events rated nearly as serious as those it is including.

(3) The conventional rate per 10,000 juveniles for the UCR index would be 48; the same computation for our index events is almost twice as high, 89.

(4) The weighted rate for the UCR index, based on the juvenile population, would be 185 and for our model is 292. The weighted rate for the UCR index, based on the total community population, would be 32 and for our model is nearly 50. In other words, the UCR index, even with weights, would contain in its classification less than two-thirds of the seriousness rate contained in our model.

(5) Within our weighting system and categories of bodily injury (A), theft (B), and damage (C) it may readily be seen that the greatest disparity in comparison with the UCR index is in Category C, 83 per cent of which would be excluded from the UCR. However, 31 and 32 per cent of the weighted rates for Categories A and B, respectively, would also be excluded. What is classified in the UCR as simple assaults and batteries constitute the major portion of the Category A exclusion; larcenies under 50 dollars, of the Category B exclusion; and malicious mischief, of the Category C exclusion.

(6) As is expected, the index events involving bodily injury (Category A) in our model have the highest mean score (5.6) with theft (B) second highest (2.5) and damage third (2.1). For all index events, the mean seriousness score is 3.3, which is only slightly and not significantly lower than the mean score for the UCR index at 3.8.

(7) Of special note is the fact that these bodily injury events excluded from the UCR index possess an average score (4.4) nearly twice as high as the greater number of theft and damage events that are included in the UCR index (2.7 and 2.4).

Tables 76 and 77 present the number of juvenile offenders, the sum of their scores, the weighted rates for offenders per 10,000 juveniles aged 7 to 17 in the city population, and the average offender's seriousness score. Similar comments concerning score and proportional variations made about index events are applicable for these tables which describe offenders. It should be noted that these tables are based on the number of juveniles involved in delinquency events and do not include the 31 juveniles from "mixed" events, in which the number of adult participants was equal to or exceeded the number of juveniles. Had the 31 juveniles been included, the total number of offenders would rise to 674; their total score, to 2275; and their average offender's seriousness score would increase from 3.3 to 3.4.

As mentioned before, there are undoubtedly other mathematical

TABLE 76. *Number, Total Scores, and Unweighted Rates of Juvenile Delinquents Involved in Index Events by Uniform Crime Reports Classification*

UNIFORM CRIME REPORTS CLASSIFICATION	CATEGORY OF EVENTS								Unweighted Rate per 10,000 Juveniles 7–17 Years
	A (Injury)		B (Theft)		C (Damage)		TOTAL		
	Number of Offenders	Score	Number of Offenders	Score	Number of Offenders	Score	Number of Offenders	Score	
UCR Index Offenses									
Criminal homicide	6	156	...	...	...	...	6	156	1.75
Rape, forcible	4	72	...	...	...	...	4	72	1.17
Robbery	37	207	18	68	...	...	55	275	16.07
Aggravated assault	51	275	...	...	...	...	51	275	14.90
Burglary	...	...	111	272	10	23	121	295	35.35
Larceny ($50+)	...	...	52	115	...	...	52	115	15.19
Auto theft	...	...	72	208	...	...	72	208	21.04
Total UCR Index	98	710	253	663	10	23	361	1396	105.47
Unweighted Rate	28.63		73.92		2.92		105.47		
UCR Nonindex Offenses									
Larceny (under $50)	1	2	138	286	2	6	141	294	41.20
Other assault	60	270	...	...	...	...	60	270	17.53
Sex offenses	3	13	...	...	...	...	3	13	0.87
Disorderly conduct	...	...	...	...	3	6	3	6	0.87
Traffic violations	...	...	...	...	1	2	1	2	0.29
Trespassing	...	...	...	...	4	8	4	8	1.17
Malicious mischief	...	...	...	...	62	125	62	125	18.12
Other	2	15	...	...	6	12	8	27	2.34
Total UCR Nonindex	66	300	138	286	78	159	282	745	82.39
Unweighted Rate	19.28		40.32		22.79		82.39		
Total	164	1010	391	949	88	182	643	2141	187.86
Unweighted Rate	47.91		114.24		25.71		187.86		

ways of treating an offender's participation in an event and consequently of distributing the gravity of that event among the contributors. When there are multiple offenders in the same event the degree of contribution by each participant to the event may be a function of the size of the group. The dynamics of such a function in situations of norm violation might well be investigated by small group research experiments. The legal distinction of principals in the first and second degree might be useful for distributing elements of a criminal even score among the perpetrators. The impact of leadership phenomena on groups of different size might be examined. But under the present circumstances we chose to assign the same seriousness score for the event to each of the participants in the event.

Table 77. Average Juvenile Offender's Seriousness Score by Delinquency Index Events and the Uniform Crime Reports Classification

	CATEGORY OF EVENTS			
UNIFORM CRIME REPORTS CLASSIFICATION	A (Injury)	B (Theft)	C (Damage)	TOTAL
UCR Index Offenses				
Criminal homicide	26.0	...	...	26.0
Rape, forcible	18.0	...	...	18.0
Robbery	5.6	3.8	...	5.0
Aggravated assault	5.4	...	...	5.4
Burglary	...	2.5	2.3	2.4
Larceny ($50+)	...	2.2	...	2.2
Auto theft	...	2.9	...	2.9
Total UCR Index	7.2	2.6	2.3	3.9
UCR Nonindex Offenses				
Larceny (under $50)	2.0	2.1	3.0	2.1
Other assault	4.5	...	...	4.5
Sex offenses	4.3	...	...	4.3
Disorderly conduct	...	...	2.0	2.0
Traffic violations	...	...	2.0	2.0
Trespassing	...	...	2.0	2.0
Malicious mischief	...	...	2.0	2.0
Other	7.5	...	2.0	3.4
Total UCR Nonindex	4.6	2.1	2.1	2.6
Total	6.2	2.4	2.1	3.3

The statistics for offenders are not presented as an alternative for the statistics for delinquent events, for the latter are those we are using as an index of delinquency. The data for offenders may be administratively useful, however, in many ways. In studies of cohorts, life histories, recidivism rates, before-after comparisons, inter- and intracommunity comparisons, and for evaluating action and therapy programs designed to promote change in individuals, offender data using a seriousness scoring system could be extremely valuable. The possibilities of refining causal and correctional analyses by means of a scale such as is used in the index are obvious. When using score values for assessing individuals and their changing or stable patterns of delinquent conduct, there may be advantage in employing the scale values for all offenses originally used in the scaling tests and not only the ones limited to the delinquency index.[4] Moreover, new offense versions can be added and integrated into the scale values through methods described previously.[5]

To summarize:

1. A scale which assigns score values to an element or elements of delinquency events is necessary. The scale developed in the present research has produced score values ranging from 1 to 26 for various elements.

2. An "index event" for use in the construction of a delinquency index is one in which a physical injury to a victim is inflicted and/or property theft, damage, or destruction occurs. It has a total score of 2 or more.

3. If both adults (18 years or older) and juveniles (7 to 17 years of age) are participant offenders in an index event, it is to be counted as a juvenile event when the number of juveniles is *more* than the number of adults.

4. The index is derived by reducing the sum of the scores of index events to a rate per unit of juvenile population (10,000, for instance).

5. Subindices for different categories of events (personal injury, property theft, property damage) are derived in a similar manner, and mean score values of events can be computed.

6. By assigning to each participant offender the total score of an event, an index of delinquents and the mean score value per delinquent can be derived.

---

[4] If this were to be done, the standard (z) scores of the offenses numbered 89–119, 121–135, 140–141, rated by the Ogontz subjects, should be converted to scale scores and divided by 16.93 to obtain the weight of each.

[5] See Ch. 17.

19
Reliability and Validity

Although the scaling analysis has followed the general theory of measurement, numbers (scale scores) assigned to delinquent events do not alone constitute an index. Our delinquency index also involved definition, from which we proceeded to classification, scaling, and finally scoring techniques applied to real events. But an index is more than a scale, a sample, or a rate. To the extent that the delinquency index is part of a whole (*real* delinquency) and is used to measure the whole, the index is similar to a sample. It is unlike a sample, however, for it is not a random representation of that whole because the items used in constructing the index have been chosen by logical judgment, statistical analysis, and a scaling procedure that have all produced a purposive rather than a random sample.[1]

Initially a representative sample of delinquent events was selected, of course, from the universe of all such events in a given city in a given year. Scaling was applied to certain units in the sample to convert them into numerical scores. Indexing spanned the initial stage of determining most of the units for conversion and the final stage of combining quantitative scores into a single measure. Our delinquency index, then, is a consequence of all these procedures and emerges finally as a weighted rate per unit of population at risk (i.e., the sum of the scores of delinquent events, divided by the juvenile population aged 7–17, multiplied by a constant.

[1] Here we are employing many of the ideas on the topic of statistical indices from the article by Edward Jackson Baur, "Statistical indexes of the social aspects of communities," *Social Forces* 33:64–75 (October, 1954).

Construction of indices is neither new nor simple. It is generally claimed that price index numbers, a related problem, originated in 1764 when Carli attempted to measure the effect of silver imports into Europe on the purchasing power of money and produced a formula comprising a simple arithmetic average of price relatives.[2] Since then, price, commodity and level-of-living indexes have become increasingly sophisticated and refined. Closer to the problems of constructing a delinquency index have been "social indices" which have been designed to measure the heterogeneity, mobility, concentration, or segregation of populations; health, through such data as mortality and morbidity; housing; welfare needs; education; or general social organization or disorganization of a community. A useful review of social indices appears in the work of Baur cited above. They all faced the problems which our delinquency index incurred, including the acquisition of data, definition and classification of units, weighting and combining components. Most of the indices have acknowledged limitations; some have endured but many have either been much revised or rejected. All have been examined for reliability and validity, and it is probably on these issues that our index designed to measure delinquency will be most carefully considered in future experimentation.

Although the scaling analysis is an integral part of the index, the two should be separately considered for reliability and validity. In Chapter 16, which described the category and magnitude scales, we have shown comparisons between different subject groups who rated offenses. While we did not use the test-retest procedure on the identical population, or the split-half method, we were able to examine the means of the distribution for the category and magnitude scales when submitted and resubmitted to similar and even different subject groups. When plotting these scales it was observed that the slope of the lines was no different for police officers, juvenile court judges, and for two sets of college students. Similarly, no significant differences occurred when the age of the offender varied or was unidentified among any of the judging groups. This invariance, therefore, meant that there was marked stability of the ratings. Moreover, after the ratings from the magnitude scale for offenders of unidentified age made by the Ogontz scores were adopted for further analysis, and after standard scores were computed for this set, a comparison of them with scores for the total population on the Primary Index Scale showed a correlation of .993 or a virtual identity.

[2] Bruce D. Mudgett, *Index Numbers* (135 pp. New York: Wiley 1952). See also, William Wasserman, *Education Price and Quantity Indexes* (ix, 166 pp. Syracuse, N.Y.: Syracuse University Press, 1963).

When a retest of twenty offense items was run on another large student population, and comparison of the standard scores for this last group was made with the standard scores of the Ogontz group, a very high correlation coefficient ($r = .986$) was found for identical offense items and for all items including those with slightly different form ($r = .987$). These coefficients suggest that the scale is highly reliable.

The seriousness of offenses involving theft was remarkably similar when two groups of subjects in the final testing stage were separately subjected to variant presentations, the one random sequential and the other simultaneous and ordered. Even in the context of all offense items used in these comparisons, the correlation was .92.

Generally, the larger the judging group, the greater is its reliability. The size of each group of raters evaluating different offenses appears in appendix tables. For no offense was the number of raters smaller than ten in any particular group. For the offender of unidentified age, no offense item was rated by fewer than twenty persons altogether. For the items on the Primary Index Scale there were no fewer than 569 raters on both the category and magnitude scales, of whom 275 used the magnitude scale. Any issue that might be raised about small numbers was overcome when (*a*) comparisons of smaller groups were made with the total population which rated items on the Primary Index Scale, and (*b*) when index offenses were presented in the final testing stage using 195 raters, 105 of whom were presented the random sequential set of offenses and produced ratings highly correlated (.987) with the ratings of previous raters.

Whether judgments which might be suggested by other groups of raters would be substantially different can only be determined by further research. As we mentioned earlier, there would be intrinsic interest in using as raters the victims of delinquent or criminal offenses, the offenders, a representative sample of a whole community, perhaps even a national sample, or any of a variety of subcultural groups. The differential perspective of particular individuals or of quite different groups would make for an interesting analysis. In this problem of the perspective of the rater as a dependent variable, psychophysical literature yields little information. Some studies have been made, of course, on personality variables that affect perspective but they offer little of value for our particular purposes at the moment.[3]

---

[3] The most direct experimental work on perspective as a dependent variable is probably that of Sherif [M. Sherif, *The Psychology of Social Norms* (xii, 209 pp. New York: Harper, 1936); M. Sherif and C. I. Hovland, *Social Judgment* (xii, 218 pp. New Haven: Yale University Press, 1961] on the development of

Relative to the question of whether any of our subjects rating offenses were previously victims or offenders, Galanter's comments on his analysis of the utility function of money are pertinent:

> . . . we have asked people about *hypothetical* increments of money, and we do not have any information about what would happen if they *actually* got the money. This is often stated as an argument against techniques of this kind, but the fact of the matter is that prior to a decision one always considers the alternatives as hypothetical and, presumably, bases his action on these considerations. To argue that we use an hypothetical situation to scale the value of money and, therefore, that the scale does not represent what people do, is to prejudge the usefulness of the scale as a characterization of the hypotheses that antedate the decision.[4]

Thus, every person makes a hypothetical judgment in any situation in which a choice is made, for the eliminated action remains hypothetical. A criminal chooses criminal behavior in advance and a judge makes his decision to convict and to sentence prior to the actions of convicting and sentencing.

It should be remembered that the ratios of score values, not necessarily the absolute numbers, have remained stable over the different rating groups used in the present study; and it is this ratio that would be important in further explorations. On the basis of our data, we would hypothesize that these relative offense score values would be preserved. To be more specific, we would hypothesize that in a replication of the magnitude and category scales, the scale values for offenses would be represented by (1) a slope not significantly different from those in our study, or, minimally (2) a straight line when plotted on semilogarithmic paper. Over time and in quite different cultures differences might occur; we are not suggesting that our final scale values or offense scores contain definitive features. But the offense items or delinquency events which we have scored are limited in number and character and represent fairly universal prescripts and prohibitions in Western culture so that we would not

---

norms. In his summary of these problems of individual perspective, Upshaw [Harry S. Upshaw, "Principles of scale formation applied to social psychological problems," *Research Previews* (Institute for Research in Social Science, University of North Carolina) 9:1–8 (June 1962)] refers to studies which indicate that somewhat religious judges can better assume the perspectives of the devoutly religious than they can that of the atheist, and that Negroes can better assume the perspective of whites than whites can that of the Negro.
[4] Eugene Galanter, "The direct measurement of utility and subjective probability," *Amer. J. Psychol.* 75:212–213 (June 1962).

be surprised to find a high degree of consistent, stable responses over a wider range of subjects than was employed in this analysis.

That our scaling analysis possesses validity, or measures what it purports to measure, is more difficult to ascertain. Logical analysis raises questions about the item structure of the scale and content validity. Previous descriptions of the scaling, which noted such things as the offense and offender items employed, conceptual clarity in expression of the items, the consistent relationships between items and scores, the correlations of scores for different subgroups, as well as the consensus of judgment by criminologists and other consultants to the study, may all contribute to the meaning of validity of both the scale and the construction of the entire index. Face validity requires general agreement that the scale and the index are convincing or plausible and the opinion of competent observers is therefore important.

We have also shown that it was possible to eliminate certain extraneous items or potential biases through design or internal analysis of the scale, because of: the stability of ratios among different judging groups, the invariance by offender age variables, the use of random ordering of all offense items for each subject, and the stability of the original set of offenses (the 21 used in the Primary Index Scale).

But if any criterion exists for testing the results of a study, then empirical analysis raises questions about concurrent and predictive validity. In reviewing the scaling of nonphysical continua we have been conscious of the fact that no physical external criterion exists with which to compare the ratings of seriousness of delinquent events. Among the other reasons discussed above for having subjects rate offenses in both the category and magnitude scales was that which permitted us to plot the one against the other. If offenses had been widely scattered on the plots, problems of choice would have arisen. There was little scattering, however, and the slopes on many different plots were consistent.

Validity through internal consistency is sometimes questionable but often useful.[5] We have selected a simple yet plausible binary criterion, and asked whether the scale values assigned on the basis of this criterion confirm our systematic but intuitive a priori impressions. We divided the 141 offenses rated by the Ogontz raters into two classes: those that involve harm, loss, or damage (Class I,

---

[5] A much stronger statement than the usual "caution," which writers warn to use when a validity coefficient is computed without replication, may be found in Edward E. Cureton, "Validity, reliability, and baloney," *Educ. psychol. Measmt.* 10:94–96 (1950).

$N = 92$), and those that involve no harm, loss, or damage (Class II, $N = 49$). In general, the expectation that Class I offenses are rated as much more serious than Class II is confirmed. Among these raw magnitude values given by the Ogontz raters (and the other rating groups are quite similar), only a single offense of the 49 Class II offenses had a scale value over 100, whereas six of the 92 Class I offenses were over that numerical value. Twenty-two (or 45%) of the Class II offenses, but only one Class I offense had a scale value less than 5, and, proportionately, about five times as many Class II offenses (60%) as Class I offenses (12%) had ratings under the scale value of 10. The lowest scale value for Class II offenses (.18) is over twenty times smaller than the lowest scale value for Class I offenses (3.79). Finally, the mean raw scale value for Class I offenses is 42.07 and for Class II offenses is 18.69. A t test for significance of difference between means ($t = 3.72$) reveals that Class I offenses are significantly different from Class II below the .01 level.

Comparison with other studies of seriousness of offenses can only be done roughly, because definitions of units are considerably divergent from those in the present study. Several checks were made, however, as crude tests to determine whether essentially the same thing was being measured. Durea, in his study of attitudes toward juvenile delinquency[6] obtained scale values for fourteen forms of delinquent behavior by having respondents designate which of a pair of offenses they considered the more serious, on the assumption that offenses would arrange themselves in a continuum from least to most serious. Ten of Durea's offenses were comparable to our own listing, and the correlation between this scale and the Ogontz mean magnitude ratings was found to be .908.[7] The plot for these points, along with their regression line is shown by Figure 18.

In an attempt at scaling offenses somewhat earlier than Durea's (and which suggested the use of paired comparisons) Thurstone obtained scores for nineteen offenses.[8] Twelve of these offenses were

---

[6] Mervin A. Durea, "An experimental study of attitudes toward juvenile delinquency," *J. appl. Psychol.* **17**:522–534 (1933).

[7] A log transform of the Ogontz magnitude scores was used in computing the correlation coefficient in order to obtain a linear relation between the ratio scale (Ogontz) and the interval scale (Durea). Using the Ogontz category scores (with no transformation needed), the coefficient remained virtually the same, .911.

[8] L. L. Thurstone, "The method of paired comparisons for social values," *J. abnorm. soc. Psychol.* **21**:384–400 (1927). Durea used much the same procedure

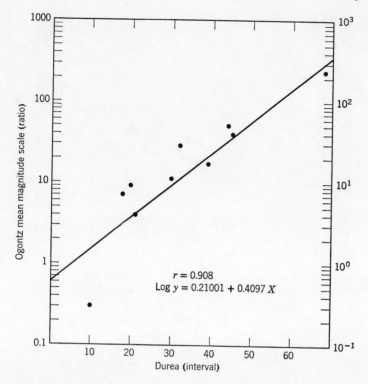

FIGURE 18. Comparison of the scale values for ten offenses rated in Durea's study with the mean magnitude scale scores of Ogontz raters.

comparable to offenses on our list, and when compared the two sets of scores yielded a coefficient of .697.[9] The plot for these points, along with the regression line is shown in Figure 19. Although there

---

as Thurstone in obtaining scale values, and the scores derived by each conformed well. Using seven comparable offenses (murder, arson, burglary, forgery, assault, larceny, and vagrancy) a coefficient of .975 was found between these two scales. It is of further interest to note that in Sweden Goesta Ekman, ["Measurement of moral judgment: A comparison of scaling methods," *Perceptual and Motor Skills* **15**:3–9 (1962)], compared Thurstone's method of paired comparisons, Case V, and Stevens's method of ratio estimation on scales of moral judgment, using 17 descriptions of "more or less criminal or immoral behavior." The logarithmic relationship reported previously was also verified for the subjective continuum in Ekman's study.

[9] One offense, adultery, was found to be quite divergent. This could be the

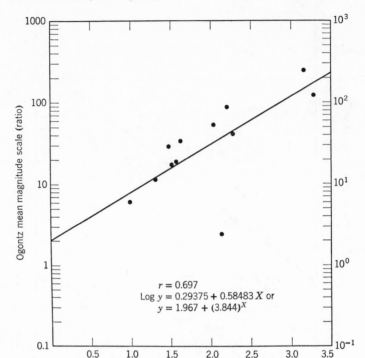

FIGURE 19. Comparison of the scale values for twelve offenses rated in Thurstone's study with the mean magnitude scale scores of Ogontz raters.

is no way of telling whether correlations are high (for there is no way of determining what "high" is in this context) these coefficients are usually considered satisfactory in similar tests for validity.

As a further effort to compare our scales with some other criterion, we used the original set of 21 offenses (partly because of their wide range, the inclusion of many index offenses, and the large number

---

result of a difference in definitions—the Ogontz students scored male adultery, whereas Thurstone gives no indication of the kind of adultery rated by his subjects. The disparity could also, however, be an indication of a change in sex values over the past three decades, since Thurstone's subjects rated adultery high in seriousness relative to the Ogontz ratings. Eliminating this offense and recomputing the coefficient resulted in a correlation of .766. The Ogontz scores were, of course, transformed by the use of logarithms. As a final note, the correlation between Thurstone and Ogontz mean category scores was .743.

of raters) with their maximum penalties described in the Pennsylvania Penal Code. (A list of these penalties by type of offense appears in Appendix E-8.) The maximum penalties were translated into 30-day units, with the death penalty assigned 43 years, which would roughly approximate the life expectancy of a white male 30 years of age, the median age common to studies in criminal homicide. The correlations of the 30-day units from the Penal Code with the log transformations of the mean magnitude scores for Ogontz and police raters were .875 and .938, respectively. These correlations are surprisingly high considering the fact that the Penal Code provides no variation in the maximum for amounts of money stolen and relatively

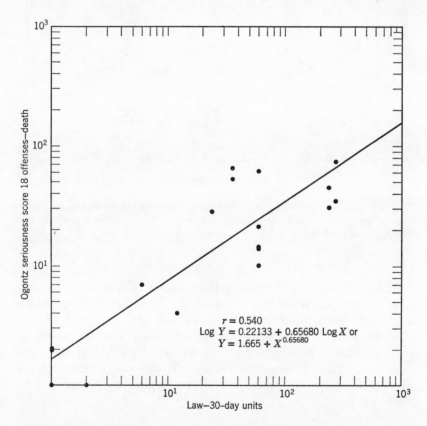

$$r = 0.540$$
$$\text{Log } Y = 0.22133 + 0.65680 \text{ Log } X \text{ or}$$
$$Y = 1.665 + X^{0.65680}$$

FIGURE 20. Comparison of the maximum penalties (in 30-day units) in the Pennsylvania Penal Code for eighteen offenses with the mean magnitude scale scores of Ogontz raters.

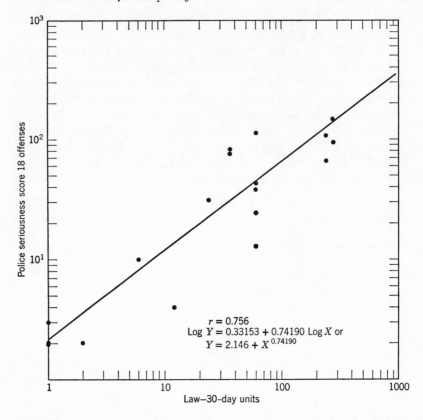

FIGURE 21.   Comparison of the maximum penalties (in 30-day units) in the Pennsylvania Penal Code for eighteen offenses with the mean magnitude scale scores of police officers.

few intervals between thirty days' imprisonment and death.   However, since the decision to set death is arbitrary, even though the procedure seems reasonable, the correlation coefficients were computed with the elimination of those offenses for which death was the maximum penalty.   The correlations drop to .540 for Ogontz and the Penal Code, and to .756 for the Police and the Penal Code.   Figures 20 and 21 show the plots for Ogontz and Police, respectively, along with the regression line.[10]

[10] In these computations, both the maximum legal penalties and the Ogontz and Police score values were transformed by the use of logarithms.

The reliability and validity of the index are partially a function of the reliability and validity of the scale values. We had already indicated some ways that, through logical and empirical analyses, the index meets the traditional standards for these tests. Crude components of the index, exclusive of the necessary refinements, are in many ways similar to those presently used in this country, in England, and in Sweden, and thereby benefit from the judgment of competent observers. We did, of course, try to recognize and to anticipate limitations of the entire study and our final index. The relative scale values for different offenses may seem disturbing to some segments of the public[11] and even to some criminologists, but the values were derived from what we considered to be firmly grounded and tested procedures. We have extracted aggravating acts from a set of delinquent events and employed the principle of additivity in scoring these events. We have not analyzed offenses for intercorrelation nor have we considered factor analysis or Guttman scaling best suited to our problems or data.[12] A time series analysis would be needed, using our weighted rates, to determine the existence of any intercorrelations and whether certain offense items might be combined.

[11] See *infra*, pp. 348–349, regarding this point.

[12] Although there is a variety of styles for scaling, our linkage with scaling analysis in psychophysics has been based partially upon the advantages of a magnitude ratio scale, not common in sociological studies. Probably the two major attempts to introduce measurement into qualitative sociological data are those of Louis Guttman and Paul Lazarsfeld whose works are well known and need not be documented here. For some discussion of the application of scalogram and factor analysis for scaling see M. W. Riley, J. W. Riley, and Jackson Toby, *Sociological Studies in Scale Analysis: Applications, Theory and Practice* (xii, 433 pp. New Brunswick, N.J.: Rutgers University Press, 1954); Samuel A. Stouffer, et al., *Studies in Social Psychology in World War II, Vol. IV, Measurement and Prediction* (x, 756 pp. Princeton, N.J.: Princeton University Press, 1950); H. J. Eysenck, "Review of measurement and prediction," *Internat. J. Opinion and Attitude Res.* 5:95–102 (1951); H. J. Eysenck and S. Crown, "An experimental study in opinion-attitudes methodology," *Internat. J. Opinion and Attitude Res.* 3:47–86 (1949); Warren S. Torgerson, *Theory and Methods of Scaling* (460 pp. New York: Wiley, 1958).

See also the critical remarks on scalogram analysis by Pitirim A. Sorokin in *Fads and Foibles in Modern Sociology and Related Sciences* (viii, 357 pp. Chicago: Henry Regnery, 1956); and the succinct discussion by Don Martindale, "Limits to the uses of mathematics in the study of sociology," in *Mathematics and The Social Sciences*, a symposium sponsored by The American Academy of Political and Social Science, edited by James C. Charlesworth, June 1963, pp. 95–121. See note 23 for factorial studies on moral values, by Rettig and Pasamanick.

Shannon,[13] Schmid,[14] and Wilkins[15] have made interesting analyses of intercorrelations of some offenses but the studies are not entirely in accord, partly because the series of offenses varied by type and time. The intercorrelations in these studies despite some contradictions seem to concur with our use of Categories A (bodily injury), B (property theft), and C (property damage) which constitute the total index. Wilkins' statement about employing legal categories raises the same questions we have suggested:

Unfortunately the legal categories under which offenses are classified for statistical purposes in this country frequently do not distinguish the degree of seriousness. For example, the value of the property stolen is not regarded as relevant to the charge of larceny. Robbery may consist of anything from a bank hold-up making national headlines to a small boy tripping up another and stealing his pocket money. The dividing line between serious and non-serious violence against the person is one which may well vary from time and from place according to the attitude of the culture in which the event occurs.[16]

If the relative degrees of seriousness of offenses were taken into account, this fact would have some effect upon previous efforts to construct indices of community disorganization. Porterfield and Talbert,[17] for example, averaged index numbers for the Part I offenses from the *Uniform Crime Reports* in their study of "social well-being." Angell limited his index to three categories of crime (murder and

[13] Lyle W. Shannon, "The spatial distribution of criminal offenses by states," *J. Crim. Law, Criminol. and Police Sci.* 45:264–273 (September–October 1954). This author used Part I offenses from the *Uniform Crime Reports* from 1946 to 1952. The highest intercorrelations were for murder and assault (.914), burglary and auto theft (.835), burglary and larceny (.786), auto theft and robbery (.771), burglary and robbery (.754), larceny and auto theft (.713). For an antecedent study of spatial distribution of these offenses but without intercorrelations, see Stuart Lottier, "Distribution of criminal offenses in sectional regions," *J. Crim. Law and Criminol.* 29:329–344 (1938).

[14] Calvin F. Schmid, "Urban crime areas I and II," *Amer. Sociol. Rev.* 25:527–542; 655–678 (1960).

[15] Leslie T. Wilkins, "The measurement of crime," *Brit. J. Criminol.* 3:321–341 (1963). Based on the intercorrelations found in England and Wales, 1946–1959, Wilkins suggested four indices: (1) serious crimes against property (e.g., burglary, breaking and entry, robbery); (2) social disorganization (e.g., drunkenness, disorderly conduct, and petty larceny); (3) serious crime against the person; (4) homicide (*a*) murder, (*b*) manslaughter. It is interesting to note that the high correlation Shannon found between murder and assault (.914) was found by Wilkins to be negative and low in England (−.15).

[16] *Ibid.*, p. 340.

[17] Austin L. Porterfield and Robert H. Talbert, *Crime, Suicide and Social Well-*

non-negligent manslaughter, robbery, and burglary) which he believed were most reliable.[18] Using heterogeneity and mobility as criteria of moral integration, he correlated them with crime and welfare effort, the two components of his moral integration index, and weighted crime twice as much as welfare effort.[19] It would be interesting to know, for instance, how a crime index using weights of seriousness for our selected offenses would affect a definition of social well-being or an effort to establish a moral integration index. The same may be said about MacNeil's[20] index for measuring vulnerability to crime and delinquency in New Jersey cities, about Buell and Robinson's index of social breakdown,[21] and Thorndike's "G-Score" for rating the "goodness of life" of various American cities.[22]

In an earlier chapter we also raised the question of what effects a more valid measurement of delinquency in a community might have on studies of causation and social action programs designed to prevent and reduce delinquency. Applying the scores as a weighted assessment of delinquent conduct to individuals might be a useful technique for analyzing changing patterns of delinquency by age, social class, and other variables as well as for providing a more refined meaning to recidivism for evaluating social intervention theory and practice.

Social research and sociological inquiry require indices which reflect the current structure and social values of society. It would not be strange, therefore, if the ratings of seriousness determined with care in the present study were not consistently maintained over long

---

Being in Your State and City (ix, 121 pp. Fort Worth: Leo Potishman Foundation, 1948).

[18] Robert C. Angell, "The moral integration of American cities," *Amer. J. Sociol.* 57:42 (July 1951). See also, Angell, *Free Society and Moral Crisis* (viii, 252 pp. Ann Arbor: The University of Michigan Press, 1958).

[19] This double weight for crime was given because the square of the average correlation between crime and the criteria was double the square of the average correlation between welfare effort and the criteria. As Baur (*op. cit.*, p. 67) points out, Horst criticized the use of this technique when there are several items, because it fails to account for the intercorrelations between items, and he recommended the least squares. See Paul Horst, et al., *The Prediction of Personal Adjustment* (xii, 455 pp. New York: Social Science Research Council, 1941).

[20] Douglas H. MacNeil, "The vulnerability index: An account of experimentation in predicting a community's crime rate," *Survey Midmonthly* 84:3-6 (January 1948).

[21] Bradley Buell and Reginald Robinson, "A composite rate of social breakdown," *Am. J. Sociol.* 45:887-898 (May 1940).

[22] E. L. Thorndike, *Your City* (204 pp. New York: Harcourt, Brace 1939), and *144 Smaller Cities* (135 pp. New York: Harcourt, Brace 1940).

periods of time and through marked shifts in the mores. It is doubtful, however, that regional variations in the United States would significantly alter the proposed index or the relative scale values. We suspect that the effort to maximize efficiency and minimize components for weighting has produced an index which might be applicable to a wide band of general cultural variants, but only further research can determine the correctness of this assumption.[23]

Studies of preliterate societies, particularly by Bacon, Child, and Barry[24] and by Brown[25] suggest that even among these societies, the most severe prohibitions of Western society are not provincial, and that a crime index not requiring legal categories, yet functioning within the cultural norms of these societies, could be a useful tool in cross-cultural analysis. Although the Bacon-Child-Barry study could not be compared with our seriousness scores because in their study the gravity of the crime was not noted, it was possible to compare six offenses for which Brown obtained scores with mean

---

[23] However, there is evidence that some basic moral values do not change substantially. Salomon Rettig and Benjamin Pasamanick, "Some observations on the moral ideology of first and second generation collective and non-collective settlers in Israel," *Social Problems* 11:165–178 (Fall 1963), concluded that relative to items examined on the dimension of criminal morality, no significant change or difference whatsoever was observed between two generations.

See also Paul Crissman, "Temporal change and sexual difference in moral judgments," *J. soc. Psychol.* 16:29–38 (August 1942); Peter G. Grasso, "Valori morali-sociali in transizione," *Orientamenti pedagogici* 8:233–268 (1961); and the following studies by Salomon Rettig and Benjamin Pasamanick: "Moral codes of American and Korean college students," *J. soc. Psychol.* 50:65–73 (Spring 1959); "Changes in moral values among college students: A factorial study," *Amer. Sociol. Rev.* 24:856–863 (December 1959); "Differences in the structure of moral values of students and alumni," *Amer. Sociol. Rev.* 25:550–555 (August 1960); "Moral value structure and social class," *Sociometry* 24:21–35 (March 1961); "Invariance in factor structure of moral value judgments from American and Korean college students," *Sociometry* 25:73–84 (March 1962).

[24] Margaret K. Bacon, Irvin L. Child, and Herbert Barry III, "A cross-cultural study of correlates of crime," *J. abnorm. soc. Psychol.* 66:291–300 (1963). This study, based on ethnographic information obtained from the Human Relations Area Files and anthropological literature, is an interesting use of judging the frequency of certain types of common offenses "made in relation to the norms of the culture under consideration" by the method of comparative ratings on a seven point scale as to relative frequency.

[25] Julia S. Brown, "A comparative study of deviation from sexual mores," *Amer. Sociol. Rev.* 17:135–146 (April 1952). In this study, also based on information in the Human Relations Area Files and other sources, a large number of preliterate societies were examined in terms of the severity of punishment for specific types of sexual behavior on a scale running from 1 (a mild penalty) to 4 (a very severe penalty).

category scale scores of the Ogontz raters. Although these are rather crude approximations, the rank order correlation between the two sets of scores was .77.[26] The important consideration, however, is that the theory of measurement, of scaling, and of index construction should contain universal application. The preservation of ratios in scale values, the choice of additive factors in the index, and the extent to which the instant scale values and scoring system can be used as a standard are presented as partially tested or testable hypotheses. Even though efficiency for use and for testing has been an important consideration throughout, accuracy has not been subordinate to simplicity.

Use of the index over time and applied to time series may be another way to determine validity. A measure may be considered valid if there is a high correlation between the predictions derived from it and what actually occurs.[27] In a sense, we have said, validity has been assured (i.e., the index measures what it claims to measure) by the proper selection, weighting, and combination of components. But predictive validity supports concurrent validity and it would therefore be desirable if experimental research could be designed to test the delinquency index for the former characteristic. "In the end," says Lundberg, "the validity of all instruments will be determined by their usefulness in serving the discriminatory purposes for which they were invented."[28]

[26] The rank order correlation coefficient is used in this situation because the scale derived by Brown is at the ordinal level.

[27] For many methodological problems similar to those faced in predictive validation of a delinquency index, see the recent analysis of techniques used by The National Science Foundation in selections of fellowships: John A. Creager, *Formation of Criterion Composites for Predictor Validation*, Technical Report No. 23 (iii, 20 pp. Washington, D.C.: National Academy of Science-National Research Council, May 1963).

[28] George A. Lundberg, *Social Research* (xx, 426 pp. New York: Longmans, Green, 1942), p. 202.

20

Measurement Theory and Delinquency

"The concept of measurement," says Coombs, "has generally meant the assignment of numbers to objects with the condition that these numbers obey the rules of arithmetic."[1] Yet, as new things are measured by new means, the definition and meaning of measurement changes. Measurement may be viewed differently by the physicist, the logician, the psychologist, and the social scientist. The requirements for assigning numbers to objects or conceptual entities range from the loosest, which is that any precisely specified rule be followed, to the most stringent, which is that numbers should be assigned only when the laws of addition are obeyed. Stevens argues that "measurement is the assignment of numerals to aspects of objects or events according to rules. . . ."[2] The only requirement he makes is a non-random assignment of numbers, for if there is no criterion for determining whether a given numeral should or should not be assigned it is not measurement. However, this rule allows definition to mean the same thing as measurement. If we define a thing we can always sort everything into two groups: those things excluded and those things included in the definition. If we define "redheads" we can sort people into two groups, redheads and persons who are not redheads. Stevens claims that this is measurement, for we can always assign a zero to persons who are not redheads and a one to persons who are redheads, and he refers to this process as measurement

[1] Clyde H. Coombs, "Psychological scaling without a unit of measurement," *Psychol. Rev.* **57**:145–158 (1952), p. 145.
[2] S. S. Stevens, in C. West Churchman and Philburn Ratoosh, *Measurement: Definitions and Theories* (274 pp. New York: Wiley, 1959), p. 24.

according to a nominal scale. Our own study does not proceed on this basis.[3]

We agree, as do many other writers, with Cohen and Nagel that definition is a step taken prior to measurement: "It is clear, moreover, that the comparison of groups by enumerating their members can be made only if the groups are themselves unambiguously distinct from one another. We therefore employ counting to make precise our ideas, *subsequent* to our having acquired sufficient knowledge about a subject to permit us to distinguish various features in it."[4]

Similarly, Churchman and Ratoosh distinguish between definition and measurement:

Definition, in general, is concerned with the systematic ordering of the conceptual scheme of science, and with the nature of the relations between different entities. Measurement has a more limited function, that of establishing metrical order among different manifestations of particular properties and of making scientific events amenable to mathematical description.[5]

We have defined classes and categories of delinquent events prior to our efforts to measure them. Those events that logical inference, supported by empirical evidence, suggested as being most consistently available for counting were designated index events. This process allowed for a separation of index and nonindex events and further permitted an exhaustive dichotomous procedure of defining events so that either they possessed a given characteristic or they did not. In this way we proceeded through ten categories with mutual exclusiveness of the primary property in each category until all events were assigned. This new classification system, however, does not provide a measurement of delinquency per se, but to be measurable some underlying order must exist in the property to be measured. We sought to measure delinquency because, along with definition, measurement in general helps to order events, promotes accuracy, leads

---

[3] For a detailed discussion of the problems involved in applying statistical measures of association to populations which are cross-classified with respect to two or more classifications of polytomies, see Leo A. Goodman and William H. Kruskal, "Measures of association for cross classifications," *J. Amer. Statistical Assoc.* 49:732–764 (December 1954); 54:123–163 (March 1959) and 58:310–364 (June 1963).

[4] Morris R. Cohen and Ernest Nagel, *An Introduction to Logic and Scientific Method* (xii, 467 pp. New York: Harcourt, Brace, 1934), p. 291.

For an opposing position that views measurement as a self-contained process, see Herbert Dingle's review of Churchmen and Ratoosh, *op. cit.*, in *Scientific American* (June 1960).

[5] Churchman and Ratoosh, *op. cit.*, pp. 3–4.

to the development of laws, permits unambiguous confirmation or refutation, and exposes significant relations among events. In this study we have been concerned primarily with a measurement theory that involves operations and assumptions only about delinquent events treated in one sense as a unitary variable. We hope, however, that substantive theories may be developed in which validly measured delinquency is one of the several variables, for substantive theory usually involves and is stated in terms of functional relations among two or more variables.[6]

Most efforts in the past to measure crime and delinquency have been content to admit, at least implicitly, that there are qualitative differences among offenses, but have failed to examine these differences for potential quantification under the assumption that different things cannot be added together. But this has meant that using legal labels for establishing criminal statistics retains equal weighting of discrete qualities of acts without thereby distinguishing among acts, either within or among categories. The distinction between quantity and quality has been clearly stated by Campbell[7] who has suggested that quantity means that $a + b > a$, and that quality means $a + b = a$. That is, a thing is a quantity if more of the property increases that property, and a thing is a quality if more of it leaves it unchanged. Thus, if a unit weighs one pound and we add to it another unit which weighs one pound, the pair will weigh two pounds; the weight of the property was increased by addition. But if we take the wetness of water as a quality and add to it more water the result will be just as wet as before; the property is not changed by the addition of more of the property. Quantities are measurable; qualities are not.

One of the major problems has been to find the ingredient for what Scott Blair[8] calls the "principle of dimensional homogeneity" when attempting to combine different items with different properties into a single measure. In criminal statistics there has been concern with the means of combining, for example, such apparently disparate offenses as larcenies and rapes. Wilkins has recently asked: "How many bicycle thefts and indecent exposures equal how many drunks

[6] See R. Duncan Luce, 'On the possible psychophysical laws," *Psychol. Rev.* **66:** 81–95 (March 1959), for a good discussion of measurement and substantive theories.

[7] Norman R. Campbell, *Foundations of Science* (vii, 565 pp. New York: Dover Publications, 1957), p. 283.

[8] G. W. Scott Blair, *Measurements of Mind and Matter* (115 pp. New York: Philosophical Library, 1956), p. 87.

or attempted suicides?"[9] And in his epilogue to a text on social problems, Merton raises the same issue,

Is one homicide to be equated with 10 petty thefts? 100? 1000? We may sense that these are incommensurables and so *feel* that the question of comparing their magnitude is a nonsense question. Yet this feeling is only a prelude to recognition of the more general fact that we have no strict common denominator for social problems and so have no workable procedures for comparing the scale of different problems, even when the task is simplified by dealing with two kinds of criminal acts.[10]

We have adopted the generally accepted view that we cannot compare events or benefit from the powerful tool of mathematical analysis unless the events which we are comparing are sufficiently alike to enable our finding a single "measuring rod" common to all of them. We can compare a foot with an inch, but we can only compare an inch with a second if we are first prepared to agree on some common ground. Blair suggests that in order to compare magnitudes which appear to be incompatible we can employ one of the following courses, even though they are not mutually exclusive nor rigidly divided from one another.[11] (1) Find a universal or ideal phenomenon linking the magnitudes, or define the scaling of one of them so as to establish a universal relation and then regard the dimensional constant as a numeric. (2) Express the magnitudes as ratios of some chosen magnitude in the same dimension. (3) Find a common "class" to which both magnitudes belong. (4) Ascribe "values" to the magnitudes in a common medium. Using these principles we can answer such questions as: (*a*) which is warmer, three fish or an overcoat?; (*b*) which is bigger, an elephant or a second?; (*c*) what quantity is three carrots plus two potatoes?; (*d*) how many canoes equal a slave? In (*a*) we can find a common phenomenon linking both fish and overcoats, which might be net calories. If we ask whether we shall be warmer if we eat three fish but do not wear an overcoat or if we forego the fish and wear the overcoat, the overcoat is probably warmer. In (*b*), if we translate the question to ask whether an elephant is bigger compared to the size of the average animal than is a second for some average time,

[9] Leslie T. Wilkins, "The measurement of crime," *Brit. J. Criminol.* 3:321–341 (April 1963), p. 337.

[10] Robert K. Merton, in *Contemporary Social Problems: An Introduction to the Sociology of Deviant Behavior and Social Disorganization,* Robert K. Merton and Robert A. Nisbet, Eds. (xiii, 754 pp. New York: Harcourt, Brace & World, 1961), p. 703.

[11] Blair, *op. cit.*, p. 115.

than we could compute the standard deviation for animal size and for times and perhaps discover that the z score of an elephant is larger than the z score of a second. In (c) we can find a common class to which both carrots and potatoes belong, namely, vegetables, and the answer is five vegetables. Finally, in (d) we could assign a value to the items, such as dollars, and determine that a slave had a higher price than three canoes.

We have taken the position in the present study that judged seriousness of delinquency is the homogeneous dimension which can allow for quantitative measurement of this phenomenon and that there are ways of ascribing values to the magnitudes in this common medium of seriousness. As we have seen in the early chapters of this book, few efforts have been made in criminal statistics to find some method for measuring what appeared to be different kinds of phenomena, but it has long been recognized that assigning equal weights to all offenses in an index is clearly an unsatisfactory solution. That differential degrees of gravity exist among criminal offenses has been perceived and explored in attempts to scale these offenses.

We have noted the early work of Mayr and De Castro to provide a more meaningful crime index,[12] but most of the efforts to scale seriousness have dealt with juvenile delinquency rather than with crime in general. Even so, most of these scales have been designed to apply the scheme to individual delinquents not to provide an index which measures the amount of delinquency in a community. This latter purpose was behind Clark's work in 1922.[13]   In 1927 Thurstone[14] provided, through the method of paired comparisons, a technique and a formula for ascertaining scale separations among different offenses. In 1933 and again 1936, Durea[15] adopted Thurstone's method and obtained a series of scale values for fourteen forms of delinquency behavior by arranging the offenses in 91 pairs and asking four professional groups to determine the more serious offense in each pair. The Cambridge-Somerville study offered a "seriousness index" used

---

[12] *Supra,* pp. 46–49.

[13] *Supra,* pp. 62–63.

[14] L. L. Thurstone, "The method of paired comparisons for social values," *J. abnorm. soc. Psychol.* 21:384–400 (1927). For a discussion of Thurstone's procedure contemporary to it, see P. M. Symonds, *Diagnosing Personality and Conduct* (xvi, 602 pp. New York: Century, 1931).

[15] Mervin A. Durea, "An experimental study of attitudes toward juvenile delinquency," *J. app. Psychol.* 17:522–534 (1933); and "A quantitative method for diagnosing the seriousness of asocial behavior of juvenile delinquents," *J. gen. Psychol.* 14:412–421 (1936). See also *supra,* pp. 63–64.

for the purpose of comparing delinquencies of a treatment group of boys with those of a control group;[16] and, more recently, concerned with the problem of "hidden delinquency," Nye[17] produced a delinquency scale employing the Guttman Cornell technique for testing unidimensionality. For many reasons discussed in the literature, the Nye scale has not been very compelling and again was not constructed as an index of delinquency over time in a given community, although efforts have been made to use the scale to compare the amount of delinquency by social class differences.[18] Using juveniles with police contacts, Shannon has made attempts to scale the delinquent behavior of individuals with first ten, then seven categories of scale type ranging from no contact with the police to contacts that include seven different kinds of offenses.[19]

The hypothesis of unidimensionality is still being subjected to further study, but again it must be emphasized that this scale is being used to estimate the amount of delinquent conduct of particular juveniles. The same may be said of the delinquent categories discussed by Havighurst et al. in *Growing Up in River City*.[20] In this study, crude and not entirely clear ratings were given for each contact a juvenile had with the police.

The ratings varied [we are told] from 1 to 4 seriousness of the offense, and from 1 to 4 for the disposition of the case—whether the individual was let off with a warning, was brought into court, declared delinquent, fined, put in

---

[16] Edwin Powers and Helen Witmer, *An Experiment in The Prevention of Delinquency* (xliii, 649 pp. New York: Columbia University Press, 1951). Fuller discussions at *supra*, p. 64.

[17] F. Ivan Nye, *Family Relationships and Delinquent Behavior* (167 pp. New York: Wiley, 1958).

[18] See also James F. Short, Jr., "A report on the incidence of criminal behavior, arrests, and convictions in selected groups," *Proc. Pacific Sociological Soc.* pp. 110–118 (1954); James F. Short, Jr., "The study of juvenile delinquency by reported behavior—An experiment in method and preliminary findings," paper read at the annual meeting of the American Sociological Society, 1955; James F Short, Jr., and F. Ivan Nye, "Reported behavior as a criterion of deviant behavior," *Social Problems* 5:207–213 (Winter 1957); F. Ivan Nye, James F. Short, Jr., and V. J. Olson, "Socioeconomic status and delinquent behavior," *Amer J. Sociol.* 63:381–389 (January 1958).

[19] Lyle W. Shannon, "Scaling juvenile delinquency," paper read at the annual meeting of the American Sociological Association, 1962. The seven offenses in the seven-category scale are contacts with the police for disorderly conduct, vagrancy, theft, liquor offenses, burglary, automobile theft, and sex offenses.

[20] Robert J. Havighurst, Paul H. Bowman, Gordon P. Liddle, Charles V. Matthews, and James V. Pierce, *Growing Up in River City* (189 pp. New York: Wiley, 1962), see especially pp. 68–88.

prison, sent to the state reformatory, and so on. The total delinquency scores ranged from 2 to 35.[21]

The delinquency records were then grouped into four categories, with Category IV, the least serious, having scores below 5, Category III with scores 5 to 8, and Categories II and I not designated by a score cutoff but with Category I, the most serious, declared "serious enough to suggest that there was real danger of a criminal career."

These efforts to scale delinquency have not been specifically concerned with our notion of a delinquency index, although they offer peripheral interest by focusing on the problems of scaling which we raised before.[22]

Our own scaling analysis is linked to the history of psychophysics, as we indicated in Chapter 15. We have used a theory of measurement that coincides with the definition by Luce:

One or more operations and relations are specified over a set of objects or events (the variable), and they are characterized by a number of empirically testable assumptions. In addition, it must be possible to assign numbers to the objects and to identify numerical operations and relations with empirical operations and relations in such a way that the numerical operations represent (are isomorphic to) the empirical ones. In other words, we have a measurement theory whenever (a) we have a system of rules for assigning numerical values to objects that are interrelated by assumptions about empirical operations involving them, and (b) these rules let us set up an isomorphic relation between some properties of the number system and some aspects of the empirical operations.[23]

Our study has made an effort to conform to this statement through the transformations which were made, and the results of the scaling tests led to our adoption of a magnitude ratio scale for use in assigning weights to delinquent events. The procedures have provided a means for extracting from a given scale score certain specific acts whose scale scores, when added together, constitute the score for the composite event.

By means of scaling we have assigned numbers to certain components of events, a process which Coombs[24] calls "mapping," and the

[21] *Ibid.*, p. 69.

[22] For two interesting anthropological studies rating crimes in preliterate societies, see *supra*, p. 332, notes 24–25.

[23] R. Duncan Luce, "On the possible psychophysical laws," *op. cit.*, p. 83. This is a particularly compelling article on nine theorems or functional equations for the laws satisfying the principle of theory construction. See the bibliography at the end of this article for additional discussions of psychophysical tests.

[24] Clyde Coombs, "Theory and methods of social measurement," in L. Festinger and D. Katz (Eds.), *Research Methods in the Behavioral Sciences* (xi, 660 pp. New York: Dryden Press, 1953).

analysis of the data has consisted of manipulating or operating on these numbers. In agreement with Luce, Stevens earlier said that "scales are possible in the first place only because there exists an isomorphism between the properties of the numeral series and the empirical operations that we can perform with the aspects of objects. . . ."[25]

The underlying theory and the design of our scale have permitted us to perform certain operations and to make various kinds of admissible transformations as part of our method of analysis.[26] "The method of analysis," says Coombs,[27] "then defines what the information is and may or may not endow this information with certain properties. A 'strong' method of analysis endows the data with properties which permit the information in the data to be used, for example, to construct a unidimensional scale."

The point is fairly obvious but often overlooked: that the method of analysis which the researcher imposes upon his data has an effect on the interpretation of the data. When attempting to assign numbers to empirical relations, the system of measurements becomes critical in the way in which the correspondence is or is not maintained. It should be clear that we are moving from the scale values to offense scores in a scoring system which embraces the concept and imposition of additivity. Our scoring techniques and the analysis of the results of scaling suggest that empirically we may treat the scale and offense scores as ratios. The question is, of course, whether such an operation is theoretically admissible. Psychologists are not agreed about the interpretation of the magnitude scale as a ratio scale. Adequate

---

[25] S. S. Stevens, "Mathematics, measurement, and psychophysics," in S. S. Stevens (Ed.), *Handbook of Experimental Psychology* (1436 pp. New York: Wiley, 1951), p. 23.

[26] In addition to the paper by Luce (*supra*, note 23), see the article by Clyde Coombs, Howard Raiffa, and R. M. Thrall, "Some views on mathematical models and measurement theory," *Psychol. Rev.* 61:132–144 (1954), which examines classical measurement theory and forms mixtures of different axioms underlying certain scales.

[27] Coombs, "Theory and methods of social measurement," *op. cit.*, p. 471. The gist of Coombs' additional remarks, however, is that if such a scale is a *necessary* consequence of the method of analysis, then the scale cannot be thought of as a characteristic of the behavior in question. He then makes a suggestion not sufficiently heeded by sociologists: "It therefore becomes desirable to study methods of collecting data with respect to the amount and kind of information each method *contains* about the behavior in question as distinct from that *imposed*. Similarly, it becomes desirable to study the various methods of analyzing data in terms of the characteristics or properties each method imposes on the information in the data as a necessary preliminary to extracting it." (*Ibid.*, p. 472.)

theory to support its use as a ratio scale is lacking, but at the empirical level it is treated both overtly and covertly as if it were a ratio scale and psychophysical experimentalists for some time have been using it as such.[28]

Part of the problem is involved in the distinction between the terms numbers and numerals, as Cicourel[29] has indicated in his discussion of these matters as they relate to sociology. The two terms are not always used interchangeably. In scaling, numerals have been assigned as conventional symbols without necessarily specifying which mathematical system governing operations or numbers is applicable. "It is possible," he says, "to develop a mathematical system which utilizes numerals to represent a theoretical system but which does not specify whether the mathematical operations developed or implicit in the system refer to any particular number system."[30]   By interpreting our results as a ratio scale we are employing a "strong" method of analysis which becomes a powerful tool for examining empirical relations. We are maintaining an assumption of isomorphism between the numbers and the class of equivalent events they represent. This now means that when we deputize numbers to reflect the seriousness of a delinquent event we are also required to refer to their relationships so that a criminal homicide is represented, for example, as being over twice as serious as a single forcible rape. As we said previously, each score represents the gravity involved in passing from lawful conduct to conduct which is unacceptable by legal norms and registers an estimated quantitative degree of seriousness of deviation. The zero point on the scale is the absence of an offense.

Sociologists in particular have been indicted for their failure to be aware that ratios in different sets may mean different things. Martindale recently remarked that in the traditional attempts to measure intensive qualities

. . . sociologists have not always avoided the error of assuming that the ratio between degrees of a quality may not be the same as the ratios of the numbers assigned to them. It is not correct to say that a student with an

---

[28] S. S. Stevens, "Mathematics, measurement, and psychophysics," in S. S. Stevens (Ed.), *Handbook of Experimental Psychophysics* (1436 pp. New York: Wiley, 1951), pp. 40–41.

[29] Aaron V. Cicourel, "Problems of measurement in sociology," an expanded version of a paper presented at the annual meeting of the American Sociological Association, 1960 (mimeographed).

[30] *Ibid.*, p. 5. See also his citation to T. W. Reese, "Application of the theory of physical measurement to the measurement of psychological magnitudes with experimental examples," *Psychol. Mon.* No. 55 (v, 89 pp. 1943), p. 8.

IQ of 50 is half as intelligent as one with an IQ of 100. The uses of numbers as identification marks, as position indicators in a series of degrees, and as signs indicating quantitative relations between qualities have rarely been kept distinct in attempts at sociological measurement.[31]

Cicourel[32] has been even more forceful:

The researcher who invokes a set of axioms (either explicitly or implicitly) which assume additivity seldom (if ever) demonstrates, operationally and theoretically, the meaning of such axioms within the object system. It is apparently enough to simply concoct some undefined, unexplicated correspondence between a set of theoretical events and a mathematical system and let the reader demonstrate for himself that the product is sensible and contributes to our knowledge. It would appear to be beneath the dignity of such writers to tell the "unsophisticated" reader what the game is all about. The fact that electing such a correspondence means that some kind of actor, some form of social order, has been assumed which must be justified in terms of sociological theory and empirical research, does not seem to worry such writers.

We have been conscious of these issues and have tried to demonstrate a correspondence between our data and the measurement system being used. Unlike the measurement of IQ which has no zero point, our model claims a zero point. It should be kept in mind that all offenses were rated relative to an anchor point and that the scale values of the components were derived from the rater rather than from the experimenter. Moreover, during the last stage of testing, in rating the gravity of property offenses, raters were presented five money values with everything else about the offense held constant. In rating assaultive offenses, raters were presented four versions of injury outcomes while everything else about the offense was held constant. The same money value in a larceny was transposed to a simple robbery with intimidation to obtain a scale value for intimidation; then to burglary to obtain a scale value for forcible entry; and from verbal intimidation to intimidation with a weapon to obtain a scale value for presence of a weapon in such circumstances. In these ways we extracted the meaning and, consequently, the numerical relations between certain properties of delinquency events. Although not all of the original judgments manifested additive qualities, ad-

---

[31] Don Martindale, "Limits to the uses of mathematics in sociology," in *Mathematics and the Social Sciences,* a symposium sponsored by The American Academy of Political and Social Science, edited by James C. Charlesworth, June 1963, p. 112.
[32] Cicourel, *op. cit.,* p. 7.

ditivity characterized both our theoretical assumptions and the operations performed on the data when applied in the scoring system. The employment of standard arithmetic principles became even more obvious when the index was produced by summing the frequency of delinquency events, which were multiplied by the score of seriousness for each event, dividing the sum by the juvenile population, and multiplying by a constant. We are aware that the numerals originally assigned to represent quantitative degrees on a continuum of seriousness are also now part of a number system which infers certain relations between these quantities. Torgerson reminds us that "measurement pertains to properties of objects, and not to the objects themselves. Thus, a stick is not measurable in our use of the term, although its length, weight, diameter, and hardness might well be. . . ."[33] We have sought to measure the seriousness of delinquency events and not all the aspects or properties of such events. The number of tangible and intangible properties of any delinquent event is enormous; we have selected certain properties for use in an index and obtained some reaction to the degree of seriousness which those properties represent. In this sense, we are measuring delinquency as Torgerson suggests one might measure a stick.

The relationship of the different types of events, because they are all delinquencies and yet possess many features not considered in the present study, may be described as homomorphic (many-one) to the degree of seriousness. But the relationship between equivalence sets of seriousness and the integers used to represent them we describe as isomorphic.

It is important to recall that *within* certain factors used from the scaling analysis additivity is not assumed. These are amounts of money and intimidation. That is, two separate theft events, each involving fifty dollars and each scored 2 are not equivalent to one theft event involving one hundred dollars, for the latter is also scored 2 under the rule of the power function of money. The first two thefts of fifty dollars each have a total score of 4. It is the transgression of the law, not only the amount of money stolen, which is rated and scored. Furthermore, intimidation is counted only once in an event involving robbery, regardless of the number of victims in that event. Thus if two robbery events occur, each of which has intimidation of one victim by an offender without a weapon and each of which is a three-dollar theft, the score for each event is 2 for

---

[33] Warren S. Torgerson, *Theory and Methods of Scaling* (460 pp. New York: Wiley, 1958), p. 14.

intimidation plus 1 for money loss, or a total of 3; and the two events total 6. A single robbery event with two victims, both of whom were intimidated by an offender without a weapon and together had six dollars stolen, is scored 2 for the intimidation and 1 for the money loss, or a total of 3. Moreover, our model index excludes all events without injury, theft, or damage and *events* of injury, theft, or damage with a total score of 1, but includes *elements* scored 1 in any event that has a total score of 2 or more. Thus, two nonindex events, each of which contains only minor injury to one victim, do not equal one index event which contains minor injury to two victims; or $(1) + (1) \neq (1+1)$ and $(1) + (2) \neq (1+2)$, etc., where the closed parentheses represent events. But the relationship *between* the score values for all elements, including those for money and intimidation, in events scored 2 or higher as well as the relationship between all events scored 2 or higher, is additive. Thus, $(3) + (2) = (4+1)$, and $(4) + (3) = (6+1)$, etc.

The relationship with which we are concerned may be expressed more formally in a traditional way. Let the symbols α, β, γ, and δ represent elements in delinquency events, which may at times contain only one such element—a simple theft of property valued at a given amount—and at other times may contain several elements—a rape, homicide, and theft, for instance. Events containing elements that, on a one-dimensional scale of seriousness, yield equivalent total scores, can be said to belong in the same set. We denote such equivalence sets by W, X, Y, and Z.[34] When the event has only one element, its score determines its set, and when composed of more than one element, the set is determined by the sum of the score values of its elements.

Such additivity was partially tested in the scaling but generally has been imposed. The alternative would be to scale all conceivable combinations of elements, and this alternative is impractical. To expedite the use of scale scores, we believe that a system of weighting and indexing requires additivity. One event, for example, may possess all elements of two other events. A robbery-murder may share the characteristics of robbery and murder separately. The relationship of the components of this event is denoted by $+$, so that if α and β denote separate [criminal] elements of the same event, $(\alpha + \beta)$ is a composite event. The fundamental relationship examined

---

[34] The equivalence sets may be thought of as being analogous to the use of H_2O, for instance, which represents steam, ice, a gallon or a gram of water indifferently.

is "judged as being at least as serious as" ($\geq$). Thus murder is *judged as being at least as serious as* a ten-dollar theft. For simplicity, if α and β denote delinquency events containing a single element, we may replace the phrase in italics by $\geq$, as in $\alpha \geq \beta$. We should then expect the following propositions to hold:

(1) $$\alpha \geq \alpha.$$

(2) $$\text{Either } \alpha \geq \beta, \text{ or } \beta \geq \alpha.$$

(3) $$\text{If } \alpha \geq \beta \text{ and } \beta \geq \gamma, \text{ then } \alpha \geq \gamma.$$

The relation is a total ordering, therefore, and (3) expresses the transitivity of the relation.

These postulates claim that every two elements or events can be compared. The question of whether (2) is satisfied in this theory is precisely the question of whether every two delinquency elements or events used in the index are judged as comparable in seriousness. Although a persuasive case might be made for the position that delinquency events with offensive elements against the person are not entirely comparable with events having offensive elements against property, the design of the scaling experiments on seriousness purposely included this kind of comparison.

In the process of addition used in the scoring, it may be noted that by definition $\alpha + \beta = \beta + \alpha$, and $(\alpha + \beta) + \gamma = \alpha + (\beta + \gamma)$, where $=$ is used to mean identity. It seems reasonable, therefore, to postulate as a connection between the relations $+$ and $\geq$ that

(4) $$\text{if } \alpha \geq \beta \text{ and } \gamma \geq \delta,$$
$$\text{then } (\alpha + \gamma) \geq (\beta + \delta),$$
$$\text{while if } also \ (\beta + \delta) \geq (\alpha + \gamma),$$
$$\text{then } \beta \geq \alpha \text{ and } \delta \geq \gamma.$$

This is simply to say that a composite delinquency event made up of two elements, each of which is judged more serious than two other elements, is more serious than the composite of the two other elements. The following rather complex statement expresses the latter part of (4) above: If, for instance, a hospitalization injury (α) is at least as serious as a money theft (β) and a medically treated and discharged injury (γ) is at least as serious as an automobile theft (δ), while the composite of the money theft and the automobile theft ($\beta + \delta$) is at least as serious as the hospitalization and the treated and discharged ($\alpha + \gamma$), then the money theft (β) is at least as serious as the hospitalization (α).

It should also be observed that we have considered nondelinquent behavior as $\bar{0}$ and that we define $\bar{0} + \alpha$ and $\alpha + \bar{0}$ to mean simply α, and $\alpha_1 + \alpha_2 + \alpha_3 + \cdots + \alpha_n \neq \bar{0}$.

Relative to the concept of multiplicity, we may denote n occurrences of an uncomplicated delinquent event, type α, by $n\alpha$ and m of type β by $m\beta$. The combination of these events is defined as $n\alpha + m\beta$. Confusion of the meaning of $+$ is avoided if we employ the crucial postulate

(5) $$n(\alpha + \beta) = n\alpha + n\beta.$$

That is, n occurrences of a composite delinquency event are equally as serious as n occurrences of each component of the composite.

We can extend these definitions to events which are gathered into an equivalence class or set, meaning that they all have the same degree of seriousness. If α is an event of the equivalence set X and β that of equivalence set Y, we define $X \geq Y$ if $\alpha \geq \beta$. We now have an algebra of types of delinquency events with the operation $+$ and the total ordering $\geq$ satisfying our hypotheses and extended to equivalence sets in the standard way, for by definition of $+$ in all cases we have for equivalence sets W, X, Y, and Z:

  I. $X + Y = Y + X$
  II. $(X + Y) + Z = X + (Y + Z)$
  III. $X + \bar{0}, \bar{0} + X = X$
  IV. If $X \geq Y$ and $W \geq Z$, then $X + W \geq Y + Z$; and if also, $Y + Z \geq W + X$, then $Y \geq X$ and $Z \geq W$.

Under the usual operations of addition and with the usual ordering, a set of non-negative integers can be assigned to delinquency elements and events. This system can be extended to an ordered group satisfying postulates (1), (2), (3), (4) and having a first element other than $\bar{0}$ which is $\geq \bar{0}$. This first element we identify with the integer 1, and, essentially, this first element is the smallest difference between elements.[35] This identification with the integer 1 induces an isomorphism between classes of events and a subset of the positive integers such that

$$\gamma(X + Y) = \gamma(X) + \gamma(Y)$$

and if $X \geq Y$, then $\gamma(X) \geq \gamma(Y)$.

---

[35] The reason that the smallest difference between elements and between events is 1 is due to our adjustment of the score values through rounding. Retaining this integer as the smallest difference is, of course, not necessary to the theory so long as the smallest difference is bounded from.

Using such an isomorphism, the least serious event being indexed is assigned the integer 2. Thus, index events can differ by 1 in their assigned integers but, as we have emphasized, there is no *index* event corresponding to the integer 1. However, two *elements* of an event, each assigned an integer of 1, constitute an index event.

Thus, distributivity is inherent in the model under the restrictions imposed. Furthermore, because all standard statistical procedures are permissible on the ratio scale,[36] they have amounted to our analyzing the assignment of numbers to the classes or sets of delinquency events in such a way as to retain this isomorphic relationship between classes of events and the numbers which represent them.

Distributivity, it is important to note, is perhaps the most controversial aspect of the model, because it implies that one homicide is more than the sum of two forcible rapes and is approximately equivalent to thirteen larcenies, each with a maximum of 250 dollars. There are only two ways out of this conclusion of a ratio scale and distributivity which are part of the model; one is a multidimensional vectorial model in which categories of crimes are treated as entirely separate. The other way is to abandon distributivity, which would mean abandoning any effort to construct an index, for then many crimes committed by one person would be different from the same crimes committed by many persons, and any idea of accumulating crimes would be virtually impossible. Equating a number of petty thefts with murder may at first seem unpalatable to some observers, but there are similar equations in operations research which have shown the mean number of deaths likely to occur in construction of any large bridge, and even with this knowledge bridges are constructed, or in moving traffic on highways at certain rates of speed. The public, when faced directly with the meaning of human life, will consider it amost infinitely precious, yet in the confusion and subtlety of complex social life this same public is forced to and does form certain equivalences. The empirical relations our subject population has given on the scale are responses which apparently are not unique and which fit the model as described.

For those who find it difficult to think of criminal homicide or forcible rape as equal to a given amount of money or number of money thefts, we suggest a look at the offenses defined in the criminal law and given punishments differing in degree of severity. In Pennsylvania, any simple theft is punishable by up to three years in prison and a forcible rape by up to fifteen years. We might con-

[36] S. S. Stevens, "Mathematics, measurement and psychophysics," *op. cit.*, p. 28.

clude that a rape is regarded as equal in seriousness to five thefts. At present the average length of time in prison spent by first-degree murderers in Pennsylvania is about 20 years, which equates one homicide with seven thefts. It is apparent that the punishments provided by law for criminal offenses of various kinds represent crude judgments by legislators of the comparative seriousness of offenses.

We are even more convinced at the end of this research than we were at the outset that only when we have an index with a quantitative scale for measuring delinquency can we give an explicit account of what we are measuring. The relatively undeveloped state of measuring instruments for such purposes in the social sciences has been an obstacle to efficient and economical research. If measurements of time, temperature, length, or weight had to be newly invented for each research analysis in the physical sciences, progress in those fields would indeed have been slow. Yet in criminology and in the social sciences generally, there has been little or no systematic theory stipulating how to select fundamental dimensions of conduct in order to measure certain social events. The efforts put into this research on the measurement of delinquency represent a recognition of this crucial role of measurement in all science.

Appendix A-1

Offense Report

(All identifying names and numbers are fictitious. Black triangle in boxes indicates items coded.)

CENTRAL COMPLAINT # 60-5443117	DIST. COMPLAINT # 34-58971		CITY OF PHILADELPHIA POLICE DEPARTMENT OFFENSE REPORT	DIST. OR UNIT REPORTING JAD		DATE OF REPORT 2-30-60	
CRIME CLASSIFICATION ROBBERY-HIGHWAY		CODE 310		DISTRICT 7	GRID x	SECTOR J	BEAT x

OFFENSE ROBBERY-HIGHWAY		CODE	DATE OF OCCURRENCE 2-30-60		TIME OF OCCURRENCE 2:00 p.m.	
PLACE OF OCCURRENCE ☐ 1-INSIDE ☑ 2-OUTSIDE 10th and Giddings Sts.			TYPE OF PREMISES - OBJECTIVE Highway - Robbery			CODE
COMPLAINANT (FIRM OR BUSINESS) James Mitciv 58/W			MEANS OR METHODS USED - WEAPONS - TOOLS Force Fist			
ADDRESS 1016 Giddings St.	PHONE QU 6 - 1574		VEHICLE USED (DESCRIBE) x			
AGE 58 YRS.	SEX ☑ 1-M ☐ 2-F	RACE W	NATIVITY U.S.	HOW ATTACKED - WHERE ENTERED, ETC. Struck with fist		
DESCRIPTION Normal		OCCUPATION Salesman		CRIMINAL'S TRAITS Highway Robber		
REPORTED BY Ira Mitciv		RELATIONSHIP Brother		PERSONS ARRESTED (NAME, ADDRESS, AGE, RACE)		
ADDRESS Same		PHONE Same		LAWRENCE 'RED' NEFFO 16/W res. 903 Suchard St.		
REPORTED TO Plm. Hollenback #0000		DATE AND TIME 2-30-60 2:00p.m.		DARRYL NEFFO 22/W 903 Suchard St.		
HOW RECEIVED ☐ 1-PERSON ☑ 2-PHONE ☐ 3-MAIL ☐ 4-SIGHT ARREST						

DETAILS AND DESCRIPTION OF PROPERTY	STOLEN VALUE	RECOVERED VALUE	CODE

ORIGIN AND DETAILS On Tuesday 2/30/60, at about 2:00 p.m. the above complainant JAMES MITCIV when at 10th and Giddings Sts. was stopped by two white males who asked him for a match. They then knocked him to the ground and beat him up and took his wallet containing $65.00 in U.S. Currency.

INVESTIGATOR: D. JONES #1637 Assigned by Sgt. Gabel on 2-30-60.

MESSAGES: ARRESTED: Lawrence Neffo, res. 903 Suchard St. and Darryl Neffo 22/W res. 903 Suchard St. charged highway robbery, larceny and RSG, and A & B arrested inside residence 4:00 p.m. 2-30-60. Pros. James Mitciv res. 1016 Giddings St. CC#60-5443117, D.C.#34-58971.

CONTACTS: James Mitciv 58/W, res. 1016, the complainant,was interviewed by the assigned inside the 34th Dist. on 2-30-60 and he stated that he had been crossing Giddings at 10th when a youth he knew, the offender, accompanied by an older person unknown to him asked for a match. Mitciv stated that they became abusive and threatened to punch him if he did not give them money. He further stated that when he refused they pushed him to the ground, kicked him and took $65 from his wallet and fled.

OFFENDERS: Lawrence NEFFO, 16/W res. 903 Suchard St. Previous record: 11/20/59, A & B, Rem; 12/1/59, Larceny, Rem. Darryl NEFFO, 22/W res. 903 Suchard St. NFR. The offenders denied taking any property from MITCIV. Darryl had the victim's wallet containing $65.00. He could offer no explanation.

ACTION TAKEN: Above contacts and Interviews. Arrest messages sent out by the assigned on Gen #91 2-3-60. 75-82,s submitted for the record. The victim was taken to Dr. Wishton for treatment and $10 was returned to him for cab fare.

EVIDENCE: One brown wallet containing $55 and personal papers sent to YSC on property receipt #95477.

CASE STATUS: CLOSED ARREST
COPIES: JAD, NCDD, FL

	STOLEN VALUE	RECOVERED VALUE	

FOUNDED ☑ 1-YES ☐ 2-NO	☐ 1-ACTIVE ☐ 2-INACTIVE (NOT CLEARED)	☑ 3-CLEARED BY ARREST ☐ 4-EXCEPTIONALLY CLEARED	TOTAL $65.00	TOTAL 65.00	INS.
POLICEMAN ASSIGNED Hollenback #0000	TELETYPE MESSAGE # Arrest #91	DATE 2-30-60	GEN. RADIO MESSAGE # X		DATE X
INVESTIGATOR ASSIGNED	DIST. OR UNIT COMMANDER		DIVISION COMMANDER		

75-49 (REV. 3-56)

CENTRAL RECORDS   6 PART

(Reduced from 8″ × 10½″)

351

Appendix A-2

Master File Card

LAST NAME	First	Middle	NICKNAME		☐ BOY ☐ GIRL

ADDRESS — BIRTH DATE

FATHER — MOTHER — RACE

SCHOOL — CHURCH — REFERRED TO

DATE	CHARGE	ARREST YES	NO	DISTRICT NO.	DISPOSITION	DATE

75-163 REV. (7/60)

JUVENILE AID DIVISION RECORD

USE REVERSE SIDE FOR ADDITIONAL INFORMATION

(Reduced from 8″ × 5″)

Appendix A-3

Juvenile Information Card

DIST.	DIST. COMPL. #	CEN. COMPL. #			ARREST	
			☐ MALE	☐ FEMALE	☐ YES	☐ NO
LAST NAME		FIRST NAME	NICKNAME		COLOR	AGE
ADDRESS			DIST. OF RES.		DATE OF BIRTH	
FATHER'S NAME	MOTHER'S NAME		SCHOOL OR PLACE OF EMPLOYMENT			
CHURCH AFFILIATION			CHURCH ADDRESS			
COMPLAINANT			SURVEY INFORMATION			
DATE OF OCCUR	TIME OF OCCUR	DAY OF WEEK	PHILA. CODE	RECORD		REFERRAL
CHARGE OR COMPLAINT - EXPLAIN CASE				OFFICE USE		
PLACE OF OCCURRENCE			OFFICER		DIST./UNIT	

75-82 (Rev. 10/59) JUVENILE INFORMATION CARD
(Original and Two Copies to Juv. Aid Div.)

(Reduced from 4″ × 6″)

Appendix A-4

Philadelphia Crime Code

PHILADELPHIA POLICE DEPARTMENT
DIRECTIVE 110
(1/1/60)

SUBJECT: PHILADELPHIA CLASSIFICATION OF PART I AND PART II OFFENSES, SERVICES AND INCIDENTS

POLICY: Philadelphia classification and codes shall be used in classifying offenses and investigations, arrests, incidents, complaints and services.

File Ref.	Phila. Code	Classification
1	*Criminal Homicide*	
	111	Wilful killing, murder and non-negligent manslaughter.
	112	Wilful killing of a felon by policeman.
	113	Wilful killing of a felon by citizen.
	114	Abortion causing death to victim, not self-inflicted.
	121	Manslaughter by auto, gross negligence of some person other than victim.
	122	Manslaughter by train, trolley, etc., gross negligence of some person other than victim.
	123	Manslaughter by negligence, other than traffic (no vehicle involved) gross negligence of some person other than victim.
	124	Manslaughter by auto, negligence of victim.
	125	Manslaughter by train, trolley, etc., negligence of victim.
2	*Rape*	
	211	Rape, forcible.
	233	Ravish, attempt rape.
	xxx	Rape, statutory. See Code 1410.

354

File Ref.	Phila. Code	Classification
3	*Robbery*	
3b	310	Highway, *no gun.*
3b	311	Highway, *gun.*
3b	312	Highway, *attempt.*
3a	313	Purse snatching, $50.00 or over.
3a	314	Purse snatching, $5.00 to $50.00.
3a	315	Purse snatching, under $5.00.
3a	316	Purse snatching, *attempt.*
3b	320	Commercial house, *no gun.*
3b	321	Commercial house, *gun.*
3b	322	Commercial house, *attempt.*
3b	323	Drug store, *no gun.*
3b	324	Drug store, *gun.*
3b	325	Drug store, *attempt.*
3b	330	Gas station, *no gun.*
3b	331	Gas station, *gun.*
3b	332	Gas station, attempt.
3b	340	Chain store, *no gun.*
3b	341	Chain store, *gun.*
3b	342	Chain store, *attempt.*
3b	350	Residence, *no gun.*
3b	351	Residence, *gun.*
3b	352	Residence, *attempt.*
3b	360	Bank, *no gun.*
3b	361	Bank, *gun.*
3b	362	Bank, *attempt.*
3b	370	Miscellaneous, *no gun.*
3b	371	Miscellaneous, *gun.*
3b	372	Miscellaneous, *attempt.*
3b	373	Taxi cab or bus, *no gun.*
3b	374	Taxi cab or bus, *gun.*
3b	375	Taxi cab or bus, *attempt.*
4	*Aggravated Assault*	
	401	Assault with intent to kill.
	402	Assault with intent to kill by auto.
	403	Mayhem.
	404	Assault and battery, aggravated.
	405	Aggravated assault and battery, by auto.
	407	Aggravated assault and battery on police officer.
5	*Burglary*	
5b.	*Residence*	
	510	Private residence, night.
	511	Apartment house, night.
	512	Hotel–motel, night.

File	*Phila.*	
Ref.	*Code*	*Classification*

5 Burglary (*Continued*)

	513	Rooming house, night.
	514	Safes, night.
	515	Attempt, night.
	520	Private residence, day.
	521	Apartment house, day.
	522	Hotel–motel, day.
	523	Rooming house, day.
	524	Attempt, day.

5a. *Nonresidence*

	530	Drug store, night.
	531	Factory, night.
	532	Gas station or garage, night.
	533	Stores (other than chain drug or liquor), night.
	534	Chain store, night.
	535	Taproom or liquor store, night.
	536	Office building, night.
	537	Safes, night.
	538	All others—nonresidence—night.
	539	Attempt, night.
	540	Drug store, day.
	541	Factory, day.
	542	Gas station or garage, day.
	543	Stores (other than chain drug or liquor), day.
	544	Chain store, day.
	545	Taproom or liquor store, day.
	546	Office building, day.
	547	Safes, day.
	548	All others—non-residence—day.
	549	Attempt, day.

5c. *Vehicle* (*from*)

	614	Non-accessory, over $50.00.
	618	Accessories, over $50.00.
	624	Non-accessory, $5.00 to $50.00.
	628	Accessories, $5.00 to $50.00.
	634	Non-accessory, under $5.00, include attempts.
	638	Accessories, under $5.00, include attempts.

6 Larceny—Theft (*except auto theft*)

Refer to Group 10 (embezzlement).

6g	611	Pocket-picking, $50.00 or over.
6h	612	Purse snatching, $50.00 or over.
6i	613	Shoplifting, $50.00 or over.
6c	615	Auto accessories, $50.00 or over.
6d	616	Bicycle, $50.00 or over.

File *Ref.*	*Phila.* *Code*	*Classification*

6 Larceny—Theft (except auto theft) (Continued)
6a   617   All others, $50.00 or over.
6g   621   Pocket-picking, $5.00 to $50.00.
6h   622   Purse snatching, $5.00 to $50.00.
6i   623   Shoplifting, $5.00 to $50.00.
6c   625   Auto accessories, $5.00 to $50.00.
6d   626   Bicycle, $5.00 to $50.00.
6b   627   All others, $5.00 to $50.00.
6g   631   Pocket-picking, under $5.00, include attempts.
6h   632   Purse snatching, under $5.00, include attempts.
6i   633   Shoplifting, under $5.00, include attempts.
6c   635   Auto accessories, under $5.00, include attempts.
6d   636   Bicycle, under $5.00, include attempts.
6b   637   All others, under $5.00, include attempts.
6f   647   Parking meters, include attempts.
6e   657   Motor vehicle tags, include attempts.

7   Auto Theft
7a   720   Auto theft, in Phila., not recovered.
7b. *Joy riding class* (auto theft in Phila., recovered within 48 hours intact, nothing stolen or damaged).
      710   Recovered by police officer.
      711   Recovered by other persons.
7b. *Auto theft in Phila., recovered in Phila.*
      721   After 48 hours.
      721   Within 48 hours, damaged or property stolen from car.
      721   Recovered by police officer (all arrests *except* for outside jurisdictions).
      722   Recovered by other persons.
      723   In Phila., recovered outside Phila., include arrests.
      724   Attempts.
7c   730   Outside Phila., recovered in Phila., include arrests. (Submit 75-48 and 75-49.)

xxx *Accessory Before and After the Fact*
      (Code crime which was aided or abetted.)

8   Other Assaults
      801   Assault and battery.
      802   Assault and battery on police officer.
      803   Resisting arrest.
      804   Interfering with an officer.
      805   Intimidating a witness.

9   Forgery and Counterfeiting
      901   Counterfeiting.
      902   Forgery.

File Phila.
Ref. Code   *Classification*

10 Embezzlement and Fraud
    1001   Embezzlement.
    1002   False pretense.
    1003   Fraudulent conversion.
    1004   Fraud (public assistance).
    1005   Passing worthless checks.
    1006   Confidence games.
    1007   Other frauds.

11 Stolen Property (Buying, Receiving, Possession)
    1101   Stolen goods (receiver of).
    1102   Transporting over state borders.

12 Weapons (carrying, possession of)
12a. Firearms
    1201   Violation uniform firearm act.
    1202   Other firearm violations.

12b. Others
    1203   Weapons (excluding 1201 and 1202).

13 Prostitution and Commercialized Vice
See Group 19 (disorderly conduct).
    1301   Pandering.
    1302   Bawdy house, proprietor.
    1303   Bawdy house, inmate.
    1304   Male bawd.
    1305   Solicitation for immoral purposes—sodomy—prostitution and assignation.

14 Sex Offenses (not commercialized)
    1401   Incest.
    1402   Indecent assault.
    1403   Corrupting morals of minor.
    1404   Minor, harboring for immoral purposes.
    1405   Sodomy, buggery (include solicitation for same).
    1406   Adultery.
    1407   Fornication and bastardy.
    1408   Public indecency (indecent exposure, obscene shows).
    1409   Minors, enticing for immoral purposes.
    1410   Statutory rape.

15 Offenses Against Family and Children
    1501   Abandonment of an infant.
    1502   Desertion of family.
    1503   Non-support.
    1504   Children, cruelty to or neglect.

16 Narcotic Drug Laws
    1601   Seller.
    1602   Possession.

File   *Phila.*
Ref.   *Code*   *Classification*

16   *Narcotic Drug Laws (Continued)*
     1603   User.
17   *Liquor Law Violations*
     1701   Illegal manufacture.
     1702   Illegal stills.
     1703   Illegal possession.
     1704   Selling to minors.
     1705   Selling on Sundays.
     1706   Miscellaneous violations.
     1707   Sale without license.
     1708   Sale after hours.
     1709   Transporting.
     1710   Maintaining unlawful drinking place (proprietor).
18   *Drunkeness*
     1801   Disorderly conduct and intoxication.
     1802   Intoxication.
     1803   Intoxication, habitual.
     1804   Intoxication, minors.
19   *Disorderly Conduct*
     1901   Bawdy house, frequenter.
     1902   Breach of peace.
     1903   Corner lounging.
     1904   Disorderly conduct. (See 2103 and 2105.)
     1905   Disorderly house, frequenter.
     1906   Disorderly street walker.
     1907   Unlawful assemblies.
     1908   Disorderly house, proprietor. (Non-vice—noisy house, parties, etc.)
     1909   Frequenter unlawful drinking place.
20   *Vagrancy*
     2001   Loitering and prowling.
     2002   Vagrancy.
     2003   Panhandling.
21   *Gambling*
     2101   Gambling device.
     2102   Gambler, common.
     2103   Gambling on highway.
     2104   Gambling house, proprietor (exclude horse racing).
     2105   Gambling house, frequenter (exclude horse racing).
     2106   Horse racing, establishment proprietor.
     2107   Horse racing, establishment frequenter.
     2108   Handbook on horses, highway.
     2109   Lottery, numbers.
     2110   Lottery, others.

File   Phila.
Ref.   Code   Classification

22   Driving while Intoxicated (1037 Motor Vehicle Code)
    2201   Operating auto intoxicated.

23   Violations of Road and Driving Laws
    2301   Traffic driving violations (arrest by warrant).
    2302   Traffic driving violations (arrest by sight).

24   Parking Violations
    2401   Traffic parking violations (arrest by warrant).

25   Other Traffic and Motor Vehicle Law Violations
    2501   624.5, operating without consent of owner.
    2502   Other MVC offenses (misdemeanor).
    2503   211.1, altering or forging title.
    2504   211.2, procure or attempt to assign title of stolen auto.
    2505   301, operator of motor vehicle with defaced manufacturer serial numbers.
    2506   304, sale of motor vehicle with defaced manufacturer serial numbers.
    2507   Turning off lights to avoid identity.
    2508   624.6, operating after license has been suspended or revoked.
    2509   624.7, operating motor vehicle after registration has been suspended.
    2510   1027-A, failing to stop after accident.
    2511   1027-B, failing to identify after accident.
    2512   1027-E, bus, trackless trolley operator failing to identify after accident.
    2513   Vehicle owner permitting intoxicated person to operate vehicle.

26   All Other Offenses
26a   2601   Abortion, criminal.
26h. Ordinances, Violation of
    2602   Animals, cruelty to.
    2603   Fireworks, selling, etc.
    2604   Fortune telling.
    2605   Ordinances, violations of (exclude those with specified coding).
    2606   Violation cigarette tax act.
    2607   Scavenger.
    2608   Sunday law violations, excluding sale of liquor.
    2609   Unnecessary noises.
    2610   False reports or requests for police services.

26j. Threats
    2611   Blackmail.
    2612   Bribery.
    2613   Extortion.
    2614   Forcible entry.
    2615   Threatening, letters, telephone calls, etc.

File	Phila.	
Ref.	*Code*	*Classification*

26 All Other Offenses (Continued)
    2616   Threats to do bodily harm.

26b. *Child Labor Violations*
    2617   Child labor violations.
    2618   Contributing to delinquency of minor.
    2619   Truancy, violation education laws.

26c   2620   City property, damage to.
26d   2621   False alarm of fire.
26k   2622   Trespassing.
26e   2623   Incorrigible.
26e   2624   Runaway.
26f   2625   Investigation, protection, medical examination.
26g   2626   Malicious mischief.

26i. *Other Than Above*
    2627   Abduction.
    2628   Arson.
    2629   Burglar tools, possession of.
    2630   Child, concealing death of.
    2631   Conspiracy.
    2632   Contempt of court.
    2633   Desertion U.S. services, AWOL, etc.
    2634   Election law violations.
    2635   Escaped prisoner.
    2637   Immigration law violations.
    2638   Impersonating an officer.
    2639   Impersonating a physician.
    2640   Indecent publications.
    2641   Kidnapping.
    2642   Material witnesses.
    2643   National Guard warrants.
    2644   Offenses other than above specified.
    2645   Parole violations.
    2646   Perjury.
    2647   Postal law violations.
    2648   Probation violations.
    2649   Riots, inciting to riot.
    2650   Thieves, professional.
    2651   Treason.
    2652   Violation city charter.
    2653   Obscene phonecalls.
    2654   Failure to pay transportation fare.
    2655   Keeping a vicious dog.

xxxx   *Accessory Before and After the Fact*
(Code crime which was aided or abetted.)

Appendix B

Crime Reporting in Philadelphia

Responsibility for the initial reporting of crimes, the collection of reports, the maintenance of criminal and other records, and the machine tabulation of approximately 2,500,000 documents yearly rests with the General Services Division (formerly the Central Records Division) of the Police Department.

INITIAL REPORTING

In order to insure adequate control over reporting, all reports must eventually be channeled through a Central Communications Room at Police Headquarters. If a citizen wishes to report an event by telephone, he may call LO 7-5100, which will connect him with a policeman in that room. Even if he believes that quicker action will result by calling the pay phones located in each police station and does so, the desk officer must promptly call the Central Communications Room. A citizen may, of course, also stop a foot patrolman, hail a cruising police car, or report an offense in person at a local police station or at one of the detective headquarters; in each of these situations a call will also be made to the Central Communications Room by phone or via the police radio system in squad cars. In other cases police officers, while on routine duty tours or in the course of special investigations, may observe an offense being committed and may take a suspect into custody. All these cases will also be reported to the Central Communications Room by telephone or police radio.

When an offense or incident is reported to the Central Communica-

362

tions Room, a police switchboard operator fills out a prenumbered "Radio Complaint Message and Incident Report," unless he judges the caller to be a prankster or crank. On this card are noted the time and location of the incident, the nature of the complaint, and the police district and sector or grid number where the incident occurred. These latter numbers can be determined from maps and a conveniently placed rotary file. The officer is able to see by a glance at a lighted control board which police cars and wagons throughout the city are available or are occupied or out of service for one reason or another. If the Incident Report Card indicates a location at 45th and Chestnut Sts., for example, the dispatcher knows that this is the 8th district, sector "L", patrolled by car 1814. If the indicator board reveals that car 1814 is not available, he selects the car which is free and assigned to the nearest sector. The card with this information is placed immediately on a conveyor belt in front of the switchboard operator and goes directly to a dispatcher who occupies a glass-enclosed booth nearby. The dispatcher makes a police radio call and gives all pertinent details of the case. He then places the IBM card in a slot corresponding to the car's number and thereby activates an electrical circuit indicating on the control board that this car is now unavailable for further assignments.

When the police apprehend an offender and bring him into the station or discover an offensive directly, the Central Communications Room is called and a prenumbered IBM card is made out for the incident involved, whether or not a car is assigned. In this way every reported incident or investigation throughout the city is channeled through Central Communications and receives a serial number, known as the Central Complaint number (C.C. number), which remains with the case until its final disposition. When the patrol car officers have completed the investigation of an incident, they call the dispatcher who takes the IBM card out of its slot, stamps the time on it, and returns it by the conveyer belt to a sergeant who sorts the cards by districts. When a number of cards have accumulated, he calls the district station in order to receive a District Complaint Number (D.C. number) for each case.

POLICE ACTION AND REPORTING

As has been noted, an officer in a patrol car or on foot patrol may observe an offense being committed or he may investigate an alleged offense or perform a police service upon receiving a radio message or a report from a citizen. At this time he fills out a complaint or

Incident Report, which indicates place, time, complainant, details of the offense, and the district in which it occurred. When he returns to the police station he gives this form to the desk officer who is responsible for assigning a D.C. number to the report, and in most offenses a Central Complaint number is also issued by the Central Communications Room. The desk officer determines the crime classification and checks to determine whether the offense was "founded" or "unfounded" and whether an Offense Report is to follow.[1]

On every call to the Central Communications Room requiring a police service, an IBM card is prepared. A corresponding Incident Report must be submitted by the district and, to make sure that this is done, the General Services Division sends to all districts daily a list of the C.C. and D.C. numbers of cases "owed" by the district. These lists are made up automatically on IBM machines after the prenumbered complaint cards are appropriately punched and fed into the machine. By the next day, most of the missing Incident Reports have been received. A "tickler file" is kept so that all of them will eventually be submitted.

In most cases, whether or not an offender has been taken into custody by the patrolman, a copy of the Incident Report is given to the appropriate detective division, which has headquarters in each police division, or to the Juvenile Aid Division. One copy also goes to the General Services Division and one is filed in the District. In cases involving persons under 18 years of age, the detectives and/or the Juvenile Aid Officers make a preliminary investigation, usually the same day, and when it is completed a typewritten *Offense Report*,[2] describing the details of the offense, is prepared by the investigator. Only one report is prepared for each offense no matter how many offenders are involved. The following information is included in the Offense Report: (1) D.C. and C.C. numbers; (2) a more accurate crime classification if the initial Incident Report erred; (3) brief notations in various boxes with such titles as "type of premises-objec-

---

[1] There are some situations, usually classed as "police services," which do not require an Incident Report, such as routine checks of stores and buildings, the transporting of prisoners or witnesses, etc., or service to the car itself. Some traffic or nonsupport cases involving a warrant, the investigation of persons, a breach of peace, corner lounging, disorderly conduct, intoxication, perjury, panhandling, vagrancy, and a number of other specified minor offenses do not ordinarily require any report beyond the Incident Report.

[2] See form 75-49, Appendix A-1. Aside from the original copy which is sent to General Services, copies are also sent to the appropriate detective division and to the District Attorney's office, except when the report is prepared by Juvenile Aid officers, in which case all copies, save the original, are retained in the J.A.D. files.

tive," "place of occurrence," "complainant" (name, address, sex, age, race, and certain other characteristics), "reported by," and "date and time"; (4) a description of the offense and radio messages sent out together with the results of the more complete investigation. If the body of the report is too long for one page, a *Continuation Report* sheet is used. At the bottom of the Offense Report the officer, by checking the appropriate box, indicates the current status of the case and whether the offense is founded or unfounded. If no one has been taken into custody and the investigation has not been completed, the case will be considered "active." It will be listed as "inactive" if the investigation has been terminated because there seems to be little or no chance of obtaining further information that could lead to the apprehension of the offender. If someone is taken into custody the case will be listed as "cleared by arrest." The status of "exceptionally cleared" is given to a case that either (*a*) results in a juvenile offender's being released with a reprimand and warning by the J.A.D. officer, or (*b*) involves an adult suspect who has since died, has been taken into custody for another offense, or has been in a mental hospital.

In the General Services Division a list of Offense Reports is prepared in the same way as the previously described lists of Incident Reports, because the submission of Offense Reports is expected for most cases which have received a C.C. number. These lists are sent to the divisions and within five days the Offense Reports reach General Services. Sometimes further investigation is required before a case is closed or an arrest is made. The investigation is then reported on an *Investigation Report*. In the event that an arrest is made, an *Arrest Report* form is used for each offender.[3] Other forms may be used on special occasions: a *Group Arrest Report* in cases involving two or more persons who are arrested for the same offense at the same time, although individual arrest IBM cards, described later, will be prepared; another type of group arrest report for intoxication; and a number of special motor accident and violation forms in compliance with the standards of the National Safety Council.

RECORD KEEPING AND STATISTICS

Every effort is made to insure the accuracy of the Incident Reports, Offense Reports, and Arrest Reports before IBM cards are prepared

---

[3] Aside from the original copy which goes to General Services, copies are also sent to its Identification Section, to the magistrate who is to hear the case, and to the defendant.

and the reports filed. Captains, lieutenants, and sergeants in the line organization may check some items or even read the reports *in toto*. When a copy of these "source documents," as they are called, arrives at General Services Division it is sent to a "Quality Control Section" where it is read by police sergeants for possible errors, omissions, wrong coding of the offense, and inconsistencies. If a mistake has been made, an *Error Correction Report* is sent to the district or division involved and the corrected report is returned. An additional check on the accuracy of the source documents is made by personnel of the Research and Planning Section, who re-interview complainants in burglary and other cases each month, with special reference to the value of the property stolen. Once these Incident and Offense Reports are complete and accurate, an IBM statistical card for the offense is punched. From this card two identical cards are reproduced by IBM machines; they are used to construct a "complainant file," arranged alphabetically according to the name of the complainant, and a "location file," based on the street address of the location where the offense occurred. Each file is kept by the year.

From the Arrest Reports submitted to General Services two files are constructed: the "defendant arrest file," continuous since 1957 and arranged alphabetically by name, and the "arrest disposition file," kept by year and arranged by C.C. number. When the source documents have been used to construct the IBM cards, they are filed separately by year and C.C. number. An additional IBM card "remedial file" without names but since 1961 including C.C. numbers is also constructed from the nonarrest Offense Reports and Investigation Reports. This last file is kept only for the current year and is thereafter destroyed.

POLICE STATISTICAL REPORTS AND THEIR ACCURACY

Police reporting procedure and reports follow strictly the standards set up by the Federal Bureau of Investigation in their Uniform Crime Reporting Handbook.[4] Statistical compilations are largely mechanized through the extensive use of IBM cards and machines in the General Services Division. Monthly reports by police districts are prepared (a) with various breakdowns for the Part 1 offenses reported, founded and unfounded; (b) by detective divisions and by the Juvenile Aid Division; (c) by "cleared" and "not cleared" offenses; (d) with comparisons between the number of current monthly offenses and the percentage "cleared" with corresponding figures for the same

[4] See Chapter 10.

months of the preceding year. Moreover, Part 1 and 2 offenses are reported by district. For both Part 1 and 2 offenses yearly totals are given for these breakdowns as well as for the age, sex, and race of persons arrested. Other miscellaneous statistics are compiled for administrative purposes and standard forms are submitted monthly and yearly to the F.B.I. for use in compiling national data.

The only figures published by the city for public consumption are those which appear in six tables in the annual report of the Police Department. One of these is a "crime index" which is actually a breakdown of Part 1 offenses for the past December, the monthly average for the year, the cumulative totals for the present and past years, and percentage changes presented both for offenses known and for those "cleared by arrest." Another table presents a monthly breakdown of Part 1 offenses which are known to the police and of those "cleared by arrest" during each month.

Because our main concern is with juvenile reporting and statistics, a detailed analysis of adult record keeping has not been made. We have made no effort to examine the actual activities of the detective divisions with the same intensity that we investigated those of the Juvenile Aid Division; however, in the course of studying that Division, it was possible from time to time to note the operations of the detectives and the uniformed squads.

The present reporting system was set up in 1954. Because it was designed by men who had considerable experience with the old system, the new one seems to have been set up with minimal opportunities to falsify district statistics to change offense categories, to avoid reporting offenses, or to engage in any of the many confusing activities that can interfere with the proper collection of police statistics. In the "old days," for example, a commanding officer who wanted to have his district appear with a good record by having low crime totals would sometimes give informal orders that some Part 1 offenses should be reported as Part 2 offenses. Occasionally, cases not cleared by arrest would never be reported to the central office. At present, when complaints are made or routed directly to a Central Communications Room and prenumbered cards prepared, such deficiencies or interference can rarely, if ever, occur. An offense category can only be changed if there is a formally recognized and documented reason, and an explanation must always be given in the body of the Offense Report. The alleged offender can only be released if the reported facts suggest a release and if the appropriate reasons are stated. Intentional falsification is unlikely to occur, not only because a written account has to be made, but also because of the variety of checks previously mentioned.

Appendix C

Instructions for Transferring Data from
Offense Reports to Study Cards

THE STUDY OFFENSE CARD

Definitions and Instructions

The staff member who is filling out the card should place his initials on the extreme upper right corner of each card.

Make out a separate Offense Card for each offense that has a different Central Complaint Number. There are three delinquency acts that are considered nonshareable and that require a separate offense card for each juvenile, even though two or more juveniles may be taken into custody under the same Central Complaint Number. These offenses are: truancy, runaway, and incorrigibility. Should two or more juveniles be taken into custody under one Central Complaint Number, use the suffix "A," "B," etc., with the same Central Complaint Number.

CENTRAL COMPLAINT NUMBER. Put the entire Central Complaint number including the year (60) which precedes the larger number.

DISTRICT COMPLAINT NUMBER. Put District Complaint Number and Uniform Crime Report classification number. The U.C.R. number should not be changed even though an erroneous classification was used originally by the police officer. (See "Corrected" below.)

Ex., 6-3387-26
   6 is the District
   3387 is the complaint number
   26 is the U.C.R. number.

OFFENSE CARD

CENTRAL COMPLAINT NUMBER :				VICTIMIZATION TYPE :

CENTRAL COMPLAINT NUMBER :

DISTRICT COMPLAINT NUMBER :   + U C R

PHILA. CODE | **CORR. :** | **NEW PHILA :** | **FORD**

PLACE OF OCCURRENCE :

DISTRICT :   **IN / OUT :**
_____ IN   _____ OUT

TIME OF OCCURRENCE :
MO. | **DAY** | **HOUR**   A M
                                                P M

VICTIMS :
          1   2   3   4   5   6   7
SEX
AGE
RACE
TYPE OF PLACE :
_____ PRIVATE _____ FIELD _____ OTHER
_____ SCHOOL _____ AUTO _____ COMMERCIAL
                                    _____ STREET

OFFENSE : | **DISCOVERED BY** | **RESULTING IN FIRST APPREHENSION BY**
POLICE DIRECT
POLICE IND.
VICTIM
VICTIM'S REP.
OTHER
DURING ACT
AFTER ACT

NUMBER OF OFFENDERS :

CUSTODY | **NO CUSTODY**
_____ ARREST | _____ ADULTS
_____ REMEDIAL | _____ JUVENILES
_____ ADULTS | _____ UNKNOWN

PROSECUTION :
          _____ COMPLAINANT FOR
_____ POLICE   _____ COMPLAINANT AGAINST

VICTIMIZATION TYPE :
                    _____ TERTIARY
_____ PRIMARY   _____ MUTUAL
_____ SECONDARY   _____ NONE

OFFENSES INVOLVING PROPERTY :
  BY VIOLENCE
  (EXCEPT AT ENTRY)_____ YES _____ NO
  FROM :   _____ PERSON _____ PLACE
  OFFENDER'S PRESENCE:_____ LEGAL
                        _____ ILLEGAL, FORCE
                        _____ ILLEGAL, NO FORCE

PROPERTY VALUE (STOLEN) :
          $

PROPERTY RECOVERY :
                    _____ NONE
_____ TOTAL _____ PARTIAL _____ UNKNOWN

PROPERTY DAMAGE :
          $

METHOD OF INTIMIDATION AND HARM :

	INTIMIDATION BY	HARM BY
GUN		
KNIFE		
BLUNT I		
PHYSICAL		
VERBAL		

INFLICTION OF PHYSICAL HARM :
_____ MINOR   _____ HOSPITALIZATION
_____ TREATED AND DIS. _____ DEATH.

SUBSIDIARY SEX ACTIVITY :

(Reduced from 8½″ × 11″)

PHILADELPHIA CODE. This is the crime code number given to the particular offense by Central Records of the Philadelphia Police Department as noted in the most recently dated source document. For listing of the code numbers, see Philadelphia Police Department Directive 110, dated 1/1/60.

CORRECTED (CODE). This block should be filled out for one or both of the following reasons:

(1) If the police make an error in classifying the offense according to the Philadelphia Crime Code, place the correct Philadephia Crime Code number here.

(2) If adults and juveniles are arrested for different offenses in the same event, classify the event according to the major offense for which a juvenile should be charged. For example, if only adults are arrested for statutory rape and a juvenile girl involved should be charged with fornication, all offenders should have 1410 (statutory rape) written in the block for "Philadelphia Code" and 1407 (fornication) written in the block for "Corrected Code."

NEW PHILADELPHIA. [Subsequently discarded.]

FORD. [Subsequently discarded.]

PLACE OF OCCURRENCE. The specific address of location where the offense occurred

Ex. 3440 Walnut Street

Ex. Corner of 36th and Walnut Streets.

If multiple places are mentioned in the text of the 75-49 report, use the address found in the block entitled, "Place of Occurrence" on that report.

In automobile theft, use the place from which the automobile was stolen.

In runaway cases, use the address from which the runaway started. In truancy cases use the address and name of the school. For incorrigibility, use the resident address of the juvenile.

In cases of carrying and concealing deadly weapons, intoxication, receiving stolen goods, illegal possession of liquor, use the place where the arrest occurred.

DISTRICT. This is the police district in which the offense occurred. If the district of occurrence is found on the report, use that district number. If the actual district of occurrence is different from the district making the arrest (see "place of occurrence" description above), it will probably be necessary to use the street directory to determine the district. (These instructions apply to all districts except the 19th. If the 19th District is recorded by the police as the district of occurrence, use the street directory to determine whether the district area should be No. 9 or No. 6.) [This instruction was necessary because in May of 1960 the 19th District was divided into the 9th and 6th Districts, which were used in our analysis for the whole year of 1960.]

INSIDE/OUTSIDE. "Inside" means inside a building or vehicle; "outside" means outside the building or vehicle. If the offense occurs in both places, use the place where the offense principally occurred. Theft of an automobile from the street should be listed as "outside." Offenses committed inside the automobile, such as theft of accessories, rape, fornication, etc., should be listed as "inside." Subways are "inside." Runaway and truancy should be listed as "outside," incorrigible as "inside."

TIME OF OCCURRENCE. This means the month, day, and the nearest hour of occurrence. If time is reported exactly on the half hour, consider the next full hour as the nearest hour of occurrence. If year is not 1960, write in. Encircle whether A.M. or P.M. If "twelve o'clock noon" write in "12 noon;" if twelve o'clock midnight write "12 midnight." In runaway cases, this means the date the juvenile first left his place of residence. In some offenses the date and time of occurrence will coincide with date and time of arrest, such as in cases of carrying and concealing deadly weapons. In cases where the specific time is difficult to determine, write in the estimated hour or time span and add "est" for "estimated." In truancy cases, list date of last truancy or if no date is reported, the date of arrest. In cases of incorrigibility, list only the month because further specificity is generally not possible to ascertain.

VICTIM(s). This category refers only to victims of a "primary" type. (See below under "Type of Victimization.")

Sex: M = male
       F = female
Race: W = white
       C = colored or Negro
   PR = Puerto Rican
      O = other
Age: as given; when unknown, use a dash (—).

TYPE OF PLACE. *Private Dwelling:* private house or apartment that is tenanted. Includes property around and belonging to the dwelling. Runaway and incorrigible should be listed as "private" when the juvenile is running away from his own home.

Commercial Building: stores, warehouses, railroad and bus stations, theaters, etc.

School: the building or the school yard. All truancies are from "school."

Street: public thoroughfare, alley, lane.

Field: parks, vacant lots.

Automobile: inside an automobile. This does not include theft of an automobile or theft of external automobile accessories.

Other: write in; for example, railroad yards, parking lots, vacant house.

OFFENSE DISCOVERED BY. "Discovered by" refers to the agent most directly responsible for bringing the offense to the attention of the public authority (the police). If a victim discovers the existence of a delinquent act and himself reports that act to the police, the act was "discovered by" the victim. If he directs another party to notify the police in his behalf, the victim is still the one who discovered the act. If it is assumed from the offense report that the decision to notify the police is made by a party other than the victim, or the victim is not willing to report or not aware of the existence of the reportability of the offense, use the party who notified the police for "discovered by."

"Police" refers only to municipal officers whether on or off duty.

"Police, direct" and "during act" refers to the fact that the police observed the instant offense.

"Police, direct" and "after act" means that police have observed evidence of commission of an offense with no offender present. (Ex. discovery of a burglarized store.)

"Police, indirect" and "during act" means in a routine check of persons, the police discover an offense. (Ex. carrying concealed deadly weapons.) This combination includes catching runaways when the police stop a boy for routine questioning and discover that he is a runaway.

"Police, indirect" and "after act" means that in a routine check of persons, the police discover an offense that was previously committed. (Ex. a package containing stolen goods carried by person stopped by police who had no prior knowledge of the theft.)

A mother who discovers that her boy has run away from home has discovered the act "during the act." Truancy generally is discovered "during the act."

OFFENSE RESULTING IN FIRST APPREHENSION BY. "Apprehension" means that the offender is detained by or is held under custody of another person or group.

In cases involving more than one offender, fill in the necessary information for the first offender apprehended.

"Victim" refers to a victim of a "primary" type. See below under "Type of Victimization."

"Victim representative" refers to store detectives, railroad police, employees of business, school teachers, et al., when these persons represent the larger, secondary establishments that employ them.

"Other" refers to any person not covered above. Write in the most precise term that designates the person making the apprehension. For example, "mother" in case of many runaways; "private citizen bystander," etc.

Cases in which the offender gives himself up for the offense for which he is charged, whether to the police or to some other person or authority, should be designated under "other" with the word "self" written in the block.

"During act" means that the first offender was apprehended during commission of the offense or while offender was present at or running away from the scene of the crime. Generally, runaways are apprehended "during the act."

In an automobile theft, "during act" refers only to cases in which the police actually observe the initial phase of the theft. If the police stop an automobile under suspicion of theft, this case is not listed as "during act."

"After act" means that the offender was apprehended after commission of the act.

NUMBER OF OFFENDERS. "Custody" means that one or more offenders were taken into custody or were available for being taken into custody by the police. "No custody" refers to persons who participated in the commission of the offense but who were not apprehended by the police. "Arrest" and "remedial" refer only to juveniles taken into custody. "Adult" refers to any participant 18 years of age or over. "Juvenile, no custody" refers to persons 17 years of age or under who participated in the offense but who were not apprehended. "Unknown, no custody" indicates that the age of the participant could not be determined.

The sum of the numbers placed on each line is the total number of individual offenders presumed to be participants in the commission of the offense.

If a group of unknown ages and number participated but were not taken into custody, place a check ($\sqrt{}$) in "Unknown."

For the sample of juvenile suspects use the following instructions in the "no custody" category:

"Adult" refers to any suspected participant 18 years of age or over. Write in the number of adult suspects.

"Juvenile" refers to persons 17 years of age or under who were suspected of having participated in the offense. Write in the number of juvenile suspects.

A check ($\sqrt{}$) means juvenile suspects in a group of unknown number.

"Unknown" indicates that the age and number of suspects are

uncertain but that *at least* one juvenile was involved.   Place a check
(✓) in this box.

PROSECUTION

___ Complainant for;   ___ Complainant against;   ___ Police.

"Complainant" refers to the person primarily responsible for the
definite statement that appears in the offense report, favoring or opposing prosecution.

Write in the proper number only when a *definite* statement favoring
or opposing prosecution appears in the report: "1" for the victim or
victim representative; "2" for a relative (parent, et al); "3" for a
school or similar agency.

Check "police" if the police officer in his official capacity appears
on the offense report as the complainant.   Check "police" also in cases
involving "mutual participation."   (See below under "Type of
Victimization.")

TYPE OF VICTIMIZATION.   "Primary" refers to individual personal
victim(s), usually of an assaultive or property offense but may include victims of certain kinds of disorderly conduct as well.   This
category includes small shopkeepers, repairmen, and other private
small family business establishments that are victims.   Some offenses
can only have primary victimization: homicide, forcible rape, purse
snatching, kidnapping, highway robbery, aggravated assault, pocket
picking, other assaults.

"Secondary" refers to large commercial establishments, such as
department stores, railroads, theaters, chain stores, churches; in short,
the victim(s) is (are) impersonalized but not so diffusive as to include the community at large.   Offenses commonly with secondary
victimization: shoplifting, burglary in chain stores, bank burglary.

"Tertiary" refers to a diffusive victimization that extends to the
community at large.   This category includes offenses against the
public order, social harmony, or the administration of government.
Regulatory offenses and violations of city ordinances are typically
included in this group.   Some offenses can *only* have tertiary victimization: larceny of parking meters, firearms violations, public
drunkenness, liquor law violations, corner lounging, gambling, violations of road and driving laws, vagrancy, false fire alarms.

"Mutual participation" refers to offenses in which there is voluntary
participation and concealment by both the offender and the other
party or parties involved in the event.   (Ex. fornication, statutory
rape, abortion.)

"None" means that the victimization is nebulous, non-specific and refers to an offense that cannot be committed by an adult. Several offenses can *only* have a victimization categorized as "none": runaway, truancy and incorrigibility.

The type of victimization for attempts to commit an offense should be considered the same as for cases of completed acts.

OFFENSES INVOLVING PROPERTY BY USE OF VIOLENCE (EXCEPT AT ENTRY). "Offenses involving property" includes all offenses designated by the Philadelphia Crime Code as thefts of property or any other offenses, such as assaults, disorderly conduct, etc., in connection with which loss or damage of property occurred.

"Use of violence" implies the exertion of unlawful force usually involving infliction of some injury or damage to person or property. Excluding force used to enter a building or car, "use of violence" includes purse snatching, even without infliction of physical harm, breaking locks on chests, safes, etc. "No violence" is involved, for example, in most shoplifting, sneak thievery, pocketpicking, burglary without causing further destruction inside the place of entry. Check "yes" or "no."

From: _____ Person; _____ Place. Check one.

"Person" here suggests that the property offense typically involved the actual presence of the victim, meaning that the victim could be aware of the offense during the act and that the offender risks observation because of the propinquity of the victim.

"Place" refers to any premise or building, as well as any kind of inanimate object, such as box, chest, safe, parking meter, and so forth without the presence of the victim.

"Presence" refers to the location, with or without entry, of the offender. "Legal" means that the offender has a legal right to be at the place where the offense is committed. If he had no such right, his presence is considered illegal. For example, an offender who is standing in the street and who extends his hand or any instrument he manipulates into a shop window is "illegally present."

"With force" means that the offender employed unlawful physical exertion (force) in order to gain entry; "without force," therefore, is the absence of this conduct. Entering through an unlocked door is "without force;" but entering through an unlocked window requires exertion, is an unusual manner of entry and should be classified "with force."

VALUE OF STOLEN PROPERTY. $_____. If the dollar value is clearly stated in the report, this figure should be inserted. If no figure appears and the object is described, an estimate should be made with "est" written after the figure. If no description of the stolen goods is available, a dash (–) should be inserted.

PROPERTY RECOVERY

_____ Total _____ Partial _____ None _____ Unknown

If any portion was recovered, "partial" should be checked. "Unknown" should be checked if no statement appears in the report. If restitution is made or promised, check the appropriate recovery.

PROPERTY DAMAGE. If the value of the damage is stated in the report, indicate in dollars or portions thereof. If the description is sufficient when no value is stated, an estimate should be made with "est" written after the figure. If no value can be estimated, place a "unk" in the space provided. If no damage, place a dash (–) in the space.

This category also includes property harmed in some way even though not removed. (Ex. malicious mischief, vandalism.) The category includes damages inflicted on property in the commission of other offenses, such as burglary, larceny, auto theft, etc.

METHOD OF INTIMIDATION BY. This category refers to a *modus operandi* in which the threat of force is used by the offender. "Threats to do bodily harm," as a legal offense, involves intimidation. Threats used to accomplish a theft, a sex crime, or any offense other than an assault *per se* (assault and battery, aggravated assault, homicide) includes intimidation. The mere display of a weapon shall constitute a threat. With the exception of verbal threats, if multiple means are used, check each one used.

"Gun" includes home-made as well as commercially produced firearms. (Ex. rifles, pistols, revolvers, air guns, zip guns, etc.)

"Knife" includes any cutting or stabbing instrument.

"Blunt instrument" refers to any object other than "gun," "knife," or "physical," as these terms are elsewhere defined.

"Physical" means the presence of (a) strong-arm tactics, such as threats with fists or menacing gestures; (b) restraint or confinement of the victim(s) by restricting physical movement.

"Verbal" means that use is made only of spoken threats. If a weapon or weapons are used to intimidate, check each one; if no weapon is used to intimidate, check "verbal."

In cases of disorderly conduct with "primary victimization," threats or intimidation should be noted under this section in order to classify the form of disorderly conduct. Similarly, "threats to do bodily harm," as a legal classification, should also be checked in order to know the *modus operandi.*

It should be kept in mind that it is possible to have intimidation without physical harm, or physical harm without intimidation, or physical harm preceded by intimidation.

HARM BY. If an offense involves any personal injury noted in the report, the method of infliction should be checked whether or not intimidation preceded the injury. In cases of multiple methods of inflicting harm, check each method used.

"Gun" means that the weapon was fired and thereby caused injury.

"Knife," as the instrument is previously defined, here means that the weapon was used to cause injury by cutting or stabbing.

"Blunt instrument" used to inflict injury refers to any object previously defined as a "blunt instrument," plus the use of a firearm for striking purposes.

"Physical" includes injury inflicted by fists, feet or other parts of the offender's body.

INFLICTION OF PHYSICAL HARM. If an offense involves any personal injury to the victim(s) noted in the report, one of these categories should be checked. If there is no injury, the lines should be left blank. If there is more than one victim, check the type of harm and identify the victim by number (i.e., 1, 2, . . . *n*).

"*Minor.*" Any result of physical violence to the person, however slight, excepting mere physical restraint as referred to under intimidation, and that does not involve medical attention, should be considered "minor." (Ex. pushing, shoving, knocking down, cutting, etc., with no medical treatment.)

"*Treated and Discharged.*" This item includes any offense following which the victim(s) received medical treatment and was not detained for further care. This category does not include routine medical examinations in connection with prostitution, fornication, statutory rape, etc.

"*Hospitalization.*" This category means in-patient care of any duration in a medical institution. It also includes any victim requiring repeated out-patient care for three or more visits.

"*Death.*" Self-explanatory.

SUBSIDIARY SEX ACTIVITY. In the block of offenses not coded as sex offenses and in which there is no specific charge for a sex offense but in which some sexual misconduct occurred, a brief statement that best describes the sex activity should be written.

THE STUDY OFFENDER CARD

Definitions and Instructions

The staff member filling out the card should place his initials on the extreme upper right part of each card.

Make out a separate Offender Card for each juvenile and adult offender taken into custody. If the offender is an adult, write "Adult" in upper left-hand box.

OFFENDER SERIAL NUMBER. Leave blank for the present. [After all cards were made out, a number beginning with "1" was assigned to each card with a different offender name.]

| | | OFFENDER CARD | OFFENDER SERIAL NUMBER : | |

NAME :				DATE :			PREVIOUS RECORD ____ NONE		D
ADDRESS :				MO.	DAY	YR.	OFFENSE		I S P
SEX :	AGE	RACE :	1						
			2						
CENTRAL COMPLAINT NUMBER :			3						
DISTRICT COMPLAINT NUMBER : + UCR			4						
			5						
PHILA. CRIME CODE :	CORRECTED CODE :		6						
CHARGE (IF DIFFERENT) :			7						
			8						
CASE CLEARANCE :			9						
____ ARREST ____ REMEDIAL									
APPREHENDED BY :			10						
____ POLICE			11						
____ VICTIM ____ DURING ACT			12						
____ VICTIM'S REP. ____ AFTER ACT									
____ OTHER			13						
RELATION OF OFFENDER TO VICTIM :			14						
VICTIM 1 ____			15						
VICTIM 2 ____									
VICTIM 3 ____									
VICTIM 4 ____									
VICTIM 5 ____									
VICTIM 6 ____									
VICTIM 7 ____									
OFFENSES INVOLVING SEX ACTIVITY WITH :									
VOLUNTARY PARTICIPATION ___ YES ___ No									
FORCE ___ YES ___ No									

(Reduced from 8½" × 11")

NAME. Place here the full name of the offender in the following order: last, first, middle.

ADDRESS. The full address of the offender's residence (Ex. 3440 Walnut Street). If the offender lives outside the jurisdiction of Philadelphia, indicate specifically by name of city, town, state as is necessary.

SEX.
   M = male
   F = female

AGE. If the offender is an adult write in age; and write in "Adult" in upper left-hand box. If the age is not given but he is a known juvenile, write in "JUV" in upper left-hand box.

RACE.
   W = white
   C = colored or Negro
  PR = Puerto Rican
   O = other

CENTRAL COMPLAINT NUMBER. See Instructions Offense Card.
DISTRICT COMPLAINT NUMBER. See Instructions Offense Card.
PHILADELPHIA CRIME CODE NUMBER. See Instructions Offense Card.
CORRECTED CODE NUMBER. See Instructions Offense Card.
CHARGE (IF DIFFERENT). This block should be filled in with a code number if the charge against the offender is different from (a) either the "Philadelphia Crime Code" number (b) or the "Corrected" Code number (c) or both.

For example, in a case involving an adult charged with adultery (1406), a juvenile charged with statutory rape (1410), and a second juvenile with fornication (1407), the Offender Card for the adult would read: Philadelphia Crime Code–1406; Corrected Code–1407; Charge, if different–1406. The Offender Card for the first juvenile would read: Philadelphia Crime Code–1406; Corrected Code–1407; Charge, if different–1410. The Offender Card for the second juvenile would read: Philadelphia Crime Code–1406, Corrected Code–1407; Charge, if different–1407.

CASE CLEARANCE. *Arrest; Remedial.* Check the appropriate line for the given offender as is indicated in the most recent source document.

APPREHENDED BY. See Instructions, Offense Card. Fill in information appropriate for each offender.

RELATION OF OFFENDER TO VICTIM. Write in as precise a designation as possible, such as: son, brother, sister, close friend, acquaintance, school mate, stranger, etc. A relationship occurs only in cases of "primary" victimization. Identify the number of the victim in cases involving multiple victims.

"Close friend" refers to a regular companion or "chum," an intimate relationship as indicated in the offense report.

"Acquaintance" means that the victim had had personal contact with the offender at least once before the offense but was not an intimate friend.

"Stranger" means no known contact between victim and offender.

In cases of mutual participation write in the bottom of this box the word, "participant," followed by the kind of relationship.

OFFENSES INVOLVING SEXUAL ACTIVITY. To be filled in for all cases with an official charge (Philadelphia Crime Code or Corrected Code) on the Offense Card, if the charge is a sex offense.

"*With Voluntary Participation.*" "Yes" means that the "victim(s)" willingly participated in the sexual activity. "No" means that the victim unwillingly participated in the sexual activity.

"*Involving Force.*" "Yes" means that the offender employed *physical* force in compelling participation. "No" means the absence of physical force.

PREVIOUS RECORD. The items in this section deal only with juvenile offenders.

If *definitely* stated that there is no previous record, check "none." If not stated either way, put a question mark before "Previous Record."

For date, write in the number for the month, day, and year. (Ex. 7/6/60, as these chronologically occurred.)

For "offense," write in the title of the previous offense for which the offender was taken into custody.

For "disposition," write in "A" for arrest and "R" for remedial.

If the offense report has insufficient information regarding dates and offenses but some indication of the number of previous arrests or remedials, encircle the total number on the left-hand column of numbers, and write in lower right-hand box the number of arrests and number of remedials if known.

If multiple offenses for the same event are listed, write in the most serious offense as indicated in ordering of offenses in the Philadelphia Crime Code.

Appendix D

141 Offense Versions Used in the Scaling Analysis

1. The offender stabs a person to death.
2. The offender robs a person at gunpoint. The victim struggles and is shot to death.
3. The offender forcibly rapes a woman. Her neck is broken and she dies.
4. The offender kills a person by reckless driving of an automobile.
5. The offender forces a female to submit to sexual intercourse. The offender inflicts physical injury by beating her with his fists.
6. The offender forces a female to submit to sexual intercourse. No physical injury is inflicted.
7. The offender drags a woman into an alley, tears her clothes, but flees before she is physically harmed or sexually attacked.
8. The offender robs a person of $1000 at gunpoint. The victim is shot and requires hospitalization.
9. The offender robs a victim of $1000 at gunpoint. The victim is wounded and requires treatment by a physician but no further treatment is needed.
10. The offender robs a victim of $1000 at gunpoint. No physical harm occurs.
11. The offender, armed with a blunt instrument, robs a victim of $1000. The victim is wounded and requires hospitalization.
12. The offender with a blunt instrument robs a person of $1000. The victim is wounded and requires treatment by a physician but no further treatment is needed.
13. The offender, armed with a blunt instrument, takes $1000 from a person No physical harm is done.

14. The offender, using physical force, robs a person of $1000. The victim is hurt and requires hospitalization.

15. The offender robs a person of $1000 by physical force. The victim is hurt and requires treatment by a physician but no further treatment is required.

16. The offender, using physical force, robs a victim of $1000. No physical harm is inflicted.

17. The offender threatens to harm a victim if he does not give money to the offender. The victim hands over $1000 but is not harmed.

18. The offender robs a victim of $5 at gunpoint. The victim is shot and requires hospitalization.

19. The offender robs a person of $5 at gunpoint. The victim is wounded and requires medical treatment but no further treatment is required.

20. The offender robs a victim of $5 at gunpoint. No physical harm occurs.

21. The offender with a blunt instrument robs a person of $5. The victim is wounded and requires hospitalization.

22. A victim is robbed of $5 by an offender with a blunt instrument. The victim is wounded and requires treatment by a physician but no further treatment is needed.

23. The offender, armed with a blunt instrument, robs a victim of $5. No physical harm is inflicted.

24. The offender, using physical force, takes $5 from a victim. The victim is hurt and requires hospitalization.

25. The offender, using physical force, robs a person of $5. The victim is hurt and requires treatment by a physician but no further treatment is required.

26. The offender takes $5 from a person by force but inflicts no physical harm.

27. The offender threatens to harm a victim if he does not give his money to the offender. The victim gives him $5 and is not harmed.

28. The offender fires a gun at a victim who suffers a minor wound that does not require medical treatment.

29. The offender with a gun wounds a victim. The wound requires treatment on one occasion by a physician.

30. The offender wounds a person with a gun. The victim lives but requires hospitalization.

31. The offender stabs a victim with a knife. The victim does not require medical treatment.

32. The offender stabs a victim with a knife. The victim is treated by a physician but requires no further treatment.

33. The offender wounds a person with a knife. The victim lives but requires hospitalization.

34. The offender wounds a person with a blunt instrument. The victim requires no medical treatment.

35. The offender wounds a person with a blunt instrument. The victim is treated by a physician but requires no further treatment.
36. The offender wounds a person with a blunt instrument. The victim lives but requires hospitalization.
37. The offender beats a victim with his fists. The victim lives but requires hospitalization.
38. The offender breaks into a residence, forces open a cash box, and takes $1000.
39. The offender breaks into a residence, forces open a cash box, and steals $5.
40. The offender breaks into a residence and steals furniture worth $1000.
41. The offender breaks into a residence and steals $5.
42. The offender breaks into a department store, forces open a safe, and steals $1000.
43. The offender breaks into a department store, forces open a cash register, and steals $5.
44. The offender breaks into a department store and steals merchandise worth $1000.
45. The offender breaks into a department store and steals merchandise worth $5.
46. The offender breaks into a public recreation center, smashes open a cash box, and steals $1000.
47. The offender breaks into a public recreation center, smashes open a cash box, and steals $5.
48. The offender breaks into a school and takes equipment worth $1000.
49. The offender breaks into a school and steals $5 worth of supplies.
50. While the owner of a small delicatessen is phoning, the offender breaks into the cash register and steals $1000.
51. The offender forces open the glove compartment of an unlocked automobile and takes $1000.
52. The offender snatches a handbag containing $5 from a person on the street.
53. The offender enters an unlocked car, forces open the glove compartment, and steals personal belongings worth $5.
54. The offender steals two diamond rings worth $1000 while the owner of a small jewelry store is not looking.
55. The offender steals $1000 worth of merchandise from an unlocked automobile.
56. The offender steals a bicycle which is parked on the street.
57. The offender illegally enters a backyard and steals a bicycle.
58. The offender breaks into a display case in a large jewelry store and steals $1000 worth of merchandise.
59. The offender trespasses in a railroad yard, tears loose $1000 worth of equipment, and steals it.

60. The offender forces open a cash register in a department store and steals $5.
61. The offender trespasses in a railroad yard, wrenches loose some fittings worth $5, and steals them.
62. The offender steals $1000 worth of merchandise from the counter of a department store.
63. The offender trespasses in a railroad yard and steals tools worth $1000.
64. The offender steals merchandise worth $5 from the counter of a department store.
65. The offender trespasses in a railroad yard and steals a lantern worth $5.
66. While in a public building during office hours, the offender breaks into a cash box and steals $1000.
67. The offender trespasses in a city motor pool lot and wrenches off $1000 worth of accessories from city cars and trucks.
68. The offender breaks into a parking meter and steals $5 worth of nickels.
69. The offender trespasses inside a publicly owned building, rips from the wall and steals a fixture worth $5.
70. The offender walks into a public museum and steals a painting worth $1000.
71. The offender trespasses on a city-owned storage lot and steals equipment worth $1000.
72. The offender steals a book worth $5 from a public library.
73. The offender trespasses on a city-owned storage lot and carries off equipment worth $5.
74. The offender picks a person's pocket of $1000.
75. The offender picks a person's pocket of $5.
76. The offender breaks into a locked car, steals, damages, and abandons it.
77. The offender breaks into a locked car and later abandons it undamaged.
78. The offender breaks into a locked car, steals it, but returns it undamaged to the place where he stole it.
79. The offender steals, damages, and abandons an unlocked car.
80. The offender steals an unlocked car and abandons but does not damage it.
81. The offender steals an unlocked car and returns it undamaged to the place where it was stolen.
82. The offender beats a victim with his fists. The victim is hurt but requires no medical treatment.
83. The offender beats a person with his fists. The victim is treated by a physician but requires no further medical treatment.
84. The offender signs someone else's name to a check and cashes it.
85. The offender embezzles $1000 from his employer.

86. The offender embezzles $5 from his employer.

87. The offender knowingly passes a check that is worthless.

88. The offender knowingly buys stolen property from the person who stole it.

89. The offender, while being searched by the police, is found in illegal possession of a gun.

90. The offender is found firing a rifle for which he has no permit.

91. The offender illegally possesses a knife.

92. The offender gets customers for a prostitute.

93. The offender runs a house of prostitution.

94. The offender is a prostitute in a house of prostitution.

95. The offender, a prostitute, has sexual intercourse with a customer.

96. The offender, a prostitute, offers to have sexual intercourse with a customer.

97. The offender has sexual intercourse with his stepdaughter.

98. A brother has sexual intercourse with his sister and thereby both become offenders.

99. The offender runs his hands over the body of a female victim, then flees.

100. The offender shows pornographic movies to a minor.

101. Two male offenders willingly have anal intercourse.

102. The offender forces a person to submit to anal intercourse.

103. The offender offers to submit to anal intercourse.

104. The offender, a married male, has sexual intercourse with a female not his wife.

105. An unmarried couple willingly have sexual intercourse.

106. The offender exposes his genitals in public.

107. The offender with immoral intent tries to entice a minor into his automobile.

108. The offender, over 16 years of age, has intercourse with a female under 16 who willingly participates in the act.

109. The offender sells heroin.

110. The offender sells marijuana.

111. The offender possesses heroin.

112. The offender has marijuana in his possession.

113. The offender administers heroin to himself.

114. The offender smokes marijuana.

115. A juvenile illegally possesses a bottle of wine and thereby becomes an offender.

116. The offender runs a house where unlawful sale of liquor takes place.

117. The offender is intoxicated in public.

118. A juvenile is found drunk on the street, thereby becoming an offender.

119. The offender is a customer in a house of prostitution.

120. A group continues to hang around a corner after being told to disperse by a policeman and thereby become offenders.
121. The offender disturbs the neighborhood with loud, noisy behavior.
122. The offender is a customer in a house where liquor is sold illegally.
123. An offender prowls in the backyard of a private residence.
124. The offender has no residence and no visible means of support and thereby becomes an offender.
125. The offender is engaged in a dice game in an alley.
126. The offender runs a house where gambling occurs illegally.
127. The offender is a customer in a house where gambling occurs illegally.
128. The offender takes bets on the numbers.
129. The offender performs an illegal abortion.
130. The offender telephones a victim and threatens bodily harm.
131. A juvenile plays hookey from school and thereby becomes an offender.
132. The offender turns in a false fire alarm.
133. The offender trespasses in a railroad yard.
134. A juvenile is reported to police by his parents as an offender because they are unable to control him.
135. A juvenile runs away from home and thereby becomes an offender.
136. The offender defaces and breaks public statues causing $1000 damage.
137. The offender throws rocks through windows.
138. The offender sets fire to a garage.
139. The offender kidnaps a person. One thousand dollars ransom is paid but no physical harm is inflicted on the victim.
140. The offender wilfully makes false statements under oath during a trial.
141. The offender makes an obscene phone call.

Appendix E-1

Mean Raw Category Scale Scores for Twenty-one Offenses, Male Offenders of Selected Age, Rated by Three Groups of Subjects

	RATING SUBJECTS							
	TEMPLE STUDENTS				POLICE			JUVENILE COURT JUDGES
	AGE OF OFFENDER				AGE OF OFFENDER			AGE OF OFFENDER
Offense Number*	13	17	27	Unidentified	13	17	27	13
1	10.8	10.7	11.0	10.9	10.97	11.00	10.96	10.95
2	10.3	10.6	10.4	10.7	10.97	10.97	11.00	11.00
3	10.8	10.4	10.9	10.7	10.88	11.00	11.00	10.65
18	9.0	9.6	9.1	9.5	10.42	10.00	10.04	9.68
20	6.9	7.7	6.7	6.6	9.67	8.83	8.93	8.60
22	7.5	8.0	7.8	8.1	9.52	9.10	9.46	8.45
28	7.8	9.0	8.8	9.0	9.61	9.03	8.74	8.94
31	8.1	8.8	8.8	8.5	8.76	8.21	8.15	7.95
32	8.4	9.1	8.9	8.8	9.16	9.14	8.04	8.28
46	7.3	6.9	6.1	6.7	8.36	7.59	7.89	7.00
52	5.5	5.4	4.9	5.1	7.33	6.57	6.63	5.63
53	5.4	5.9	4.6	5.0	6.56	5.70	6.42	4.80

Mean Raw Category Scale Scores for Twenty-one Offenses, Male Offenders of Selected Age, Rated by Three Groups of Subjects (Continued)

Offense Number*	TEMPLE STUDENTS AGE OF OFFENDER				POLICE AGE OF OFFENDER			JUVENILE COURT JUDGES AGE OF OFFENDER
	13	17	27	Unidentified	13	17	27	13
74	6.8	6.2	5.7	5.9	7.48	7.10	6.59	6.55
80	5.8	5.8	5.2	5.0	5.72	5.55	6.00	4.65
82	6.4	6.4	6.5	6.8	5.91	6.50	5.19	4.25
90	3.2	2.5	3.0	3.0	4.64	4.07	3.89	1.83
121	1.8	1.6	1.9	1.3	2.38	1.69	1.78	1.32
122	2.6	2.8	2.8	1.9	4.91	3.79	3.56	3.35
123	2.8	3.0	3.7	3.8	4.16	4.41	5.93	2.55
133	1.8	1.9	1.8	2.1	2.42	2.07	2.67	1.78
137	3.1	4.3	3.8	4.3	3.45	3.34	3.89	2.75

RATING SUBJECTS

* Description in Appendix D.

Appendix E-2

Mean Raw Magnitude Ratio Scale Scores for Twenty-one Offenses, Male Offenders of Selected Age, Rated by Three Groups of Subjects

Offense Number*	PRIMARY INDEX SCALE**	TEMPLE STUDENTS AGE OF OFFENDER 13	17	27	Unidentified	POLICE AGE OF OFFENDER 13	17	27	JUVENILE COURT JUDGES AGE OF OFFENDER 13
1	242.	171.	202.	334.	389.	279.	200.	144.	196.
2	221.	111.	174.	301.	368.	296.	176.	142.	193.
3	290.	158.	185.	342.	673.	367.	187.	153.	199.
18	100.	68.5	70.0	108.0	118.0	104.0	132.0	90.7	93.1
20	52.8	28.9	35.2	50.6	24.4	57.9	73.9	61.6	62.2
22	64.0	39.3	51.4	73.8	46.0	60.6	82.2	66.6	71.2
28	76.0	42.2	61.0	105.0	87.4	68.2	87.9	72.8	62.4
31	60.5	45.7	56.2	68.5	78.8	41.4	71.9	53.3	54.7
32	66.1	53.5	54.1	81.0	69.1	55.1	75.6	63.8	64.2
46	41.8	30.3	39.3	36.8	34.1	42.1	48.4	47.2	43.9
52	23.3	13.7	20.6	17.0	14.0	28.2	34.3	24.5	28.6

Mean Raw Magnitude Ratio Scale Scores for Twenty-one Offenses, Male Offenders of Selected Age, Rated by Three Groups of Subjects (Continued)

390

	PRIMARY	RATING SUBJECTS							JUVENILE COURT JUDGES
		TEMPLE STUDENTS				POLICE			
	INDEX SCALE**	AGE OF OFFENDER				AGE OF OFFENDER			AGE OF OFFENDER
Offense Number*		13	17	27	Unidentified	13	17	27	13
53	16.7	10.2	16.4	16.4	14.5	23.3	16.6	17.9	12.8
74	31.0	20.6	30.8	33.6	23.1	35.3	34.1	25.8	42.5
80	11.5	11.6	10.0	10.8	10.1	14.9	11.3	12.7	11.0
82	24.3	7.74	23.9	46.9	24.8	21.8	27.2	18.7	12.7
90	5.00	2.01	3.32	3.75	5.43	10.9	9.17	4.34	1.45
121	2.50	0.511	2.17	1.23	2.13	3.78	4.88	4.10	1.11
122	3.90	2.75	3.18	1.74	0.306	10.1	8.63	4.82	2.72
123	8.70	2.66	4.07	4.46	8.70	10.8	14.3	14.3	3.72
133	2.00	0.393	1.76	0.534	0.686	4.91	3.55	3.10	0.937
137	7.00	4.29	8.16	9.27	6.98	7.51	8.74	4.69	3.25

* Description in Appendix D.
** The Primary Index Scale, composed of these 21 offenses, is the mean of the geometric means for the four offender versions (13, 17, 27 years old, and unidentified age) among the four rating groups (Temple students, Police officers, Juvenile Court Judges, Ogontz Students). In short, the Primary Index Scale is the arithmetic mean of the ten geometric means found in Appendix E-2 and E-4 for these offenses.

Appendix E-3

Mean Raw Category Scale Scores for 141 Offenses, Male Offenders of Unidentified Age, Rated by Police Officers and Ogontz Penn State Center Students

OFFENSE NUMBER*	RATERS Police	RATERS Ogontz	OFFENSE NUMBER*	RATERS Police	RATERS Ogontz
1	10.86	10.86	33	8.54	8.16
2	10.91	10.00	34	8.60	6.82
3	10.93	10.32	35	8.4	7.09
4	9.73	8.82	36	8.45	7.83
5	7.00	9.16	37	7.36	6.36
6	10.18	7.54	38	8.45	5.82
7	9.36	6.00	39	7.00	4.36
8	10.64	8.27	40	6.54	5.83
9	9.73	7.27	41	8.91	4.00
10	9.36	6.91	42	8.82	5.70
11	9.64	8.16	43	5.00	5.08
12	8.54	7.45	44	7.64	5.73
13	8.36	7.00	45	6.36	3.82
14	10.09	6.91	46	8.23	5.93
15	9.36	6.64	47	5.27	3.82
16	8.09	7.16	48	6.36	6.42
17	8.54	6.18	49	5.45	3.64
18	10.18	8.34	50	7.00	6.42
19	8.64	7.09	51	6.54	6.33
20	9.09	6.02	52	7.50	4.08
21	10.18	7.64	53	6.38	4.18
22	9.40	6.75	54	5.64	5.73
23	8.82	5.36	55	6.64	5.64
24	9.18	6.36	56	4.64	2.73
25	9.27	5.82	57	5.18	2.82
26	9.09	5.64	58	7.64	6.09
27	6.73	5.50	59	8.82	5.54
28	8.84	7.73	60	7.18	4.18
29	9.82	7.54	61	4.73	3.26
30	9.09	7.36	62	7.36	5.45
31	8.11	7.53	63	7.82	5.45
32	8.33	7.82	64	3.91	3.50

Mean Raw Category Scale Scores for 141 Offenses, Male Offenders of Unidentified Age, Rated by Police Officers and Ogontz Penn State Center Students (Continued)

OFFENSE NUMBER*	RATERS		OFFENSE NUMBER*	RATERS	
	Police	Ogontz		Police	Ogontz
65	5.64	3.83	104	2.91	3.30
66	6.36	6.58	105	3.36	1.82
67	6.73	5.00	106	4.45	5.00
68	5.27	2.73	107	9.45	7.09
69	4.64	3.92	108	5.64	2.90
70	5.64	5.18	109	9.82	6.45
71	7.00	5.36	110	9.64	7.91
72	3.91	2.27	111	8.54	5.72
73	3.91	4.00	112	7.27	6.08
74	6.73	5.67	113	8.82	4.54
75	4.36	3.81	114	7.45	5.75
76	6.00	7.33	115	3.91	1.90
77	6.40	4.50	116	3.64	3.91
78	6.09	4.18	117	1.60	2.00
79	5.54	7.25	118	3.45	2.54
80	5.48	4.38	119	2.18	2.42
81	4.09	3.27	120	2.82	2.45
82	6.13	5.54	121	1.86	1.40
83	5.73	5.45	122	2.31	2.60
84	7.18	4.27	123	5.31	3.51
85	6.36	5.09	124	2.59	2.09
86	2.50	3.25	125	1.36	2.00
87	6.40	4.09	126	2.91	3.54
88	6.90	4.45	127	3.09	2.82
89	6.36	5.08	128	3.82	2.36
90	3.21	2.44	129	9.91	6.91
91	4.40	2.64	130	4.91	4.58
92	7.00	4.00	131	2.54	1.82
93	6.18	4.64	132	6.90	3.82
94	3.73	3.18	133	2.33	1.84
95	3.36	2.73	134	3.82	2.42
96	3.18	3.66	135	2.54	1.82
97	8.00	4.45	136	5.90	4.73
98	7.09	4.92	137	3.37	2.98
99	5.45	4.45	138	8.00	4.09
100	8.36	5.64	139	9.27	8.27
101	7.00	4.18	140	6.45	7.58
102	9.36	6.09	141	5.45	3.45
103	5.36	4.25			

* Description in Appendix D.

Appendix E-4

Mean Raw Magnitude Ratio Scale Scores for 141 Offenses, Male Offenders of Unidentified Age, Rated by Police Officers and Ogontz Penn State Center Students

OFFENSE NUMBER*	RATERS Police	RATERS Ogontz	OFFENSE NUMBER*	RATERS Police	RATERS Ogontz
1	272.	236.60	33	167.5	95.39
2	265.	179.90	34	57.06	19.19
3	318.	308.60	35	69.31	27.59
4	89.51	25.02	36	163.9	71.31
5	297.8	145.40	37	172.4	43.94
6	396.3	114.20	38	75.88	37.20
7	98.68	51.99	39	169.5	19.24
8	581.7	72.07	40	115.5	37.27
9	129.1	77.86	41	81.79	16.64
10	99.93	44.91	42	115.6	31.98
11	196.4	107.00	43	72.72	15.87
12	139.4	36.21	44	234.9	29.93
13	210.5	49.22	45	50.76	13.27
14	446.6	62.00	46	65.2	30.23
15	110.9	78.96	47	112.7	23.29
16	167.5	60.03	48	120.1	34.32
17	122.3	35.58	49	35.48	9.49
18	147.0	73.35	50	110.6	29.24
19	99.12	71.34	51	69.74	34.92
20	93.4	35.34	52	38.3	13.75
21	136.1	30.05	53	24.6	14.05
22	104.0	44.93	54	118.8	23.63
23	79.16	29.98	55	47.07	21.84
24	78.66	61.56	56	18.18	5.29
25	218.3	34.36	57	13.64	7.37
26	69.45	16.65	58	62.51	22.23
27	123.5	38.79	59	65.05	23.91
28	111.0	61.75	60	39.17	14.32
29	100.1	57.96	61	13.57	5.10
30	388.5	68.81	62	38.63	22.88
31	80.8	53.48	63	66.78	23.59
32	74.8	65.11	64	46.46	13.06

Mean Raw Magnitude Ratio Scale Scores for 141 Offenses, Male Offenders of Unidentified Age, Rated by Police Officers and Ogontz Penn State Center Students (Continued)

OFFENSE NUMBER*	RATERS		OFFENSE NUMBER*	RATERS	
	Police	Ogontz		Police	Ogontz
65	19.38	6.52	104	3.74	2.35
66	172.2	36.13	105	3.50	0.37
67	56.49	21.43	106	53.80	27.56
68	73.14	12.59	107	369.1	33.75
69	45.07	13.50	108	20.00	0.18
70	91.34	33.04	109	450.8	84.32
71	54.88	19.62	110	125.4	142.20
72	9.55	3.79	111	101.9	10.14
73	45.32	13.27	112	68.57	88.89
74	42.9	20.97	113	81.68	8.03
75	76.81	11.30	114	53.81	37.64
76	39.88	36.51	115	15.11	2.66
77	22.92	11.79	116	16.48	8.15
78	18.58	10.38	117	1.02	0.38
79	39.88	36.47	118	5.25	4.18
80	13.3	9.75	119	11.34	3.14
81	8.95	9.76	120	8.86	1.35
82	31.4	27.88	121	4.11	1.16
83	39.62	22.74	122	3.13	1.40
84	40.26	18.08	123	20.0	3.95
85	51.37	33.36	124	2.85	0.43
86	32.42	8.51	125	4.12	5.05
87	30.87	15.40	126	13.41	19.03
88	27.35	6.08	127	10.77	2.35
89	67.37	27.28	128	11.51	3.38
90	7.93	2.00	129	434.3	40.44
91	12.53	8.16	130	53.11	41.16
92	44.22	9.39	131	2.51	0.31
93	56.21	5.29	132	42.80	4.06
94	11.58	10.56	133	3.60	0.78
95	4.28	1.16	134	7.16	8.70
96	18.96	10.53	135	3.94	1.94
97	76.96	16.39	136	31.69	28.96
98	35.32	48.18	137	10.0	6.86
99	39.59	18.69	138	76.50	52.03
100	89.92	14.19	139	704.7	83.13
101	117.2	6.67	140	42.95	69.37
102	120.1	48.94	141	29.16	2.17
103	18.51	27.46			

* Description in Appendix D.

Appendix E-5

z Scores and Standard Deviations for 141 Offenses on the Magnitude Scale, for Male Offenders of Unidentified Age, Rated by Ogontz Penn State Center Students

OFFENSE NUMBER*	z SCORE	S.D.	OFFENSE NUMBER*	z SCORE	S.D.
1	1.28633	.38367	33	.99383	.46153
2	1.18441	.44859	34	.48232	.43427
3	1.43103	.48353	35	.71778	.37049
4	.51568	.94945	36	.74478	.53295
5	1.37419	.43119	37	.58021	.52415
6	1.16383	.81017	38	.37656	.32882
7	.79102	.46565	39	−.07127	.44280
8	.96204	.24943	40	.19300	.41668
9	1.00629	.39742	41	.34147	.48791
10	.57296	.26285	42	.79417	.28389
11	.88268	.43148	43	−.49966	.43438
12	.85691	.16488	44	.23043	.32390
13	.31038	.60284	45	−.13167	.65567
14	.87756	.34855	46	.25551	.42265
15	1.00237	.37967	47	.05897	.46606
16	.57520	.53935	48	.08448	.57662
17	.84035	.26005	49	−.35241	.58331
18	.74872	.30434	50	−.03293	.56214
19	.87231	.44660	51	.14434	.44387
20	.30394	.36793	52	−.20068	.39587
21	.75474	.30401	53	−.24295	.40128
22	.48947	.31673	54	.09088	.40969
23	.18969	.43815	55	.49262	.46272
24	.69813	.50050	56	−.98226	.71926
25	.37596	.48733	57	−.70566	.66672
26	.37235	.52783	58	.21276	.54505
27	.19669	.61133	59	.56715	.40977
28	.54731	.26577	60	.24447	.47433
29	.88409	.74545	61	−.86371	.67538
30	.92179	.25918	62	.53512	.39812
31	.48151	.42951	63	.58236	.40960
32	.60673	.34477	64	−.72306	.53809

z Scores and Standard Deviations for 141 Offenses on the Magnitude Scale, for Male Offenders of Unidentified Age, Rated by Ogontz Penn State Center Students (Continued)

OFFENSE NUMBER*	z SCORE	S.D.	OFFENSE NUMBER*	z SCORE	S.D.
65	−.23834	.57614	104	−.62266	.93014
66	.18198	.53796	105	−1.75659	.73556
67	.06427	.50971	106	−.08329	.69802
68	−.49947	.61754	107	.51481	.90635
69	−.66774	.56531	108	−1.44474	1.28872
70	.37165	.47872	109	1.03406	.53972
71	.15682	.46730	110	.99374	.65820
72	−1.07129	.69198	111	.37706	1.13981
73	−.51019	.67975	112	.87942	.88138
74	.08427	.38384	113	.11168	1.10186
75	−.70100	.91606	114	.23601	.56375
76	.16755	.46740	115	−1.38131	.90128
77	.10378	.48692	116	−.34437	.64538
78	−.00131	.37073	117	−1.86098	.88845
79	.23831	.55017	118	−1.09981	.50732
80	−.41142	.38670	119	−1.67789	1.36496
81	−.56944	.50290	120	−1.00028	.96650
82	.17793	.45956	121	−1.39756	.56012
83	.06286	.57321	122	−1.26420	.75710
84	−.00841	.52107	123	−.88873	.76955
85	.37554	.33889	124	−1.45913	.54830
86	−1.06228	.87299	125	−1.50902	.64468
87	.26302	.56986	126	−.00410	.51180
88	−.27736	.66041	127	−.91397	.75135
89	−.01448	.64250	128	−.92591	.86399
90	−1.11969	.65324	129	.66705	1.05997
91	−.88562	.74372	130	.13549	.62410
92	−.41970	1.15615	131	−2.10149	.69716
93	.06242	.90720	132	−.28220	.40895
94	−.55169	.95723	133	−1.45183	.61326
95	−.96175	.85131	134	−1.20414	1.16856
96	−.80781	.94095	135	−1.60558	.85575
97	.24545	.83712	136	.21873	.44433
98	.32538	1.07107	137	−.62010	.45193
99	−.02401	.67401	138	.67636	.43302
100	−.27963	.74578	139	1.11636	.44072
101	−.64510	1.17417	140	.71966	.80446
102	.57076	.48887	141	−.49741	.78040
103	−.10085	.75499			

* Descriptions in Appendix D.

Appendix E-6

Offense Versions Used to Obtain Discriminatory Score Values for Selected Offenses

A. *Without breaking into or entering* a building and with no one else present, an offender takes property worth *$5*.

B. *Without breaking into or entering* a building and with no one else present, an offender takes property worth *$20*.

C. *Without breaking into or entering* a building and with no one else present, an offender takes property worth *$50*.

D. *Without breaking into or entering* a building and with no one else present, an offender takes property worth *$1000*.

E. *Without breaking into or entering* a building and with no one else present, an offender takes property worth *$5000*.

F. An offender *breaks into* a building and with no one else present takes property worth *$5*.

G. An offender *without a weapon* threatens to harm a victim unless the victim gives him money. The offender takes the victim's money ($5) and leaves without harming the victim.

H. An offender *with a weapon* threatens to harm a victim unless the victim gives him money. The offender takes the victim's money ($5) and leaves without harming the victim.

I. An offender inflicts injury on a victim. The victim *dies* from the injury.

J. An offender inflicts injury on a victim. The victim is treated by a physician *and* his injuries require him to be hospitalized.

K. An offender inflicts injury on a victim. The victim is treated by a physician *but* his injuries do *not* require him to be hospitalized.

L. An offender shoves (or pushes) a victim. The victim does *not* require any medical treatment.

M. An offender forces a female to submit to sexual intercourse. No other physical injury is inflicted.

N. An offender takes an automobile which is recovered undamaged.

O. The offender is found firing a rifle for which he has no permit.

P. An offender prowls in the back yard of a private residence.

Q. The offender is a customer in a house where liquor is sold illegally.

R. The offender disturbs the neighborhood with loud noisy behavior.

S. A juvenile runs away from home and thereby becomes an offender.

T. A juvenile plays hookey from school and thereby becomes an offender.

Appendix E-7

z Scores and Standard Deviations on Sequential and Simultaneous Tests for Selected Offenses on the Magnitude Scale, for Male Offenders of Unidentified Age Rated by University of Pennsylvania Students

	z SCORE		STANDARD DEVIATIONS	
OFFENSE*	Sequential	Simultaneous	Sequential	Simultaneous
A	−0.13996	−0.28833	.54240	.48231
B	0.02638	−0.15972	.36028	.39219
C	0.10246	−0.00851	.35616	.35812
D	0.42092	0.36287	.32036	.34918
E	0.53782	0.50644	.35718	.40379
F	0.23976	0.06531	.40889	.41850
G	0.39025	0.25243	.35502	.36502
H	0.69031	0.49256	.34291	.35749
I	1.67593	1.70444	.59642	.60800
J	0.86467	1.15042	.39174	.53846
K	0.55921	0.80198	.50983	.50733
L	−0.66700	−0.08797	.88898	.61238
M	1.14990	1.21157	.52143	.61360
N	−0.00015	−0.16053	.37388	.34599
O	−0.79464	−0.84947	.64527	.65817
P	−0.47565	−0.44884	.62772	.61788
Q	−1.04146	−0.89696	.74923	.70440
R	−1.11835	−0.99194	.68200	.54956
S	−1.07152	−1.19767	.74425	.71110
T	−1.34889	−1.45808	.72347	.68309

* Description in Appendix E-6.

Appendix E-8

Comparison of Maximum Penalty of Twenty-one Offenses in 30-Day Units from the Pennsylvania Penal Code with Mean Raw Magnitude Scores of Police and Ogontz Raters

OFFENSE NUMBER[a]	PA. PENAL CODE MAXIMUM PENALTY	MAXIMUM IN 30-DAY UNITS	POLICE SCORES	OGONTZ SCORES
1	Death[b]	600	272	237
2	Death[b]	600	265	180
3	Death[b]	600	318	309
18	23 years	276	147	73
20	23 years	276	93	35
22	20 years	240	104	45
28	5 years	60	111	62
31	3 years	36	81	53
32	3 years	36	75	65
46	20 years	240	65	30
52	5 years	60	38	14
53	5 years	60	25	14
74	5 years	60	43	21
80	5 years	60	13	10
82	2 years	24	31	28
90	30 days	1	3	2
121	$10 $\cong$ 30 days	1	2	1
122	60 days	2	2	1
123	1 year	12	4	4
133	$10 $\cong$ 30 days	1	2	2
137	6 months	6	10	7

[a] Description in Appendix D.
[b] Death was assigned an upper limit of 600 30-day units.

Appendix F

The Scoring System

Information needed for scoring events. In order to score the events in the tripartite classification (A, B, C), the following items, in so far as they are applicable to a given event, must be collected and recorded by the police during the investigation.

1. The number of victims who, during the event, receive minor bodily injuries or are treated and discharged, hospitalized, or killed.

2. The number of victims of acts of forcible sex intercourse and the number of such victims who are compelled to participation in the act by threats with a dangerous weapon.

3. The presence of physical or verbal intimidation or intimidation by a dangerous weapon of persons during events other than those in which forcible sex acts occur.

4. The number of premises forcibly entered.

5. The number of motor vehicles stolen.

6. The total amount of property loss during an event through theft, damage or destruction of property.

Attention should be recalled to the fact that the *only* events that, so far as an index of delinquency is concerned, need to be considered are those in which some personal victim receives bodily harm or in which property theft, damage, or destruction actually occurs.

No event can be scored, of course, until all pertinent information required for scoring it has been secured and recorded.

THE SYSTEM ILLUSTRATED

The scoring system can best be described by a form which contains all the elements that are scoreable and which is clarified by definitions of these elements and illustrated by the method of scoring.

SCORE SHEET

Identification number(s): _____

Effects of Event: I   T   D   (Circle One)

Category of Event: A   B   C   (Circle One)

Elements Scored 1	Number x Weight 2 3	Total 4
I. Number of victims of bodily harm		
(a) Receiving minor injuries	1	
(b) Treated and discharged	4	
(c) Hospitalized	7	
(d) Killed	26	
II. Number of victims of forcible sex intercourse	10	
(a) Number of such victims intimidated by weapon	2	
III. Intimidation (except II above)		
(a) Physical or verbal only	2	
(b) By weapon	4	
IV. Number of premises forcibly entered	1	
V. Number of motor vehicles stolen	2	
VI. Value of property stolen, damaged, or destroyed (in dollars)		
(a) Under 10 dollars	1	
(b) 10– 250	2	
(c) 251– 2000	3	
(d) 2001– 9000	4	
(e) 9001–30000	5	
(f) 30001–80000	6	
(g) Over 80000	7	

Total Score

IDENTIFICATION NUMBER(S).   This is the number which is given to a particular event. It may be a central complaint number, a district number, or some similar number. If the same event is represented by more than one such number, all numbers should be recorded, so that the event can be scored as a whole. In most cases an event will be described in complaint and investigation reports carrying but one identifying number. In some cases, however, one event may become the subject of reports with different numbers, two or more such reports describing the same event. If, for instance, in a rape event with two victims, each victim gives rise to a separate report on the event, it would be necessary to coordinate the two reports before the event is scored or it might incorrectly be scored twice.

CLASSIFICATION OF EVENT. Circle the appropriate letters. In order to permit the construction of sub-indices of delinquency for comparative use, events should be classified according to effects they produce. An event may involve (*a*) *only* personal injury to a victim or victims, (*b*) *only* the theft of some property or (*c*) *only* property damage, but personal injury may be associated with theft or damage or both, and theft may be associated with damage. Therefore, note should be taken of these combinations, because it may be considered desirable to compute separate indices for events involving *I* (personal injury); *I* and *T* (theft); *I* and *D* (damage); *I*, *T*, and *D*; *T*; *T* and *D*; and *D*. Other combinations are also possible, such as all events involving *I*; *T* but not *I*; and *D*, but not *I* and *T*. Below the two items noted for classifying events, the score sheet is divided into four columns. Column 1 contains a list of the elements that can be scored, even though most events will include only one or two of these elements, and Column 2 lists the number of instances a particular element occurs in an event. Column 3 gives the weight assigned to the element. Column 4 is reserved for the total score for a given element; this is derived by multiplying the figure in Column by the figure in Column 3. By adding all figures in Column 4, the total score for the event is found.

I. NUMBER OF PERSONS INJURED. Each victim receiving some bodily injury during an event must be accounted for. If there are three victims and one suffers a minor injury and two have to be hospitalized write "1" in Column 2 opposite I(*a*) and "2" opposite I(*b*). Physical injuries usually occur during assaultive events but they may be a by-product of other events—reckless driving, for instance.

I(*a*). *Minor injury.* An injury that requires or receives no professional medical attention. The victim may, for instance, be pushed, knocked down, or mildly wounded—minor cut, black eye, or bruise.

I(*b*). *Treated and discharged.* The victim receives professional medical treatment but is not detained for prolonged or further care.

I(*c*). *Hospitalized.* The victim requires in-patient care in a medical institution, regardless of its duration, or out-patient care during three or more clinical visits.

I(d). *Killed.* The victim dies of his injuries, regardless of the circumstances in which they were inflicted.

Note: An event resulting in bodily harm may also present other elements listed under Sections IV, V, and VI on the score sheet and either under II or III. *All* elements of the event must be scored. The injury for instance, may have occurred during a rape or a robbery when intimidation is always present, and may have followed upon a forcible entry to a building and have been accompanied by theft of a motor vehicle and other property of specific value.

The injunction regarding the scoring of all elements of an event applies not only to those resulting in bodily harm but to all events of Categories B and C as well.

II. SEX INTERCOURSE BY FORCE.   Occurs when a person is intimidated and forced against his will to engage in a sexual act—rape, incest, or sodomy, for instance.   The victim is usually a female.[1]   An event may have more than one victim, and the score of the event depends on the number of victims.   A continuous relationship such as may occur in forcible incest is to be counted as one event.   The number of victims is entered in Column 2 opposite II.

A forcible sex act is accomplished by intimidation.   The weight attached to the act includes the element of physical or verbal intimidation, but if a victim is forced to engage in the sex act under threat with a dangerous weapon (see III below), additional weight is given to the act.   Intimidation by weapon is scored only once for each person intimidated during the event of a forcible sex act.   If only one is intimidated by weapon, write "1" in Column 2 opposite II(a); if more than one person is intimidated in that manner, write in the proper number.

The victim of one or more forcible sex acts during an event is always

---

[1] If the victim is under a certain age and is mentally deficient the law often considers a sexual act as a forcible one even when the victim is not in fact forced. The Model Penal Code is explicit in this matter and seems to be a good guide. It includes in rape, sexual intercourse with a female victim who is unconscious or is less than 10 years old. In "gross sexual imposition," the Code includes the fact that the male offender "knows that she [the victim] suffers from a mental disease or defect which renders her incapable of appraising the nature of her conduct . . . " (*Model Penal Code,* Philadelphia: The American Law Institute, 1962, Article 213, Section 213.1). The point we wish to emphasize is that what is generally meant by statutory rape but which involves a mentally capable victim willingly engaging in a sex act should *not* be included under our meaning of "sexual intercourse with force."

assumed to have suffered at least a minor injury. Even when medical examination does not reveal any injuries, write "1" in Column 2 opposite I(*a*). This score of "1" should also be given if the victim is examined by a physician only in order to ascertain if venereal infection has occurred or for prophylactic reasons.

III. INTIMIDATION OF PERSONS (other than in II above). This is an element in all events in which one or more victims are threatened with bodily harm or some other serious consequence for the purpose of forcing the victim(s) to obey the request of the offender(s) to give up something of value, to assist in an event that leads to someone's bodily injury or to property theft, damage, or destruction, or to witness such an act. Robbery is the classical example. Ordinary assault and battery, aggravated assault and battery, or homicide are *not* to be scored for intimidation. Intimidation is scored but once in these events regardless of the number of victims or the number of offenders.

Physical or verbal intimidation. Physical intimidation means the use of strong-arm tactics, threats with fists, menacing gestures, physical restraint by pinioning arms, etc. Verbal intimidation means spoken threats only, not overtly supported by the display of a weapon.

Intimidation by weapon. Display of weapon, such as a firearm, a cutting or stabbing instrument, or a blunt instrument capable of inflicting serious injury.

Write "1" in Column 2 opposite III(*a*) or III(*b*). If both kinds of intimidation occur, score only III(*b*).

IV. NUMBER OF PREMISES ENTERED FORCIBLY. As used here, forcible entry means the unlawful entry, even when not by "breaking," of a premise of a private character to which the public does not have free access, or the breaking and entering of a premise to which the public ordinarily had free access. Such an entry is in itself an event to be scored if it causes some degree of damage to property—a broken lock or window, for instance—even though it is not followed by an injury to a person or by theft or damage to property inside.

Usually only one distinct premise will be entered, such as a family dwelling, an apartment, or a suite of offices, but some events may embrace several such entries. The scoring depends on the *number of premises forcibly entered during the event and occupied or belonging to different owners, tenants, or lessees.* Contrary to the "hotel rule" used in the Uniform Crime Reporting system, each hotel room, motel, or lodging house room broken into and occupied by different tenants should be scored. If a building was forcibly entered and further entries made inside, the total number of entries scored should include the forcible entry of the building, even when the building belongs to someone who is victimized by a further entry inside. Write the appropriate number in Column 2 opposite item IV.

V. NUMBER OF MOTOR VEHICLES STOLEN. Enter in Column 2, opposite V, the number of motor vehicles stolen during an event. Usually there will be one only but there may be several if a garage is broken into and more than one vehicle is stolen, for instance.

By motor vehicle is meant any self-propelled vehicle—automobile, motorcycle, truck, tractor, locomotive, or airplane. Disregard self-propelled lawn mowers and similar domestic instruments from this section, for the value of these is scored under Section VI.

VI. VALUE OF PROPERTY STOLEN, DAMAGED OR DESTROYED. Regardless of the type of event scored and the number of victims, find the *total value* of all property stolen, damaged, or destroyed during the event, whether it is wholly or partly recovered and whether or not the loss is covered by insurance. Write the figure "1" in Column 2 opposite the proper bracket in VI(*a–g*).

Motor vehicle thefts require special handling. If the vehicle is recovered undamaged and nothing is stolen from it, *there is no loss to be scored.* The theft itself has already been given a weight of 2 under V. If not recovered, the loss is the value of the vehicle and contents. If it is recovered damaged and/or property has been taken from it, the loss is the sum of the cost of the damage and the value of the stolen articles. The amount of loss should be added to the value of other property values lost during the event, before scoring, if more than the vehicle and its contents were taken.

CLASSIFYING AND SCORING EVENTS

Illustrations of how the proposed scoring system works are given below. For the purpose of showing how it differs from that of the Uniform Crime Reporting System, the problems have been copied from the *Uniform Crime Reporting Handbook* issued by the Federal Bureau of Investigation. The problems as originally stated generally do not contain all the information needed. Hypothetical data have been supplied in the brackets. The symbols in the column headed "Elements" refer to the items as numbered in Column 1 of the Score Sheet reproduced on an earlier page. Circles around the letters *I* (Injury), *T* (Theft), or *D* (Damage) indicate the presence of these attributes in an event.

PROBLEM 1. "A holdup man forces a husband and his wife to get out of their automobile. He shoots the husband, gun whips and rapes the wife [hospitalized] and leaves in the automobile [values $2000] after taking money [$100] from the husband. The husband dies as a result of the shooting."

SOLUTION. UCR—1 non-negligent criminal homicide.

Proposed Scoring
Effects of Event: Ⓘ Ⓣ   D
Category A. Bodily Injury

ELEMENT	NUMBER	WEIGHT	TOTAL SCORE
I(c)	1	7	7
I(d)	1	26	26
II	1	10	10
II(a)	1	2	2
V	1	2	2
VI(d)	1	4	4

Total Score   51

The husband was killed (26); the wife was raped (10), threatened with a gun (2), and sustained injuries requiring hospitalization (7). The car was stolen (2). The total value of the property lost, car and money, was $2,100 (4).

PROBLEM 2. "Two thieves break into a warehouse [damage, $20] and have loaded considerable merchandise [worth $3,500] on a truck [worth $3,000]. The night watchman is knocked unconscious with some blunt instrument [treated and discharged]. The thieves drive away in the stolen truck."

SOLUTION. UCR—1 robbery.

Proposed Scoring
Effects of Event: Ⓘ Ⓣ   D
Category A. Bodily Injury

ELEMENT	NUMBER	WEIGHT	TOTAL SCORE
I(b)	1	4	4
IV	1	1	1
V	1	2	2
VI(d)	1	4	4

Total Score   11

Forcible entry (1), injury to night watchman requiring treatment (4), theft of motor vehicle (2), and loss of $6520 in value (4).

PROBLEM 3. "Three men break into a public garage [damage $20] after closing hours. They steal cash from the garage office lockbox [$50.00] and two automobiles from the shop [one worth $1500 and the other $3000. The latter was recovered undamaged with nothing stolen from it; the other was not found]."

SOLUTION. UCR—1 burglary.

Proposed Scoring
Effects of Event: I (T) (D)
Category B. Property Theft

ELEMENT	NUMBER	WEIGHT	TOTAL SCORE
IV	1	1	1
V	2	2	4
VI(c)	1	3	3

Total Score 8

Forcible entry (1), two motor vehicles stolen (4), total loss of property $1570 (3).

PROBLEM 4. "An automobile containing clothing and luggage valued at $375 is stolen. The car is recovered [undamaged] but the clothing and luggage are missing."

SOLUTION. UCR—1 auto theft.

Proposed Scoring
Effects of Event: I (T) D
Category B. Property Theft

ELEMENT	NUMBER	WEIGHT	TOTAL SCORE
V	1	2	2
VI(c)	1	3	3

Total Score 5

Motor vehicle theft (2), loss of property $375 (3).

PROBLEM 5.   "An automobile [worth $2000] is stolen and a short time later it is used as a getaway car in an armed robbery [netting $50.]."

SOLUTION.   UCR—1 robbery and 1 auto theft.

Proposed Scoring
Effects of Event: I   Ⓣ   D
Category B. Property Theft

EVENT	ELEMENT	NUMBER	WEIGHT	TOTAL SCORE
1	V	1	2	2
	VI(c)	1	3	3
			Total Score	5
2	III(b)	1	4	4
	VI(b)	1	2	2
			Total Score	6

As stated, the problem indicates that there are two events, each to be scored separately.   In the first event a car was stolen (2) worth $2000 (3).

In the second event a hold-up with gun (4) resulted in a total loss of $50 (2).   If the events had been of such a nature that they could have been scored as one event, the total score would have been 10 instead of the combined score of 11 because of the method of scoring total property loss during an event.

PROBLEM 6.   "Answering an 'armed robbery in progress' broadcast, police are engaged in a gun battle with 3 armed robbers; one of the bandits is killed and the other two captured.   [Presumably no one was injured except the robbers]"

SOLUTION.   UCR—1 robbery.
Proposed Scoring.   If no one was injured except the robbers, this would be a Category B (I   Ⓣ   D) event, if theft had actually occurred before the police arrived.   If so, the event would be scored for intimidation by weapon (4) plus the score or weight for the value of property taken, which if the total amount were $300 for instance (3), would total 7 for the event.   If the robbers failed to carry out their crime, because the police came before any property had been taken, the event would be considered an attempt and not scored at all for index purposes.

PROBLEM 7.   "Three men murder one person."

SOLUTION.   UCR—1 non-negligent criminal homicide.

Proposed Scoring
Effects of Event: ⓘ   *T   D*
Category A. Bodily Injury

ELEMENT	NUMBER	WEIGHT	TOTAL SCORE
I(*d*)	1	26	26

PROBLEM 8.   "Answering a 'riot' call, police find that seven persons were in a fight.   A variety of weapons are strewn about.   None of the participants is particularly cooperative.   Each one claims innocence but is vague as to who is responsible for the assault.   Three of the seven are severely wounded [all were hospitalized, presumably the others were not injured enough to receive medical attention] and receive emergency medical treatment."

SOLUTION.   UCR—3 aggravated assaults.

Proposed Scoring
Effects of Event: ⓘ   *T   D*
Category A. Bodily Injury

ELEMENT	NUMBER	WEIGHT	TOTAL SCORE
I(*c*)	3	7	21

If any of the others had received "minor injuries," that element should also be scored.

PROBLEM 9.   "Forty persons are present in a nightclub when it and the 40 persons are held up by armed bandits [taking a total of $1800]."

SOLUTION.   UCR—1 robbery.

Proposed Scoring
Effects of Event: I   Ⓣ   *D*
Category B. Property Theft

ELEMENT	NUMBER	WEIGHT	TOTAL SCORE
III(*b*)	1	4	4
VI(*c*)	1	3	3

Total Score   7

PROBLEM 10.   "Three men strong-arm and rob a man on the street [of $20]."

SOLUTION.   UCR—1 robbery.

Proposed Scoring
Effects of Event: I   ⓣ   D
Category B. Property Theft

ELEMENT	NUMBER	WEIGHT	TOTAL SCORE
III(*a*)	1	2	2
VI(*b*)	1	2	2

Total Score   4

PROBLEM 11.   "You receive a report from 3 separate women on 3 separate days. All say they were knocked to the ground and their purses stolen. On the fourth evening, police arrest a man who had just tried to grab a woman's purse after hitting her in the face. He admits the attempt and three robberies on the previous days."

SOLUTION.   UCR—4 robberies.

Proposed Scoring. This problem presents interesting aspects. The events are obviously separate ones to be scored separately, but their classification and scoring depend on information pertaining to each but not specified in the problem. It would appear that all the victims received some injuries, even mild ones. If so the events would all be category A (ⓘ ⓣ   D) events and the degree of injury should be scored. If the value of the purse and its contents varied in the events, this could also affect the size of the score for each event.

PROBLEM 12.   "Six rooms in a hotel are broken into [total damage $60] by 2 sneak thieves on 1 occasion. [The total value of property stolen from the rooms, occupied by different tenants, amounted to $1200.]"

SOLUTION.   UCR—1 burglary.

Proposed Scoring
Effects of Event: I   ⓣ   ⓓ
Category B. Property Theft

ELEMENT	NUMBER	WEIGHT	TOTAL SCORE
IV	6	1	6
VI(*c*)	1	3	3

Total Score   9

There were six forcible entries (6) and the total value stolen was $1260 (3).

PROBLEM 13. "One night a building is broken into [damage $10]. In all, 21 offices (rooms or partitioned spaces) are ransacked. These offices are occupied by (1) a lawyer, (2) a doctor, (3) Apex Co., and (4) Elite Co., who do not share their space and are not related in a business way [and who presumably kept their premises locked, and who altogether lost $6,000 and had property worth $100 damaged]."

SOLUTION. UCR—4 burglaries.

Proposed Scoring
Effects of Event: I (T) (D)
Category B. Property Theft

ELEMENT	NUMBER	WEIGHT	TOTAL SCORE
IV	5	1	5
VI(d)	1	4	4

Total Score 9

There were four forcible entries plus the forced entry of the building (5) and a total of $6,110 stolen and in damages (4).

Index

PATTERSON SMITH SERIES IN
CRIMINOLOGY, LAW ENFORCEMENT, AND SOCIAL PROBLEMS

1. Lewis: *The Development of American Prisons and Prison Customs, 1776–1845*
2. Carpenter: *Reformatory Prison Discipline*
3. Brace: *The Dangerous Classes of New York*
4. Dix: *Remarks on Prisons and Prison Discipline in the United States*
5. Bruce *et al.*: *The Workings of the Indeterminate-Sentence Law and the Parole System in Illinois*
6. Wickersham Commission: *Complete Reports, Including the Mooney-Billings Report.* 14 vols.
7. Livingston: *Complete Works on Criminal Jurisprudence.* 2 vols.
8. Cleveland Foundation: *Criminal Justice in Cleveland*
9. Illinois Association for Criminal Justice: *The Illinois Crime Survey*
10. Missouri Association for Criminal Justice: *The Missouri Crime Survey*
11. Aschaffenburg: *Crime and Its Repression*
12. Garofalo: *Criminology*
13. Gross: *Criminal Psychology*
14. Lombroso: *Crime, Its Causes and Remedies*
15. Saleilles: *The Individualization of Punishment*
16. Tarde: *Penal Philosophy*
17. McKelvey: *American Prisons*
18. Sanders: *Negro Child Welfare in North Carolina*
19. Pike: *A History of Crime in England.* 2 vols.
20. Herring: *Welfare Work in Mill Villages*
21. Barnes: *The Evolution of Penology in Pennsylvania*
22. Puckett: *Folk Beliefs of the Southern Negro*
23. Fernald *et al.*: *A Study of Women Delinquents in New York State*
24. Wines: *The State of Prisons and of Child-Saving Institutions*
25. Raper: *The Tragedy of Lynching*
26. Thomas: *The Unadjusted Girl*
27. Jorns: *The Quakers as Pioneers in Social Work*
28. Owings: *Women Police*
29. Woolston: *Prostitution in the United States*
30. Flexner: *Prostitution in Europe*
31. Kelso: *The History of Public Poor Relief in Massachusetts, 1820–1920*
32. Spivak: *Georgia Nigger*
33. Earle: *Curious Punishments of Bygone Days*
34. Bonger: *Race and Crime*
35. Fishman: *Crucibles of Crime*
36. Brearley: *Homicide in the United States*
37. Graper: *American Police Administration*
38. Hichborn: *"The System"*
39. Steiner & Brown: *The North Carolina Chain Gang*
40. Cherrington: *The Evolution of Prohibition in the United States of America*
41. Colquhoun: *A Treatise on the Commerce and Police of the River Thames*
42. Colquhoun: *A Treatise on the Police of the Metropolis*
43. Abrahamsen: *Crime and the Human Mind*
44. Schneider: *The History of Public Welfare in New York State, 1609–1866*
45. Schneider & Deutsch: *The History of Public Welfare in New York State, 1867–1940*
46. Crapsey: *The Nether Side of New York*
47. Young: *Social Treatment in Probation and Delinquency*
48. Quinn: *Gambling and Gambling Devices*
49. McCord & McCord: *Origins of Crime*
50. Worthington & Topping: *Specialized Courts Dealing with Sex Delinquency*
51. Asbury: *Sucker's Progress*
52. Kneeland: *Commercialized Prostitution in New York City*

PATTERSON SMITH SERIES IN
CRIMINOLOGY, LAW ENFORCEMENT, AND SOCIAL PROBLEMS